《韦卓民全集》编委会

顾　问：章开沅
主　任：马　敏

编委会成员：（按姓氏笔画顺序）
　　　　　　马　敏　　王世鹏　　刘占峰　　刘明海
　　　　　　刘家峰　　余子侠　　张　舟　　张卫国
　　　　　　李良明　　李艳鸽　　范　军　　段　维
　　　　　　赵子柳　　高新民　　唐有伯　　曹方久
　　　　　　熊桂玉

湖北省学术著作出版专项资金资助项目

韦卓民全集 第十卷

教育实录

余子侠 郑刚 整理

韦卓民 著

华中师范大学出版社

图书在版编目(CIP)数据

韦卓民全集·第十卷/韦卓民著;余子侠,郑刚整理. —武汉:华中师范大学出版社,2016.7

ISBN 978-7-5622-7227-4

Ⅰ.①韦… Ⅱ.①韦… ②余… ③郑… Ⅲ.①韦卓民(1888—1976)—全集 Ⅳ.①C52

中国版本图书馆 CIP 数据核字(2015)第 315664 号

韦卓民全集·第十卷
ⓒ 韦卓民著　余子侠　郑　刚整理

责任编辑:章光琼	责任校对:王　炜
编辑室:学术出版中心	电话:027－67863220
出版发行:华中师范大学出版社	社址:湖北省武汉市珞喻路 152 号
电话:027－67863426/3280(发行)	027－67861321(邮购)
传真:027－67863291	
网址:http://www.ccnupress.com	电子信箱:press@mail.ccnu.edu.cn
印刷:湖北恒泰印务有限公司	督印:王兴平
字数:524 千字	封面设计:甘　英
开本:710mm×1000mm　1/16	印张:32.75
版次:2016 年 7 月第 1 版	印次:2016 年 7 月第 1 次印刷
定价:98.00 元	

欢迎上网查询、购书

敬告读者:欢迎举报盗版,请打举报电话:027－67861321

总　序

　　历经 20 年以上两代华师相关学者曹方久、高新民诸教授的辛勤搜集、整理、校订、编辑,《韦卓民全集》终于出版问世。这是华中师范大学出版社的又一壮举,也是这位前辈大家给我们留下的一笔丰厚学术文化遗产。

　　韦卓民先生不仅是一位卓越的大学校长,还是一位学贯中西、博古通今的杰出学者,其重要业绩在于中西文化之沟通。他毕业于华大前身文华大学,并曾先后就读于哈佛、伦敦、牛津、柏林等世界著名大学。他以毕生精力营造中西文化交流的桥梁。正如年轻一代学者王宏维所描述的那样:"集翻译、研究、教学于一体,熔'三大批判'于一炉,风雨如磐,运动迭起。精译、深耕、勤教,始终无怨无悔。"1915 年,韦先生以英文撰写《孟子之政治思想》,取得文华大学文学硕士学位,可以看作是其学术生涯的发端。随后陆续发表的《佛教净土宗以信得救的教义及其与基督教之比较》(1920)、《孔门伦理》(1929,博士论文)、《中国文化之精神》(1947)等论著,则是这一事业的继续发展。上个世纪 50 年代中期以后,他身处逆境,而沟通中西文化致力更勤,译著笔耕始终未辍,如《康德哲学介绍》(1956)、《亚里士多德逻辑》(1957)、《培根与其〈新工具〉》(1956)、《康德哲学浅说》(1972)、《黑格尔〈小逻辑〉讲稿》(年代不详)等。这些学术业绩多侧重于介绍西方传统文化的精华,特别是对亚里士多德、培根、康德、黑格尔等人哲学名著的翻译、阐释与导读。早在 1928 年他就说过:"有机体须从其环境吸收并同化一些要素,而且只有在吸收及同化的过程不断的情况下,才可能有生命。'综合'一词是很重要的。它意指我们须对我们要综合的文化有完整的分析,比较其优缺点,然后造成一个有机体的整体,以保存两种文化的优点。我们必须这样做,而且必须以母体系统为新结构的间架。这是精神创新的工作……又是多么伟大的工作。"(《东西文化之综合问题》,据台北韦卓民纪念馆译文)这些话陈义甚高。他是这样说的,也是这样做的,而且是以自己的全部生命投入这项伟大工作。或许可以说,不理解这一点就不懂得真正的韦卓民。

诚然,韦卓民是一个虔诚的基督徒,但他信仰而非偏执,更没有流于浅薄的迷信。其根本原因就在于他是一个真正的哲学家,在精神世界更着重于理性的超越,既超越世俗,也超越宗教。正如香港年轻一代学者陈广培所曾指出:韦卓民眼中的基督教与中国社会文化的关系,"隐含着'他者'的伦理视野",其终极探究乃是整个宇宙与人类文明的存在与变化。但他并非沉溺于幻想,而是立足现实,关切现实,理解现实。所以他在基督教对华传播问题上,极力主张必须根植于中华文化土壤。用我自己的话来表述,就是"主归中华应该先于中华归主"。作为基督徒,他当然希望"将远东拥有世界最悠久历史的这个国家的优良文化,带到主的神坛前,作为对主的奉献"。因此,他自己坦然承认:"我毕生研究,都在导致去发现怎样使中国文化基督教化。"但他毕竟又是一个经过长期科学训练的现代哲学家,他对基督教的信仰,虔诚而非迷信,从不认为任何经典就是绝对真理,而多数传教士与基督徒信奉与传播的也不一定就是真正的教义真谛。所以,他摒弃西方中心主义,特别是许多欧美差会在华传播基督教过程中所拘守的专断与偏执。我认为,他在学术上致力更多的还是对西方近代哲学名著的译介与诠释。即使是在神学方面,也是反复强调并致力于基督教的中国化,即根植于中华文化。

韦卓民一生最为辉煌的时期是 1945—1947 年。抗战胜利后,华中大学返回昙华林,重整家园,百废待兴,并且雄心勃勃制订十年发展计划。在此期间,他曾应邀赴美讲学,先是作为鲁斯世界基督教讲座教授(The Henry W. Luce Visiting Professorship of World Christianity),发表题为"让基督教在中国土地上生长"(Rooting the Christian Church in Chinese Soil)的系统演讲。随后,又应 Hewell 基金会邀请,在 Andoer-Newton 以及波士顿的圣公会多次演讲,主题是"中国文化之精神"(The Spirit of Chinese Culture)。这些系列演讲,均于 1947 年在美国结集出版。

这次讲学,规格甚高,声誉颇隆。韦卓民以前在耶鲁大学的老同事,曾任美国历史学会与美国教会史学会会长的赖德烈教授(Kenneth Scott Latourette),为其演讲文集撰写序言,高度评价说:"韦博士了解中国文化的精神,有同情而深度的睿智,同时他又是一位基督徒,在向英语世界里,阐述中国文化之深处,实在罕与其比。"赖德烈1910—1917年曾在中国雅礼学院任教,是上个世纪30—40年代美国中国史与教会史研究的领军人物,他对韦卓民的评价绝非礼仪性的客套,而是由衷的倾服。韦卓民虽然专攻西方哲学,但其中国文化根底甚深,长期教授逻辑学、代数与几何、政治学、哲学、神学等课程,早已具备中西跨文化研究(他自己称为"综合")的坚实基础,即使对欧洲早期汉学大家也不盲目崇信。韦卓民曾指出:"由于不够严谨地解释中国文字中若干名词,或是无意地把若干我们自己的意见掺杂到中国哲学宗教文献之中,我们假中国文化之名,表达我们自己的思想。……如此我们犯了理解上的谬误,翻译上的谬误,这尤其是在引用上最恶劣的谬误,因为在翻译原著时,你等于有效地告诉读者,这是原作者的意思。……最著名的汉学家,往往是最大的罪人。但是谁肯带头来批评呢?"他只有自己带头来批判,并且指名道姓地以这些"饱学之士"为例,如"19世纪的Legge(理雅各)与Ross(罗约翰),20世纪的Bruce(卜道成)和Rawlinson(乐灵生)"。他有意不提当时仍然在世的某些"饱学之士"的名字,算是给他们留点面子。

韦卓民在对外文化交流过程中显示出可贵的自觉与自信,他有足够的底气向西方学界挑战,因为他中文底子极好,熟读四书五经;又精通英、德、法、俄、希腊、拉丁等文字,不仅对西方相关经典著作钻研颇深,而且阅读涉猎甚广。例如,英国史学大师汤因比的巨著《历史研究》尚在陆续撰写出版之中,他就在演讲涉及人类文明兴衰时多次引用其论述,而当时中国史学界研究汤因比者还寥若晨星。韦卓民对西方"饱学之士"的批评,并非局限于经典中个别词语翻译的考订纠误。他特别强调:"我要指出的,不只是语言文字而已。整个的文化背景,必须也要加以考虑,诸如思想形式、思想规则、研究方法、哲学、宗教、艺术及社会结构等。"(以上引文均据老校友沈宝寰译文)因此,这种批评就不是口舌之争,更不是意气之争,而是力图实现层次更高而收效更为深远的东西文化高层交流。韦卓民的演讲不仅面对美国,而且面对世界;不仅面对基督徒,而且面对全人类。

韦卓民虽然是基督徒,但也是教育家与哲学家,他投入精力与思考更多的毕竟还是学校教育与哲学研究。教育使他进入世俗,哲学使他超越宗教;他追求美好的理想,但始终立足于现实,立足于中国的土地,厕身于中国的人民。因此,不像那些专业的神学家与偏执的布道者,他公开而真诚地履行现实社会的公民承担。抗战爆发后,他不断以英文撰写时评文章,向全世界介绍中国人民团结抗击日本疯狂侵略的真实情况,勇敢地表明反对法西斯主义的政治立场,比如1938年6月在美国《耶鲁评论》(Yale Reviews)上发表《抗战初期中国的若干问题》(Questions about China),1940年于重庆发表的长篇英文通讯稿《抗战时期中国的教育》(Education in Wartime China),1941年春发表于《基督王国》(Christendom)杂志的《中国战争对中国文化的影响》(Cultural Effects of the Present War in China),1941年3月在中国广播电台发表的广播词《学者在战争中的任务》(The Role of Scholars in the War)等。特别是这篇向美国人民发表的广播词,再次重申:"在中国所发生的战争,只是极权与民主间大战的先锋。过去一年半来的事实,证实了我的看法,中国正在作战,而且决心继续作战,直至正义和世界道德得到维护为止。"作为一所西迁云南大理的大学之校长,他还自豪地向世界宣布:"透过坚持不懈的努力,中国的高等教育,不仅在战时得以维持,而且在一些重要方面还获得了显著进步,特别是许多研究所和高等学府向大后方落后地区的转移,产生了很好的影响,使得过惯了沿海各地生活的师生们,有机会熟识内地的生活。这种情形本身就是一种具有深远意义的教育,文化得以广泛散布,现代思想得以传播,水准较低的学校,在和进步的省份迁来的大学接触后,也因此提高了程度和效能,其结果将是战后会出现一个更教育化的中国。"在这些平实而又恳挚的话语中,我们可以看到一个真正的爱国者,一个终生奉献教育的老校长,一个胸怀世界的卓越中国公民。

但是抗战结束以后,人们还没有从胜利的喜悦中醒悟过来,国民党反动派就发动了史无前例的大规模内战,而政府腐败与战祸绵延,迅速使广大民众再次陷入痛苦深渊。韦卓民与成千上万善良的知识精英一样,逐步放弃了对于国民党政府的幻想,同情民主运动,保护进步学生,并且毅然拒绝国民政府迁校台湾的指令。他与华中大学广大师生一起,迎接了新中国的诞生,并且接受人民政府的命令,断绝与外国差会的联系,把学校由私立改为公立,以后又顺应全国性院系调整,与中华大学、中原大学等校合并,改制建立华中师范学院。他确实自觉地努力适应新社会,新政府也确曾给予重视并委以领导建校的重任。但是由于朝鲜战争爆发,美国成为敌国,而中国选择"一面倒"的亲苏外交政策。在抗美援朝热潮中,教会大学被定位为"美帝侵华文化堡垒",其校长也相应被定格为"帝国主义文化侵略代理人"。在肃清"亲美"、"崇美"、"恐美"思想运动的高潮中,韦卓民成为理所当然且火力集中的靶子,并且从此离开学校领导岗位,成为一般教师。1957年他被错划为"右派"以后,在政治上更受歧视,"十年动乱"期间亦为当然的批斗对象,直至1976年以后才经过平反恢复名誉。但好景确实不长,不过两年,这一代学术宗师就溘然与世长辞。

应该承认,韦卓民1949年以后这将近30年之久的漫长岁月确实是一个悲剧,但悲剧并非个人原因造成。根据我个人亲自接触与文献检索两方面的了解,过去无论如何屈辱痛苦,俨然成为众矢之的,他都能以平和的心态、超脱的胸怀,似乎顺应而又有内在定力地坦然应对。他天性幽默,语言风趣。记得"文革"时期,他作为"批斗对象"每天都要挤公交车从昙华林到南湖校本部"集中学习"。吃中饭排长队时,有人好心提醒他的铝制饭盒已被挤扁,他微笑轻声回应:"人都扁了,何况饭盒?"这就是真实的韦卓民,一位伟大的哲学家、教育家。在那种是非颠倒、蒙冤受屈的岁月,仍然保持着学者的尊严与人格魅力,甚至在集中学习的"牛棚"里仍然照常写作不辍。

俱往矣,过往的岁月,已逝的往事!大江东去,浪淘尽千古风流人物。刘知几云:披沙拣金,时有获宝。评文如此,评人亦然,只要是真金,迟早总会闪耀炫目光芒。出版社领导嘱我作序,哲学与神学浅薄如我,何必贻佛头著粪之讥。但曾忝任后辈校长,毕竟有所相知,于公于私,义不容辞。感慨万端,直抒胸臆而已。不当之处,尚祈多界贤达不吝批评教正。

章开沅
乙未初冬 年方九十
于南湖实斋

韦卓民引领我们走向康德
——代出版前言

在中国,伟大哲学家康德的著作和思想正在被越来越多的人所熟悉、所掌握,他那博大精深的思想在中华民族精神进程中的魅力已逐步展现。

韦卓民先生对康德哲学在中国的传播起到了巨大的作用,他在康德哲学"东渐"过程中的关键性地位是不可磨灭的。

20世纪甫始,梁启超发表《近世第一大哲康德之学说》一文,首次向中国人系统地介绍了康德。

"五四"新文化运动前后,张颐先生率先将康德和黑格尔的哲学带进了中国大学的课堂,张铭鼎等许多老一辈的学者致力于康德哲学的介绍和传播,在文化理论界掀起了一个热潮。

20世纪30年代以后,国内陆续翻译出版了康德的一些原著,它们是:《纯粹理性批判》(胡仁源译,1931年,商务印书馆)、《实践理性批判》(张铭鼎译,1936年,商务印书馆)、《道德形而上学探本》(唐钺译,1937年,商务印书馆)。与此同时,也出现了一些有价值的研究专著和论文,如郑昕先生的《康德学述》(1946年,商务印书馆)。

从"五四"到中华人民共和国成立前,尽管康德哲学得到了一定传播,但正如贺麟先生所评论的:成效不大,深度不够,范围狭小,"以致最后谈康德的仅有学术界为数极少的几个人"[①]。这种情况之所以产生,恐怕与学术界对康德哲学原著的系统翻译和介绍工作做得不够有莫大关系。

20世纪60年代,这种情况得到了很大改善。康德的三大批判中译本陆续出版:《纯粹理性批判》(蓝公武译,1960年)、《实践理性批判》(关文运译,1960年)、《判断力批判》(宗白华、韦卓民译,1964年)。中国人终于可以用中文一窥康德批判哲学体系的全豹了。接着,商务印书馆又出

---

① 贺麟:《康德、黑格尔哲学在中国的传播》,见《贺麟选集》,吉林人民出版社,2005年,第461页。

版了三本解释康德原著的译作。即是韦卓民先生翻译的《康德〈纯粹理性批判〉解义》([英]斯密著,1964年)、《康德哲学著作选译》([加拿大]华特生编选,1963年)和《康德哲学讲解》([加拿大]华特生著,1963年)。

《纯粹理性批判》是批判哲学的根基,是康德的扛鼎之作。尘封20多年的蓝译《纯粹理性批判》的问世,对想学习康德而又无条件直接阅读原文的莘莘学子,就像久旱后之甘露①,它成了哲学系学生和哲学研究者案头必备之书。读懂康德,特别是他的《纯粹理性批判》,是十分艰难之事。入门需要引领,康蒲·斯密的《康德〈纯粹理性批判〉解义》,像他英译的康德原著一样,是一本国际公认的权威著作,近一个世纪以来,广泛流传,经久不衰。这一著作汉译本的出版,对康德哲学的传播,无疑又是一场及时雨。试问,有志于研究康德的学者,有几位没有读过这本《解义》的呢?这本书当时"内部"出版,印数很少,可谓洛阳纸贵,得之者将它作为珍品收藏。直到20世纪90年代,有的学校因难觅此书,为教学需要,不得不内部翻印,可见它的价值和作用。

同期出版的其他两本华特生讲解康德的译作,也是对学习、研究康德极具参考价值的读物。《康德哲学原著选读》(原书1888年出版)编选了"三大批判"和《道德形而上学基础》四本原著中的若干章节。作者认为这些包括了康德系统思想的一切要点,对初学康德哲学的人很有帮助,可以为进一步研究康德哲学作好充分准备。这本书曾作为加拿大的大学教材,美国的大学也采用过。《康德哲学讲解》(原书1908年出版)是作者用前书作为基本教材向大学生讲的讲稿,积20年的教学经验整理而成。作者认为把这两本书结合起来向学生传授康德哲学,是"比较成功的一种试验结果"。韦卓民教授也正是用过华特生的教本和经验讲授康德哲学的。

以《解义》为标志的上述三本讲解康德哲学的著作,对促进康德哲学的教学、研究的重要意义,是显而易见的。它们的翻译出版,在康德哲学东渐史中,如果不能说"不亚于",那也是"仅次于"康德原著翻译出版的一件大事。在短短的两三年内,韦卓民先生向世人贡献了包括《判断力批判》(下册)在内的四本有关康德的译作,这在当时无人能出其右,可以说,

---

① 20世纪30年代出版的胡仁源的译本是公认读不懂的。

解放后国内引进康德哲学最早、最多、最有力者,实应首属韦卓民先生。这些事实已然可以确定:在康德哲学在中国传播的第三个阶段①中,韦先生起到了发端奠基的重要历史作用。

但韦卓民先生所从事的康德哲学的传播、研究工作远远不止于此,人们以前知道得太少了。

韦卓民先生是一位学贯中西、融汇古今的大学者。他在中外哲学史、逻辑、教育和宗教神学等领域中均有很深的造诣与丰硕的建树。在西方哲学史领域,韦先生着重研究了四个人,即亚里士多德、培根、康德和黑格尔。关于这四位哲人,他均有遗著留下,但花时间最长、耗精力最多的乃是康德。在他留下近百部(篇)达七八百万字的中英文遗稿中,关于康德哲学的竟占了二分之一左右。这些足以证明,20 世纪中期,国内关于康德哲学的传播和研究,韦先生确实是首屈一指的。

韦先生之所以花大力从事康德哲学的传播和研究,是因为,他把康德看作西方哲学思想发展中承前启后的最关键人物。他认为,研究西方近代哲学中的人不管谈什么哲学问题,都必须追踪到康德。在他讲授康德、黑格尔哲学时,讲到康德,不时会流露出一种激情,这是他讲黑格尔时所没有的。他曾向王元化先生讲过,他对康德的评价远远超过黑格尔。当然,在那极"左"的年代里,他在称颂康德的同时也不得不从政治角度斥责过康德几句,这是可以理解的。

韦先生在 1957 年突遭厄运后,从居住几十年的校长楼移居一间斗室,工资陡降,生活条件急剧变差,但他从容对待,一心扑到对康德等人的研究上,到"文革"前,数年内以惊人的速度译出有关康德的专著竟达 10 部,300 余万字(同一时期,韦先生还撰写和翻译了 4 本关于黑格尔哲学和逻辑学等方面的著作达 100 万字左右)。这个时期,是中国最需要理性和人性的时期,也是他在康德的研究中成就最多的时期,也许这并不是偶然的。商务印书馆慕其名向他约稿,由于"文革"爆发,只出版了 4 部,这可以说是学界的一大损失。此后 10 年,这位耄耋老人在蹲牛棚、下农村、

---

① 贺麟先生在《康德、黑格尔哲学在中国的传播》中把康德、黑格尔哲学在中国的传播分为三个时期:早期为从变法运动到五四运动,中期为从五四运动到全国解放,后期为中华人民共和国成立之后到现在。

挨批斗、受凌辱等更为恶劣的境遇中仍念念不忘康德、黑格尔,笔耕不辍。在那令知识分子濒于崩溃绝望的岁月,他鼓励难友说:"要有信心,做学问不能停下来!"像其他中国学者一样,韦卓民先生也以自己的人格谱写了康德、黑格尔东渐史上悲壮的一幕。

我们看到,韦先生关于康德研究的遗著中,绝大部分是译著,是康德的原著和对原著解读的著作。他认为,要真正认识康德哲学一定要读原著,特别是他的"三大批判",这是康德哲学思想的精髓。韦先生曾著文专门分析"三大批判"的前提、基础和背景,提出了独到的见解。他认为"三大批判"中的《纯粹理性批判》是重中之重,代表了康德在哲学史上的地位。五六十年代,他在"康德哲学讲座"上,主要讲的是《纯粹理性批判》。他着重分析了该书的主题思想"验前综合判断怎样成为可能的?"这一课题的理论来源、内容实质和解决途径。正是因为想要帮助国内学子更好、更深入地学习这部名著,才知难而进,重新翻译这本最难读的书,以克服当时已有译本中的缺陷。在此前后,他还翻译了两位英国学者讲解《纯粹理性批判》的两本专著(即《康德〈纯粹理性批判〉解义》和《康德的经验形而上学》);特别在"文革"前夕,又翻译了康德为《纯粹理性批判》所撰的简写本《一切未来形而上学导论》。这些都说明了他对这一名著的异常重视。

但是韦先生并不是单纯为翻译而翻译,而是把研究寓于翻译之中,翻译的过程也就是他的研究过程。当年他讲康德、黑格尔哲学时,对一些重要概念、词语,总是反复地从结构、词根讲到语义,从英文、德文追溯到拉丁文,给人的感觉似乎有点"咬文嚼字"、"烦琐考证",但只要用心体会,就会领略到其中的奥妙和深刻。

下面仅举两例:

例一,"a priori"一词,国内一般都译为"先天",韦先生认为是错误的,因为"a priori"在拉丁文中并无"与生俱来"之意,康德用这个词更无此意。韦先生在译此词时,先译为"先验",后一再琢磨,觉得也不妥当。因为在康德著作里多年来已用"先验"来译德文的"transzendental",如果再用它来译"a priori",就混淆不清了。于是他反复推敲,最后决定创造一个崭新的词语"验前"来译"a priori"。从字面上看,二者似无甚区别,实际上意思却大不相同,"验前"更符合康德的原意。韦先生在"文革"中还专为此写过一篇文稿。韦先生的这一翻译,目前已得到许多学者的认同。例如中国人民大学的钟宇人教授在来信中写道:"康德所用'a priori'一词,蓝译本译为'先天的',影响很大,其实是不确切的。韦先生根据原拉丁文与对康德用意的深入研究,创译为'验前的',很符合康德所说'绝对不依赖于经验的'原意。"

例二,《纯粹理性批判》第二版序言中康德有一句名言:Ich musste also das Wissen aufheben, um zum Glauben Platz zu bekommen。20世纪的五六十年代,国内都把它译成"我否定知识,以便给信仰扫清地盘",并据此认定康德是个反对科学知识的信仰主义者。韦先生说,这根本不是康德的原意,是英译者错误地把"aufheben"译为"deny",国内有人据英文而译为"否定",是跟着别人犯错误。因此韦先生根据对德文"aufheben"与"Glaube"词义的考察,及对康德思想主旨的理解,把这句话译为"我要扬弃知识,以便替信念留有余地"。近年来,随着对康德哲学研究的深入,学术界对把"aufheben"译为"扬弃",把"Glaube"译为"信念"尚有不同的意见。但若留意到当年韦先生这样译,至少表达了康德既未否定知识,又给信仰扫清地盘的意蕴,从而为康德在中国的"错案"平了反,也就不难体会他的苦心了。

对康德哲学中的概念、术语,乃至重要句子,像这样苦心推敲、决不含糊的例子还有很多很多。正如韦先生说的,他在翻译时"以信为主",用尽心思忠实于原著,不能为了追求"达"、"雅"而损伤原著本意。为了更忠实于原著,他始终不断地修订自己的译文,刻苦钻研、精益求精,正如他所说的,做学问一定要有一种"主见不可无,成见不可有"的独立与创新精神。这种精神在当今弥漫着浮躁、浮夸气氛的学术界,尤其值得提倡,值得推崇。

韦卓民先生在康德哲学研究领域卓有成效的工作,辉煌的成就,是他一生事业的重要组成部分。韦卓民先生乃是为了一个宏伟的工程而奋斗终生的。这个工程就是营造一座宽广而坚实的融通中西文化的桥梁。早在70年前,他已明确了这一奋斗目标。1928年他在伦敦所作的一篇演讲中声称,融合异质文化是各民族文化发展的规律,而在当时的我国,"融合中西文化则是中国走向现代化而必需的、富有挑战性的工作"。他还旗帜鲜明地申明:在吸收西方文化时,我们反对妄自尊大的"保守派",也要反对崇洋媚外的"洋化派"。如果说,解放前他在融合中西文化方面所做的工作主要是通过在国内办教会大学、宣讲基督教神学和在国外讲解与介绍中国传统优秀文化的话,那么,解放后他就把主要精力放在西方哲学史的译介上来了。原来,他研究、译介康德哲学正是站在这个高度来进行的!他常说:我们要在学习西方哲学时做到取长补短,以便更好地发展中国的哲学。他在上世纪50年代就曾多次说过:在欧洲,有些小国都翻译、出版了柏拉图、亚里士多德、康德、黑格尔等哲学大师的"全集",而我们至今还没有一套,这同我们这个文明古国的地位是极不相称的。他立志要弥补这一缺陷。本来他已具备优越的主观条件,既"通晓古今",又"学贯中西",仅外语就精通英、德、法、俄、拉丁文等七八种。可他并不满足,仍自谦说"差距很大"。其实,他是在鼓励我们努力奠定扎实的功底,以铺设他理想中的"桥梁"。他还认为,在介绍西方文化、西方哲学时,要避免把西方的观念"解说成中国的观念",过分追求中国化、通俗化,以致把人家的文化变质变味。我们体会他的意思是,在学习康德这样的西方哲学时,一定要力争学到原汁原味的康德思想;要努力体验领会德国语言的特征及其文化背景;设法逐渐领会康德的思维方式从而弄懂其实质,真正做到沟通中西,优势互补。

在这方面,韦先生开了先河,做了榜样,引领我们走近了康德,也引领我们走上了民族文化复兴的宽广大道。

唐有伯　曹方久
2006年6月24日

目 录

中 文

基督教学校的行动方向 …………………………………………… 3
华中大学 1933—1934 年度校长报告书 …………………………… 5
与华中大学一年级学生谈话 ……………………………………… 7
抗战时期中国的教育 ……………………………………………… 11
学者在战时的任务 ………………………………………………… 21
如何成为一所基督教大学 ………………………………………… 25
致华中大学校友函 ………………………………………………… 29
《华中大学二十周年纪念特刊》发刊词 …………………………… 31
华中大学史略 ……………………………………………………… 32
为中国教会培养有学识的领导人——中国基督教教育的前景 …… 37
华中大学前途之展望与规则 ……………………………………… 44
今后基督教中学应取的政策 ……………………………………… 48
华中大学向毕业同学劝募食米二百石救济学荒启 ……………… 51
奉令呈复本校教学训育各实情 仍祈鉴核指示以便改进由 ……… 53
华中大学基本精神 ………………………………………………… 55
四十年来我国基督教的高等教育 ………………………………… 58
同学中对于下乡参加土改工作一点顾虑的解答 ………………… 65
土改学习小结 ……………………………………………………… 67
我所亲历的欧美高等教育 ………………………………………… 71
武昌文华书院及其后身华中大学 ………………………………… 77
浅论科学研究的方法 ……………………………………………… 91
中文通信数通 ……………………………………………………… 100

英　文

Whither Christian Education?	109
Hua Chung (Central China) College	115
The Role of Scholars in the War	122
Semi-Annual Report to Board of Trustees Known as Board of Founders and Board of Directors of Hua Chung College (Wu Chang) in Kweilin, Kwangsi, China	127
Three Years of Chinese Education in War Time	135
Education in Wartime China	151
What Makes a College Christian	166
The Future of Christian Education in China	172
Development of Hua Chung College after the War	182
President's Report to the Board of Directors, Hua Chung College, Hsichow, Yunnan, for the Year 1943—1944	203
A Memorandum on the Planning of the Christian Colleges in China After the War	216
Annual Report on the Work of the Department of Chinese Literature and History in Hua Chung College for the Year 1944—1945	232
Report Regarding Hua Chung College Given at the Yale-in-China Trustees' Meeting in New Haven on January 26, 1946 by President Francis C. M. Wei	239
Training Educated Leadership for the Church in China	244
The President's Annual Report for the Academic Year 1946—1947 Hua Chung University, Wu Chang, China	258
The President's Annual Report for the Academic Year 1947—1948	277
Comments on the Report of the Committee to Study the Progress of the Ten-Year Plan for Hua Chung University	293
英文通信 175 通	296
1. To F. E. Hawkins (December 2, 1929)	296
2. To Mr. Hutchins (April 2, 1930)	297

目 录

3. To Dr. E. H. Hume (July 17, 1930) ·················· 299
4. To Dr. Edward H. Hume (November 10, 1930) ············ 300
5. To Canon Anson Phelps Stokes (February 2, 1931) ········ 301
6. To Mr. E. Fay Campbell (February 26, 1931) ··············· 301
7. To Dr. Edward H. Hume (November 30, 1931) ············ 303
8. To Rev. A. P. Stokes (December 4, 1931) ················· 304
9. To Mr. E. Fay Campbell (January 5, 1933) ··············· 304
10. To Dr. Edward H. Hume (February 1, 1933) ············ 305
11. To Mr. E. Fay Campbell (February 8, 1933) ··············· 306
12. To Mr. Francis S. Hutchins (May 9, 1933) ··············· 306
13. To Prof. S. M. Gunn (December 18, 1933) ··············· 307
14. To Dean Wallace B. Donham (November 6, 1934) ········ 309
15. To the Directors, Alumni, Parents of Students, and Friends of Hua Chung College (1935) ····················· 310
16. To Mr. Richard D. Weigle (September 19, 1935) ········ 313
17. To Mr. R. D. Weigle (November 6, 1935) ··············· 314
18. To Mr. Richard D. Weigle (March 11, 1936) ··············· 315
19. To Mr. Richard D. Weigle (March 16, 1936) ··············· 317
20. To Mr. Richard D. Weigle (April 27, 1936) ··············· 318
21. To Mr. Richard D. Weigle (June 1, 1936) ··············· 318
22. To Rev. Edwin C. Lobenstine (August 28, 1936) ········ 319
23. To Mr. Richard D. Weigle (September 12, 1936) ········ 320
24. To Dr. John W. Wood (September 12, 1936) ··············· 321
25. To Mr. Richard D. Weigle (November 20, 1936) ········ 322
26. To Dr. Sherman (January, 1937) ························· 322
27. To Mr. Richard D. Weigle (May 3, 1937) ··············· 323
28. To Mr. Richard D. Weigle (March 3, 1937) ··············· 324
29. To Dr. P'u Hwang (January 4, 1938) ····················· 325
30. To Dr. P'u Hwang (January 17, 1938) ··················· 326
31. To Professor David Hsiung (January 19, 1938) ············ 327
32. To Professor Paul C. T. Kwei (January 19, 1938) ········ 328
33. To Rt. Rev. Logan Roots (February 4, 1938) ············ 329
34. To Dr. P'u Hwang (February 4, 1938) ··················· 329

35. To Mr. Richard D. Weigle (May 3, 1938) ………………… 331
36. To Rev. A. M. Sherman (September 13, 1938) ………… 331
37. To Members of the Board of Founders
    (December 5, 1938) ……………………………………… 333
38. To Dr. E. C. Lobenstine (January 19, 1939) …………… 334
39. To Rev. A. M. Sherman (January 21, 1939) …………… 335
40. To Mr. Robert A. Smith (August 12, 1939) …………… 336
41. To O. S. Lyford (November 8, 1939) …………………… 337
42. To Mr. Robert A. Smith (November 9, 1939) ………… 338
43. To Mr. Oliver S. Lyford (November 16, 1939) ………… 339
44. To Francis S. Hutchins (November 20, 1939) ………… 340
45. To Mr. Robert A. Smith (January 8, 1940) …………… 341
46. To Rev. E. C. Lobenstine (January 22, 1940) ………… 341
47. To Professor Serge Elisseeff (February 15, 1940) …… 343
48. To Rev. Arthur M. Sherman (March 18, 1940) ………… 344
49. To Mr. Robert A. Smith (June 7, 1940) ……………… 345
50. To Mr. Robert A. Smith (August 13, 1940) …………… 348
51. To Professor Serge Elisseeff (August 14, 1940) ……… 348
52. To Mr. Robert A. Smith (September 2, 1940) ………… 349
53. To Mr. Oliver S. Lyford (September 21, 1940) ……… 350
54. To Mr. O. S. Lyford (October 12, 1940) ……………… 351
55. To Mr. Robert A. Smith (January 8, 1941) …………… 352
56. To Mr. Robert A. Smith (January 29, 1941) ………… 353
57. To Rev. J. T. Addison (February 12, 1941) …………… 354
58. To Dr. Arthur M. Sherman (April 3, 1941) …………… 357
59. To Mr. Oliver S. Lyford (May 7, 1941) ……………… 360
60. To Rev. A. M. Sherman (June 10, 1941) …………… 360
61. To Mr. Robert A. Smith (June 10, 1941) …………… 361
62. To Mr. Robert A. Smith (June 20, 1941) …………… 363
63. To Mr. Robert A. Smith (July 9, 1941) ……………… 364
64. To Mr. Joseph I. Parker (July 11, 1941) …………… 366
65. To Mr. Oliver S. Lyford (October 28, 1941) ………… 366
66. To Rev. Arthur M. Sherman (November 6, 1941) …… 369

目 录

67. To Rev. A. M. Sherman (January 13, 1942) ············· 372
68. To Mr. Oliver S. Lyford (January 27, 1942) ············· 373
69. To Mr. Robert A. Smith (February 11, 1942) ············ 374
70. To Mr. Oliver S. Lyford (March 11, 1942)············· 375
71. To Dr. Joseph I. Parker (May 29, 1942) ··············· 376
72. To Mr. Oliver S. Lyford (June 11, 1942) ··············· 376
73. To Mr. Oliver S. Lyford (September 29, 1942) ············ 377
74. To Mr. Oliver S. Lyford (October 8, 1942) ············· 378
75. To Mr. Oliver S. Lyford (October 13, 1942) ············· 379
76. To Mr. Oliver S. Lyford (November 5, 1942) ············ 380
77. To Dr. Edwin C. Lobenstine (November 10, 1942) ······ 381
78. To Mr. Oliver S. Lyford (December 8, 1942)············· 382
79. To Mr. Oliver S. Lyford (January 26, 1943) ············· 383
80. To Rev. A. M. Sherman (January 26, 1943) ············· 386
81. To Mr. Oliver S. Lyford (March 4, 1943) ··············· 387
82. To Mr. Oliver S. Lyford (May 1, 1943) ··············· 388
83. To Dr. Frank Price (June 17, 1943) ··················· 389
84. To Mr. Oliver S. Lyford (August 10, 1943) ············· 391
85. To Mr. Oliver S. Lyford (August 24, 1943) ············· 392
86. To Mr. Oliver S. Lyford (September 7, 1943) ············ 393
87. To Mr. Oliver S. Lyford (October 5, 1943) ············· 394
88. To Mr. Oliver S. Lyford (November 9, 1943) ············ 395
89. Report of Various Conversations at Hua Chung (Late November 1943) ····························· 397
90. Hua Chung College Plan for Development after the War Submitted by President Francis C. M. Wei (February 15, 1944) ······························· 398
91. To Mr. Oliver S. Lyford (February 22, 1944) ············ 400
92. To Professor Serge Elisseeff (March 9, 1944) ············ 401
93. To Miss Rachel Dowd (March 14, 1944) ··············· 402
94. To Dr. William Fenn (March 14, 1944) ··············· 403
95. To Mrs. Ida Williams (April 4, 1944) ··················· 404
96. To Mr. Oliver S. Lyford (April 25, 1944) ··············· 404

97. To Dr. Lobenstine (May 16, 1944) ……………… 405
98. To Dr. Charles H. Corbett (June 22, 1944) ………… 406
99. To Mr. Oliver S. Lyford (July 31, 1944)……………… 406
100. To Mr. Oliver S. Lyford (August 15, 1944) …………… 408
101. To Mr. Oliver S. Lyford (September 14, 1944) ……… 409
102. To Rev. Edwin C. Lobenstine (September 19, 1944) …………………………………………………… 410
103. To Dr. Charles H. Corbett (October 3, 1944) ………… 410
104. To Mr. Oliver S. Lyford (October 12, 1944) ………… 411
105. A Paragraph from Dr. Wei's Letter N. Y. 98 of November 9, 1944 ……………………………………… 413
106. To Mr. Oliver S. Lyford (February 22, 1945) ………… 414
107. To Mr. Oliver S. Lyford (March 20, 1945) ………… 415
108. To Rev. Earle H. Ballou (March 20, 1945) ………… 416
109. To Miss. Rachel A. Dowd (April 19, 1945) ………… 417
110. To Dr. Charles H. Corbett (April 19, 1945)………… 418
111. To Mr. Oliver S. Lyford (May 4, 1945) ……………… 418
112. To Rev. James Thayer Addison (June 19, 1945) ……… 419
113. To Dr. Arthur O. Rinden (February 1, 1946) ………… 419
114. To Rev. A. M. Sherman (August 28, 1946)…………… 421
115. To Mr. Oliver S. Lyford (September 11, 1946) ……… 423
116. To Mr. Earl Fowler (October 7, 1946) ……………… 424
117. To Mr. Oliver S. Lyford (October 15, 1946) ………… 425
118. To Rt. Rev. William P. Roberts (November 11, 1946) …………………………………………………………… 428
119. To Mr. Rev. A. M. Sherman (November 12, 1946) … 429
120. To Mr. J. Earl Fowler (November 15, 1946) ………… 431
121. To Mr. Oliver S. Lyford (December 3, 1946) ………… 432
122. To Mr. J. Earl Fowler (December 17, 1946) ………… 433
123. To Rev. Arthur M. Sherman (February 12, 1947) …… 433
124. To Mr. Oliver S. Lyford (March 10, 1947) …………… 434
125. To Mr. J. Earl Fowler (May 1, 1947) ……………… 434
126. To Mr. Oliver S. Lyford (June 4, 1947) …………… 436

目 录

127. To Mr. J. Earl Fowler (September 15, 1947) ………… 437
128. To Mr. Oliver S. Lyford (September 26, 1947) ……… 438
129. To Mr. Oliver S. Lyford (October 18, 1947) ………… 440
130. To Mr. W. Reginald Wheeler (September 15, 1947) … 442
131. To Professor Kenneth S. Latourette (January 17, 1948) … 443
132. To Mr. Oliver S. Lyford (January 23, 1948) ………… 444
133. To Mr. J. Earl Fowler (January 29, 1948) ……………… 445
134. To Mr. Oliver S. Lyford (March 9, 1948)……………… 446
135. To Mr. J. Earl Fowler (March 23, 1948) ……………… 448
136. To Mr. J. Earl Fowler (April 13, 1948) ……………… 448
137. To Rev. Arthur M. Sherman (June 1, 1948) ………… 449
138. To Mr. J. Earl Fowler (July 28, 1948) ………………… 449
139. To Mr. J. Earl Fowler (August 16, 1948)……………… 452
140. To Mr. J. Earl Fowler (October 5, 1948) ……………… 453
141. To Dr. William P. Fenn (October 26, 1948)…………… 454
142. To Mr. J. Earl Fowler (November 4, 1948) …………… 457
143. To Mr. J. Earl Fowler (November 16, 1948) ………… 458
144. To Mr. J. Earl Fowler (November 23, 1948) ………… 459
145. To Dr. Robert J. McMullen (December 7, 1948) ……… 460
146. To Mr. J. Earl Fowler (December 14, 1948) ………… 461
147. To Mr. J. Earl Fowler (December 21, 1948) ………… 462
148. To Dr. Robert J. McMullen (January 4, 1949)………… 463
149. To Mr. J. Earl Fowler (January 10, 1949) …………… 464
150. To Rev. Robert J. McMullen (January 26, 1949)……… 465
151. To Dr. Robert J. McMullen (February 9, 1949) ……… 466
152. To Dr. Robert J. McMullen (February 17, 1949) …… 467
153. To Rt. Rev. Jno. B. Bentley (February 24, 1949) …… 468
154. To Dr. Robert J. McMullen (February 24, 1949) …… 469
155. To Dr. Robert J. McMullen (March 3, 1949) ………… 471
156. To Dr. Robert J. McMullen (April 19, 1949) ………… 472
157. To Mr. J. Earl Fowler (April 19, 1949) ……………… 473
158. To Dr. Robert J. McMullen (April 26, 1949) ………… 474
159. To Dr. Robert J. McMullen (May 3, 1949) …………… 476

160. To Dr. Robert J. McMullen (May 10, 1949) ········ 477
161. An Excerpt from a Letter from President Francis Wei (May 31, 1949) ········ 478
162. Excerpts from a Letter from President Wei, Hua Chung University (June 7, 1949) ········ 479
163. Excerpts from a Letter from Francis Wei, Hua Chung University (July 21, 1949) ········ 481
164. To Dr. Arthur M. Sherman (August 11, 1949) ········ 482
165. Letter from President Wei, Hua Chung University (August 11, 1949) ········ 483
166. Letter from Francis Wei, Hua Chung University (September 2, 1949) ········ 483
167. Letter from Francis Wei, Hua Chung University (September 9, 1949) ········ 485
168. Letter from Francis Wei, Hua Chung University (September 21, 1949) ········ 486
169. Letter from Francis Wei, Hua Chung University (January 31, 1950) ········ 487
170. Letter from President Wei, Hua Chung University (March 9, 1950) ········ 489
171. To United Board Office (March 14 and 21, 1950) ········ 490
172. Excerpts from a Letter from President Wei, Hua Chung University (August 29, 1950) ········ 490
173. Excerpts from a Letter from President Wei, Hua Chung University (November 29, 1950) ········ 491
174. Letter from President Wei, Hua Chung University (January 17, 1951) ········ 492
175. Letter from Francis Wei at Hua Chung University (February 13, 1951) ········ 493

出版后记 ········ 495

中文

基督教学校的行动方向*

不管现在的环境如何困难,我相信教会中小学应该继续存在下去,其理由如下:

第一,我相信现在这个时期是一个过渡时期,这一段时期有多久却很难说,如果我们基督教教育工作者能做出最大的努力,做适当的正确的工作,这种惧怕的和不信任的态度是不会长久的。政府对基督教将采取更自由灵活的态度的日子不久就会到来。遵照政府法规和减少原则牺牲是该赞扬的,等待着好日子到来吧!

第二,在现在形势下,在小学和初中进行基督教工作并非完全不可能。我们常说基督徒教师会造成基督徒学校,再没有比这更明确的真理。想想我们每天每日与儿童接触的影响,即使他们在课外时间,在课堂以外,并不进礼拜堂做礼拜或听讲道,但是也有可能把我们学校的学生聚在一起搞宗教活动或把他们带进星期日圣经学校。不仅仅我们的学生,连学生的亲友也有可能,想一想我们有许多接近家属的机会并由此开创了在家庭中做基督教工作的道路。除了这种方式外,用别的方式是行不通的。最后想一想我们基督教教育工作者在居民中,使人看得很清楚的基督教教徒的品德。正是这样我们才能开办学校,关心儿童。

第三,即使我们把形势估计得最坏,不能正面地、公开地做宗教工作,但是,如果有了教会的小学和初中,我们至少可以保证一件事,即我们把这样多的儿童放在我们学校读书,他们就不至于受到随时都可以蔓延全国的反基督教的宣传。

第四,即最后一点,我们应归功于基督徒家长,帮我们维持了一些小学和初中,政府不能剥夺家长在家里教他们的子女他们所要求的宗教的权利。然而,如果儿童们过多接触在学校中的反基督教的或十足的世俗主义的宣传的影响,家庭中宗教教育的效果必然会受到损伤。

---

* 此文原载《教育季报》第 22 卷第 4 期(1930 年 10 月)。

我料想,办初中的困难局面将会到来。那儿的学生将不能进入外面的任何教堂,他们也太年幼了,自己也不能参加学校以外的宗教活动。唯一的办法是使学校小、效力高,使得师生之间的紧密接触得到保证。

我们不应当关闭我们的好学校,除非我们委派自己的教师成为不可能或者基督教教徒不准当教师。

华中大学 1933—1934 年度校长报告书*

　　我们有限的学生给予的学费只是一笔小额收入。可是收学费将会违背我们本身的宗旨。由于1926—1927年的革命，1931年的水灾，国内与国际形势的混乱，华中区贫困了，很少学生交得起学费。如果我们的收费增加，我们便会失去一些来自本地基督教会的我们的好学生。即在比中国经济上更发达的其他国家，也很少高校教育机关能够主要靠收费来维持自己的。作此企图将非我们大学之福。

　　我们迄今未从地方或中央的中国政府得到任何津贴，没有任何与中国有利害关系的基金团体曾给我们当前预算以任何津贴。虽然我们得到"洛克菲勒基金"来作我们一些教员、奖学金和作特别研究的小额津贴之福庇。我们的校友寥寥无几，而且他们中许多在教会或学校工作，这使他们不能给本大学以大量款项的捐助。

　　可是，中国公众在开始对我们学校发生兴趣。去年我们预算不足，一个包括大多数是汉口的商人的本地中华委员会曾负责给中国文学讲座筹募一笔捐款；同时该委员会在支付中国文学系主任的薪金。在上海的"耶鲁俱乐部"也在开始在中国的耶鲁旧友和朋友中，给我们的"耶鲁在中国理学院"的一个讲座筹划一笔基金，来表示赞成他们的美国校友的工作。后者多年来在为中国人之福利而支持"耶鲁外国教会"。当然要多过一个的燕子才能造成春天。但这些对我们工作的表征是最令人鼓舞的。

　　我们的方针是：学生第一、二学年的功课应在较为宽广的基础上，而剩下的两年应较为集中。从而，我们要求学生后两年中，全部功课的四分之三专心研究主要科和次要科或有关科目，而在第三、四学年中受到主要科中最低限度必修功课之三分之二。

　　我们一方面要忠诚于我们创办的原则，另一方面忠诚于中国的法律。

---

　　* 原件为手拟草稿，故而字迹模糊，意思不全。此处所载，仅供参考。特此说明并致歉。原件现藏华中师范大学档案馆。

我们尽可能忠诚地遵循"校董会"("创办人"会所任命的)为本大学所制定的政策；但同时我们设法尽我们所能执行南京教育部的一切法规。

诚然，我们在大学中没有公开宣称的训练牧师课程，然而要完成这种训练是可能的，而且我们正在考虑用各种方法来进行。

训练牧师的机会从没有像今天这样大的。职业训练日益为政府所强调了。同时，在最近上海基督教中学全国会议上，校长们请求"全国基督教教育促进会"安排由基督教大学发给在教育学科方面具有最低限度训练的学生以师资证书。当我们短期训练农村师资的计划，由于与那现在有着一个农村纲领的华中区基督教学校的合作而付诸实现时，我们在这方面的服务即将进一步扩展。

可是还有另一方面具有远大而有效结果的服务可能性的，就是为商业服务的教育。汉口是一个大商业中心。随着机械交通的改进和铁路干线——特别是粤汉铁路的完成，我们这里势必成为国内最大的商业中心，即所谓中国的芝加哥。我们的毕业生将如我们各组成大学的一样，愈来愈多投进商业界中去。一种像我们学校所能给予学生的具有基督教理想的经济与商业的良好训练，将供给像汉口这样的中心的领导人物——他们将不仅是中国而且是全世界之福。我们与商界的忠实关系将使我们处在这种工作的有利的基础上，同时在今后十年或十五年的开始阶段中，必然看见给经济商业系的支持愈来愈多。因为，今后的支助定会来自其毕业生及商店，当他们更充分认识这样的训练对于商业的健康发展的价值的时候，就不用提到其他一些可能性了。所顾及的已够和我们的朋友资助人共同抱有我们所负担的工作是必需的这个感觉："收获诚然丰富，但劳动者寡少。"

与华中大学一年级学生谈话*

今天我要讲的是关于大学性质及本校组织两点,大家来到这里,必定都知道大学到底是做什么的,也必定想到进大学里来究竟预备做些什么。教育部规定,大学是以研究高深学问,培养专门人才为宗旨的学术机关,其任务非常重大。

一个现代国家的教育,常依其阶段分为三个等级:

(一)初等教育

(二)中等教育

(三)高等教育

初等教育是基础教育,其目的在于普遍地推行义务教育,树立公民教育的基础。中等教育是以培植社会各项团体之领袖人才为目标,不单只在于造成一批好国民,使其能服务社会服务国家而已,且更应灌输他们更多的知识及其与社会国家的关系。至于大学教育,则更较前述二者高过一层。它是中等教育所不能研究到的教育,是以作为特殊贡献为依归的教育。

我国教育已经普遍到了什么程度,迄今尚无确实统计。根据初步的调查结果:我国有四千一百多万儿童应该接受小学教育,但是现在实际入学的儿童不过一千一百余万,竟有三千万儿童失学,这是一个非常严重而待解决的问题。就教员而言,这三千万失学儿童,应该需要一百多万才够分配,而求这样巨量的师资,目前绝难办到。中学教育更不堪言,我国现时中学生不过五十余万;美国人口仅及我国四分之一,尚有七百多万中学生,我们与之比拟,相差实在太远。至于大学和专科学校学生数目更少。据抗战前之统计,全国人数尚不能超过四万,由此可知,我国教育程度距离理想目标实在太远,至此又令我想到大学生与出路的问题上来:大学生

---

* 原文题为"韦校长与一年级学生谈话",刊载《华大桂声》第1卷第1期(1938年10月1日),由许俊千、袁明清、胡润清记录整理并发表。

人数既少到这样,尚有人整日价地闹喊着"无出路",时在今日,正值国家遭逢厄难,社会情形也变动得比较厉害,在这种时代要一个比较适意的职业,的确不甚容易,惟可怪者,许多大学毕业学生有事竟不能做,甚或不肯做。学生不能干,学校应该负责研究其不能干的理由。质言之,社会并非没有工作,而多是毕业学生不肯去干。大学生若求享乐,定难找到出路,若求真实服务,则到处都是机会。

其次我要谈到华中本身上来。华中究竟是哪一种学校呢?大家都知道,在国内高中以上的学校有两种:一为大学与独立学院,一为专门学校。依教育部规定,后者以两年或三年为修业期,所施教育,是应用某种事业之一种技能(农专、图专皆属其列)。至于大学,则有文、法、商、教育、理、工、医、农等八院。文学院分中外文学、史地、音乐等系;法学院分法律、政治、经济等系;商学院分理财、会计、银行等系;教育学院分心理、教育行政等系;理学院分物理、化学、生物、天文、地质等系;工学院分机械、土木、工程、矿冶等系;医学院则有医生、看护、公共卫生等训练;农学院则有农林、畜牧等科。教育部规定,大学至多分设以上所述八院,不能再有第九之设立;若只办三院,则需设有理、工、医、农中之任何一院,方得称为大学。我们设有文理教育三院,所以也称大学。某生在某学院毕业即授以某种学士,惟经济学系虽属文学院,却授以商学士,故共有四种学位的授予。教育部对于大学课程,正在规定,我们学校前两年的课程仍旧一样,并无多大限制,不过四年之中,非修满一百四十六学分不能毕业,本来课程之名称,学分之数目,院系之多少,无需多事规定,其要者乃在于如何健全学生学术头脑,以及养成特殊技能。

我国大学普遍可以分为两种:一为欧洲大陆式,一为美国式。就一般而言,国、省立大学多近于欧洲大陆式(大陆学生如德国,须经过十二年学历,方可升入大学,我国亦然);其不同者是我国大学修业期为四年,德国大学只两年。德国大学教育与其他国家确有不同,凡学生毕业考试及格,论文合格者,即授以哲学博士学位(柏林大学神学院例外),但德国教育确能造就许多专门人才,德国的九年中等教育,全为准备升大学之阶梯。中学毕业学生对于求学工具以及基本知识均已获得,故能进入大学领受专门教育而不感觉半点困难。我国中学未臻完善,大学若采用这种教育方式,必属难能;观乎我国之中等教育,对于一切基本学科,尚未筑成相当之基础,就中文程度而言,至大学仍需学习,外国语言能力,更属不够。这种情形在德国是绝对没有的,他们高出我们的程度,实在惊人。据我校英文系教员多年研究的结果,以湘、鄂、皖、赣诸省中学校之学生平均程度为标准,年来投考华中之英文入学考试,仅相当于美国高中一年级程度,这是一种非常落后的现象。今日中学生所习之数学,程度虽加紧提高,但成绩竟不如从前的了,其原因在于中学课程太繁,时间不充分,故以我国此种中学基础,去模仿欧洲大陆国家之大学制度,是只有百弊而无一利的。我们正看出这种弊病,所以特求极力补救。课程一项,不在于繁多——盖世上一切知识,绝非在这四年中即可以研究得精通的,其要者乃在于在此四年修业期中,打定一个基础,使学生以后能继续研究学习。我国大学亦有仿效美国制度者,这大都以教会大学为多。美国大学教育制度,十余年来,日求改善,我国竟模仿其陈旧不适用的制度,殊属失计。观乎美国大学生多无专门技能,苟进一步从事专门研究,作学术上之贡献,至少尚需受三年研究院教育。美国一般人最珍视时间,而于教育上,则确不免过于浪费,德国中学毕业生,入美国大学只需两年,便可卒业,由此可知美国十六年的教育,仅相当于德国十四年的程度,其时间之浪费可见。直到前几年感受了经济的不景气,推进教育才注重节省光阴。

华中自改组以来,不过九年,惨淡经营在谋养成学生研究学术的态度与门径,使其毕业以后能够继续研究,深求学术上之造诣,以贡献社会国家。大家都知道,办学校首在经费充裕。世界上绝对没有大学是仅依学费收入,便可以应付一切的。我们每年的经费大概是二十多万,和别的大学比较起来,恐怕是最少的了,但我们是在刻苦经营,尽量地推行服务人群社会的工作,所以前四年教育部派员来校观察的时候,批评我们是"以最少的金钱,办最多的事业"。如工资之节省,教员多兼职而不兼薪等,都是我们吃苦实干的实例子,欲以少数金钱,举办最多的事业,我们设立一系,即切实为之,决不苟且敷衍。至于学生所纳各费,以每年计,尚不足学校为他花用的数目的十分之一,故人家以为多收学生,学校即可增加收入,是为大误。抗战发动前,我校本拟于今年度容纳学生两百人,而今则决不愿收足此数,并希望不超过一百六十人为好,学校每年花用二十多万，教育百多个学生，平均每人花费千余元。希望各同学随着我们全体教职员，本着苦干实干的精神求学。我们聘请教员不在乎讲课之动听悦耳，而在谋学生学术上之增长。我校原则上，不聘兼任教员，不收走读学生，目的在使师生间随时可以析疑研究，多有切磋的机会，去年提倡导师制，亦是本着这个目标，故不在乎学生之多，在使学生多有与教员接近的机会。

几年来我们所举行之中期考试，是在测验学生于第一、第二两年中，于所习科目及基本治学工具，已否养成相当的根底，中期考试，除英文和国文之外，再就其本系所规定之科目，加以考试；考试科目共五项，五项之中，必有两门是修满过十二学分，三门修满过六学分的。

至于学校将来的发展，今天暂且不讲，一来是短于时间，一来也是不愿谈多空理想，我们办学校的精神各方面大家都能体会得到的。实事求是是华中办学的基本精神，希望大家要深加注意。

抗战时期中国的教育[*]

  多少世纪以来，中国人就秉承了古圣先贤的教诲：深信人活着不只是为了饮食，而是为了国家的生存必须竭尽所能去维护吾人从古到今所积聚的经验。他们体会到国运是依存于一个有教养的领导阶层，基于邦国之服务乃是凭借学识，而且经由其服务不但可以光耀门楣，更且沾益了其据以崛起的社会。主要的是基于此一传统，方使学识之炬，代有传人，教育工作从未中断，而无视于国运的振疲。

  此一值得中国人骄傲的教育传统应追溯到公元前一千年。古时生计简朴，教育即可于阅读先人遗留下来的书籍中获得，故尔教育事工即使在战时也不受干扰。当时只要有一位塾师和几本书就足够推行教育下一代的工作了。可是过去半个世纪中，中国的教育制度乃是因袭西方的，教育不再是一个简单的事情了。校舍更精美，设备更昂贵而且不易搬动，不像以前的只要一位塾师和少数的学生。现在我们拥有不少教职员和人数相当庞大的青年学子需要我们去照顾。像这样的一个教育机构及其工作，很容易因为任一严重的社会或政治的动乱而致中断或遭干扰。因此，当日本于1937年发动侵华战争以来，中国采取了抗战政策，政府所面临的一个问题就是在这个存亡绝续的全面战争中，如何继续我们的教育计划。

  1932年的沪战乃至1931年东北同胞所遭受的惨痛经验在告诫我们，敌人对于我们的教育设施是毫不留情的。只要有机会，第一个受到攻击和破坏的就是学校。面对此一情况，如何保全我们的教育力量，实在是一个很大的课题。战争持续而我们的军队继续诱敌深入，教育工作不可能停顿下来等待战事中止。另外还有一个更严重的问题，是要计划陷于敌后的人民的教育。敌人当然会榨取沦陷区青年人的心智。面对此一可能，吾人应否将学校和学生统统迁往后方？或是干脆关闭学校，而将在学

---

  * 此文原为英文，1940年发表于重庆。后经作者的学生蓝乾章译成中文，刊载于在台湾出版的《湖北文献》第54期（1970年）。

青年送上前线作战？中国不是一个富庶的国家，国库的每一分钱都应当用于战争，以保卫国家。我们就让这些青年人的心智随着战争的持续而呈休耕的态势呢，还是用各种方法勉励在极端困苦的环境下仍能继续我们的教育工作？过去三年在战争中的中国教育是一部史诗，将为中国人民子子孙孙永志不忘。

大专院校的迁徙

自从1937年夏季以来，中国教育所发生的事情，要言之，当诿因于中国文化的富饶淳厚以及中国人民真正喜爱和平的德性。仅就高等教育的机构而言，在抗战以前即设立的108所大专院校中，目前只有14所还能在外国租界中或是为敌军侵占的城市中（如北平）勉强维持，这些机构在外国教会主持下还能继续办理。77所原来设立的大专院校都从战区迁往大后方，俾使弦歌不辍，其中包括国立的、私立的和基督教会所办理的。

任何人若体验过一个机构的被迫搬迁，将知这实在是一件不愉快的事。房舍当然是搬不动的，所有的家具也不得不丢弃，科学仪器和设备大都是易脆或是过于笨重而无法搬运，图书要装箱而且沉重。在战时，运输困难，就算能够运送，搬运整座图书馆甚或小部分的图书，所需运费之高昂，实足惊人。可是搬迁一所学院或一所大学而抛弃其藏书和教学设备，那还有何用！在敌人封锁了大部分的海港后，避处内地的学校如欲补充图书仪器，即使可能，也是昂贵的。其次是搬迁教职员及眷属和学生的问题。这77所机构中，每一单位平均有100位教职员，而每一位教职员的家庭约为四人到五人。跟随学校迁移的学生人数平均为300人。此一概略而低微的估计（由于缺乏精确统计，我们只能做此估计），意味着38,500位教职员及其家属和同等数目的学生，总计是77,000人的迁入内地，而这个数字还不包括国民小学。

我们到底为什么要搬迁？这当然不是为了校产，那些都是搬不动的，但是战争初期在上海、苏州、南京和旁的地方，经验告诉我们，当地的妇女和儿童处于敌骑之下是不安全的。敌人对于知识分子和学生是不友善的，如果这些人不幸陷入敌人之铁蹄，撇开身体所受的折磨不说，其精神上的痛苦将是无法忍受的。不是为了崇高的目的而牺牲性命更且牺牲人格,是无法辩白的。

　　国外的友人时常问我,何以这些学生不去从军或是参加其他战时工作以保卫国家,反而将他们迁入内地接受教育?难道政府不需要大学教授在战时提供技术的知识吗?这个说法可以说对,也可以说不对。在1937年以前,中国尚未充分备战,欲将我们的生产力一夜之间转入备战状态,谈何容易?而且我们的军械多自国外输入,大学教授不能立刻变为工厂的专家,然而许多教授都参加了战时工作,而且成千成万的学生也参加了陆军和空军。有一件事中国不虞匮乏,那就是人力。政府认为将所有的学生派赴前线,其代价终究是太高了。试想把他们培育到大学程度需要十几年的时间,而且全国的人口中,大学生仅占万分之一。他们若都在战场上被屠杀,那么战后国家的精神生活中势将出现严重的缺口,斯时重建的工作将对全国的才俊责以重任,似此情景曾于第一次世界大战结束后英、法两国的经验充分昭告世人。我们当前的口号是"抗战建国",假使我们的抗战忽略了复兴,那不啻自毁立场。中国现代化的伟业始于抗战前不久,必须于战争结束后完成,所需的长期训练绝对不可中止或遭到严重的阻碍。主要的是基于此理,使得高等教育的机构向内地迁徙,绝非逃避战争,而且配合政府抗战的计划以为战后国家的重建。这个代价是高的,而且所受的苦痛也是很大的,但是为了这场自卫和自保的圣战,这只不过是一部分的牺牲而已。

　　中日战争爆发之前,全国有108所高等教育机构,其中有42所为大学(每校至少设有三个学院)、34所独立学院和32所专科学校,其分配如次:

	国立	省立	私立	小计
大学	16	7	19	42
独立学院	5	8	21	34
专科学校	6	16	10	32

　　中日战争爆发以后,沿海各省以及扬子江下游和中游的教育机构都受到威胁,甚至于这些地区的城市在尚未被敌军占领以前,由于日以继夜的空袭,任何教育工作都无法进行。然而有些学校在如此困难的情况下继续上课,一直等到必须撤离的时候方才停止。

由于残忍的空袭和敌军于占领沿海和扬子江中下游城市后的暴行,教育机构的校舍和教学设备所受到的损失是无法估计的。纪录和手稿被破坏,校舍被焚毁,若干珍贵的善本书籍甚至被敌人掳去作为战利品。不幸的是40％的独立学院和大学,不论其为纳税人或他种情形所支持的,都设在上海、北平、南京和广州。这些大专院校都在战争爆发后的一年半的时间内全部沦陷敌手;其中有42所被迫选择是否迁往内地,或是在外国势力保护下和严重阻碍下继续办理。究竟是选择了迁校所遭受的苦痛大呢,还是选择了留在原地忍辱苦撑的苦痛大?实在难以判定。

然而高等教育机构的迁入内地并不是一种灾难。他们是迁移到了文化落后的地区。知识和技术意念的普及帮助了内地的迅速现代化。这些外地高等学府的迁入,促使落后地区的学校在教学水准上和效率上都获得改进。大专院校的师生大都是在沿海大城市中长大的,有机会和本国落后地区的生活接触,使他们能于亲身体会的经验中学习到重视祖国所面临的问题。许多教授由于环境所迫,要去应付新的问题,而这些答案绝非仅为西洋人使用的课本中所能觅得,更非彼等携归的欧美各大学课堂中所讲所做的笔记。简单而欠精确的设备也非全然无益,基于此理,教学也许更有兴趣而且更有实效。

可是,虽然政府已尽全力去减轻学生在战时刻苦求学所遭遇到的困难,情况依然很严重,而且战争若持续下去会更加恶化。许多青年势须离乡背井徙入自由地区。他们的家庭已丧失了收入,因此不能够接济他们。物价不断上涨,仅就膳食费而论,许多地方都昂贵得惊人。值得注意的是处此情景,91所大专院校1938年春季注册学生的总数占了战前108所院校注册总数的74％。1938年一年中,有6所院校复校,使这97所院校的注册总数达到了战前总数的95％。1939年有102所院校开课,可是本年的统计还无从获致。这一点充分说明了中国高等教育大无畏的精神以及中国政府及人民的决心——不让敌人攻破其文化前线。我们的抵抗是坚忍的,而且我们深信最后的胜利必属于我们。我们继续培育青年人,因此一旦战争结束,我们就可立即展开重建的计划。由于战争扩大,政府需要更多有学识的人去担任不同的工作,我们的愿望是在自力更生、在薪火相传中供给政府所需的人才。

失业教师的征用

政府和私人团体虽然已竭尽所能支援教育,但是仍有少数学校被迫停办,而且那些还能勉强支持的学校不得不减少教职员的名额,并紧缩开支,因此大专院校的教师遂大批失业。政府在1937年秋初就面临这一难题。教育部着手登记这些失业的教师,并且负责分配他们的工作:(1)"群众运动"或"青年文艺运动"的编辑;(2)国立编译馆担任译书工作;(3)在继续办理的学校充任临时教员,由教育部发给薪金;(4)充任偏远地区的地方教育主管。以前担任过大学教授的教师每月津贴法币100元至120元,视当地的生活程度而定;至于以前是大学讲师或专科学校教师者,每月津贴法币50元。截至1938年7月中日战争爆发一周年为止,报告中指出有447位大学教授接受政府此项周济。

另外还有流亡学生的问题,他们逃离了入侵的敌军,可是他们既无工作,又兼身无分文,远离家乡,无依无靠。于是政府通过教育部向他们伸出援手:依照年龄和各人以前所接受过的训练,有些被安置在不同的战时工作中,其他则发给旅费回到他们原来就读的学校,由于学校内迁,致关山阻隔。更有一些遣送到邻近的学校,认做流亡学生或寄读生。

然而这些流亡学生和许多其他学生,由于家乡陷敌,接济中断,或因战争的关系未能全力供给其子弟,必须获得资助始能入学。政府乃给予彼等膳食贷款,每月自7元至14元不等。1937至1938学年度,有4,256名学生领受此种贷款。1938至1939学年度增为5,372名,而1939至1940学年度增至6,384名,此一数字表示大约有13.5%的大专学生领受政府的补助。

对留学生的援助

政府也关注海外的留学生。当然他们也因为战事而使来自家中的接济受到了影响。许多留学生实际上完全得不到金钱上的接济。1938至1939学年度在北美洲的留学生总数为1,872名,其中有许多人是自费,可是他们的收入由于外汇的调整和家庭的财务不振,都受到了影响。政府补助每人法币700元作为返国的旅费,或让他们暂时渡过3个月的难关,直到他们能够重新做必须的安排。有300位留学生曾经接受了政府此种金钱上的援助。

从1938年起本国学生不准出国留学。政府只核发护照给那些到外国学习军事学、医学或工程学的学生。战前几年,教育部曾指令出国留学只限研究生。国内大学几乎各个学院都有大幅度的改进,如果还要送青年学子到外国去念大学,无异浪费金钱。他们应该先在国内念完大学,然后到外国去仅就他们认定的专门学科继续攻读,并选定何校可以获得最佳的训练,以便日后从事该项工作。如果出国只是为了炫耀,那简直是愚蠢,而且在战时这种事情是应该停止的了,尤其是此种炫耀如今似乎已迅速消失了。即使在今日的战争情况下,我们许多的大专院校仍旧能像西方一般的大学一样,各种学科都能给予青年很好的教育。一个学生在他心智尚未成熟以前就出国留学,其于中国文化背景的丧失,有胜于他可能在国外旅行而与另一文化接触所获得的益处。战争唤起了政府当局的注意,认为我们大量派遣留学生的政策必须重新厘订。

高等教育所受战争的另一影响是公立大专院校的合并。像北平的北京大学、清华大学和天津的南开大学3所大学合并起来,由北徙南,首先迁到长沙;继以战争持续而且华中地区受到威胁,复迁昆明,改称国立西南联合大学。同样的,其他在北平的国立大学迁到陕西,合并成为国立西北联合大学。由于3所工业专科学校的合并,新成立1所工学院。另有3所医学院也合并起来迁入内地上课,以避战火。这些院校的合并,全是为了我国高等教育的延续,如果不是为了战争,决不会想到更不会实行合并的办法。

当此战火弥漫之际,政府新开办了6所师范学院。以前国内有5所高等师范学校,培育中等学校的师资。后来这些高等师范学校,除了设在北平的一所外,不是关闭了就是并入了一所大学,成为一个学系。此后,我国的中学师资就委由大专院校培育。战前不久,教育部指令大学生之欲充任中学教师者,必须修习若干教育科目方为合格。1938年教育部制定了一套新的培育中学师资的计划。根据这一计划,政府有责任和权利培育中学师资。在新设立的6所师范学院中,5所是附属于国立大学的,第6所则系设于湖南的一所独立学院。前此设立的师范学校和大专院校的教育学科系(不论是由政府或其他情形设立的)全部停办,只留下两所私立大学所设立的和一所省立的师范学校。这说明了政府的政策是尽可能将大学程度以下的教育掌握在政府手中。这不仅是一个试图使中学教育标准化因而提高其水准的措施,而且也是必须的和我们所渴望的,这个措施实际上乃是达到了集中管理中等学校的一个步骤。这个办法只能在战时行之有效,斯时一般民众,尤其是教育工作者都极愿支援政府在抗战期间全力创造一个联合一致的阵线,其结果更是足以说明战时中国的知识分子是坚决支援政府的。

新课程

这次中日之战也使政府能够公布大学及独立学院各学系的部定课程标准。在此以前,高等教育机构实际上是可以随心所欲地讲授,在大学四年中所有的学生只有三民主义、体育和卫生三科在每学年度中每周必须上课一次,男生接受每周二小时的军事训练,为期一年;而女生则接受每周二小时的护理,否则不准毕业。对于这些必修科目,姑且无论你如何看法,它们并未干涉到大学安排课程的自由。自然会有滥用此种自由的情形,但是对于那些以高水准和良好训练传授学生为职志的机构——而且他们都诚恳地办到了,此种自由应是吾人想要达成目标的最好途径。

政府下定决心要使高等教育维持一个高水准,甚至于尽可能地提高其水准。多年来中学生都必须通过政府所举办的毕业会考。此种毕业会考本质上是一个使全国的中等学校达到大约一致的水准的量杯,进而改进中等教育。

迄至今日,大专院校的水准,距达到一致的目标尚远。多年以来政府一直想施行若干改革,但是直到一年以前,才使大专院校有了一个部定的标准。本年政府鼓励学生去参加大学所授各种科目的甄别考试,而且同一地区高等教育机构的学生得竞选品学优良奖,吾人愿观其成。毫无疑问,这些考试如果适当地执行,对于我国的高等教育一定会产生良好的影响。我们切盼标准化,但绝非统制,因为高等教育,一经统制,将丧失活力。应该允许有变化和实验,尤其是现代教育的全盘计划在今日来说,对于我国还是很新颖的,只有凭借我国悠久的文化,及其特殊的和多样的需要,在长远使用不断试探的过程中,才能为我国的高等教育求得正确的政策和方法。

导师制度

教育界在战时的另一个创举,乃是教育部于1939年春颁布了中上学校导师制的施行。兹将有关导师工作的部分译成下文:

(1)为了改善当前过分着重知识传授的教育制度,并促使师生的关系更趋密切,教育部计划采行古老的导师制,于我国的中上学校内仿效英国牛津大学和剑桥大学的实施办法。

(2)一校中每一班级分为若干小组,每组应由学生5至10名组成,并由校长指派专任教师一人负责督导。校长尚须派定主任导师或设立训导处(组),以负责全校导师和科际间的事务。

(3)导师应注意各生在学习过程中心智与品格的进展及其身心的发展,给予指示与劝导,以保证该生之正当发展,进而培育其健全的品格。

(4)除了个别指导以外,导师应利用闲暇时间和假日,集合其负责的一组学生举行会议或野餐,施以参与团体生活的指导。

加强职业教育

这次战争显然使教育主管当局集中注意力于职业训练的重要性,而这或许是我国现代教育中最弱的一环。不过,在过去3年间,中央政府创办了9所职业学校,而且由教育部直接管辖。所授科目包括造纸、制革、染整、养蚕、电讯、汽车工程、畜牧和农业经济。会计、兽医和卫生行政也有讲授。此举旨在提倡轻工业,并且开发本国资源,以应付战争的需要。

职业学校是让学生接受较长时间的课程,而又不致拖长他们的结业年限。以前职业学校的课程是属于所谓的美国"短期大学"的标准,修业时间是两年或三年,而且这些学校只收高中毕业生,那就是说,在他们接受职业训练之前已经读过12年书了。1938年教育部施行了一个新方案,使职业学校可以招收初中毕业生,即是说他们已经受过6年的初等教育和3年的中等教育,他们以后得受5年的职业训练。这种较长时间的专门训练应能产生较好的效果。不过,有一个困难却是希望这些只有15岁年龄的学生能够决定他们愿欲接受的专业训练。若能于职业学校的5年中多讲授一些基础科目,而使专业训练逐年增加,如此或可排除此一困难。

根据我国的教育行政制度,中学是由当地(省、市或区)政府拨款和管理,虽然这些地方的主管是透过教育部所派任的省政府教育厅长而接受中央政府教育部的一般监督。当战事蔓延到某一省份时,省立、市立或区立的中学就纷纷迁往后方恢复上课。如此当可照料不少学生,可是许多家庭自沦陷区迁徙到内陆各省去,虽然远离敌人的铁骑,但是当地的教育并不发达。成千成万的中学男女学生背井离乡地徙入内地的城镇,他们的父母将子弟送到自由地区,一方面是为了安全,另一方面则是继续他们的学业。自由中国的中等学校,特别是一些离国军阵地不远的城镇的学校,所收容的流亡学生几乎到了人满为患的地步。其中有几所私立学校,尤其是基督教会所办的中学,有办法迁往内地,并可对于此种拥挤而又必须充分收容的现象提供部分的解决。但是像这样的学校并不多,而且需要救济的情形不断增加。为了应付这种急迫的需要,中央政府开办了13所国立中学,分别设立于河南、四川、陕西、甘肃、湘西、贵州和江西各省。根据最新的报告,这些国立中学总共收容了3万名学生。

沦陷区的教育

中国历史上从来就没有发生过人民因为逃避入侵敌寇而大批迁徙的现象,可是这一次的数量之庞大却是空前的。然而大部分的人仍旧留在沦陷地区。许多人由于种种原因无法迁移,经济困难使他们必须留下来,这只不过是其中的一个原因而已。若干中学的适龄儿童可能很幸运地能够到距离国军阵地不远的学校就读。即使敌人限制人民离开沦陷区,也无法阻止聪明机智的中国人千方百计地设法克服这些困难,遣送青年人逃离魔掌。然而事实上有许多男童和女童,特别是国民小学的适龄儿童,他们年纪太小,不能离家,敌人一日不撤去,他们只有被迫失学。有些儿童或能在家中得到父母的教导。这个古老的私塾制度乃是延聘一位老师到家中来，但只教导几名学童，如果能够不让敌人干扰而有效施行，或可拖延沦陷区青年的教育，直到抗战胜利。除此以外似乎别无他法。让有组织的教育受制于一个怀有敌意的势力，而其整个的意向和宗旨乃是在摧毁中国人的民族精神，这简直是不可思议的。我们为儿童未能获得学习阅读和习字的机会这一事实而感到悲愤。但是学习读和写，本身并不是教育，而且只为了获得求生技能也不能认做是教育。千百年以前我们先贤留给我们更好的教训：我们必须不计任何代价去阻止敌人假教育之名榨取我青年人的心智。榨取人类心智的行为是违反教育的基本原理的。因此在沦陷区惟一可行的方法是无须试图实施任何有组织的教育，只要让青年人在家中接受教育，并使国族的理想在家庭中生生不息。当儿童长大到可以回到自由祖国，重新呼吸到新鲜空气的当儿，政府应给予照顾并使彼等继续求学的机会。因此，教育部修订了以前的入学规程，使意欲升学的学生经过甄别考试而无需如前的提出较低学校的毕业证书。假如此一方案经正常施行，而且为环境所迫留在沦陷区的人民与政府合作，我们深信他们定能合作，将能使我们下一代的学龄儿童免除敌人有毒的影响——其目的乃在从根本上感染中国人，破灭国家的生命。

　　际此生死存亡之秋，中国人民的教育实系我们抵御外侮的文化前线。本文限于篇幅，未能对遍及全国的社会和大众教育提出详尽的报道。贴在墙壁上的报纸，战争的影片，新闻卡通，战讯的广播，战歌的教唱——这一切都是爱国教育的本质，而且深具有利的效果。本文纯系对战时中国的正规教育而论，更重要的是抗战三年，吾人虽然遭受横逆处于极端的困苦中，仍能完成许多因应措施。

学者在战时的任务*

我很高兴能够有机会从我们的战时首都重庆,向我在美国的朋友们讲话。

我访问美国回来已经两年半了。两年半来,世界情势变化真大;记得我在美国的时候,我告诉朋友们说,在中国所发生的战争,只是极权与民主间大战的先锋。过去一年半来的事实,证实了我的说法,中国正在作战,而且决心继续作战,直至正义和世界公道得到维护为止。

当1937年夏天,中日战争爆发的时候,我刚好在国外。我和许多人的看法相反,我当时确信,我们中华民族在英明领袖蒋委员长的领导下,必将战斗到最后一刻,战争将是持久的,虽然我知道我们的国家没有战争准备,但是我对我们的最后胜利充满了信心,因为我也知道我们人民的士气以及战争的起因,我们是接受我们的敌人的挑战,战争并不是因我们而起的。

我从美国回来的时候,战争已经进行了整整一年,我目击一切,产生了我的信念,没有任何困难能挫折我们人民的意志,没有任何敌人能动摇我们对政府的信心,城市一个接一个地陷落于敌人之手,我们一时无法抵抗敌人的飞机和机械化部队的进攻,我们的装备确很落后,可是情形正在改善,我们很快就会有更多训练良好的部队投入战场。我们将在适当的时机,进行大规模的反攻。我们现在对战争的最后胜利比以往更有信心,正如在美国的朋友们对我们赢得战争的能力比以往更有信心一样。

过去三年半来,有数百万人,其中大部分是知识分子和熟练的技工阶层,由沦陷区撤退到内地去。中华民族正以崇山峻岭作为自然屏障,在继续抵抗日本的侵略,并且开始进行国家重建的积极工作,建设规模如此之宏伟,只有亲眼看到的人才会相信。战争创造了新中国,它也给予我们

---

* 此文系抗战期间作者在重庆中央广播电台的广播词(见文后"附录"),原文载《台湾圣公会通讯》第24卷第7期(1968年7月)。

新生。

有很多事可以说明这点，因为时间的关系，我在这里只谈一点，那就是高等教育。我最了解这方面，我可以根据亲身体验来谈。

中国的高等教育，在战前已经有了相当的进步，假若这种进步没有中断，我们很快就会赶上美国的大专学校。但是战争迫使我们许多最好的高等学府撤退到内地，在那里教育落后，环境也不顺利。

在 1937 年，我们有 108 所大专学校，其中只有 9 所是原来就在我们现在所说的自由中国地区。其余的有一半由占领区撤退到西南方和西北方，四分之一留在北平、天津、上海继续开课，这几个地方日本人的影响还不算严重，还有 22 所被迫关闭了。

但是目前很多已经关闭的学校，又在自由中国地区复校，政府也针对战争的需要，设立了一些新的学校。目前大专院校达 113 所，比战前还多。大专学生总人数在战争初起时有些减少，但是这三年来，则已稳健地增加，现在已经接近 1937 年春的数目了。

两年半前，我还在美国的时候，朋友们常问我，也许现在也仍在问，为什么大学生不上战场保卫国家，而撤到后方去。一部分大学生已经参加作战，而且更多的正在走向前线，但是中国并不缺乏人力资源，我们已经有五百万武装男儿，还有更多的正在训练中。我们政府考虑到让所有的大学生去参战，代价太大，培养到一个大学生的水准，要花很多年时间，一万个人当中才有一个大学生，要是大学生都战死了，当战争过后，迫切需要调动国家的才俊来进行重建工作时，国家的知识命脉就会严重地枯竭。中国现代化的伟大任务已经开始，而且一定要完成。这个任务，需要受过现代化智能训练的男、女青年，这种训练将不惜代价继续下去，故而政府采取以最大的代价来维持高等教育的政策，故而高等学府迁到内地，这并不是想逃离战争，甚至是害怕日军的屠杀，而是考虑到为将来重建国家而实施一部分抗战计划的缘故。

我上面说过，战争爆发以来，政府设立了一些新的大专院校，政府也拨了一笔相当大的款项来济助被这场战争殃及的老师和学生。很多私立中学和大专学校都由沦陷区迁到了中央政府现在所在地的四川省。食物昂贵，对师生都造成了严重的生活影响。政府采取特别措施，拨了一百万元专款来济助他们。自由中国其他地区的流亡学生,这三年来也受到同样的济助,刚刚几天前,当我们亲自听到在国民参政会议上报告,说政府尽管有严重的财政困难,教育预算还是比战争初期高出百分之三十的时候,我们真是受到了极大的鼓舞,这是政府决心要使教育发挥最大功能的最显明的表示。

但是政府虽作了努力,大学教师和大学生的生活困难,还是严重。很多学生是由沦陷区流亡出来的,不是家庭破散,就是穷困不堪,再也付不起在校的伙食费,有的完全和家人隔绝。战时的食物,经常都是问题,有营养不良的威胁,物价天天在飞涨,文具用品很贵,书籍几乎买不到,几个学生合用一本书,流亡大学发觉要是尽力设法搬运图书,费用太贵,科学仪器有的太重,有的易碎,不堪大卡车长途颠簸运载,因此带出来的很少。迁留的时间一久,图书和设备的缺乏越来越成问题,化学物品和其他供应品用完了,很难再行补充,很多实验没有办法做,老师们势须要像无米难炊的巧妇一样,运用智巧来克服这些困难。

牺牲总是有代价的,困难激使我们动脑筋,我们常常由较深远的学术研讨,转而孜孜于切身的问题,但是没有一些起码需要的书籍和仪器,这些实际的问题是不能解决的。美国的朋友们,能否给予我们珍贵的援助,供应更多的图书和科学仪器呢?

这些困难问题,就是战时中国的高等教育上所遭遇的。但是就像我们前方战士那样,我们所持有的,是无畏的精神和坚强的决心。

透过坚韧不懈的努力,中国的高等教育,不但在战时得以维持,而且在一些重要的方面还获得了显著的进步,特别是许多研究所和高等学府向大后方落后地区的转移,产生了很好的影响,使得过惯了沿海各地生活的师生们,有机会熟识内地的生活。这种情形本身就是一种具有深远意义的教育,文化得以广泛散布,现代思想也得以传播,水准较低的学校,在和进步的省份迁来的大学接触后,也因此激发,提高了程度和效能,其结果将是战后会出现一个更教育化的中国。

为了战时的需要,我们的高等教育已经作了很多调整,在战争结束后,也将要作更多的调整,但这一切都是为了国家的最高利益。

附录：

　　这是韦故校长卓民于一九四一年三月在重庆中央广播电台的广播词，他以国民参政会参政员及校长身份，向全国及国外广播，原名"The Role of Scholars in the War"，并载于同年四月《战时中国》杂志。我们校友都知道韦故校长一生淡泊仕途，只在专心教育，传播基督福音，所以在抗战期间，他历经长途艰苦，把学校迁徙深入云南大理之喜洲镇，俾师生远离城市尘嚣，潜心研读，但他热爱国家，仍不时奔走于欧美，及战时首都之重庆。或争取美国与其他友邦之同情与援助，或向政府作教育上之献议。我们从这篇广播词里，可以回忆到三十至四十年代抗战时高等教育的艰难之状，也仿佛可以听到韦故校长关心国家前途及高等教育的呼声。岁月悠忽，今隔三十余载，哲人已远，遗泽犹存，本馆译载之余，真不胜感念追慕之情耳。

（台北）韦卓民纪念馆谨诚

如何成为一所基督教大学*

对我们学院而言,这个问题最为重要。本文将从学校管理的观点出发,对此进行论述。

许多年来,正如学院学年行事表中所说的和学院在教育部注册所介绍的那样,办校的目的是"向中国青年提供高水准的大学教育,发展学生的个性和能力,使其成为中国忠实有用的公民,为帮助建立和加强各自在道德、智能、体格和人道主义方面的团体,实现创办学校的各个传教团体的共同目标做好准备"。这项声明以法定意见的形式由纽约的创办委员会制订,并逐字翻成汉语,呈递政府认可。学院正是以这个表现办校目的声明,注册成为教育部所属的一所大学。

我们的学校是作为中国基督教运动的一部分而创建的一所基督教学院。十五年前提出注册问题之前,无人曾明确询问过办校目的。对政府而言,这是所教育学院,政府关心的是其教育效率和规范。在这方面,我们完全遵守政府的规章。不过,注意一下办校声明的最后一句:"实现创办学校各个传教团体的共同目的。"这句话暗示了什么呢?

它暗示着学院是作为中国基督教运动的一部分而创建的,为的是在中国人中传播基督教,给教堂提供牧师,给教会活动的不同部门安排领导人员,帮助制定明智合理的政策,以便实现中国个人、社会的基督教式生活计划,促进世界基督教文化发展。同时也是为了思考当今世界基督教徒面临的问题,设法找出解决办法。我们的作用既是行政性的也是预言性的。我们必须帮助开展中国教会的工作,引导国内基督教徒的思想。

要完成这样的作用,我们还有许多困难。其中,最严重的困难并不是政府对私立教育机构的管理。实际上,根据规章,学院可以进行宗教训练。不过,参加者必须是自愿的。此外还可以在选修的原则下讲授宗教

---

* 原文为英文,题目是:What Makes a College Christian,刊在 *The Chinese Recorder*,1941年3月。

课。在接到政府命令以及各系、所实行新课程之前,我们遇到的困难很小,除了少数人坚持要进行几乎是词义矛盾的强制性礼拜和给每个学生开设宗教指导的必修课。无论有无政府规定,为了真正的礼拜和诚实的学识缘故,我们都不应为之。不过,即便是教选修课,在所有学院、大学一致实行的新课程,也未给它留下多大余地。这当然剥夺了我们的学术自由。但是,即使有这些限制,我们依然可以开办名副其实的基督教学院,发挥宗教作用。只要我们拥有这样的教员,基督教的声望就不会严重受损。这些教员乐于做出必要的努力,用基督教的观点来讲述课目内容。相信这完全不会与教学效率或学术水准有抵触。十五年前,政府关于私立学校注册的规章还在讨论中时,我个人就认为,只要能自由选择学校全体人员,我们就仍有能力开展基督教教育工作。无论政府如何规定,只要给我能胜任教学和研究的基督教员就行。我们没有什么好害怕的。

但这正是情况关键之所在。倘若不算神学院和其他基督教会主办的职业学校,中国目前的基督教学院有十二所之多。若要尽力保持学术的高水准,在各学科方面我们是否有足够多的基督教学者充实学校?只有不知情况和不关心学术水准的人才会予以肯定答复。

传教士的需求

由于这个原因,今后若干年里,我们必须呼吁国外历史悠久的教会派遣足够数量的传教士到中国基督教大学任教。我们需要担任教师的传教士,因为,在中国基督徒中无法找到足够多能胜任的学者。但是,我们需要的传教士是在学科上受过良好训练的,他们到这里来,不只是为了教书,而且有明确无误的基督教传教目的。在已发表的各项声明中,我向来坚持,一所基督教大学三分之一的教职员是传教士,其余人员应尽量为基督教学者。

我们不是没有留心这样的事实。在某些情况下,一个人是否为基督教徒纯粹是个称谓问题。但是,倘若有人自称是基督教徒,那就意味着某些基督教方面的事情他得去做。只要自称为教会一员,他就无法公开反对基督教,并因此得参加到基督教运动中去。

就目前环境而言,要让所有大学的人员都为基督教徒,当然是不可能的。也许在某些意义上是不合需要的。有些非基督教徒人员,有着真挚的意向和堪称楷模的品格,可以鞭策那些自称是基督教徒的人员。作为大学的管理者,我会毫不犹豫问心无愧地任命非基督教学者到校任教,附加条件是他们不反对我们成为基督教大学的努力。当然,这是消极的说法。积极的说法是,每位基督教职员必须清楚自身的职责,尽力保持工作的基督教特色。有时,我发现很难在两者之间作出任命选择:一位是基督教徒,但学识浅薄;一位是优秀的学者,却非立誓的基督教徒。我们必须永远牢记,倘若在学校的课堂上表现不佳,我们的基督教影响将是有限的。在对学生施加基督教影响之前,我们必须首先成为优秀教师。当然,会有些例外,但这不失为一条很好的工作准则。

财政资助

基督教大学目前以及未来都将面临的另一问题是财政资助。高等教育是花费颇多的投资,随着时间的推移,还会愈来愈昂贵。水平要提高,效率要增长,人员要加强,图书馆和其他方面的设备必须得到完善。所有这些都要花钱。仅提供一所有三个院系大学的适当预算数字,甚至像我们这样一个学院的有限项目的预算数字,是无用的。根据管理经验,我个人估算,像我校这种规模的学院,至少需要贬值前价值三十万元国币的资金。这笔资金远远超出中国教会的财政能力。何况,目前世界正处于难熬时期,无人知晓,须过多久,国外的教会才会提供必要的援助。

目光短浅的基督教大学管理者不会为之担忧。倘若目前的一些资金来源干涸,从哪里才能得到资助?高等学府不可能只靠学生的学费生存。我们必须仔细考察一下自立的基督教教育机构,一定是在什么地方有毛病。某些自立的基督教学院应当被关闭。是否应当寻求政府愈来愈多的补助津贴?倘若走这条路,最后,学院完全成为政府大学,而这自然不是我们所期望的。国内外一定有我们可以得到资助的基金会。不过,谁掌握了资金,谁就能控制政策。许多原本带着基督教意图创建的学校,在主要依赖非教会资金生存和发展后,失去了宗教特点。有许多先例,尤其是在美国的,我们不应效仿它们。当然,有人会问什么是世俗资金。我的回答是,世俗资金是将上帝排除在外给予和花费的钱财。就连我们这样一所基督教学院也需要利用政府资金，正如许多年来我们一直所做的那样，接受资金，但不与基督教特色抵触，我们可以利用任何种类的资金，只要它不附带修改基督教计划的接受条件。就基督教大学而言，甚至校友资助也未必总是纯粹的幸事。英国和欧洲大陆的大学并未依赖校友资助，那些国家的大学毕业生捐助学校并非母校之缘故，而是因之值得投资。这种精神应当得到鼓励和赞许。希望我们的毕业生会愈来愈支持学校。同时，也希望他们把学校看作无愧于他们慷慨的基督教大学。他们资助它，不仅因其教育效率，而且还因其基督教影响。

不过，还需很长时间，我们才可以开始依靠毕业生的捐献和捐赠生存。在这之前，捐赠基金似乎是顺理成章的出路。但是，筹集这样的基金，必须注意无任何减少学校及其工作的基督教特色的附带条件。

知晓了这些困难，我们的政策就应当是限额招生的高水准的有限计划，一方面能保证工作得到充足的财政资助，一方面能保证离校之前，每位学生都能被感化，并在更广阔的世界代表我们。

结束本文前，我还想提及另一个值得密切注意的问题，这就是生源供给。中国有基督教小学、基督教中学、基督教大学，可它们并非在同一计划里为同一目的而共同运转。这看来简直是荒谬的。我们需要统计数字表明有多少儿童在结束了基督教小学的课程后，会进入基督教中学就读，基督教徒学生在基督教中学所占百分比是多少，占多大比例的基督教中学毕业生上了基督教大学。除非大部分学生受过某种基督教训练，否则我们不可能有基督教大学。大学四年的时间是不够培养学生基督观念的。让基督教中学毕业生去上非基督教大学，而让基督教大学录取大部分非基督教中学学生，无疑是浪费时间和精力。若想让中学的基督教训练成果得到保存，大学的工作有效，两者就必须统一起来。我们必须认真考虑基督教教育的整体计划并进行修改。

卓民不想占后文之先，但本文结束前，仍须简言几句。在我们这样的基督教学院里，教学和研究应紧密结合。各科教师须牢记基督教宗旨。某些情况下，须设置专事研究的教授职位，以解决世界所需基督教解答之问题。

致华中大学校友函*

各地校友公鉴：

暴日侵我，五载不遂，恼羞成怒，转向南进，为时不过两月，而香港、马来、星洲各地，相继失守，缅甸为我对外惟一交通孔道，亦岌岌可危。我校迁处迤西，原为后方之最，忽当前方之冲，顾安全犹可无虞，工作仍得进行，上月秒，曾专函奉告，谅达左右，而足纾怀念。此时我援缅大军，已云集前线，与敌交绥，我校处境，益臻牢固，尤堪告慰。

惟有一事振触于怀，应向我各地校[友]吁请援助者，即在校学生生活艰窘，达于极点，丁兹危局，尤如水益深，如火益热！盖抗战五年，经济破产，民生凋敝，富者变穷，穷者益困。我校为培植人才，蔚为国用，对于来学子弟，津贴其盘川，资助其膏火，豁免其历来所应缴之学杂各费，实已尽校力所及之能事。故在校学生目前所需之费用，厥为膳食一项。然即此一项，因币值低落，物价狂涨，每人亦月非百元以上不济。中产之家，何堪支此！而我校学生，大都来自沿江、沿海与南洋各地，其经济来源早经告绝，纯赖学校奖学金与政府贷金维持学业者，固居绝对多数，即一二素封子弟，畴昔聊堪自给者，近亦以沪、汉、港、澳、南洋等处之交通绝断，而悉陷绝境。学校财力有限，所设奖学金及津贴，虽已超过战前预算六七倍，然终属杯水车薪，不能顾复周全。冬暖号寒，年丰啼饥，人生惨境，见诸学府，每一念及，辄为怛恻不已！

窃思民胞物与，吾儒怀抱，解衣推食，仁者职志。在校诸生，倘遇晏婴脱左骖而相赎，若逢冉子分秉粟以相优，不仅越石原宪，此日之辛苦可以稍杀，他年成德达才之功，亦必藉是而立也。我校各地校友，类皆学有专长，身膺重寄，虽在此离乱之际，或亦有室家之累，然笃念同门之谊，赖以先进提携后进，忧人之忧，急人之急者，当亦大有人在。忧患愈急之日，正团结弥坚之机，不惟慷慨解囊，多多益善，即滴涓之惠，亦整装之腋。孔子

---

* 此函为作者于1942年2月25日所拟，现存华中师范大学档案馆，标题系编者所拟。

云：" 当仁不让。"又云："有能一日用其力于仁者,未有力不足者。"基督亦云："施比受更为有福。"本年爰拟由各地校友捐集同学救济奖学金国币五千元。博施好义,幸勿后人！捐款由五元至千元,皆所拜赐,并请以邮政汇票或银行支票直寄本校会计处,至所感祷,专此布臆,即颂

文祉！

校长　韦卓民　谨启

民国三十一年二月二十五日

《华中大学二十周年纪念特刊》发刊词*

　　大学之设，不徒为培植后学已也。讲授之余，必有事于学术之探讨，以求增进世界之文明，开阔知识之领域。故华大同寅，素以学术研究相砥砺，军兴以还，播迁万里，图书仪器，残缺不全，研讨之功，未敢自信间有一得，亦不轻易示人，以沽薄誉。盖学问之道，点滴未清，不免见笑大雅，贻误后生也。年来研究结果未刊行问世者，以此以故，兹值学校成立二十周年纪念，同人等乏刍荛之献，谨搜集旧作十余种，汇为一编，为学校寿，且以就正于海内明达。行将付梓，同人索发刊词于予。予不文，爰述同人治学不苟之精神，及斯编发刊之大意，以弁编首，是为序。

民国三十三年十一月一日　韦卓民

---

* 此文载《私立武昌华中大学二十周年纪念特刊》，原件现藏武汉大学档案馆。

华中大学史略*

华中大学成立于今二十年矣。合文华、博文、雅礼、湖滨、博学五大学而成。朔其历史,二十年实不足以尽之也。既自海禁大开,中西互市,欧风东渐,国事日繁,清廷有见于西学之亟待讲求,乃于同治元年(公元1862年)创设京师同文馆,以为欧西语文人才之培养。斯时也,英美教会亦感于世界大同之推进,宜先求中西文化之沟通,遂以设立学校为首务。同治十一年(公元1872年),圣公会首创文华书院于武昌。无何,遁道会有博文书院之设立汉口,伦敦会亦举办博学书院。为此三者皆教会学校,在吾国之先河,而武汉遂斐然为华中区新教育之中心矣。戊戌、庚子以后,吾国新学风气日益蓬勃,光绪二十九年(公元1903年),清廷颁布张文襄公奏定学堂章程,废除科举。时文襄公总督湖南(广),门下多新学之士,故于鄂坦广设学校。新学之兴,武昌实其嚆失,而文华书院亦于是年扩为大学,分备馆、正馆,盖采上海南洋公学正备馆之制也。文华大学规模狭小,然学风整肃,教员中旧制留学日本东京者数人,刘静庵(即周谷城《中国通史》之刘家运,见通史下册一一○面)、陈亚龙二先生,其最著者也。每值课余,辄为学生谈论革命。由是革命空气弥漫全校,学生假教会救世军宣教名义,星期日整队出行,集市民布道,语多讽刺清廷。光绪三十一年,员生举办学生军,成立军乐队,以音乐陶冶学生军国民精神。其军歌有"一腔热血儿意绪多,怎能够坐视国步蹉跎。指日挥戈,好收拾旧山河"之句。时复来岁,列队游行街市,唤起民众,武汉人之热血动容。又刊行《文华学界》,为吾国学生定期刊物之先声。文字中隐有革命宣传意。编者用新中国之新国民、先觉者、法兰西士等笔号,在学校附近设日知会(周著《中国通史》下册一一○一面认为一知会),盖取顾炎武《日知录》意也。阳为阅书报社,实则一革命之秘密组织也。督署时加注意,遣官僚子弟来校肄业,意图侦察。然学生举动隐约,且以教会学校关系,投

---

* 此文载《私立武昌华中大学二十周年纪念特刊》,原件现藏武汉大学档案馆。

鼠忌器，终无之何。惟寒暑假，学生归家出城时，警察严搜衣箧，然皆有先备，无迹可寻。而静庵、亚龙二师，竟于辛亥前先后殉国，未克目睹民国成立。又同学数辈，亦以革命罹难。此一页光荣历史，外间知之者盖寥寥也。武昌博文书院大学院，成立于光绪二十八年。然以大学班时断时续，不如文华大学之自光绪二十九年始岁有学生毕业，发达较为明著耳。清末雅礼会设雅礼学校于长沙。民国三年，雅礼大学成立。雅礼会者，美国耶鲁大学校友所创办，外人团体在吾国设立学校而纯为国际私人文化事业者也。湖南兴办新学，雅礼大学贡献实多，其自然科学与医学之倡厥功尤伟。民国六年，复初会创设湖滨大学于岳阳。其时汉口博学书院亦有成立大学部之议，以经费困难未果。此华中大学前身各校历史之崖略，故曰华中大学之历史不足以二十年尽之者此也。

民国十二年，华中区各教会大学慨于力量分散，力谋集中人力经费以宏效率，乃有合并之议。然兹事体大，坐言而起行问题滋多，如联合大学应取何名，校址宜湘宜鄂，联校成立原有各校不免无形隐遏，各校校友不谙分则弱合则强之旨者，纷纷发起护校运动。而各校负行责任之校友，又感于联合之不容稍缓。双方争持几致决裂。其卒底于成者，少数先知先觉任怨任劳之功也。联校成立于民国十三年秋，名曰私立武昌华中大学。先仅文华大学，武昌博文、汉口博学两书院之大学部加入，以武昌蛇山麓昙华林文华大学原址为校址，设文、理、商、图书四科，教职员十数人，学生不盈百。办理未久，正谋扩充，而武汉政变以起，先是国民革命军北伐，湘鄂响应风起云涌，民族自觉焕然一新。讵民国十五年冬，少数激烈分子希图攫取政权，摧残文化不遗余力，湘鄂公立、私立学校先后停闭。华中大学坚持至翌年五月，既而武汉学生会强迫学生参加破坏工作，华中大学不忍坐视莘莘学子误入歧途，遂于五月十八日解散学生，转学宁沪各大学，而学校充容力谋改组，迟迟未能恢复。此华中校史之第一期也。

民国十八年秋复校，长沙雅礼大学、岳阳湖滨大学相继加入，始成立今日华中大学之五组合体，校史第二期开始。学校组织，一本国民政府颁布之私立学校及大学法规，设校董会，成立三学院，曰文、曰理、曰教育，增聘教员、充实图书仪器，预计五年以树立纯朴之校风，建设学校强健之基础，校园之扩大、校舍之壮丽，则未遑及。民国二十年，呈准教育部立案，所谓校舍制、导师制、中期考试、毕业总考者,当时均者(著)部章以外,而华中已先后举办历年。部派专员、督学来校视察,奖勉有加,同人乃知实事求是不无定评,益自策励,力求学生程序之提高,学校风气之纯洁,期于无负国家社会。民国二十三年,卓民应美国芝加哥、耶鲁、哈佛、哥伦比亚等大学特约讲座之聘赴美讲学,未便与在美设立者大会商校址之推广、校舍之添建,询谋佥同发起募捐,在美一年收获颇多。而所得益,不仅在数十万美金之捐款,而在友邦人士对我国文化复兴之同情。彼邦学校界知有华中大学亦始于是年。学校发展进入第三期矣。原用文华大学旧址,位于武昌废城东北隅,面积约百亩,民国二十四年购城外民地百余亩。以废城基蜿蜒于新旧地之间,新校舍建筑甚感不便,乃于民国二十五年冬呈准湖北省政府暨教育部,承购废城基地五十余亩,新旧基地始获毗连。民国二十六年鸠工庀材,拟于新地建大礼堂、图书馆、音乐馆、文理商教四院及教职员住宅若干栋,期于二年竣事。而七月空前世界大战起于我卢沟桥,建筑工程遂无形停顿,时卓民已于六月杪赴英伦参与世界基督教大会,后有美国耶鲁大学客座伦理教授之聘,一年后始能返国,校事由教育学院黄院长秋浦博士代理。战祸日剧,全校员生敌忾无后国人,惟有抗战不忘建国,建国首重教育之旨,弦歌不敢中绝。迨民国二十七年夏,敌逼武汉,乃奉命移校西迁。八月,员生挟一部之图书仪器,经粤汉路越衡阳沿新成之湘桂路抵桂林。卓民亦由美飞抵香江,急趋桂垣,匆匆择定桂林乐翠路李子园为校址。九月开学,讵十月广州、武汉相继沦陷,寇焰益炽。十一月后,敌机狂炸桂林,[校舍、设施]频频被毁,警报略无虚日,图书仪器移贮防空洞内,[对师生教学]影响甚大,乃集员生谋再迁徙。桂省当局亦皆谓然。而交通困难远行不易,幸员生不辞跋涉,遂决购卡车,自行搬运,计划已定,仍俟学期结束,乃乘寒假取道镇南关,经越南,北抵昆明。当是时,滇垣原有云南大学,而西南联合大学、中法大学亦早来迁,华中大学乃决迁滇西,择大理喜洲为校址。喜洲背苍山面洱海,清静幽僻,远离尘嚣,物产富庶,民俗纯厚,距新辟之滇缅公路仅三十余公里,国外器材输入较易。于此避地,可不违持久抗战之旨。遂于五月初在喜洲寺庙三所复课,七月中放暑假。计阅一年,举校播迁者再,长征八千里,而总计学生缺课不满六周,占全学年五分之一,员生坚苦,至可钦佩也。滇西中学程度较低,本校重质不重量,招生匪易,故民国二十八、二十九两年学生人数减少,三十年学校迁滇既久,闻风来学者日久(多),且全国学生程度皆不如战前,本校亦莫从按图索骥,乃取录较宽,三十年至三十二年遂复桂林时之名额,然比诸昔日武昌之人数逊色多矣。物价继长,教员生活日困,民国三十年太平洋战争爆发,尤形剧烈。虽薪俸津贴时有增加,然按物价指数,则同人月入实与时递减,故枵腹从公者虽多,然弃而之他者亦所难免。民国三十二年,教员人数最少,比战前全校专任教员之三十九名,计缺其五,而职员仍旧。三十三年,则教员人数已复抗战前一年之旧观,学生人数超过抗战前名额,比抗战第一年第一学期仅少二十八名。岂胜利在此否极泰来欤,抑在校同人努力之所致也。自民国二十七年武昌西迁,至三十二年暑假止,六易寒暑,此为华中大学史之第四期。其第五期则自今年始云。

抗战七年,欧战结束已见端倪,西南太平洋日寇屡遭挫折,盟军近且以菲岛之捷闻矣,吾国河山指日可复,同人兴奋之余,草拟战后学校扩大计划万言,已获设立者大会与校董会之同意,略分七项:一,维持现有三院也。各系增设讲座,充实设备,教员以教学与研究并重,学生期于程度之提高。一,扩充经济商业系为商学院也。武汉为全国工商业枢纽。国计民生之发展,世界永久之和平,系于工商政策者颇多。经济专门人才关系甚重,不可不从事培养,储为国用。一,增设音乐系及附设音乐专科也。我国音乐不振,亟待提倡,各级学校音乐教员最为缺乏,民众社会教育于音乐是赖,音乐专门人才之培养急不容缓。一,恢复神学教育也。文华大学原有神学院之设,自该校并入华中大学以来,神学教育早经停顿。盖神学乃以历史科学方法研究基督教之学科,基督教入华千三百年,所传教义未能与我国文化思想融合,误解滋深,不有本国瞻学贯通中西之士为之精研探讨,基督教之在吾国难免枘凿,故高深神学之研究实为教会大学当务之急。一,新校舍之建筑计划宜早完成也。校舍建筑,既以二十六年战争中止学校迁返武昌原址,范围扩大,学生增多,即原有校舍不毁于敌,新校舍之建筑亦宜积极推进。一,教员宜多予以深造之机会也。师资缺乏为全国教员(育)普遍之现象,故本校决定,教员出国留学或在国内研究之经费列入常年预算,以谋师资之充实、学术之提高。一,校舍制、学校导师制之务切实施行也。大学教育,不限于知识一隅,欲求健全之人格,必有赖于师生间之共同生活,故导师制尚矣。而导师制之收效,实赖于校舍制之推行。全校学生分数十人之小组,以学舍为其生活之中心。舍各有长,择教员之善于指导学生者数人,助舍长为导师,朝夕观摩,潜移默化,如是则吾国旧时师生之感情庶可复见于今日之学校矣。综上七端,为华中大学战后发展计划之荦荦大者,果能一一见诸实行,则学校前途未有艾也。华中大学前身各校之历史光荣,成立后二十年之经营惨淡,略具于是。若夫历年各同事努力,于风气之树立、学术之推进,与夫两次长途播迁,皆未于文中一一详叙以扬其功绩者。盖自晦不彰学人素志,当不以卓民之忽略而责之也。兹值成立二十周年有纪念册之刊行,编辑同人嘱述校史以附编末,谨就所忆,书以报命云尔。

为中国教会培养有学识的领导人*
——中国基督教教育的前景

  现在无需为基督教教育作任何辩护。基督教在哪里强盛,就会在哪里对中国民众的生活和思想产生影响。在了解了这一点后,你就会发现有这样一群男女,他们已从基督教学校毕业,成为教堂牧师、医生或教会执事。在校的岁月中,他们树立了理想,懂得去献身教会,热爱上帝。随便翻翻中国的《名人录》,给人留下印象的是曾受过基督教教育的人数,尽管测验可能不太可靠,或者同任何一位毫无偏见的政府或工商界的明智人士交谈一下,你就会明白大体上是否有反对教会教育工作的批评。目前的危机是基督教教育面临的一次严峻考验。无论在何处,教会要是在重要的中心势力强大,基督教要是能战胜困难,展望未来之时有自信和乐观的办法,那么,那里的教会一定已为上一代人的所有层次的基督教教育投入了人员和资金。在过去的三十年里,中国教会的力量与其对教育的忠诚成正比。

  限于短文的篇幅,无法详述上世纪基督教教育的历史。初期的基督教教育规模很小。从满足时代需求的尝试失败时起步,它已稳固发展到目前的规模,基督教教会世界传教机构在一九三八年发表的统计说明调查报告的"表四"中列出下列有关中国地区(包括满洲)的数据。

小学(所)	2,887	学院(所)	13
学生总数(名)	182,110	学生总数(名)	6,131
中学(所)	270	中等学院(所)	17
学生总数(名)	43,482	学生总数(名)	686
专门学校(所)	118	幼稚园(所)	113
学生总数(名)	4,348	学生总数(名)	5,815

---

 * 原文为英文,完稿于 1946 年 4 月 27 日,题目"Training Educated Leadership for the Church in China"。打印原稿现藏于华中师范大学档案馆。

圣经培训学校(所)	141	教师培训学校(所)	58
学生总数(名)	4,440	学生总数(名)	2,629
神学学校(所)	32		
学生总数(名)	1,032		

这些是非常重要的数据,显示了基督教教育对变动中安危未定的中国的影响,体现了国内外教徒们对这个试图变得再次年轻的古老国家所做的贡献。正如一位作家贴切地描述:"数据后的人类生活表明了主在世上教会的行动。"

但是,当我们把目光从回顾中转开,超越现在,展望未来时,我们能否确信中国基督教教育的一切都发展得很好?目前,基督教教育者们在政府设定的课程和规章下叹息。这些抱怨是否有理,我们暂且不去理会。不过,也曾有段时期,距今并不遥远,也并非短暂,基督教学校和学院完全自由,可以遵循任何教育政策,采用任何制度,自由地设置课程,执行纪律,或者根本不做上述任何事情。从这段试验或不如说是碰运气时期中,我们是否继承了适应中国人需要的教学方法?任何实用的课程?或确定了经受时间考验的新目标?我们的风纪也许比同一城市的其他学校要好些。而且,也许在牺牲了一些用教育观点来看同样重要的课目后,我们的英语课也教得比其他学校好。目前,我们的许多学校仍旧满足于这样的成绩。如果一所小学的学生坐满了周末的教室和礼拜日邻近的教堂,那么,该校将被认为是欣欣向荣的,其他任何理由似乎都不重要。中学则收取高额学费,支付低薪给教员。不管教学效率如何,只要条件允许,就尽可能增多入学人数,因为自立是成功的主要评判标准。以前,学院都以美国同类大学为典范进行效仿,而今的目标却是成为国立大学。到处都是要求职业教育的呼声,因为这在当今是时尚。无人认真考虑,我们是否有这类学校所需的人力、物力。也根本无人仔细想过为什么基督教教会要赞助职业教育。新时期明显缺乏基督教教育连贯一致的政策。我们无法再碰运气,所以只好盲目遵循。

可能会听到急切的反驳。从最初开始,基督教教育的目的就是传道,至今仍如此。是的,但我们需要的是更宽容的福音派教义观念,并且应当探究其含意。衡量传道是否成功,我们看重的是受洗礼的人数,还是基督教对人们生活和思想的总体影响？基督教要想在中国成为创造力量，仅仅是靠年年增加基督教教徒的人数，还是靠改变这个国家的文化？我们的教育工作有助于革新中国社会吗？通过基督教学校和学院的努力，基督教精神是否深刻而有效地渗入中国人的生活中，使其成为起作用的内部力量？基督教教育应当有这样的目的。

有了翘首以待的目标，我们是否像做学问那样，研究了农村地区和城市地区中国人的生活？是否研究了中国在社会、政治、经济方面的制度？亦或中国的哲学思想和宗教信仰？中国人的幸福生活观和对人类命运的信念？如果没有做这些工作，反而在基督教学院里忙着培养更多的技术专家，让他们去种更多的庄稼，养更肥的猪，或修更宽的马路，建更坚固的桥，做更清楚的账目，搜集更多令人难忘的统计数据，甚至，去制造更耐用的墨水，更卫生的肥皂，那么，尽管这些活动对团体和国家的幸福很重要，基督教教育已失去了自己的目标，即在基督教根源的真理之光中重建人类生活。这并不是提倡基督教教育只应关心由教会直接主办的活动，正如笔者在一九三八年为世界传教机构所写的统计调查报告说明中提到：

"有基督教动机的社会工作者、有基督教准则的记者和有基督教观点的作家可以创造奇迹，教会应当为这些人培训尽一份力。我们渴望看到基督教教义被应用到商业、工业和政治中。多一些教育事业机构吧，让它们教授的经济学、历史学和政治学接近基督教的观点。现代世界不是怀疑基督教和科学能否共处吗？那就让教会对科学研究真正发生兴趣，鼓励它的那些前途远大的青年男女热心于对各种科学的追求。"

当然，我们不能因为那些引人向往的途径而见树木不见森林或失去目标。基督教教育只有一心一意，坚定地盯住自己的最终目标才能取得成功。

再者，我们必须坐下来算算基督教教育的费用，免得打下地基后却发现无法完工。基督教教徒们会向任何有益的工作伸出援助之手。但要满足国家教育的所有需求，则无疑远远超出了教会的能力。我们应当只做那些我们能做得最好的事，做那些对我们的事业至关重要的事。在教育方面，我们不会去重复政府的努力，甚至不做对其修补的工作，我们有自己明确而极为重要的职责。就这种职责而言，如果我们不去履行，旁人是不会去做的。我们必须把基督教信仰教给我们的孩子,并尽可能地帮助其他儿童对之有所了解;要为我们的年轻人准备勇敢无畏、生机勃勃的基督教生活,并在他们生活的团体中宣传这种生活;要让我们的青年男女坚定地追求上帝的真理,并用现代语言对之做出明智而非虚伪的解释,这就是我们应在基督教教育中力争所做之事,否则,这些事将无人完成。这是我们义不容辞的职责。未来基督教的成功取决于它的履行。在此过程中,我们要向主做出证明。这证明将远远超出对个人经历自吹自擂的价值。如若需要,事后又感到后悔的那种牺牲,这应当是中国未来基督教教育的指导准则。但是,如何用有限的资金和精力执行职责呢?

让我们先看看基督教小学的情况。我们应当尽力维持一九三八年报告中的学生总数为十八万二千一百一十人的二千八百八十七所小学吗?毋庸置疑,在满足中国小学教育的主要需求方面,教会所做的,皆为崇高的贡献。在中国,年龄六至十二岁的儿童中四分之三的儿童没有上学。他们应当在校且按法律规定应当上学。这个国家没有足够的学校供其上学,而因此所造成的中国文盲人数,十年后将达到英国人口总数,二十五年后达到美国人口总数。

可是,许多年里,日本却没有基督教小学。在土耳其和墨西哥,政府规定不准开办这类学校。而今民族主义的浪潮已席卷整个世界,除非目前的战争给中国留下全新的教育前景,我们才能期待在日本、土耳其和墨西哥发生的情况将在中国很快消失。让所有的儿童在统一的公立学校制度下接受普通教育,这个目标深得民心,政府将不遗余力地实现它。

不过,要实现这个目标可能还需等些年。这期间,可允许民间公民团体在政府的管理和监督下开办小学,那么这将可能成为基督教服务的一种形式。当地的基督教团体应当接受挑战。无论情况如何,不管有无基督教小学,当地的教会须愈来愈重视儿童的宗教教育。应当把主日学校和其他形式的教会教育活动办得有声有色、有效率,使之不与政府规定抵触,除非在校外都禁止对儿童进行宗教教育。而这种情况在中国又不大可能发生。

教会的中等教育问题又是另一种情况。因目前未得中国罗马天主教会的统计数字,只好先看看非天主教教会的情况了。中国大约有六十万名受过洗礼的基督教教徒,不足总人口的0.2%。这些教会照顾到的儿童大约只占全国小学生的1.5%,不过,这已十倍于他们在初等教育中应占的分量。而9%的中学生在基督教中学上学,是基督教初等教育的六倍之强。

无论中国教育者还是中国当局,都不能忽视或轻视这个事实。如果没有了基督教中学,中国的教育体系将出现严重的缺口,而且,在很长时间内这个缺口无法得到填补。在中等教育领域中,同样不大可能有一套严格统一的公立学校体系。每年的小学毕业生不断增多,因而还需很长一段时间,政府才能给所有想接受中等教育的儿童提供上学的机会。如此一来,这一层次的私立学校很可能会占一席长久之地。

但是,无论是基督教学校,还是非基督教学校,中学一直是中国教育体系中最薄弱的一环。一度曾有某些基督教中学因训导学生有方而享有盛誉,但情况很快就变了。为了从学费中获取更多收入争得早日自立,招生人数持续猛增,直至学校庞大得难以管理。教学水平下降,纪律松懈,标准降低,在某些学校,基督教教育徒有虚名。学校吸引的是豪门子弟。而且由于他们的学费支撑着学校,这些子弟决定了学校生活的主调。

我们也许不得不集中力量。因此,没有必要保持一九三八年前已有的二百七十所基督教中学,而是开办更多一些好学校。这些学校师资力量强,资金充足,并且有更多的基督教教徒。自立是学校力争的好事,但为了确保自立而牺牲学校宗教特点和教育实力却是危险的。战争前,基督徒学生在中学里的平均人数约占总数的30%。这样的比例能够充分保证学校里的基督教氛围吗?应当让多少比例的基督教中学毕业生进入基督教学院学习,从而保存在校时对他们进行的基督教教育,而不是让他们远离基督教影响,使教育的成果消失殆尽?要得到更好的效果,基督教中等教育和高等教育之间应当有一种更紧密的联系。

总的来说,基督教势力在中国职业教育方面成绩不太理想。随着目前国内工业的发展,职业学校很难开办下去。职业教育应该是实践教育,应由工业界中有实践经验的人来任教。但是这样的人很少,而且难以适合教学工作。从其他国家的经验来看,开办职业教育的最佳方法就是同工厂联系起来。如此一来,就应当先有基督教工业,而后才有基督教职业学校。

但是,这个问题需要立即引起我们的注意。教会的许多年轻人需要职业培训。一九三八年的二百七十所基督教中学有四万五千四百八十二名学生。这些中学无疑应当有同样数量多的基督教教徒,但只有33％的学生信奉基督教。这个事实表明了大批到了上中学年龄的基督徒儿童未在基督教中学上学。其中的一个原因,也许是主要原因,就是学生家庭支付不起孩子的学费。职业学校可以满足这些儿童的需要。由于这是个较难的新领域,我们应当先在试验的基础上开办少数几所学校进行尝试,在这些学校取得成功后,可随之再开办更多所。

对基督教高等教育来说,最需要的莫过于人们对未来更加清醒的认识。我们在建立类似英国的牛津、剑桥或美国的哈佛、耶鲁那样的私立大学吗?如果是这样,我们在中国能有十三所这样的大学吗?充足的来源将是什么?或者,也许我们应当少点雄心而满足于开办一些类似美国教会学院的大学。难道还不值得一试吗?特别是在我们不得不把有限的资源分散到十三所大学后,这样的体系制度在中国还会有什么继续存在的价值呢?

究竟什么是基督教高等教育的目标?应当先把它弄清楚,然后再制订政策,设计要实施的合理计划。至少可以这样说,我们目前胡乱应付的办法代价昂贵。我们当然不应只满足于继续培养技术人员,因为这并非我们的专职。我们的资金和精力应有更好的用处:去试图影响动荡的国家和千百万民众的命运。难道稍微改善一下几百人的生活就算成功了吗?我们不愿低估基督教学院的价值,甚至是现在这样的价值。无论国家还是教会都不能没有它们。不过,在基督教高等教育中,我们是否利用了有效资源去取得最佳效益?只满足所在地区眼前的需求是不够的,难道我们不应该瞄准大学教育部门可能实现的最高标准,而非仅仅满足于一般好?只有这样,才能期望基督教高等教育有永恒的价值。但最重要的,是不要忘了我们的特殊贡献,即处理问题的基督教态度。除非向我们的学生反复灌输这一点,否则我们就失去了开办基督教学院的目的。要实现目的,我们需要的不仅是用于教学和研究的更好的设备,不仅是使我们工作效率维持最高水平的更多充足的基金,最重要的还要有更雄厚的师资力量。它主要由中国基督教学者组成。这些学者懂得基督教高等教育的目标,并致力于在世间建立天国的伟大工作。假如有这样一批中国学者,那么基督教高等教育的其他所有问题就会迎刃而解。

　　基督教高等教育的顶点自然是神学教育。无论基督教教育如何发展,神学教育必须保留下来,这是基督教运动的生命力的依靠所在。但无疑这是中国基督教教育发展最差的部分:神学教员中,中国人最少;课程适应中国国情情况最糟;其教育标准则更无法与欧美的相提并论。有多少神学院里的教师能够在讲授圣经时,指导学生参阅原文并就原文提出个人创见?有多少神学院让教授主讲解释基督教教旨的,即一般称之为系统神学的课程,并且这些教授不但通晓西方基督教和哲学思想,还精通中国的哲学和中国宗教的历史及现象学?我们需要有这样的教师引导和激励中国神学院的学生从事基督教宗教的科学研究,将其阐释并介绍给中国人民。但我们离这个目标还很遥远,也许比中国教授们同他们在化学或物理、历史或哲学领域的目标离得更远。与其他学科相比,神学教育的目标更难实现,可是这并不能成为我们懈怠的借口。要达到目标,中国必须有自己的基督教神学,教会将因之更富强,也只有这样,中国基督教教育才不会失去目标。

一九四六年二月二十七日

华中大学前途之展望与规则*

　　本校成立于民国十三年，民国十六年武汉政变，停顿二年。民国十八年秋复校，扩大组织，惨淡经营，至民国二十三年，规模始具。购省有废城基地50余亩，及城基外毗连之民有地百余亩，谋校址之扩充，新校舍之落成，鸠工庀材，正拟实现建筑新计划之第一步，讵抗战军兴，除女生宿舍之一部分，及教职员住宅四栋，草率完工外，主要建筑不得不中止进行。然教学工作，仍在武昌继续一学年，备受敌机轰袭之威迫，民国二十七年夏，乃奉令内迁。内迁伊始，勾留于桂林者一学期。民国二十七年入冬以后，敌机狂炸桂垣，学校谋教学及学术研究之安定，于民国二十八年一月，再迁云南，择大理喜洲镇为临时校址，租借地方之祠堂庙宇、民间房屋为校舍，因陋就简，求物力之省节，以符抗战国策。故滞留喜洲八载，除国币5,000元外，未曾动支校款，作临时建筑，用心良苦，迤西僻处一隅。太平洋战争爆发以后，安南缅甸相继沦陷，交通阻塞，本校迁出之图书仅百分之二十，科学仪器仅三分之一，补充困难，员生感觉不便，而教学与研究之效能，不让其他后迁大学，全校努力之功也。民国三十四年，敌寇投降，三十五年四月，学年功课全部结束后，乃复员武昌原址。五月杪，员生及迁出之图书仪器全部到达，九月底在武昌开学，计男生307名，女生140名，全校学生共447名，专任教职员67名。

　　列表如次：

文学院

国文系8人	外语文系8人	经济商业系5人
历史社会系5人	哲学心理组2人	宗教组3人
		共31人

---

* 此文原载《华中通讯》第1卷第1期（1947年3月）。当时作者接任华中大学校长已近二十年。

理学院
  生物系4人   化学系5人   物理系4人
  数学组2人

                          共15人

教育学院
  教育系5人   音乐组4人

                          共9人

专任职员 12人

  现任教员55人中,有博士学位者15人,硕士学位者14人,得有学士学位者26人,阵容比战前为盛。然去十年计划之标准尚远,当按学校经济力量,逐渐加强。

  查本校战后之十年计划,系于民国三十一年,由校董会驻校临时执行委员会与校务会议、联席会议所订。历时年重,几经商榷,稿凡数易,乃提出于设立者大会及校董会,民国三十三年,始由设立者大会及校董,予以原则上批准,原文冗长,都万余字,兹择其荦荦大者数点,述之如下:

  第一,文、理、教育三院现设之八系计:

  文 学 院:国文系 外语文系 历史社会系 经济商业系

  理 学 院:生物系 化学系 物理系

  教育学院:教育系

  宜极力充实,求师资数量与质量之双方注重,图书仪器之增加,学生程度之提高,研究精神之发展。

  第二,文学院之经济商业系,应于最短期间,扩充为商学院,一以符民国二十年本校立案时呈准教育部之组织计划,一以供应武汉地区工商业各部门急需之专门人才。

  第三,现时文学院之历史社会系,偏重历史,其社会学各学程,多未遑及。因吾国社会学有系统之研究,尚在初期,而社会学为富有地方性之学科,借镜于欧美各国社会研究之材料,本无不可,然取他人之课本,以教中国之学生,未尝见其得计。故本校社会学之研究,宜先设社会学研究讲座,从事于社会学各部门之探讨,搜集材料,为将来教学之张本,盖学问之道,未可躐等也。

第四,文学院现设之哲学各学程,仅足以应教育部论理①、伦理等课必修之用。心理学亦只设教育学院学生之必修及选修学程。哲学一科,欲成专系,宜与历史政治经济之基本学程配合,以期学生之研究,实际与理论兼顾,明理所以致用也。

第五,本校为基督教大学,不可无基督教文献与典籍、教义与组织之研究,故神学尚焉,宜于教育部私立大学规程范围以内,设新旧约圣经、基督教历史、基督教教义、基督教实践神学各讲座,分配于文学院各系,开设高深之学程,对基督教及其他宗教,作科学之研究,由学生自由选修,所以使宗教之研究科学化,亦所以培养教会富有新智识之人才也。

第六,理学院之数学组,宜扩充成系,以强固自然科学研究之基础。生物研究,宜与国内之医药卫生各组织密切合作,以增进生物学之实用。化学系物理系,宜一方面注重基本原理之训练,一方面谋与各生产机关取得联系,学以致用,专精探讨,利国福民,明体达用,固二而一者也。

第七,吾国旧学,礼乐并重,然时至今日,礼涉空虚,乐经弛废,以言乐理,寥无几人,以言教育,师资缺乏,故音乐人才之培养,实为当务之急。何况基督教之精神表现,基督徒之公共崇拜,有赖于音乐者甚多。教育学院之音乐组,现仅为教育系学生准备教育之功课,宜速扩充成系,以培养音乐人才,并附设专修科,以宏音乐师资。

第八,教育学院现有之教育系,似嫌其偏重中等学校师资之培养,而教育科学之研究,未遑发展,故教育学之研究,宜成一系,师资培养,另为一系。

上列八端,其第一、第五、第七、第八,现正着手推进,其余四项,尚在筹划阶段,其进展之速度,一视学校经费增加多少为转移。此关于本校院系之计划也。

至于全校学生人数,战前总额仅达 240 名,抗战开始,迁桂迁滇,与华中区各有关中学交通隔绝,西南各省,中学程度比较低落,每年招生,虽降格以求,取录新生,仍寥寥无几,其始也,学生人数渐减,民国三十二年以后,乃逐年增加,胜利后一年,仍留云南喜洲,学生名额,达 280 余人。复

---

① 论理即逻辑。民国时期学校教育将逻辑学称为论理学。

返武昌,本学年秋季招生,各地投考者4,000余人,惟以各种限制,全校男生亦仅307名,女生140名,共447名。而本校一向不收走读生,宿舍容量无多,男生惟有连床叠铺,极形拥挤。此后学生名额,逐年增加,至校董会所定之最高额800名为止。故男女生宿舍之添建,为最迫切之一问题。

且也,大学教育,不止于课室、图书馆、实验室,还有赖于师生间之观摩,同学间之社交生活,而宿舍云者,不惟饮食起居之所,实学术商榷之地,所以学为士学为人也。于是宿舍合理之建筑尚焉,宿舍之严密组织尚焉。本校之理想目标在此,其实现还以待诸他日。

若夫新校舍之建筑,需款孔多,尚待筹措。教授任教多年者,应给假游历研究。后进教员之宜于深造者,应栽培鼓励,皆在十年计划之中,刻已着手实施矣。

夫学校树人之地也,树人百年,其道远,其任重,是则本校之战后十年计划,仅具什一之初步,广大精微,尚未也,愿与吾校同人,先后同学,共勉之。

今后基督教中学应取的政策*

办理学校必先有其理想,由此理想,乃生宗旨,宗旨既明,政策乃定,计划始立,本末始终,有不容或紊者。

中国政府自办学校,及外国教士在华开办学校,其动机随时代而皆有转变。就教会今日办学之动机而论:一、因鉴于社会一般学校,办理上殊欠优良,故教会兴办学校,以补救之;二、中西各国办理教育,其宗旨均失之偏畸,侧重于身心之锻炼,而忽略灵性之陶冶,基督教认为基于此等宗旨所造出之人才,尚非全能,故欲办理一种完善学校,教学时对学生身、心、灵各方面,期求其平衡发展;三、一般社会不能供应教会需要,因教会仅属社会之一部分,而又自有其特殊之需要,不能全靠社会予以满足,如神学校、圣经学校等,教会乃不得不自办之。

时至今日,教会办学动机,较之五十年前,已显有不同。当戊戌政变之前,国人多故步自封,对西洋学术,不愿接受,迨后东西交通大开,接触日繁,迫于需要,遂设方言馆,以培植通译人才,以后更以事实需要,遂创办江南造船厂,并于各省开办武备学堂,以树国防,及培植军事人才。然眼光至为浅短,仅顾及一时,毫无远大计划。同时外人鉴于中国一般人士思想之闭塞,对新式学校皆裹足不前,乃仿我国义塾之制,开办若干义塾式学校。即以文华书院论,在初创时,实非学校,盖不过一教会传教机构耳。其办学动机,乃以教会为目的,而办学仅其手段之一,实即以科学祛迷信,便其传教已耳;同时亦借此培植传教人员,岂有他哉!迨戊戌政变后,鄂督张之洞奏办学校,培植通晓时务人才,以英语为外国文主修科。教会乃抓住此一机会,办理新式学校,盖仍本其第一动机也。从此教会学校,遂进入一新的阶段。

民国十一年,我国颁布教育宗旨,颇趋向于狭隘之国家主义;民国

---

* 本文系作者的一篇演讲词,由雷蕙亭笔记,刊载于《文华月刊》第7号(1947年5月31日)。

十七年,教育宗旨复趋向于物质化,偏重自然科。是时,教会办学旨趣亦一变而为:(1)宣传教义;(2)灌输科学,沟通中西文化;(3)以灵性管制物质;(4)促进世界大同。故基督教各级学校,皆以贯彻此旨为其目标。

至于基督教中学,顾名思义,当有以异于其他中学。基督教中学,仅致力于普通科之设立,而不办理职业学校者,其原因当不外下列三种:(1)非一般家长之需要,家长多希望其子女作升学准备,故不乐令其子女入职业学校。(2)职业学校因师资缺乏及设备艰巨,不易办理完善;此不独教会为然,即政府亦何莫如是。(3)入职业学校之学生多非出诸本意,有机即行转学。究之此种现象,是否合理,明眼人自能知之,此处姑不具论。总之,中学教育办理完善,即中等人才赖以造成;职业教育非教会必办之事工,即有办之者,亦仅含救济与提倡之意义耳。近年国家对职业教育已渐知注意,固勿庸教会之越俎代谋矣。

今日教会中学政策,如已有上述之合理理想,正当动机,且合于教会宗旨,则在实施上,当注意下列三点:

1. 身之教育——关于学生之身体训练,当不仅限于体育,而于其营养方面、身体缺陷方面,均应密切注意。学校当局应聘有食谱专家,以调剂学生食品之种类,及其应备之营养成分,并聘请防治专家,以防治学生身体上之缺陷。此种教育如非一校独力所能办,可联合数校共同办理之。我教会中学果能办此,即可表现出在教育上之特殊贡献。

2. 理智教育——关于理智方面之教育,当包括有:A. 教学,B. 自修,C. 读书习惯,D. 心理治疗,E. 课外阅读,F. 职业指导,G. 业余运动,诸要项,而课堂所授科目,依本人所见,尚属次要。盖中学最成功之教育,即在使学生于出校后,能自己读书。兹将上提诸项分别略论如下:

A. 教学:依我国现行部颁中学课程标准而言,中学生负担实属过重。教会学校适应无方,使学生颠蹶匍匐于课程重压之下,毫无回旋发展之余地,论者谓教会学校迄少培成杰出人才,此乃其最大原因。故今日教会中学,对教学方面,课程之编排,宜细心研究,分别轻重,以作教学取舍之标准。自另一方面观之,中学任务,乃在使其毕业生达到升学目的,故一般教会中学生之升入大学者,其程度均感太差,此教会中学教学失败之另一证也。

B. 自修：教会中学教师任课均较繁重，其精力多用于应付课堂，每每无暇及此。

C. 读书习惯之养成：同上。

D. 心理治疗：学生中常发现有顽皮或偷窃等不良行为者，非尽生性恶劣，不可救药，亦有因心理上具有病态，而产生不良行为者。此类学生，教师宜于平时默察其状态，注意其言行，相机施以心理治疗，自可化莠为良，收训导之奇效，固无须出以"勒令退学"或"开除学籍"之下策也。

E. 课外阅读：宜鼓励学生尽量利用课外时间为之。

F. 职业指导：在中学时代，即当注意，以免升入大学时，不知所择。

G. 业余运动：办法同E项。

3. 灵性教育——教会中学最重大之使命，乃养成学生基督教人格。所谓基督教人格即：一、始终保持，随处表现之不可磨灭性；二、人人平等；三、人格高于物质；四、有标准——基督，亦即所谓价值表之教育也。此项教育之施行，着重于人格之感化，非可以言说收效也。教师等须于日常生活、学校行政中随在寓潜移默化之旨，如行政经费、经费来源、收支状况、员工待遇等，无一不含教育之意味，则老师之行德风，学生之德草，草上之风必偃。但学校当局，亦应减轻老师课业上之过重负担，俾有余力及此；而老师亦应负起其神圣任务，鼓起其宗教精神，随时行道，示范学生，则灵性教育，庶有成果。或曰，事固应办，奈乏金钱何？曰：金钱固不可少，但非绝无办法。倘能细心研究开源节流办法，则解决经济之途径，正不难觅得也。如缩小学额，节省开支，即其一端，盖教会开办学校之宗旨，乃以之培植社会优秀青年，吾人又何必为人作嫁，专替一般发国难财者，教育其子女耶！

华中大学向毕业同学劝募食米二百石救济学荒启[*]

战乱相寻,历十余载,迄无休止,民力凋敝,民生迫蹙,已有年丰啼饥,岁暖号寒之势;今夏淫雨肆虐,有天皆漏,无地不浸,谷物鲜登,农事徒劳,嗟我小民,益救死不遑矣。人命危浅,朝不虑夕,树人百年,力谁能胜?故本年投考大学人数,较之往年,业已锐减;而肄业学生,声请休学者,亦踵相接。望黉舍而趑趄,临中道而彷徨,学子苦闷,孰愈于此!斯文不振,人道沦亡,载瞻前途,不寒而慄!寻坠绪,绍绝学,早为学人之本分;济危扶倾,解衣推食,亦吾儒之美德。在此学术文化不绝如缕之会,慷慨解囊,救济学子,我毕业同学,似责无旁贷。本年六月二十五日校友会席上,卓民爱有向先后同学筹募食米二百石,救济在学学生之议。盖学校经费有限,虽已极力提高下年度奖学金额,下学期超过三千金圆之数;然受经济压追(迫)之学生,因之不能继续学业者,尚有百人之多。故区区奖学金,对于空前学荒,实不无杯水车薪之感。语曰:莫为之前,虽美而不彰,莫为之后,虽盛而不传。务望我各地同学,本爱护母校之热忱,扶植后进之素志,或自身捐输,或转为劝募,各尽所能,共襄义举。一腋之孤,千金之裘,不仅清寒学子,拜德不尽,学术文化,亦利赖无穷矣。倘承捐款请于九月半以前汇交本校会计处,并指明为救济学生之用,是为至祷。

校长 韦卓民 拜启

附文:

母校救济学荒工作尚在办理
望未资助校友继续捐输

为救济母校一般清寒同学,而由校友总会申请母校向我各地校友筹募食米二百石事宜,业由母校当局办理。闻进行以来,承我各地校友热烈

---

[*] 此文系身为华中大学校长韦卓民致全体校友的一封公开函。原载《华中通讯》(复员后)第3卷第3期(1948年10月20日)。发函起因见文后"附文"。

响应,解囊助学,成绩已相当可观。此匪特说明我校友对救济事业之热情,亦即宣示诸先进爱校不后人之衷心,良可感佩!

查救荒工作,现尚赓续办理,望未资助校友,发挥力量,继续捐输,俾此光荣事业,克底于成(至于捐助结果,当于下期本讯刊出)。

兹恐少数校友因地址更动,而未目睹八月二十六日由韦校长发出呼吁,用特转载于后:(见前文——编者)

奉令呈复本校教学训育各实情仍祈鉴核指示以便改进由[*]

案奉大部三十七年十一月一日高字第五九八九六号训令,略以学校对学生教学与训育方面,有应行加强实施之点,特标举指示,仰遵办具报,等因;祗悉。查指示各点,本校均早有严格规定,绝不通融变更,谨将有关各项规定,逐一呈复如次。

甲、教学方面:(1)本校每学期开学放假,向按学校历进行,从未更改一日半天。上课点名,有专员逐课巡回执行,并将巡查结果,当堂请各教员签字证明。学生缺课,各课均以其一学期内之学分数为最多时数,时限一满,即先由教务处予以警告。某一课程缺课逾限,即勒令停习。停习课程超过学生选修学程半数者,即勒令休学。学生事假,一学期不得超过两星期,准假与否,且须视其事故之重要性如何为断。病假,一学期不得超过学时六分之一,更须缴呈医鉴。(2)教员缺课须由各教员负责觅时补授,因事请假逆料不能补授者,则须事先觅人代授,并须由校核准。其预定教学实验进程,概须如期完成,由各院系逐层负责;监督考验,不得敷衍分毫。(3)考试:本校每学期设有期中考试、学期考试,二年级终了,晋升三年级时,设有中期考试,四年终了,设有毕业考试,均较部订规程为严。任何考试,绝不容学生规避,不容学生反对。考试不及格者,或留级或斥退。

乙、训导方面:(1)本校采用宿舍制与导师制,除分设男生训导长与女生训导长各一人外,每宿舍均设宿舍主任一人,副主任一人或二人,另聘导师若干人,合为训导委员会,解决学生一切生活问题,并对其身心各方面之发展情形,随时加以积极适当之指导,务使学生生活安定,思想行为悉合正轨。(2)一切学生课外活动组织,概须聘请教员一人或二人为顾问,呈报学校备案,各组织如出版刊物,除自负言责外,所有文稿,并须由其顾问审核。

---

[*] 此文系身为华中大学校长韦卓民回应国民政府教育部关于加强学生教学与训育的"指示"(背景详情参见文后"附文")。原载《华中通讯》(复员后)第3卷第4期(1948年12月25日)。

(3)本校学生外出,除佩戴校徽外,一律给有学生证;如外出经夜不能返校者,不妨碍课业,亦须在学生外出簿上登记去向,与预定离校返校之时间。

(4)本校学生宿舍,绝对禁止留客膳宿,违者即予严惩,从不宽假。

以上各种办法,本校均已编为章程,即拟付印。是否有当,尚祈鉴核加以指示便知改进,至为德便。

谨呈

教育部部长朱

校长韦卓民

附文:

母校教学训育最近实施概况

[本社讯]母校复员武昌,瞬将三载,所有校内教学、训育种种活动,及经常推行事务,均能依循常轨,平静进展,无所滞碍,师生弦诵未尝一日中绝。据悉,学校近奉部令,以学生教学与训育方面应行加强,并指示各点,仰遵办具报等由,业经学校查照最近训教情形,据实呈复。兹将教育部令知各点,及学校呈复原文,分别探录于次,关心母校同学,由此当可窥见母校最近教学、训育概况,从知校中弦歌不辍,实非出于偶然;苟非学校当局,及师长同学,融为一片,精诚合作,不克臻此。

部令关于学生教学与训育应行加强各点,指示如下:

(一)教学方面:(1)每学期寒暑假期终了,务须按时开学,学生上课,应实行点名,考核勤惰,未经请假,无故缺课之学生,应切实查明扣分。(2)各科课程,务于规定时期授毕,实验实习,必须切实办理,教员缺课,亦须设法补授。(3)学校各种考试,应按时举行,学生不得借故避免。

(二)训育方面:(1)积极倡导各种增进学术、有益身心之课外作业,纳学生生活于正轨,一切课外作业组织,悉由学校派员指导,否则令其停止活动,或予解散。(2)学生在校或外出,应一律佩带证章,以资识别,由训导处随时注意抽查。(3)非本校学生,绝对不准参加学生伙食团,并不得在校内寄宿,主管人员应随时巡查,如有擅留校外人士寄宿者,一经查明,即予以记过,或其他严厉之处分。(4)学生请假办法,应由校严格执行。

学校呈复教育部原文如下:(见前文——编者)

华中大学基本精神*

基本精神三大要素

母校组织机构,办事系统,皆沉浸于一种基本精神,亦即基督教精神;其发皇于举校教育设施,及日常生活行事者,则具有三大要素:一曰民主精神,二曰守法精神,三曰负责精神。三者互为因果,交织纷陈,贯注于全校生活行事之内,衍为数十年来一贯校风,使一校生机,赖以维持不坠。

民主精神使决事允当

民主精神,弥漫校中,足使决断事理,公允明当。故本校行政大端,皆决于校务会议(The Senate),其教务设施,皆决于教务会议(The Faculty Meeting),事有专责,则设各委员会以司之。凡事之来,不论巨细,必由该管机构公同处理,由会中人员各抒所见,自由辩论,务使事理,折衷至当,而后有所决断。但一经决断,行之必果。是以决事之前,会中辩论毫无保留,既经决断,则会外无所訾议。年来校事处理,能力求允当,而事之推行,无所阻滞者,职是故也……华中师生工友有如家人,日常相处,一出于诚,互相爱重,尤特别尊重各人意见与人格。不论何时何事,其相与接触,必视人为"人",而不为"机械"。诚以一家之人,各有独立人格,其行事与意见,自不免于分歧,有可容忍者必尽量容忍,人苟独行其是,一意孤行,自当独承其责,自食其果。斯亦民主精神之一,行于本校则然也。

守法精神使行事有常

守法精神为法治精神所由立,人类群居,有之则治,无之则乱。人人守法,则行事有常,使事循正轨,不相踰越。故本校历年规则与习惯,或为"成文法",或为"习惯法",一经树立,人皆竭力遵循,谨守勿失,盖各种法程规律,胥由有关在职人员,审慎制定,无不出于公意。制定之后,即生约

---

* 此文系作者于1949年3月27日在华中大学朝会训示全校学生时阐述华大"基本精神"之要点。原载《华中通讯》(复员后)第3卷第6期(1949年5月5日)。

束力量，为人所必守，不容遂私循情，而稍有出入，虽校长亦无权更改一字，遑论他人。以是华中大学一家之人，咸以守法为荣，坏法为耻。苟日久法敝，不适于用，可由有关人员，重议修改，苟其法一日未更，即一日有效。故华大有可修改之法，而不容有越法之行。数十年来，形成风气，事循常轨，皆此守法精神所致。其他习惯诸法，虽无明文规定，人亦自然行之，习以为常，蔚为优良校风。驯致校事推行，用力少而收效宏，亦职是故耳。

负责精神使事无弛废

本校事事推行，胥由专人分层负责。盖人各有所职掌，不相侵越，亦互不干涉。在职务范围之内，各贵忠于所守，克尽其职。是以校事万端，无所废弛。而校长有如家长，于事之推行，有监理督促之责，无越俎代庖之理；其于人人尽职之时，且力尊其独立意向，使各发抒个性，展其所长……师长教学，必竭其知虑，展其专长，而以旷废敷衍为可愧；各级职员，多由师长兼任，虽负荷繁重，从无闲言，且常以诿卸责任为羞；各级人员，执行所事，恒不避劳怨，而以去重就轻，因应圆滑为耻；即在校工友，司其职责，亦莫不以忠实自勉。故全校用人少，而事无弛懈，皆负责精神所使然。

此三种精神互相配合，行乎自然，施之教育，使有形无形，融贯于同学生活行事之中，以变其习行，去其旧染，生其新机，即为华中大学所以为国尽忠，树立有用人才之一道。盖数十年来，国事不振，人多因循泄沓，积弊已深，多由缺乏此三种精神而然。大学生受教四年，于耳濡目染之时，当深察此种精神之重要，非独珍惜拥护，且当习为常行，俾出校之后，见诸行事，以矫时弊，期于国事万一有补……学生出校，将为国家异日领袖人才。一旦任事，使无民主精神，决事何由允当；使无守法精神，法治何由而致；使无负责精神，事业何由开展！若学生在校，行事不负责任，出校何责可负？在校不知守法，出校何法能守？在校不娴于民主精神，出校治事何从实践民主之则？其势必至与世浮沉，推波助澜；见人不负责，我亦敷衍；人以不守法为荣，我亦舞文弄法，以遂其私；人皆专断，擅作威福，我亦武断专横，唯己独尊！以此展转流毒，国家生机丧尽，国脉乃斩。本校忾于国家危机，教育流弊，故于作育人才之时，必于民主、守法、负责三种精神特别重视,无所通假。此固华中大学基本精神所在,为在校同学所当深知,亦毕业校友恒以自勉者也。

附文：

  四月十八日星期一,本刊将发稿付印时,值韦校长假朝会之便,向全体同学讲述母校组织机构,特探志其内容大要于次：

  本校自民国十三年,由前文华、雅礼、博文、博学、湖滨等五大学团体,联合组织成立,迄今不过二十五年。其办学宗旨,在推本基督教精神,遵循我国教育法令,兼采英美各大学教育特长,泯除地域、种族及文化思想之偏见,欲以养成牺牲服务,不偏不倚,顶天立地之人才。故所有教育设施,皆纯以学术立场,为促进人类前途幸福而发；不事党争,不谋私利,不为任何其他企图所蔽。本校设立者大会(Board of Founders)为贯彻斯旨,经依法组设校董会,并选派校长及会计主任,综理校政及经济事宜。校内各院系组织,胥遵我国"大学法"办理,而校政大端掌于校务会议,教学诸事掌于教务会议,使责有专司,事决于多人,克收集思广益之效。至各院系经常事务,则由院务会议、系务会议分别掌理,其他专一事务,别设各种委员会专门掌理。故事无大小,皆非决于一人。而校长职责,仅在监理全校事务之推进。苟事有越法,校长以法绳之,若循正轨,即不得干与。故校中诸事,皆循民主、守法与负责精神积渐推进,欲使同学耳濡目染、潜移默化,以此养成顶天立地之有用人才！

  本校一贯风气,欲以至少金钱,作至多事业。下年度经常费预算,大氐(抵)不过银币十五万元,折合美金,平均不过十万元,惟修建等费不计在内。此皆由各国有关教会或学术团体及私人捐助而来。此外,承教育部津贴,本年计金圆券二千三百元,同学所缴各费,除膳费外,用于教学及其他生活事项者,全年不过银币四十余元,欲以此至少之费,作至多之事,自非力事搏节不可,而每生在校四年,学校所贴补之费为数甚巨。但为贯彻办学宗旨,养成有用人才,本校设立者大会终亦乐予挹注也。

四十年来我国基督教的高等教育[*]

一

我国的基督教高等教育已有 80 余年的历史,这还是仅指革新的基督教范围而言,至于中国的天主教教育,因材料不易得,故未计及。所谓高等教育是一种比较模糊的说法,因为公元 1903 年以前,我国的新教育制度尚未建立,无所谓高等教育,所以基督教教会团体举办的学校程度,也并未明白地划清。

革新的基督教团体或个人为中国青年举办学校,历史可说是悠久的。远在公元 1813 年,其时有英国伦敦会教士在马六甲为华人开办学校,可为我国基督教学校之滥觞。1830 年以后,美国教会人士开始致力于在中国的基督教教育,他们最早的一个学校,是 1839 年在澳门开办的。鸦片战争之后,海禁大开,五口通商,外人来华传教,突飞猛进,基督教教育随之增加,但所收录的学生,类多失学的贫寒子弟,学校的规模和程度都谈不上,却是不得不说是我国教育的别开生面,打破了当时传统的八股教育作风。

这个在中国初期的基督教教育,可分为两个时期:(1)自 1842 年至 1877 年为第一期。在这 35 年间,教会的学校,大都是外国传教士因着随时随地的需要,办一种义塾(或义学)性质的学校,明显地缺乏任何计划和组织。(2)1877 年之后至 1903 年为第二期。基督教教育初具规模,办教会学校的人士,感觉到团结和合作的必要,于是在 1890 年有基督教教育会的组织,从事于教本的翻译和编纂,由上海江南制造局代印,比较大量地介绍西洋的科学。1902 年(光绪二十八年),当时所谓《奏定学校章程》出现,基督教所办的学校在制度上才有所适从,原来开办的基督教学校,大体上根据《奏定学校章程》改组推进。一方面固然要培养在中国教会所

---

[*] 此文原载《金陵神学志》1950 年为纪念南京金陵神学院成立 40 周年所发的特刊。

需要的人才,另一方面,是介绍西洋的科学。因为当时在中国谈基督教,最大的阻力是社会一般人的迷信和缺乏世界的眼光,惟有介绍现代的自然科学,才可希望破除迷信,并改正那夜郎自大的狭隘思想。

一件可注意的事,也是后来抱着狭隘的态度去办基督教学校的人所应该知道的,就是19世纪上半叶在马六甲开办的基督教学校。章程里有一条说:"来校的青年,并不强迫信基督教,亦不强迫参加任何宗教仪式,只需参加学校的公开演讲。"初期办基督教学校的人,是比较开明的。后来的人反变本加厉,开倒车了。

二

严格一点说,基督教高等教育是在公元1864年才开始的。那年有山东登州书院的设立,学生寥寥无几;到1873年(留存最早的实录)也只有10个学生;1882年有华北协和书院的设立,学生7人;上海圣约翰书院创设于1894年,学生6人。足见当时基督教高等教育之筚路蓝缕。到了1903年,基督教高等学校已有11所,计山东5所,后合并为现在的山东济南齐鲁大学;北京2所,后此两校与北京汇文女子书院(创设于1905年),都并入1917年开办的燕京大学;杭州1所,为今日杭州之江大学的前身;上海1所,即圣约翰书院;武昌2所,即文华书院和博文书院,后于1924年并入现在的华中大学。所以从各大学的前身算起,济南齐鲁大学、北京燕京大学、杭州之江大学、武昌华中大学,是历史很悠久的,而以现有的学校单独来算,上海圣约翰大学是最老的。

1903年后,苏州东吴大学(1904年)、广州岭南大学(1906年)、上海沪江大学(1909年)、南京金陵大学(1910年)、成都华西(协合)大学(1910年)、岳阳湖滨大学(1910年)、长沙雅礼大学(1914年)、福州华南女子大学(1914年)、南京金陵女子大学(1915年)、福州协和大学(1916年)相继成立,一直到现在还继续地进展。

这13所基督教大学,在1910年后的近十年中(当时原有学校有些尚未合并,所以有16所),学生总数不到2,000名(1919年统计只有1,595名),但逐年增加,到1937年抗战开始时,学生总数已超过6,000名,一直到现在还在逐年增加。抗战爆发后,除上海圣约翰、沪江两大学未离上海,华西大学在成都不需迁移外,其余十校均先后迁入内地。日敌投降后,学校纷纷复员,迁返原址。各个迁移的大学校舍图书仪器损失惨重。但复员后三数年,大都恢复旧观。解放战争期间,除一所大学部分南迁之外,其余 12 所大学,稳步地在原址继续工作,以表示其信任人民和服务人民的决心。

三

上面所述的基督教大学,在 1926 年以前,校长和其他重要的负责人,几乎全数是外国人,就是一般的教职员当中,中国人比较有地位的还占少数。1924 年 2 月各基督教大学在南京金陵女子大学举行基督教大学会议,到会代表将近 250 人,而中国人只占五分之一。但是这次会议之后,一般的观感,都认为基督教各大学,不是缺乏中国国籍的人才,乃是以前在学校负责的外国人,不肯尽量地罗致和信任,结果是 1926 年以前,各基督教大学所教育的学生,除少数的例外,大都不中不西,不今不古,和中国的社会格格不入,更谈不上结合中国的实际,供应中国的需要。而当时的社会上却拥挤地送子弟到基督教大学,原因是:(1)国内公私立大学在那军阀当权的时代,一般的教学和校风都很坏,而基督教大学比较好,能得社会的信任;(2)在帝国主义侵略的势力之下,精通英文是谋生的一种工具,基督教大学,教英文是有办法的;(3)1910 年—1920 年,留学外国,最为时髦,潮流已从德、法、日转向英、美,尤其是趋向美国,而基督教大学英文既教得比较好,又和美国接近,所以许多基督教大学几乎成为留美的预备学校!

其实,1926 年之前的基督教大学,也不仅注重英文英语,当时各基督教大学的课程,每校都设有:国文、英文、化学、物理、历史、宗教;除一二校外还都设有:生物、数学、社会、教育;比较不充实的是:政治、经济、社会、哲学。余如法文、德文,东亚语文如日文,则是绝无仅有而已。至于俄文、印度语文,皆所忽略。科学如天文、地理、地质,只徒有其名目。医学是从起头就注重的;农、工等科则提倡稍后,乃经费不足之故,教育与商学仅后起之秀耳。

这种分析说明了 1926 年以前的基督教大学,在外国人主持之下,办学的宗旨极为模糊,他们自己在本国学的是什么,在中国提倡的也是什么,除少数人比较有点眼光之外,基督教大学干的什么事,为谁辛苦为谁忙,主观是马马虎虎的。1903年前后,基督教高等教育是为基督教教会培养干部,那是清楚的。1903年之后,尤其是1910年—1920年,基督教高等教育已冲破了培养教会干部的樊篱,注意到一般的高等教育。而教育立场看不清楚,却是很危险,易于受人利用的。同时所教的不切合当时的实际,结果除学生所学的英文尚可实用外,其余课目大都看为具文。这是1926年前的基督教大学失败的基本原因。

四

1926年是国民革命军北伐的一个年头。1927年南京国民政府成立,多少还留着一点革命的朝气,教育部严厉执行私立学校立案的规定,颁布私立学校规程,于是一向行政权在外国人手里的基督教大学,便面临一个严重的问题:那就是立案与否的问题。

这本来不是一个完全新的问题。自从1922年,我国教育界已经很尖锐地感觉到,一个独立的国家容许外人在国土内设立学校,丝毫不受所在地政府的管理,而受教育的又是我们中国的青年,这是绝对不合理的。于是有当时所谓"收回教育权"的运动,弥漫全国。头脑陈腐的教会人士,动辄引用不平等条约所载的"治外法权"以为掩护。但教会的中外人士,开明的也不少。例如,1925年4月份的英文《教育杂志》(教会刊印的),社论中便有这几句话:"无论我们干的是什么,留下来不干的又是什么,教会办教育的人绝不可依赖所谓治外法权去维持基督教的学校,那种作风是自取灭亡的。"1925年4月1日至2日基督教全国教育协进会开会,也通过议案,"认为外国教会在华工作人员享有特种权利,是应及时彻底加以检讨的"。即早在1922年教会来华的教育访问团的总结报告,亦认为在中国的基督教学校应以"更有效,更基督化,而更中国化"为其目标。

虽然在1925年以前的满清和北洋军阀政府,对于少数愿意申请立案的基督教学校,因着种种顾虑,置之不理,但是到了1925年那一年,北洋军阀政府也曾颁布过基督教学校立案的条例,大要有五点:(1)校名须冠以"私立"字样;(2)校长必须是中国人,但原来校长若是外籍人,须有中国人为副校长,向政府申请立案;(3)校董之中半数必须是中国人;(4)不得以传教列入办学的宗旨;(5)课程须遵照政府的规定,并不得以宗教课为必修科目。

这些学校立案条例颁布后,基督教教育会于1925年4月开会时,大家认为第一、第二、第三点和第五点的前半,应由各基督教学校立即实行,并且建议凡愿意向政府申请立案的学校,应自行申请。

南京国民政府成立后,颁布私立学校立案条例,比北洋政府的条例更加严厉,校长必须是中国人,校董三分之二以上须是中国籍。于是立案问题在1926年—1930年间,成为基督教大学所面临的一个大问题。却是到了1932年,除了一个例外,基督教大学都遵照规程完成了立案手续。虽然如此,有几个立了案的基督教大学对政府讲,校长是中国人,而学校行政权和财政权照旧操在外国人手里,一直到抗战胜利,各校复员之后,还是这样。以学校论,是阳奉阴违,以政府论,是明知不问。却是立案酝酿几年之后,基督教大学大都逐渐地变为由中国人办理的学校,形式和内容都渐渐多与我国国情结合。但是校舍的浮华,课程内容的外国成分太重,和我国实际脱节,学生思想趋向英美,大部分学生生活奢侈,因之有形无形、有意无意地为他人所利用,是不能完全否认的。

但是话要说回来,基督教大学的教员、学生,主观上是爱国的。平时尽管自由散漫,到了国家民族的严重关头,他们爱国的热烈情绪表现,还是不落人后的。无论任何学生爱国运动,基督教大学的学生,总是踊跃参加;抗战军兴,除一二所基督教大学环境特殊外,都纷纷后迁,不愿意和日敌妥协,准备抵抗牺牲到底;还有一二所基督教大学,据我所知,八年抗战之久,未曾有过一个毕业学生沦为汉奸的。可以说基督教大学过去培养的学生,大部分是爱国的。不过因立场不十分稳定,观点易于游移,充分地表现着革命不彻底的作风,犯了旧社会中知识分子最大的毛病。至于80余年的基督教高等教育,在我国首先提倡科学,介绍西洋文化,在某种程度上鼓励青年的牺牲服务精神,学校办理认真,校风严正,在恶势力统治之下,坚持一种严格的学术态度,都是优良的成绩是不可磨灭的。我们可以用上面所说的这些话作为1922年"收回教育权"运动之后,一直到我国大陆解放之前,基督教大学将近20年经历的检讨总结。

五

毋庸讳言的是，基督教高等教育，起初是为着培养在中国的教会所需要的干部人才而办的。当然教会所需要的人才不止于传道的人员，还有医药、教育、社会服务、农、工、商等等。范围是随着教会为人民服务的机会和社会的需要而转移的。但是传道为教会的基本工作，所以训练传道人才是基督教高等教育绝对不能少的一部分，那就是神学教育。

革新的教会神学教育程度参差不齐，各教会的政策大相悬异。有些教会主张大量培养传道人才，几乎不问学生文化水准；有些教会认为要搞好教会，必须尽量提高传道工作者的教育程度，所以神学教育要和一般的基督教高等教育程度至少相等，研究神学的学生，入学程度须和高级中学毕业相等。本文论高等教育，故只讲到后一种的神学教育。

在我国的高等神学教育，是在 19 世纪末年才提倡的。到 1926 年，全国的革新基督教教会办有神学院科 10 所，以组织论，在基督教大学成为一院的有 3 所，即：济南齐鲁神学院、成都华西（协合）大学宗教学院（现独立为华西协和神学院）、北京燕京大学宗教学院；在基督教大学成为一科的有 3 所，即：上海圣约翰大学神学科、上海沪江大学神学科、武昌华中大学前文华大学所办神学科；独立神学院 4 所，即：南京金陵神学院、福州协和神学院、广州协和神学院、濼口信义神学院。除此 10 所神学院科外，以后中国圣公会在无锡办有中央神学院，嗣后迁南京，今在上海。但 11 所神学院科中，严格地以高中毕业或更需在大学修业一年至三年才能开始研究神学的，只有 5 所，其余大都以"同等学力"为任意招收学生的烟幕，影响中国神学的发展和降低传道工作者的水准甚多。

上面所谈到的神学院科，所教的课目，类多机械地沿袭英美神学院的传统课程，有些并简直教《圣经》，略及其他课目，只是一种变形的圣经学校，讲不到神学的研究。教员多是外籍的传教士，思想陈腐，眼光狭隘，为一憾事，其结果就是中国教会的神学人才缺乏。1926 年后，虽然有过神学教育的相当努力和改进，但青出于蓝的神学学生尚不多见，为中国神学前途隐忧，亡羊补牢，现在似嫌太晚！而真正觉悟的有几人呢？

六

我国大陆解放之后的今日,已进入一个新的时代。今年6月人民政府中央教育部在北京召开了第一次全国高等教育会议,经过中央文教委员会和政务院的仔细审查,已将会议结果颁布为高等教育五大文件。我们的基督教高等教育,应如何展开五大文件的学习,根据新的高等教育精神,响应人民政府的号召,本着新民主主义的文化教育政策,培养具有高度文化水准、能掌握最高的科学文化的成果、全心全意为人民服务的建设人才,是我们当前的任务。过去几十年的基督教高等教育若有什么成功,我们不应自满,更不可骄傲,所有的偏差和失败都由于当时旧社会的恶劣环境和我们自己的主观模糊,现在可不计较,只依照圣保罗的遗教,"忘记背后,努力面前",基督教高等教育的前途还是光明的。

作者附言:

南京金陵神学院,成立40周年,发行纪念特刊,嘱卓民撰《四十年来我国基督教的高等教育》一文,卓民不才,本无以报。然卓民任教母校,今冬适满四十寒暑,回思既往,惭悚良多,又有不能已于言者!文中容有愤慨语,实自述之辞,非敢厚责前贤也。

同学中对于下乡参加土改工作
一点顾虑的解答*

我们在学校学习过土改十几天之后,大概都认识到土地改革是广大农民的要求,是建设新中国必须经过的一个阶段,是革命必须有的过程,是根据共同纲领第三条要"有步骤地将封建半封建的土地所有制改变为农民的土地所有制",是"发展生产力和国家工业化的必要条件",是我们人民的一件伟大的事业,我们人民应该以热爱祖国的情绪,服务人民的决心来参加,并应抱着通过参加土改的工作来提高自己、改造自己的希望来参加土改的工作。

一般而论,时到今日,我们全校的同学已经了解土地改革的重要性,压倒目前任何其他的任务。我们全校同学已经深深地体会到,就是放下六个月在课室中和实验室的学习,去参加土改工作,实际地来认识农村的情形,和广大农民接触,和劳动的农民过六个月同甘共苦的生活,在工作和斗争中去体验土地改革的意义,总的收获一定有利于我们土改完成返校后的业务学习。却是有少数的同学,尤其是少数的物理系、化学系、生物系、音乐组的同学,以为放下了六个月的业务学习,土改后返校只上三个半月的课,一定不能完成一整个学年的课程,更不问一整个年头的实验,三个半月的教与学不是敷衍了事,功课"减而不精",便是把许多功课堆在一起,"食而不化"。

这种顾虑,正如王副主委①在启发报告中讲过"不是反动的顾虑","而是好学生的顾虑"。却是这种顾虑是大可不必存在的。我在这里不再强调地讲,土改工作一定会将我们师生的业务效能大大地提高,三个半月的教与学一定不仅仅等同于土改前的三个半月,我更不必再次在这里强调地讲,假使不好好去过土改关,不但六个月课室的业务学习没有多大的

---

* 原文刊载在《华大生活》,1951 年 10 月 13 日(星期二),第 2 版。
① 指其时华中大学负责人之一王自中。

价值，就是更长时的业务学习，也等于无用。我所要强调讲的，是同学对于老师、对于学校、对于政府信任应有的态度。华大的老师和华大的领导部门对青年学生、对政府、对人民、对祖国是负责任的。六个月土改归来，作了总结之后，三个半月的教与学，能否完成一学年的任务，一九五二年本科和专修科应届毕业的学生，所学的成就，到了一九五二年八月总结起来，应否毕业，不是同学的问题，而是老师负责制的问题，校长负责制的问题。到时老师是要忠诚老实地向学校行政部门作报告，学校也要忠诚老实地向中南教育部转向中央教育部作报告。应届毕业的学生应不应该毕业的问题，是要分层负责地来解决的。只要同学对老师和学校有信任，又何必有应该不应该毕业的顾虑呢？同学们，可以已矣！

什么才算是大学毕业的程度呢？能机械地决定吗？不说现在全国高等学校各系科课程还没有由中央教育部最后规定，所规定的只是一般原则性的东西，就说是规定了每课的内容还须长期才能全国划一。原则上我们大学第一、二年的功课是为学生在所专修的学术树立一定程度的基础，训练学生去掌握研究学术的工具，第三、四年的功课只是在专门学术中举例地示范教学生，指导深入和提高的轮廓和途径，给学生一个学术的地图，一部前进的指南，一堆打开学术门户的钥匙。因此，到了第三、四年本科各系学生所应该从老师那里得着的不是功课里量的问题，而是质的问题。当然时间长一点从质来讲，深入和提高可以加强，但不能有任何绝对的标准。大学毕业不是学习的结束，反之，正是在各毕业生从事实际工作，在各人不同岗位上更加结合实际去自学，去将学校所学的来提高深入。毕业后指导我们学习的不是老师，而是广大的群众。我们在实际工作中来学习，不是靠学校举行考试来鉴定成绩，而是依靠周围的群众，我们服务的对象，来评定我们的工作。这种学习是继续不断死而后已的，和三个月、六个月在学校的学习比起来，真是不可同日而语。

至于第一、二、三年级的同学，更不需顾虑了！假使土改后三个半月功课不能学完，下学年的教学计划必须照顾到，绝不会叫学生躐等以进。学习是有计划、有步骤、循序渐进的，只要同学信任老师、信任学校，学业的问题是可以解决的，又何必顾虑？让我们轻松愉快地去参加土改工作吧！

土改学习小结*

一、自从今春政府号召各大专学校教工下乡参观土改工作,我听过了各地的参观团,路过武汉市,在武汉市人代会协商委员会招待席上的讲话,我心里便起了一种下乡看看的要求,但总因学校职务放不下来,未能下决心下乡去。

九月中从中南教育部潘部长在本校改制委员会席上,得知我校师生参加土改工作的消息,我心里第一个反应乃是考虑工作时间的问题,对于土改的政治性,因为去年列席中南军政委员会会议,听了首长所关于土改的报告和各地完成了土改的报告,又在小组经过比较长期的文件学习和讨论,又经过湖北省人代会李先念主席和其他首长关于土改的报告,各地准备土改情形的报告,和多[几]天小组的学习和讨论,又加上了多次武汉市协商委员会召开关于土改的座谈会和各界的座谈会,我是比较清楚,从未怀疑过土改政策的正确和重要,一直就拥护土改的。

但谈到我校全体师生下乡参加土改工作时,心里便发生矛盾了,主要是时间的问题。假使全校师生下乡时间只是两个月的话,本年度寒暑假缩短,绝对不妨碍教学计划,问题不大。若是时间为三个月,而据武汉市郊区土改委员会代表有一次在市协商委员会土改座谈会席上的意见,三个月尽可以完成土改整套的工作,那末,我心中便从三个月作算。一直到十月十日,我的看法都是这样。

分析我当时的思想,主要是土改工作和学校业务起了严重的矛盾。假使土改和业务思想能够统一起来,我的愿望便可达到。下乡只三个月的话,这"矛盾"是可以统一的。校中的同事,大多数也是这样的要求,纷纷向我反映过,于是我三个月下乡的主张愈发坚定,初期酝酿参加土改的工作是从这点出发的。这是由于我负责学校行政多年,型[形]成了一种"稳健"性和保守性,总想两头都将就一点。

---

* 原文为作者的手稿,现藏于华中师范大学档案馆。

拿六个月来下乡参加土改,当时我觉得问题是多的,尤其是今年改制后,开学迟,十月开学,十月五日尚未正式上课。下乡的六个月,又摆在一整个学年的中间,两个学期都受着严重的影响,不说一年的教学计划无法精简完成,甚至一个学期的学业还要很吃力地去精简,尤其理科各系的实验无法补足,土改与业务起了严重的矛盾。

另外还有一个问题严重着在我心里存在,就是我校改制,原华大和原中大教院才开始合并,我们要搞好团结合作的工作,下乡六个月,到明年四月底返校,从头再搞起,岂不是工作要延迟将近一年?

岂不知思想转变是不知不觉中很快的。十月十日(?)①王副校长带回来中南教育部决定了我校下乡六个月的消息,我很愉快而轻松地接受。现在我回忆起来,主要是我对于潘部长指示的信任,同时,这决定是中南教育部在中央指示下的决定,学校行政的责任问题便解决了。

我回头来,拿出来《高等学校暂行规程》一看,看到第一条宗旨为:"以理论与实际一致的教育方法,培养具有高级文化水平,掌握现代科学和技术的成就,全心全意为人民服务的高级建设人才。"第二条又有:"进行革命的政治及思想教育,肃清封建的、买办的、法西斯主义的思想,树立正确的观念和方法,发扬为人民服务的思想。"然后我好像恍然大悟! 培养具有高级文化水平、掌握现代科学和技术成果、全心全意为人民服务的高级建设人才的任务,我个人是清楚地了解,并愿意去努力完成的。但是,我过去由于多年在旧社会工作型[形]成的偏差,也是过去"超政治"企图的偏差,只看重了"高级文化水平"和"现代科学和技术成果",没有认识为培养全心全意为人民服务的建设人才,首先需要,而且必定彻底地做到"肃清封建的、买办的、法西斯主义的思想",才是进行革命的政治及思想教育。那末,肃清封建的、买办的、法西斯主义的思想,还有方法比全体师生六个月下乡土改更为有效吗? 六个月的时间,正是拿来完成我们学校的主要任务,哪里会和学校业务起什么冲突? 所谓矛盾就不成为矛盾,只是狭义去看业务的矛盾。

两校合并后团结合作的工作,即是原来两校的教职干部、本科专修科

---

① 原文如此,特以说明。

的学生,混合编队,"并肩作战""甘苦共尝"。六个月土改工作的经验正好促进我们彼此间的认识,加紧我们的团结和合作。土改六个月后归来,全校定有一家人的感觉和情绪,恐怕比在校工作一年还要有效。十几天学习土改(文件)的过程中已经是初步见效了。

  学校问题的解决,在我个人思想上一个月来,是有了上述的转变。至于我个人对于土改文件学习的体会,一部分是在中南军政委员会以下各级人民政府召开的会议席上,经过一年多的学习,自己并作过多次的传达报告,另一部分是此次半月来在听启发报告和再次、再三读学习文件所体会的:(1)土改主要固然是消灭数千年根深蒂固的土地封建制度,建立土地为农民所有的制度,帮助农民翻身,解放和发展农村生产力,实现城乡经济交流,为祖国工业化开辟道路。但是土改还要认为是建立人民民主专政的政治建设重要的一个环节。同时是消灭反革命分子和帝国主义走狗的防空洞。换一句话说,当前的抗美援朝、土地改革、镇压反革命三大任务,是互相关联、不可分划的。没有人民志愿军在朝鲜的辉煌胜利,我们就不能在后方安心进行土改的工作;完成土改,发展农村生产,城乡交流,繁荣经济,正是有力地打击帝国主义、保卫世界和平。(2)我过去一年多学习土改文件,虽然有过从和平土改的错误思想转变过来认识到土改是一场剧烈的革命战争,但是因为书本的文件学习,甚至于开会讨论,总不免教条主义,不和实际相结合。这次决心下乡六个月参加工作,学习的时候和听报告的时候,就细心去在个人思想上结合到要做实际工作和个人自己的问题,结果学习好像更有深刻的体会。(3)过去尽管学习土改政策、拥护土改政策,但同时听到各方片面的传说和谣言,难免有动于中,多多少少觉得有的地方,因为干部的不能正确地掌握政策,弄到"糟得很"。这次刘政委的报告帮助我来认识"糟得很、好得很"是不同立场的看法。由于看的角度不同——农民立场和地主立场、封建秩序的看法和建立新秩序的看法——所以看到的就不同。我们要从农民翻身的立场来看,从建立新的秩序观点来看。(4)"分别对待"是对我很大的启发。这不是一种"花样",乃是集中力量打击敌人、分化敌人的方法。我到了农村实际工作中要好好学习这一点。(5)依靠贫雇,团结中农,中立富农,消灭地主,不是平铺的,是有步骤地依靠而团结、团结而中立,才好好地大力地消灭地主。(6)黄居易主任所讲的工作八个步骤,讲到"合理合法"对我的启发很多,是过去学习中所没有注意到的。其余文件里面许多点都是这次半月来学习所体会到的。

  下乡吃苦问题我一直没严重考虑。我虽不生长[在]真正的农村,而是生长在中山县的一小镇市,却是抗战期间曾在偏僻的滇西住过六七年,滇缅公路上跑过多次,吃与住不大讲究,随适[遇]而安。但是我怕冷,冬天没有火就大大不舒服,这是我最大的顾虑。我虽不计较吃什么,但年老齿落,许多东西嚼不烂,消化不了。但是每餐只要有点咸菜,我相信农民的饭,我是可以吃得饱的。我下乡土改主要是工作,从工作中学习农民、学习青年、学习群众。我相信一定能学到许多东西。我保证我尽量争取学习的机会,虚心地向农民、青年、群众学习,和农民、青年、群众一起来搞土改的工作。一方面站稳贫雇农的立场,执行土改政策;另一方面提高个人的警惕,防止我的小资产阶级思想从中捣乱,服从组织领导。依靠群众,重新做一个小学生,实际工作中体会马克思列宁主义和毛泽东思想,真正投身到革命大队伍里面去。

我所亲历的欧美高等教育*

我于1918年9月进哈佛大学研究院,1919年7月取得哲学系的 M. A. 学位。研究一年以后,于1920年7月回国。

美国的大学一般要求入学的学生修毕旧制八年的小学和四年的中学或新制六年的小学和六年的中学,各科大学的入学考试合格,才能入学。由于各大学入学考试的程度不同,入学后四年大学的课程与毕业的要求也就各各相异,结果就是比较优良大学毕业生的成绩与比较差的大学毕业生的成绩相差很远,几乎不能同日而语。

当时我国留学美国的学生,很少是正式通过美国大学的入学考试加以修完四年大学的课程、按规定毕业的。多半是在国内大学修业一二年入美国大学插班或在国内大学毕业后,找到某大学承认其大学毕业资格,入该大学的研究院,一年后,按该大学的规定,取得其硕士学位,如果继续再读两年或三年,就能取得博士学位。这些所谓高等学位,需看它们是哪个学校的学位,而且还要看是哪科哪系的。即使同一个学校、同一个科(系),如果时代不同,师资变易,学位的价值是大不相同的。比方以哲学这科而论,在20世纪头10年与20年代里,大家都承认哈佛大学无疑是第一流的。可是在第一次世界大战结束以前的哈佛大学的哲学系与战后的哈佛大学哲学系相比较,其师资有很大的分别,因之学生所受的锻炼就有所不同。即以该校研究院的哲学系而论,专修哲学史或逻辑的功课,其质量与心理学的功课质量相比较,或与全系的社会伦理学的功课质量相比较,据作者亲身的体会,是有相当大的距离的。但是以全时代的美国各大学的哲学系师资与其学生的成绩而论,则不能不说哈佛大学总胜一等,绝大多数的美国大学是不能与之相比拟的。如果我们远隔重洋,不明真相,以为美国各大学的硕士、博士学位代表同一的学术水平,这是完全错

---

* 此文根据作者20世纪50年代介绍自己留学生活、我国留学生情况以及欧美高等教育的讲稿的第四部分整理而成。全文共有五部分,其中前两部分已遗失,第三部分讲述留学美国人数多的原因,第五部分根据当时政治需要,对留学生所受的"资本主义教育"的毒害进行了批判。

误的。至于留学美国三五年,没有取得学位的留学生,我们就无从衡量了。可能是造诣很深,也可能是一无所得,那就要看他们回国后在学术工作上的具体表现了。

美国各大学的本科与研究院,一般是规定学生每学期按各科(系)的要求选四五门课程,研究生必须每学期选一门功课是研究讨论课(称为Seminar)。有些大学的课程是以学分计算的,如一门功课每周上课3小时,则一个学期的课程算作3个学分,5门课程就是15个学分。但是研究生一般只选4门功课,甚至3门,其中如果1门是研究讨论课,每周上课连续2小时,那么选这种课的学生,每周上课的时间可能少至7小时。

普通课由教师(教授或讲师)讲授,指定参考书,大都每周须阅读约30页,所以一个研究生如选4门课的话,每周平均要读一百二三十页的参考书。大都临时小考两次,学期考一次。以五等或三等或合格与不合格两等记分。本科生和研究生在这方面是一样待遇的。

参加研究讨论课的学生限定不超过12人。学期开始时先由领导教师(限于教授)说明研究的范围与其主要的问题,各学生认定研究的题目,按教师指定的秩序,每周由一个学生提出研究论文,大约五千至一万字,预先至少一周交由参考室保管,该课教师与学生在参考室阅读,做好笔记,准备提问与批评。上课时,提出论文的学生以扼要的话语,在大约30分钟内,说明论文的内容与所得的结论,然后由其他学生轮流提问与批评,提论文的学生须立即答辩或解释,最后由教师总结。研究讨论课的成绩是根据所提的论文、答辩的情况与对他的论文提问与批评而定的,此外没有考试。

选普通课的中国留学生写英文不够流利的还没有多大妨碍,只要阅卷的老师能够明白所写的大意就行了,但参加研究讨论课的学生,如果短语不熟练是有很大的困难的,尤其哲学与其他社会科学课是这样。

大学本科一般不要求写毕业论文,硕士的毕业论文也很简单,不限定是对学术有贡献的,只是心得而已。博士论文原本是代表学术贡献的,但是美国大多数的大学是很广泛地解释"贡献"这词的。调查三四十个中国留学生初到美国时对美国生活适应的问题,总结这三四十个学生所填的表格,就是一篇博士论文了!还有不少是比这更容易办到的。社会科学博士论文的材料搜集与写作一般需时只一个学年,而且写论文的学生,同时还得听两三门课。自然科学的研究生还有实验室的研究方法锻炼,而人文科学的研究生大半是靠他们的天才。

硕士学位大都要求一种外语(即使中国留学生也不能算英语为外语,更不能算汉语为外语),博士学位一般要德、法语口试及格,但能口译本专业的参考书而没有严重的错误就算了事。很少中国留学生在取得博士学位之后阅读德、法文的参考资料。

以上是我国在美国各大学的留学生20世纪初至20年代的一般学习情况。

再说英、德、法三国的中国留学生和高等教育。我所亲身知道在英、德、法三国的中国留学生是限于20世纪20年代的,而且又限于英国的伦敦与牛津两大学和法国的巴黎大学与德国的柏林大学。在德、法的见闻所及容有挂漏,即使在英国两所大学的阅历,亦难免主观,聊志个人几十年后的回忆,这是须请读者原谅的。

我在哈佛大学时就羡慕当时英国哲学家霍布侯斯的治学方法的缜密,于1927年秋赴英从他学习前,得知他在伦敦大学经济学院主持讲座。到伦敦大学后,我声明想师从这位教授,所以我就被学院分派到他的名下为研究生,霍教授便是我的指导教师了。经霍教授考察过我过去的学历,便向大学评议会承认我在美国哈佛大学哲学博士候选人的资格,免除了取得这种资格所规定的考试。经过一次谈话,霍教授让我立即草拟博士论文大纲。这大纲拟就后,经过他的修改和指示,我除了在经济学院和附近的两个学院听三门有关我的论文的哲学与社会学课外,遵照他的嘱咐在英国博物馆附设图书馆搜集论文材料并进行写作。我赴英之前,对于我拟写的论文《从欧洲哲学看中国儒家伦理学思想二千年的发展》,曾搜集了一些材料,到英国后,只需加以适当的补充,向讲课的教师请教。第一个学期内(英国大学的学年分为三个学期)向霍教授提出论文写成的一部分。伦敦大学哲学博士论文的写作在数量与质量上至少能代替两个学年的时间,而且对所研究的学术部门是有创造性的贡献,其程度达到大学评议会认为能代表该大学哲学博士论文的水平,才算为合格。其初步评定由指导教师决定。所以这第一个学期我的部分论文的写作能得到指导教师的比较好评,对我是极大的鼓舞。

一学期后,霍教授叫我不再听课。但我仍继续听两三门的哲学课,包括霍教授自己所讲的课在内,而霍教授认为我听课是浪费时间,应把全部精力放在论文的研究与写作上面。那就是说,作为一个研究生来说,我的任务是进行自行研究,每个学期提出写成论文部分的初稿,交由指导教师批阅,而且每学期至少和他有一两次关于研究问题的讨论,且这种讨论是相当磨人的。指导教师每每在我的研究写作中指出种种材料的不足或推理的不正确,必须予以改正。纠正推理的缺点尚属容易,而补足材料的不足往往感到麻烦。比方有一次,霍教授要我寻找我国宋朝朱熹的哲理思想有无受过古希腊亚里斯多德的思想的影响,并指出其历史上联系的线索。这是一个难题。比较两家的哲学思想并不很难,但寻找历史上具体的接触就不易了。只这一个问题就花了我好几个月的钻研,经过多次和专家学者的访问与通讯,最后在德国柏林大学由于伏朗克教授的帮助才得到关于这个问题的初步线索,可是依然没有彻底澄清。我将所有的心得写出来,寄回伦敦霍教授,他回信说:"够了。既然到此为止,没有别人对于这问题比你掌握更多的材料,而这又不是你的主要问题,就暂时搁下罢。"这是他指导我的方法,即主要是要我发挥自己的主观能动性,对问题的解决多想方法,不依靠导师。他不止一次对我说过:"研究这问题的是你,而不是我,我只代表学术界对你的研究方法和成果的严格批评,由你去应付。这是锻炼研究生的方法。指导教师不应有太多的帮助。你能毕生依靠指导教师吗?"这种方法我认为是正确的,对我的教益是不少的。

由于我赴英以前就已搜集大部分的材料,用英文写作对我来说也不困难,我所需要的多半是从霍教授学习钻研的方法,因而我在一个学年零两个学期之内便将全部论文写成了,其中一个长达三个月的暑假和一个多月的春假是在法国巴黎大学听课与研究的(因英法两大学春假时期不同,而巴黎大学是有暑假课的),一个学期在柏林大学。这是因为伦敦大学的研究生有权取得指导教师的许可,花两个学期的时间在其他国家进行研究。

既然我在第五个学期写成了论文,并由指导教师的评阅批准,向大会评议会提出,剩余的工作只是准备口试。而为了口试的准备,霍教授认为我只需阅读欧洲最近出版的有关刊物,不必太过紧张,所以他就破例向大会提议让我去牛津大学随意听课一个学期,然后回伦敦大学参加口试。博士毕业口试,其内容主要是论文的答辩,英国各大学聘请校外专家考查博士候选人。这个关口我顺利地通过了,而哲学博士的学位是次年才授予的。

以上是我两年在英、德、法研究的回忆。现在我说说我留学美国与欧洲的几点感想。

(1)留学外国取得学位有没有价值呢?我认为在外国的学校按其规章取得学位,表示达到一种里程碑,也是和所在国的同等程度的学生较量,有助于我们学习的努力并检查我们研究的成绩。这并不等于说,在国外不取得学位的留学生就毫无成就。研究所得是一回事,而通过按章的考查再取得学位是另一回事。没有学位并不等于没有成绩,而学位仅是某种成绩的表示。不应以学位来完全代表成绩。而且同一种学位并不能一律代表同等的成绩。

(2)有人认为某国的学位总要比某另一国同样学位价值更高,我却认为这种评价是错误的。依我个人本世纪初至20年代实际的经验来说,美国最好的大学本科毕业生的程度一般比欧洲著名大学的大学本科毕业生的程度较低两年。那就是说,英国著名大学的 B. A.,法国著名大学的 Licencié 和德国的 Ph. D.(哲学博士)比美国著名大学的 B. A. 在专业程度上高出两年。但我说的英国 B. A. 是指专业(honours school)的 B. A.,而不是一般的 B. A. (pass degree)。同称 B. A. 并且是同一所大学同时所分发的,其程度的不同是不可以道理计的。又如苏格兰四所大学本部毕业所给的学位都是 M. A.,即在名称上相同于伦敦大学毕业后继续研究两年考试合格的学位,而又相同于英国地方大学伯明翰、曼彻斯特等本科毕业后继续研究一年考试合格的学位。但是英国著名的古老牛津与剑桥两大学的 M. A. 是在取得 B. A. 之后,从大学入学时起算,经过五个学年、无须再通过考试,只交规定的金额——50 英镑左右,便可取得的,因此在牛津与剑桥,有时一个人花了五个学年考取大学毕业的 B. A.,就可以同时交费而领取 M. A.,那就是说,牛津与剑桥的 M. A. 在学术成绩上简直与 B. A. 没有分别。这样欧洲大学毕业的学位,其名称是不一致的,而英国大学毕业的学位尤其是这样！这是大学本科毕业学位的情况。

谈到所谓美国与英、德、法的高等学位，那就更是令我国内一般人不能明了了。

大学的研究院只是美国才有的。英、德、法大学都没有研究院，只有研究生，但不设专为研究生的课程。这些国家认为大学毕业的学生在专业上是已经有了基础的，无须再去听课，应该能独立研究。德国的大学毕业生取得了博士学位，此外并没有什么所谓高等学位。在法国大学毕业，一般是五年后，提出科学论文，审查合格，便取得国家的博士学位。在别国大学毕业的人，其资格是法国所承认的也可以向法国的大学提出科学论文，取得博士学位，但这是大学的博士，而不是法国国家的博士。这两种博士是有区别的。英国的哲学博士已在上面讲过了。其实在第一次世界大战前，英国各大学许多年来已经没有哲学博士的授予，大学毕业后按各大学的定章取得 M. A. 的学位也就够了。这原是中世纪的观念。所谓 M. A. 就是 Master of Arts（拉丁文 Magister Artium 的简写），而拉丁文的 magister 就是教师的意思。这与博士又有什么分别呢？"博士"乃是古希腊文 doctor 之汉译，而 doctor 原来也就是教师的意思，和 magister 是没有区别的，只不过一个是拉丁文而另一个是希腊文而已。三级学位在美国是 19 世纪与 20 世纪之交产生的，其 M. A. 原是仿英国的制度，而 Ph. D. 是仿德的。先学英而后学德，所以就有 B. A.、M. A.、Ph. D. 这三级学位。第一次世界大战后，为了吸引美国出国的学生，英国才复兴久已停止颁发的 Ph. D.。可是在哲学博士学位恢复后，M. A. 与 Ph. D. 在英国各大学仍有要求上的不同。除牛津、剑桥与苏格兰大学之外，一般可以说，M. A. 是听课而通过考试来取得的，需进行研究，即有论文，但不要求有创造性的贡献。而 Ph. D. 是以学术研究为标准的，重点完全是在研究的创造性成绩上。

武昌文华书院及其后身华中大学*

在旧中国,帝国主义者以办学为名,对我国进行文化侵略。文华书院及其后身华中大学,则是他们在武汉的重要据点。

我于1903年进入文华书院读书直到文华大学毕业,接着又在文华大学、华中大学担任教员、教授、副校长、校长,先后达48年。其中,还到美国的哈佛,英国的伦敦、牛津,法国的巴黎,德国的柏林等大学当研究生,获博士学位。又应聘到美国芝加哥、耶鲁、哥伦比亚等大学担任特约讲师与客座教授。以中国基督教代表的身份两次参加世界基督教在英国举行的代表大会。以中华圣公会的代表身份参加在美国召开的两次总议会。因而对外国教会来我国"传道"和兴办学校的因由有所了解。

文华书院和文华大学

武昌文华书院,是由美国基督教圣公会创办于1871年10月2日。校址原在武昌横街头,后于19世纪90年代迁到武昌花园山,即现在的昙华林。

书院之所以取名"文华",是因为美国圣公会派来中国传教的第一位主教,中国姓姓"文",后来的主教在武昌办了这个学校来纪念他。结合高尚典雅的中文"文章华国"的含义,定名为文华书院。

文华书院开办时,教会拉学生上学,全部费用由书院供给,第一年不过14名学生,第二年才24名,第三年增到30名,到第九年即1880年也只有90名。

教会出钱办学,出钱拉学生,是以培养教会传教人才为目的。大约1878年,就曾专门开设了一个神学班,后来发展成为文华大学的神学院。从神学班、神学院出来的人,有很多分派到各地传教,不少成为圣公会主

---

* 本文原稿撰成于1964年,后刊载于政协武汉市委员会文史学习委员会编:《武汉文史资料文库》第4卷(教育文化卷),武汉出版社1999年8月版。

教、会长、会吏。

从 1903 年到 1911 年,我在武昌文华书院度过了我的学生时代。

1903 年,我随父亲由广东香山(现中山县)来武汉,那时我 14 岁了,已读过七年私塾,读过四书五经、《古文观止》,学过英文、算术,只是英语不能"会话",所以初进书院,被编到最低班。

那时书院监督(即院长)是英国人翟雅各。全院只有外籍教师 4 人,中国教师 7 人。共有学生 144 人,分 7 个班。每班每周有汉文 10~12 小时,分为古文 4~6 小时(作文在内),读经书 3 小时,史纲 3 小时。英文 10~12 小时,分为读本 6 小时,文法作文 4~6 小时。数学(算术、代数、几何)6 小时。地理(下一、上一、二、三班)或欧洲史(四~六班)2 小时,理化(五、六班)2 小时,每周共大约 33 小时。每日上课 6 小时,上、下午各 3 小时。星期六下午不上课。

功课中注重英文、数学,而对中文学习则视同儿戏,老师讲得不起劲,照本宣读,学生则无心听课,大都偷看英文书或公开看小说。教中文的老师待遇也远不如教英文、数学的老师,月薪少得多。当时英文、数、理、化老师月薪 50 元(银元,以下皆同),中文老师仅 30 元。所以文华学生,除在进文华以前中文已有根底外,很多人连一封信都不会写。

大学生中有英语练习会,大学生一律参加,每星期五晚开会,练习英语讲演、辩论,或听教师、来宾用英语作专题演讲。

文华高中学生的英语,已初步熟练,大学生则能自由运用,对答如流。高中除本国语文、历史课外,其余各科全用英语课本,教师全用英语教课。大学更是如此。可以说,文华学生的英语,的确是不错的。

为奖励学生,每年年终结业时,每班有第一名、第二名奖,均以书籍为奖品,在举行毕业典礼时一道颁发。每年还举行中文比赛一次,也发第一、二、三等奖。前三名的文章贴堂展出。

辛亥革命前,中学可以跳级。我进校时因为英语会话不好,进了最低班次。但我在私塾中读了七年,中文程度较高,入学后,除加紧学习英语会话外,英语、算术以及"格致"(生理、理化)等课,我都应付自如,成绩甚好,接连跳了几级,用四年时间学完备馆(中学)六年的功课。1907 年春升入正馆,即大学了。

中学可因成绩不良而留级,大学只计学分,学分满定额而平均在60分以上的可以毕业,可领取学士学位的文凭。

学校对学生管理是严格的。中学有领班制,领班(总领班)由校长从五、六班的学生中选出,不论是否信教,不问功课好坏,只问是否操行好。领班向校长负责,协助校长与舍监管理学生,每星期六上午早餐后,全中学领班集合在校长室向校长汇报一周的学校情况以及学生操行。

一般学生平时不准出校门。星期六下午全校无课,可以请假,但要校长批准,限即晚六时半返校,参加晚祷。

文华春季始业为上学期,秋季始业为下学期。每年有暑假两个月,寒假一个月。每逢端午、中秋两节各放假三天。在这四个假期中,学生可以自由回家,寒假学生不准留校。

文华规定,所有学生,不论信教与否,一律参加宗教活动,不得违抗。1903年,湖广总督张之洞曾派人来校磋商,愿付双重学费让他的孙子到文华学英语,只不参加宗教仪式,但未得到允许。宗教仪式每日早晚两次,每次大约半小时,按圣公会的公祷文进行,由校牧(会长)或牧师(会吏)领导举行,学生按规定坐、立、跪如仪。

每逢星期日,有宗教仪式三次,学生一律强制参加。其时间内容是:上午6点30分圣餐(非信徒只参加前段),9~10点圣经(非宗教仪式),10点30分~12点大礼拜。下午6~6点30分晚祷(中学生参加),7~8点大学生英文礼拜。大礼拜和英文礼拜都是圣职人员讲道。

文华书院向学生收取的学杂费,在当时是比较高的。1903年,我为全自费生,每学期交纳50元。那时每人每月膳费不过一至二元,一学期按4个半月计算,大约8元。那么学校在每个学生身上可收入42元,不能说不高了。但就学院来讲,全自费的学生约为2/3,有1/3"吃教"的学生全免费或只收膳食费的。因而要完全依靠对学生收费来维持学校开支,还是不够的。然而"醉翁之意"在于传教,在于培养为其所用的"洋才",外国老板也就乐于施舍、解囊。

文华书院于1909年申请美国立案后,改称"文华大学",中国学校要申请外国立案,这难道说是什么治外法权?这是外国学阀在我国领土内称王称霸,其处心积虑,更是昭然若揭。

文华学生生活:伙食较好,早餐稀饭,三小菜,午、晚两餐干饭,四菜,两荤两素。食堂纪律严肃,有舍监管理,8人一桌,同时开动。校舍、寝室和公共场所,整齐清洁。学校设有医药室,可随时给学生看病。中学生平时不准离校,养成了以校为家的习惯,也形成与世隔绝的状况,而耳闻目见,尽是外国的教会的东西。文华的学生生活方式虽不完全是外国式的,也不是中国式的,因而养成一些学生与我国社会格格不入,脱离实际,向往西洋,鄙视本国,缺乏革命思想,只有某些改良主义的要求。

教会的潜移默化

文华书院强迫学生参加宗教仪式活动,强迫学生听圣职人员"讲道"。但不强迫学生入教,甚至在学校供职多年的教职员工,也有不少人没有入教。只要你不公开反对教会,那些传教士就乐于利用你。且以此作为一种口实,说明他们办学并不歧视不信教的教员。就我自己说,从1903年到1911年在文华读了八年书,一直未加入教会。接受洗礼,信奉基督教,那是我毕业后留校任教一学期以后的事。

当初,我的父亲知道文华书院是教会办的,他一再叮嘱我说:"学他们的英文便好,千万不要吃洋教,卖掉了祖宗。"因此,我对教会学校引人入教,是时刻提高警惕的。

礼拜的机械仪式和干枯的说教,诚然不能动人,但那些不文不白大都词句鄙俚的"颂主圣"诗,配上好听的音乐,却能起些作用。每人随着众人唱歌,开始只是唱歌,继而听唱音乐,有美感。久而久之,似乎那些教义有点意思,不像初听起来那么可笑,不知不觉地某些教义灌到我的心里来了。后来想了一下,其主要原因:基督教作为一种宗教,好像比我国社会上流行鬼神迷信较为合理,而细玩其所说伦常道德,以似儒家的"慎终追远""恕以待人""亲其亲以及人之亲,子其子以及人之子"的大端道理。文华英国校长翟雅各好像了解我的思想,他曾读过我国的某些古籍,不时叫我在这方面加以研究。我的1911年1月大学毕业论文,以《中国古籍中的上帝观和祭祖的研究》为题,旨在证明古书中的上帝观接近于一神教,而祭祖乃是慎终追远,不是宗教。这篇洋洋万言的论文,正适合翟雅各的胃口,大加捧场,刊登在本校英文季刊《文华评论》(Boone Review)上,并立即被转载于上海各教会出版多年的《教务杂志》(Chinese Recorder)季刊里,在编辑部的前言里特别声明这是中国人第一次写的文章。这就大大地拉了我一把,使我与教会接近。

在这以前我读中学的时候,学校来了一位美籍化学教师 Richard,原是美国耶鲁大学的理科硕士,为人和蔼,关心学生。一些患着小毛病的同学,要去院里的一所教会小医院就诊;那里病人多,唯一的苏格兰籍医生,性情粗暴,使许多患病的同学碰了钉子。而这位美籍老师,却自己备了一些普通药品,亲自给同学们看病,热情照护,感动了很多同学,更感动了我。我想这岂不是"博爱为德"的典型表现吗?也就是基督精神吧!

我在精神上已渐渐为基督精神所俘虏,文华大学毕业后,我就彻底违背了"不要吃洋教"的父教,向基督投降——接受洗礼了。

我在文华读书时,一向成绩好,名列前茅,早为英籍校长和其他英美籍教员所注意。刚毕业,就被破格聘用为大学一年级的数学教员和高中高年级的英、数教员,月薪 80 元,比以前的教员多 30 元,我自以为了不起。一年之后,我不过 23 岁,又被任命为备馆(即文华大学中学部)代理堂长,尤觉高人一等而沾沾自喜!校长翟雅各又叫我自修西洋哲学史、政治经济思想史,由他自己和另外两个英籍教员作为我的导师,要我注意研究古罗马和近代英国政治上的变革,鼓吹"不流血革命"。接着又要我担任大学的形式逻辑、西洋哲学史、比较政府学和政治学的讲课。这时我不仅成为教会学校——文华大学所重视的人物,而且为直辖文华大学的教会——圣公会所重视了。从此以后,我竟成为教会中的重要人物。辛亥革命后我花了几年工夫,向文华大学写了一篇题为《孟子的政治思想》的硕士论文,用英文写出,于 1915 年在上海广学会出版。这就更加巩固了我和教会的联系,在全国教会中提高了地位。

1918 年,圣公会主教吴德施(Roots)替我在美国哈佛大学研究院取得一名[个]助学金[名额],那年夏季,我赴美国留学。1920 年回国,晋任文华大学哲学教授。

日知会与《文华学界》

1904—1905 年间,一些有排满兴华革命思想的人,利用教会作掩护,在文华书院附近的花园山高家巷圣公会的另一教堂里开办一所阅书馆,名叫"日知会",实际成为宣传革命排满的机关。平时任人看书看报,每逢星期六和星期日开会,有人前来演讲,宣传排满、兴汉和建立共和国的道理。有些同学前往参加,其中就有在备馆五、六班讲汉文课的三位老师。另一位是在正馆教诸子学的刘静庵先生。这位刘老师,端容正色,沉默寡言,在课堂上,两眼半开半合,严肃地讲解庄子、墨子诸书,毫不涉及其他问题,尤其不谈时务、不讲政治。但到日知会开会时,他却慷慨激昂大谈其革命排满。后来刘先生被捕入狱,清朝官吏曾企图治以死罪,因刘先生是教会学校的老师,有关方面和部分学生呼吁教会出面营救,经美籍主教吴德施通过汉口美领事馆电北京美公使馆转圜,使得清廷对刘先生不敢杀害,判为永远监禁,后病死狱中,不失为辛亥革命的先行火种。

与此同时,文华书院的学生在教师余日章先生的指导下,办了一个定期刊物——《文华学界》,不时登载一些涉及宣传革命排满的文章,我当时是《文华学界》编辑部的成员,也是经常用笔名"法兰西士"写这类文章的学生之一。

另有一部分学生,以传教为借口,组织"十字军"(亦称"教世军"),举旗结队,吹号打鼓,走到黄鹤楼、阅马场等人多的地方进行"说教",实际则间接宣传革命。

有时上街的队伍还高唱自己的军歌:

愿同胞团结个英雄气,唱军歌。
一腔热血儿意绪多,
怎能坐视国步蹉跎,
但望指日挥戈,
好收拾旧山河!

《文华学界》的言论、"十字军"的活动,引起了清廷官吏的注意。湖北巡警道冯少竹的儿子冯建统进入循道会办的博文书院,由于文华、博文学生之间的密切联系,从那里刺探着文华学生的革命活动消息。

1906年冬季,我和几个同学带行李出城回家被军警拦住检查行李,目的在于搜查革命证据,逮捕《文华学界》编辑部成员。为此,必须设法应付,我和编辑部成员一道找英籍监督翟雅各要求辞去编辑职务,洋人愕然,问我们何以有此一举。我们告以上述情况,他又问:"你们是不是革命党?"其实我们宣传革命完全出于爱国热情,没有加入革命组织,齐声答应:"不是。"他便说:"那么,有学校保护你们,只要小心你们的行李有没有藏着宣传革命的书籍。《文华学界》是我们学校的刊物,与政治无关。"我们听了,感到有恃无恐。

革命排满的爱国情绪,是当时我国汹涌澎湃的时代潮流,是任何力量都阻挡不住的。教会和教会所控制的学校,自然也限制不了。可是,当他们假惺惺地营救刘静庵,假惺惺地为《文华学界》编辑部人员壮胆,我们还真以为外国教会及其传教士真心同情我们爱国革命,这使我们受到了麻痹。可见帝国主义者对我国文化侵略起了相当大的作用。

华中大学创立缘起

1924年华中大学在武昌文华大学的基础上正式成立。新成立的校董会选定孟良佐为校长,并推定我为副校长兼教务长。

为说明华中大学建立的缘起,这里简要介绍一下教会在我国的情况。当时,基督教在我国派系复杂分歧,美英帝国主义统治阶层为便于对华进行文化侵略,希望教、会合一。

美国以穆德(John. R. Mott)为首的基督教青年会乃是最好教、会合一的桥梁。基督教青年会运动原发生于英国,而盛行于美国。青年会声称,不分教会的宗派,不问教会的教义和历史,不拘任何一种的礼拜仪式,其口号是"非以役人,乃役于人"。就是说单纯为社会服务。这个口号是最适合帝国主义作为欺骗的工具。穆德在美国垄断资本家的支持下,连续召开过世界基督教代表大会,旨在促进教、会合一。

1922年,在上海举行的中国全国基督教数千人的代表大会,我曾作为代表参加,会上鼓吹教、会合一。代表大会成立了一个执行委员会——中国基督教协进会,其经费全是穆德筹自美国的,成为促进中国教、会合一的具体机构。首先以教会所办医院和学校,尤其是教会大学合作作为教、会合一的先河。因为在中国的国立、省立的各大学没有上轨道的时候,教会学校还能吸收一些学生。但在本世纪20年代开始,公立各大学越办越好,私立大学除少数"野鸡大学"外,也在日有改进。教会大学有鉴于此,就不能不集中力量,力图巩固,免遭淘汰。

教会大学调整合并的初步计划是分全国华北、华东、华南、华西、华中五个区:

华北有北京的燕京大学与济南的齐鲁大学。

华东有南京的金陵大学、金陵女子文理学院,上海的圣约翰大学、沪江大学,杭州的之江大学和苏州的东吴大学。

华南有广州的岭南大学,福州的福建协和大学。

华西有成都的华西协和大学。

华中有武昌的文华大学、博文书院大学部,长沙的雅礼大学,岳阳的湖滨大学,益阳的信义大学。

上述教会大学之中,力量最分散、内容最空虚则是华中区的几所大学。其中历史较久、基础较为巩固的要算武昌文华大学和长沙雅礼大学,其他大学都以这两所大学的马首是瞻。但是真正洽谈合并时,困难很大,这是因为文华大学是美国圣公会经营的典型教会大学。雅礼大学虽具有教会大学色彩,实际上是美国耶鲁大学一些毕业同学组织的私人团体——"雅礼会"所创办的,不属任何教会,加之在长沙开办日久,不愿离开,而作为文华大学后台的美国圣公会,以武汉为两湖传教事业中心,更不愿意外迁。在华中区的其他几个大学,也都徘徊不前。

当时鼓吹教会大学合并最力的外国传教士,以汉口圣公会吴德施声望最高,文华大学校长孟良佐野心最大(孟于1917年继翟雅各为文华大学校长)。他们奔走联络,几经磋商,得到汉口英国循道会和伦敦会的支持,将博文、博学两个书院的有关学部与文华大学合并,改为华中大学。

新合并而成立的华中大学,渺小得极为可怜!全校教师在文华中学兼职的占过半数。还有在教会兼职的,合零为整,共计只有12个教员,大都又是学无专长,不能称职的。以图书计,虽有中、美书籍各三四万册,有用或无用的中外文期刊十多种,但却没有添置的经常预算和计划。至于科学仪器,物理、化学、生物,其价值不过2万元。据雅礼大学校长胡美对我说,雅礼还比不上华中,其他教会大学也大都如此。

1926年北伐军经湖南到达武汉,作为帝国主义对华文化侵略的教会学校纷纷停办。华中大学在1927年5月也呈准革命政府,宣告停办。到了1929年,湖南的雅礼大学、岳阳的湖滨大学,都无意恢复,相继将其教员、学生和图书、仪器合并到华中大学。这时华中大学的后台有:汉口的美国圣公会、英国循道会、英国伦敦会和岳阳的复初会和长沙的雅礼会。喧嚷多年的华中区教会大学合并的企谋,真正实现了。

华中大学的兴盛时期

按照英国大学教授7年中有一年带薪休假之例,圣公会资助我赴英进入伦敦大学当研究生,在霍布侯斯(Hobhouse)教授指导下继续研究哲学。学院还承认我在哈佛大学两年研究生的学历。我在英国留学两年,在伦敦大学规章许可之内,用了大半年时间赴法国巴黎大学和德国柏林大学听讲。我的博士论文提前一个学期在德国完成,并由我的指导教授霍布侯斯审阅通过,完成所需要通过的考试,取得博士学位。霍布侯斯教授叫我把剩下的几个月时间用到牛津大学借读,听哲学课。

圣公会支持我去美国留学,是另有用心的。因为,英国教会传教士向来在学术上看不起美国人,也看不起留学美国的中国人,如果美国教会要想同英国教会合作,就要找一个能在学术上沟通美英思想的人,如能找到一个在学术上能够压倒英国传教士的中国代理人,那就最理想不过了。我获得英国伦敦大学的博士学位,又在著名的牛津、柏林、巴黎大学听过课,满足了美国圣公会传教士对我的期望,也达到了英国传教士对华中大学校长资格的要求,对完成华中区教会大学合并有所帮助。

合并后的华中大学,有文学院、理学院、教育院三个学院,共有教职员24人,学生57人。

校舍全部是圣公会的,合作的循道会、伦敦会也拿出一点钱和就近拨出几栋房扩充了校舍。

校董会通过全校开支预算为5,000元,全由学生学费收入开支。这时学生学费每人每年两学期100元,宿费40元,膳费60元,是颇为昂贵的,一般家庭不能负担。图书杂志以及图书馆(即文华公书林)的一切开支,则由公会负担,与图书馆专科学校共同使用。

在华中大学后台的五个单位名为合作,实则貌合神离,彼此推诿,各有打算,随时准备拆伙。在这种情况下,我这个"全权"校长,要想有所作为,处处受到阻碍。要求校董会通过校舍、图书、仪器的经费,特别是通过各单位所负担教职员的工资,传教士们严重限制了校长的实权。

如何摆脱传教士们的束缚,巩固校长的职权。我认为,首先要不通过教会,由校长自行筹集学校经费和建筑费、设备费;其次就是要由校长直接和这五个单位在美英的教会组织取得联系而不通过它们在中国的代理人。为了达到这个目的,除获得我国教育部和湖北省政府每年一二万元的补助之外,还争取得中美、中英"庚子赔款"委员会的每年二三万元的"津贴"。我认为最大的希望,要算设法由我自己的努力以增加美英教会的直接拨款,并取得美英两国的私人捐助。

1931年我应邀去美国芝加哥大学在哈士卡尔基金讲座作特约讲师,主讲中国儒家的伦理学。同时美国耶鲁大学也约我去在该校主办的暑期中学行政人员比较教育讲习会讲课。暑期后又在该校研究院作为伦理学客座教授一年。利用这个机会,我和美国圣公会、雅礼会和复初会董事会及其主要人物取得联系,打破了在中国的传教士的中间隔阂。美国圣公会与复初会增加了对华中大学的常年捐助,并募得扩大校址所需购买基地的用款,以及计划的文学院大楼建筑费。从此,学校经费虽然少,但是相当稳定,学校得到了稳步前进的基础。

1931年国民党教育部正式批准华中大学立案。

从1929年至1935年这6年中,华中大学由24个教职员增加到60多人,男女学生由57人增加到200人,总算有所发展。

在此时期,学校的制度建立起来了。学生升级毕业必须通过严格的考试,大学头两年四个学期的功课,必须按各系规定全部读完。考试合格,学校还要举行一场非常严格的"中期"考试,包括中文、英文和两项专业,是算两年学习的总账。"中期"考试不及格的,仍须重读第二年的功课。学生读完三、四级全部功课在班内考试合格后,学校又要举行一次统考,算整个四年的总账。在管理上,男女学生分开住宿,每宿舍设主任,负责管理宿舍的工作。平时学生不准离开校园,外出必须告假,这样养成一种认真读书的校风。1935年以前的六届毕业生都获得较好的成绩,学生品德上从未出现过较严重的问题,博得社会的信任。

教师分为助教、讲师、副教授、教授四级,升级由校务委员会所选出的

12名教授组成专门委员会，按固定条例经过讨论后，以不记名投票逐一通过办理，任何人不得干涉或更改。以此促进教师钻研学术，杜绝幸进。

会计主任和校长一样，由校董会选定，对校董会负责，按校董会每年所通过的预算开支，任何人不得干涉，校长也无权更改预算。教职员的工资，会计处绝对按月照聘书规定分送。

校务会议和院、系会议每月召开一次。处理各自范围内有关事务，关于课程的兴废、修改与实施，由全体教师组成的教务会议讨论处理。

1937年七、八两月，世界各教会在英国牛津大学与苏格兰的爱丁堡举行代表大会，我为中国各教会代表人之一。我到达英国后，"七七"抗日战争爆发了。我匆匆参加两次[教]会(议)之后，又应美国耶鲁大学之请作第二次客座教授讲课，为华中大学进行募捐，没能收到较大的效果。我心里盘算着学校搬迁的事，向在美国的华中大学设立者大会提出一笔搬迁费的预算，也没有结果。

从抗战内迁到复员故地

抗战开始后，我正在英国，极力主张华中大学迁往后方，写信向代理校长建议，再向校董会提请讨论。可是校董会受美国圣公会代表孟良佐的错误思想的影响，认为我国不能支持长期的抗战，即使日寇打到武汉，对美英教会合办的华中大学，也不会进行摧残。很多人受其影响，都主张不过早迁移。直到武汉各校开始后迁，华中大学才开始准备。1938年7月我由英转美，得知学校已决定迁往桂林，我按学校所提出的搬迁预算，筹足款项汇回武昌。

当我由美国飞香港转道到达桂林时，已是8月15日，学校师生先几天到了桂林，当询及搬迁情况，才知从武昌运来的图书不过百分之四五，仪器不及四分之一。当即决定派员回武昌抢运，而水陆交通业已阻塞，损失甚大，这才使大家痛恨，上了帝国主义分子孟良佐的当了。

学校在桂林初步安定之后，开始上课，师生员工，精力充沛，表现了同仇敌忾的爱国情绪和团结合作的大家庭精神，令人感动！可是从10月下旬起，日机频繁空袭桂林，学校几乎不能上课，于是又不得不作再次后迁之计。

经校务委员会决定,再迁云南,后经派员调查确定为喜洲坝。

1939年元月全校教职员工、家属和图书、仪器分批乘汽车经河内转昆明再到喜洲坝。喜洲坝在大理城北40里,风景幽美,确实是个"世外桃源",我们在这里闭门办学,为时七年有半。抗日战争胜利后,于1946年5月才启程迁回武昌原址。

我为了要去国外劝募重建校园的款项,抗战刚结束,即应美国哥伦比亚大学协和神学院之聘,先行离开喜洲坝,第三次赴美讲学。1946年6月由美赴英。8月下旬,由英乘飞机经印度到达武昌时,华中大学已经准备在9月初开学了。

华中大学算是复员了,但要真正开学上课恢复旧观,还有一段很长的距离。

第一,从1929年至1937年,华中大学学生程度有着大幅度提高,毕业学生,都是经过无数次严格考试的。迁云南极西的后方,那里中学生少,程度低。如要经过严格筛选,就无法招收学生,所收大学一年级学生,甚至高中一年级程度都不能达到,经过学校教学、考试,在校读了四五年甚至有读了六年的还不能达到华中大学原毕业生的水平,也只得降格让他们毕业。

第二,偏处滇西的喜洲坝七八年,生活单调而且艰苦,许多资学较优的教授、副教授和喜欢活动的青年教师,相继远走高飞,特别遭到削弱的是物理、化学、生物三系,其他各系教师也不得不降格以求。

第三,经过日寇七年蹂躏,武昌校舍"徒空四壁",连地板都被拆掉了,房屋的修理、安装,图书仪器的添补,需费巨大,不能即时筹到。

以上三个问题是华中大学复迁武昌的刻不容缓,而又非一朝一夕可以完成的事,也是最伤脑筋的事,从1946—1949年解放前,都没有得到称心如意的解决。

司徒雷登阴谋破产

在中国的教会大学,受着在美国的中国教会大学联合托事部的接济和支配。

这个联合托事部的主席范杜生,是哥伦比亚大学协和神学院院长,

1945年就任院长典礼时,刻意反共、坚持侵略我国、臭名远扬的杜勒斯在会上大吹法螺,另一个支持他的是美国国际特务、《时代》和《运气杂志》的老板兼总编辑路斯(Henry C. Luce),而给这些家伙提供关于中国教会大学的消息,设计合并教育(会)大学,制订实施办法,以适应美国帝国主义进行文化侵略的,则是司徒雷登。

司徒雷登(John Leighten Stuart)的父亲是在中国传教多年的美国传教士。司徒雷登1876年生于浙江杭州,善操中国语言,返美受过大学教育与神学教育后,又回到中国教《圣经》的《新约》和希腊文,1919年被派为燕京大学校长。其主要任务是拉拢我国的高级知识分子,培养"民主个人主义者"。他在燕京大学设所谓"社会服务系",主要培养基督教青年会的干事这类推动教、会合一的人才。

中国教会大学托事部1945年在纽约拟订的计划,据我所知,是由司徒雷登草定的。

这时,我在哥伦比亚大学讲学,学校原以为我会带家属来,给我配给一所教授正式住宅,计有两间大卧室,一大间膳厅连客厅,一间书房、浴室、厨房,一切设备俱全,我个人住不完。而那时纽约旅馆拥挤,收费昂贵。司徒雷登正在纽约,通过学校院长的介绍,我原在国内早已认识,我同意和他同住。当时,我忙,他也忙,夜间见面寒暄几句,从未深谈。司徒雷登对联合托事部的事缄口不言。

同年的四五月间,司徒雷登和马歇尔一道乘马歇尔的专机返回中国。这使我大为诧异,一个普通传教士,能和马歇尔如此亲近吗?可见他有着美国政府的后台。由于他对华文化侵略有功,那年七月就被委任为美国驻华大使。

司徒雷登虽然狡猾,仍不能一手遮天,他的计划后来还是暴露了。该计划分两部分:第一部分是联合托事部准备向抗战时迁往后方的教会大学施舍一笔复员费,要各教会大学唯命是从;第二部分则是合并教会大学的阴谋的实施。它规定在中国只能有5所教会大学。

燕京大学,是华北的唯一大学。济南齐鲁大学只留下在济南的齐鲁医学院,其他院系合并燕大。燕大设文、法、理、工和神学五个学院,各学院不但系别多,而且都有不止一个研究所,为其他各教会大学,除医学院外，培养师资。从而使燕大成为各教会大学的"母机制造厂"，控制和领导全中国的教会学校。

尤其毒辣的是，司徒雷登特别重视燕大的法学院，其规模简直是一个法政财经学院。它培养法律、政治、财政、经济、外交、新闻和社会工作人才，准备透入我国政治和其他各个领域中去。

除把燕京大学建成为领导教会大学外，还准备建立华东、华南大学，稳住华西大学，华中大学则在可有可无之列。

华东大学，合并原有的南京金陵大学与金陵女子文理学院为第一部，设文、理、农三个学院，以农学院为主。合并上海圣约翰大学、沪江大学、杭州的之江大学和苏州的东吴大学，设文、理、法、商、医五个学院，但不设研究院。联合托事部以经济手段向各大学施加压力。

华南大学，旨在合并广州岭南大学、福州协和大学和华南女子文理学院，设文、理、工、农、医五个学院，不设研究院，只限大学本科。

华西大学照旧，只设文、理、医、牙四个学院，系别尽量裁减。

华中大学，按联合托事部计划，准备不办。由于纽约华中大学设立者大会的支持，托事部才列入计划，只设文、理、教育三个学院，八个系。

司徒雷登之所以这样做，主要是要合并分散的教会大学，集中力量，以与我国公、私立大学抗衡，争学生，抢青年。进一步把培养好的服务于帝国主义政策的人，渗入我国各个组织中去，左右我国的发展路线，真正成为帝国主义的殖民地。

1949年，在中国共产党的领导下，中国人民推翻帝国主义、封建主义和官僚资本主义三座大山，中国人民站起来了。司徒雷登大使侵华计划，也包括他的文化侵略一起破产。他在中国，没有什么事做了，只好夹起皮包走路。

(1964年稿)

浅论科学研究的方法[*]

"科学研究的方法"这个题目很大,涉及面很广,我这里仅根据个人体会浅谈两个问题:一是介绍我本人在国外做科学研究的一些经验;二是泛论科学研究的方法、步骤和应注意的问题。

一

我大学毕业时(1910年),曾搞过科学研究,但只是一种尝试,很肤浅。后来在欧美留学做研究生时,才算真正搞科学研究,经受了比较严格的科学锻炼。

当时欧美一些发达国家研究生的研究方式主要有三种:1. Seminar;2. 教师定期指导下的个人研究;3. 写学位毕业论文。现按个人经验介绍如下:

1. Seminar

Seminar 相当于研究班、研讨班、研究小组等,源于德国。实际上各国的 Seminar 都不尽相同,我们现在的"课堂讨论"也是其中的一种形式,是苏联因袭俄国而传入我国的。在德国大学里,每个研究生专业的 Seminar 都有专设的研究室、资料室和指导教师的个人研究室。我在柏林大学时由于不是正式研究生,只旁听过一个 Seminar。随后在美国哈佛大学研究院,每学期至少参加一个 Seminar。每个 Seminar 通常有10个研究生参加,每周举行研讨会两次,每次 2 小时。研究生轮流提出论文,大家针对论文提出问题讨论、争辩;然后由指导教师作总结。这是一种很好的学习、研究和争鸣的方式。我通过 Seminar 初步练习了搜集材料、组织材料和熟悉文献的方法,锻炼了提出问题、分析问题和解决问题的能力。特别要指出的是我学会了鉴别材料真伪,分辨第一手材料和

---

[*] 本文系华中师范大学曹方久教授根据作者20世纪60年代一次报告的草稿加工整理而成,具体时间、地点和对象均无记载。曾发表于《华中师范大学学报》1990年第2期。

第二手材料的方法,明确了参加学术讨论的基本要求。当我们争论问题时,老师很注意争论时的礼貌和态度。他很反对意气用事,以感情代替理论;要我们培养学术涵养与风度。他说,大家尽可以从不同的角度或方面提出不同的乃至尖锐的反对意见,坚持自己的意见,但同时必须有礼貌地尊重并认真考虑别人的不同意见,如果自己有错误,就要立即承认并修正,不应强词夺理,把维护个人的"面子"置于探讨真理之上。

2. 老师指导下的个人研究

在美国,一般讲,只有具有一定科研基础的研究生才能开始个人的研究。指导个人研究的教师是在学术上造诣比较深,知识相当渊博的教授。我读哈佛大学研究院时,在一位70多岁的老教授指导下从事个人研究,他对我要求十分严格,同学们都认为他很厉害,不容易接近。我听他讲授一年的课后,他才让我搞个人研究。每周对我个别指导两小时,布置一周的学习和研究的任务,指定必读的参考文献,有200页左右;读完后,按规定的时间到他的研究室汇报并回答他的问题。他首先要我简要地汇报读书心得和发现的问题,当我谈到某个问题时,他就要我谈这个问题的另一方面或与此有关联的其他一些问题,要我一并分析。汇报之后,他用半小时的时间对我的汇报进行分析、评价;虽然也有肯定,但主要是批评我的不足和谬误,最后布置下一周的任务。

老师布置的下一周的文献资料每每和上一周的不同:或深度不同,或观点不同,或采用的方法不同等等。在下周的定时指导时,他就要我指出上下两周文献资料异同之处,如二者观点不同,就问我的观点如何? 赞成谁? 反对谁? 并说出理由和根据。这样一来,每周的定时指导都是一场考试,为了对付这两个小时,我必须天天紧张地学习,刻苦地钻研,反复地思考,兢兢业业不敢稍有懈怠。我正是在这位严师的指导下,较快地掌握了专业知识,锻炼了我对待学问严谨认真的科学态度,提高了独立进行科学研究的能力。可惜的是,由于其他原因我未能在他的指导下写学位论文。我的学位论文是后来在英国伦敦大学完成的。

3. 写毕业论文

当时英国的大学指导研究生的方式和德、美两国不同,即主要通过写毕业论文来指导。毕业论文与Seminar的论文不同,Seminar也要求写论文,但只是习作性的短篇,一般万把字即可,只解决一个较简单的问题。而毕业论文则是系统性的长篇论文,要求解决前人未解决,甚至未涉及的问题,从而对本专业能作出创造性的贡献。

那时,博士生的毕业论文规定至少要用两年以上的时间。研究生从拟定大纲,搜集、整理和组织材料到写出初稿,每一个环节都要送指导老师审阅并照老师的意见修正,这样按部就班地下来,通常要3年至4年才行。如果材料搜集不很棘手,或事先已经大体搜集就绪,其他环节也比较顺当,两年也可能完成。

在伦敦大学时,导师指导我写博士论文的过程中,很注意培养我搜集材料和研究问题的方法与能力。以下几例可见一斑。

在搜集材料问题上,老师只对我进行一般性的提示,而不具体告诉我搜集哪些材料,怎样和到何处去搜集。他认为,研究生是作为专家来培养的,而未来的专家应该了解本专业各方面的情况;如果还要老师指出论文材料的范围、出处以及搜集的方法,那怎能培养出合格的专家?因此,老师指导我搜集材料时,总是让我"钻烟囱",等我"钻"得差不多了,他才说,这里不够,那里不行,要我再去"钻"。开始,我把搜集的材料送他审阅,他说不行,不够。我请教他,应该再如何搜集?他幽默地说:"在这个问题上,你是专家,我是外行,我只代表学术界对你提意见,找毛病,评论你研究成果的价值,你不要依赖我给你更多的东西。"我对老师的这几句话印象十分深刻,使我认识到,独立研究是一个研究生首先的和起码的职责,不具备这个条件就根本不配当研究生。

有一次,在我送审的提纲中提到,陶器在公元前约5世纪至3世纪发明于中国,而后才传入东欧。此问题本与我的论文主题无大关系,但碰巧这个观点同英国一位地质学家和一位陶器专家的观点相左。我的老师对此情况颇感兴趣,乃鼓励我深入钻一下这个问题,搜集更多的材料以证实自己的看法,并敢于向那两位专家挑战。我本是研究哲学的,现在要我去钻陶器的发源地及其传播的历史,不免离开我的本行和研究主题而进入地质、考古的领域了,牵涉面太多、太广。但我必须遵照老师的教导去做,我一头扎进图书馆,广泛搜集资料,访问有关专家、学者,终于写出一份有分量的材料,证明了我的观点,驳倒了那两位专家。事后我体会到,老师并不是要我离开本题去钻牛角尖,搞枝节问题;而是借这个问题培养我独立地广泛搜集各种有关资料的能力,开阔我的视野,扩大我的知识面,同时培养我以严肃的科学态度敢于向权威挑战的勇气和创新精神。

还有一事启发颇大:在写论文的过程中,我发现我国宋代的朱熹和古希腊亚里斯多德在一些重大哲学问题上相类似。那么,他们的思想有没有历史的联系?朱熹是否受过亚里斯多德思想的影响?但两位哲人在时间上相距1,700多年(一为公元前5世纪,一为公元12世纪),空间上又远隔重洋,何止万里?加上语言文字的差异,决不能因为两位在哲学思想上有相似之处,就轻率地认为有师承关系。虽然,我国和欧洲早在朱熹之前1,400多年已开始通商,但物质的商品交换和抽象的哲学思想的交流毕竟不是一回事。所以,对此问题必须作深入的研究,在掌握大量材料的基础上待证据确凿、理由充足,而后才能作出实事求是的结论。这一问题原来也不是我的论文的组成部分,甚至并无什么直接的联系,但老师却要我作进一步的研究,弄清楚两位哲人究竟有无师承关系,能确证其有固然是成绩,如确证其无当然也是成绩。

在老师的鼓励下,我满怀信心地钻研进去。开始我依据一定的材料,提出了亚里斯多德的思想在朱熹以前传入中国的三个可能性。我的根据是,唐太宗时,大秦景教、伊斯兰教和佛教这三派宗教曾相继传入中国,而宗教语言和哲学语言是有关联的。那么,当时在欧洲盛行的亚里斯多德的哲学就有可能随着这三种宗教之一而传入中国,这就有了三种可能。我按照科研逻辑的方法、步骤,依次验证这三个假设;重新钻研了亚里斯多德和朱熹的有关著作,阅读了上述三种宗教的有关典籍、文献、历史。当时我只掌握了大秦景教和佛教的一些资料,但对于伊斯兰教,我只知一部古兰经,特别是对于它传入中国的历史,却一无所知。我不得不请教内行、专家,或登门拜访,或以信函方式求教(英国学者很愿意用通信方式来回答或讨论问题)。我用了半年时间的钻研、考证,首先否定了其中两种可能性,最后只剩随大秦景教传入这一可能还有一点影子。那时,我到德国请教柏林大学Franke教授(我过去的老师),他找到一篇尚未发表的内部传阅的论文,文中提到亚里斯多德的著作有可能于公元7世纪时通过大秦景教从叙利亚传入中国,但缺乏具体材料证实。这样,这唯一的可能也不过只是一条据以追查的线索而已,它是不能作为肯定结论的充足理由或论据的。当时,在这个问题上,国内外再没有人比我掌握的资料更多了,因此,我完全可以作出亚里斯多德在朱熹以前没有传入中国,因而两位哲人没有师承关系的结论。这是一个消极的否定性的结论,而科学研究中,真正按科学方法得出的一个否定性的消极结论也是重要的,其价值并不亚于一个肯定性的积极结论。而且更重要的不是在这个问题上得出什么结论,而在于经过半年时间对这一问题钻研,我不仅读了不少书籍资料,掌握了更多的专业知识,而且大大提高了钻研问题的能力,学会了科学研究的方法。

我在国外做研究生的四年生活中,体会到一个研究生的首要任务,不是听课,甚至不是读许多书,而是在有经验的老师指导下学习科学研究的方法。大学毕了业的人应该具备自学的能力,知道读什么书,如何读书,不需要花多的时间去听课。我虽然也听过不少课,读了不少书(每年约读100本专业书,杂志在外),但我收获最大的则是得到严格的科学训练,锻炼了科学研究的方法。

上述国外培养研究生的三种方式主要是根据个人的经历,有很大的局限,且均为资本主义国家的情况,我们可作为参考,批判地吸取采用。

二

人们从事一门学科的研究都包含三种不大相同的活动,即:学习、钻研和科学研究。三者是蝉联的、交错的,而在性质上则是有所不同的。

"学习"是一种很广泛的活动。人一生下来,从吃奶起,便是学习的开始。婴儿时期的种种活动,对周围事物的逐步了解、认识,都是步步深入的学习。此后,上小学、读中学就更是学习了。进了大学,学习的范围、内容和质量有了很大的变化,走出教科书和老师所教的圈子,要读许多参考书、报纸杂志,还要走向社会考察、实习,到实验室亲手做实验,这就从比较单纯接受性学习阶段进入高一层的学习,我把这种比较复杂性的学习称之为"钻研"。随后,在钻研中每每发现不能解决或不完全能解决的问题或者人们在过去未接触过的新问题;以解决这些问题为目的的再学习、再钻研,并用种种科学方法和科学手段来解决问题的过程,我才称之为

"科学研究"。科学研究的结果一定是为本门学科或专业作出了或大或小的创造性的贡献。因此,学习、钻研和科学研究是有机关联着的三种活动、三个阶段。由学习发展到钻研,又由钻研发展为科学研究是一个逐步升高、逐步深化的过程。当然,三者并不是截然分开的阶段,是你中有我、我中有你的互相交错的活动。前面的活动是后面的基础,包含有发展为后面的契机;后面的活动是前面发展的必然结果,并包含前面于自身之中。很明显,离开学习和钻研的科学研究是不可想象的;对于一个研究者来说,也不存在单纯的学习或单纯的钻研,而必须在一开始的学习和钻研中,捕捉将要在科学研究中所要发现和提出的问题,为以后的选题打好基础;否则走了弯路,浪费光阴,事倍功半。

在广泛学习、深入钻研基础上开展的科学研究必定是从发现"问题"开始的,没有"问题"就没有科学研究。确定了要解决的"问题",也就确定了研究的方向,确定了研究的对象。一般在学习和钻研时是会碰到、发现许多问题的,但并不是所有的问题都可以作为科研的对象。我认为,在选题时要作如下的考虑:

第一,确定为科研对象的"问题"不是灵机一动、随心所欲的问题,也不是冥思苦想出来的问题,而是本学科或本专业在继续向前发展中所碰到的障碍或困难。研究的目的在于排除这些障碍,克服这些困难,为科学的发展创造条件;这样的"问题"才有价值,有实践意义。

第二,作为科研对象的"问题"之提出应是合理的、合逻辑的、同已知的事实不相冲突的。

现以康德在《纯粹理性批判》一书中所研究的中心问题为例来说明以上两点。康德认为,当时哲学认识论面临着一个十分棘手的问题,即:自然科学知识都是综合经验而来的"综合判断";按说,经验的知识是没有必然的普遍有效性的,只有"验前的"(有人错误地译为"先天的")知识才有必然的普遍有效性;可是,自然科学的公理、定理、定律等在事实上又具有这种必然普遍有效性;这应如何解释?他认为,这说明事实上存在着"验前的(先天的)综合判断"。可是,这种"验前的综合判断"是怎样成为可能的呢?这就是康德在《纯粹理性批判》一书中所要解决的根本问题。这一问题的提出符合哲学发展的内在逻辑,是十分合理和顺理成章的。须注意：他的问题并不是"验前的综合判断有无可能",而是"验前综合判断如何成为可能的"。因为事实上存在着这种判断,谁也不能否认;关键是在他以前谁也没有说明这种判断是怎样成为可能的。这个问题的提出和解决在哲学认识论的发展史上有十分重大的意义,这是康德的一大功绩。

第三,作为科研对象而提出的问题应是前人未曾解决或未完全解决的问题。因此,当提出一问题作为研究对象时,就要首先弄清楚该问题是否有人提出过、研究过？解决的情况如何？这就要求广泛深入地查阅有关文献资料,摸清来龙去脉。查阅专业杂志时,其前号越多越好,以自然科学为例,世界上历史最久的杂志是英国皇家学会的《年报》(*Proceedings of the Royal Society*),有两百多年的历史。据说,我国藏有完备一套的只有清华大学。虽然为了研究现代自然科学的某一个问题,不一定非要查阅两百年前的记载不可,但至少近几十年的资料是要查阅的。我们现在研究自然科学、历史、哲学、宗教等方面的问题,最感头痛的是文献资料不足,每每数典而忘祖。当然,在科学研究中,应该勇于创新、破除对古人的迷信,但是决不应因此而割断历史的联系,不尊重前人的研究成果,干出枉走弯路、白费力气的蠢事。

"问题"正式确定之后,按照一般的步骤就要根据事实和已有的资料,对所提的"问题"设想出一种或几种可能的答案,这就是"假设"。"假设"是对"问题"作出的、有一定盖然性的结论,但暂时还提不出确认这一结论的充足理由。尽管"假设"只是假定的解答,但在知识的发展上却有很大的意义。科学理论最初都是作为"假定"而产生的,都必须经过"假设"的阶段;从而任何科学都是通过合理的科学"假设"而向前发展的。恩格斯说过：只要自然科学在思维着,它的发展形式就是假说。当然,不仅自然科学,而且人文科学也是如此。

提出"假设"时须注意以下几点：

其一,须"持之有故,言之成理"。所谓"持之有故",即指"假设"的提出须依据事实与已有的科学原理。那些凭主观臆造、任意杜撰的假定不是我们所说的"假设"。所谓"言之成理",乃指根据这一"假设"所推断出来的东西能得到说明;能说明与解释的现象越多,其盖然性程度越高。当然,"假设"所引申出来的现象即使存在,并不等于它已是确实可靠的理论;因为这些引申出来的现象可能是其他原因引起的。所以一个"假设"虽然"持之有故,言之成理",它仍然只是盖然性的而不是科学理论。

其二,"假设"虽有事实和客观的依据,但它毕竟是人们对于要解决的问题的主观意见。所以,一个严肃的科学工作者就要勇于在事实面前修正错误,乃至放弃已判明为不正确的"假设",改弦更张,提出新的合理的"假设"。如果坚持己见、顽固偏执,就不是科学的态度。所以,主见不可无,而成见则绝不可有。

其三,在某种情况下,一个"假设"表面上似乎和某些事实相违。但事实有简单与复杂、现象与本质、假象与真相等差别。那些没有经过认真观察、分析和筛选的"事实"还不能说就是事实;一般的所谓"事实"之中,常伴有假象等杂质,一经把这些杂质清洗之后,面貌可能大大改观,甚至面目全非了。如有人说他的确看见了"鬼",他认为这是"事实"。但当真相大白后,他所谓的"事实"已不复存在。因此,如果发现某"假设"与事实相违,就需要首先考查并追究这一"事实"是什么样的事实,是真相还是假象,是现象还是本质;而要做到这一点,就必须下一番苦功夫才行。

其四,一般情况下,提出一个"假设"不应同已知的公理、原理、定律或规律相矛盾。但必须注意两点:(1)虽然不应相矛盾,但也不是要求基本同一,不是要求提出的"假设"直接可以从某已知的原理推演出来。因为如果可以直接推演出来,就说明"假设"与已知原理基本上是同一的东西,没有任何创见与新意,因而也不是什么科学的"假设"。如果一篇论文表面上似乎对某个问题提出一个假定、设想,而究其实质不过是对某原理、原则的解释与说明,这就没有什么科研价值。(2)如一假设和已有的科学理论发生了冲突,不可过早而轻率地否定和放弃此一假设。爱因斯坦最初提出相对论的假设是和牛顿的定律相矛盾的,但相对论这一假设成了新的科学理论,丰富、发展、扬弃了牛顿的理论。非欧几里德几何学的假设并未因与公认的欧几里德几何学相矛盾而被否定,反而发展了几何学。哥白尼的"太阳中心学说"开始只是一个科学假设,它直接与托勒密的"地球中心说"相冲突,但最终被否定的不是"太阳中心说"而是曾被认为神圣不可侵犯的"地球中心说"。科学正是通过否定打破旧的、不完备的理论,证实新的、更完备的科学假设而向前发展的。

其五，提出科学的假设固然要有破除迷信、勇于创新的精神，但最基本的仍然是尊重事实、实事求是的科学态度。绝不可借口破除迷信而怀疑一切、否定一切。

"假设"的提出与形成，只是解决"问题"的初步阶段，科学工作要继续下去，还要发展假设、检验假设，最后形成真理性的结论。这往往是个漫长的过程，有时一篇论文即可解决一个问题，有时可能需要很多论文和专著来解决；假设需要实践长期地、反复地检验，甚至经过多少年，几代人才能形成科学理论。

科学研究所经历的道路每每是迂回曲折的，研究工作是十分艰苦细致的工作，要付出极大的心血，要作出很大的牺牲，有时刻苦努力很久却收获甚微；可是科研成果正是这样一点一滴逐渐积累起来的。科学研究中通常是一环套一环的，没有止境，一个问题解决了，或者尚未完全解决，就又发现了新的问题；解决了一个小问题又冒出一个大问题；有时一个大问题似乎已经解决，但仔细一检查，原来还有许多小问题尚未解决。往往越钻问题越多，"剪不断，理还乱"，深感自己知道的太少、太少，而未知的却很多、很多。在科研的道路上，既要自信，但又不能自满；既要虚心，但又不能心虚。要充满信心，谦虚谨慎而大胆地钻进去，走下去，最终一定会出成果的。

中文通信数通

阴嘉贤弟英鉴：

　　三月九日并十一日华函均悉，适因公赴沪未即裁答，歉甚。母校现须聘长于教育、社会经济政治及生物各学科之教员，以留学在研究院以上者为合格。待遇即视资格为转移。大概月薪由壹佰伍拾元起，采年功加俸制以次递升。希尽量特色为盼。

　　弟台天资聪颖、矢志向学，无任欣慰，倘有机缘，玉汝于成。兄自竭力相助也。此复即颂

时祺

1931 年 3 月 20 日

克诚先生道席：

　　刻为充实抗日力量计，中央对高中以上男女学生决分别施以军事及看护训练。敝校男生军事训练早已施行，惟女生看护训练因无老师尚付缺如。素仰台驾赤心爱国，敢恳每星期一下午四时半，派贵院经验宏富之看护士一员前来敝校指示一切（以一小时为限），可否之处，敬祈裁处。感祷。此颂

时祉

弟　韦卓民
1931 年 12 月 7 日

民安先生道鉴：

　　辱赐教并面允兼道任本校军事教席，欣感无尽。查该项课程本校每周实授三小时，一小时学科，二小时术科。术科二小时分四次，于每星期一、二、三、四晨七时上课，学科一小时则定在每星期二下午一时上课。月薪三十元。全年以十个月计算。本学期即自二月份起薪。前已面陈，谅

邀,明察惟恐遗忘,用再赘渎。再,本校不另用聘书,即以此为正式聘函,合并声明专肃敦聘。敬祈履诺见复,至为祷企。藉颂
时祉

弟 韦卓民 谨上
1933年元月

鹭宾先生道席:

　　顷由武汉大学时昭瀛、游国恩两先生绍介,闻悉台端道德文章为现代所仅见,无任景慕,极欲屈驾来敝校担任国文功课:国文、作文改文(大约两堂学生共五十人每周一次)、国学概论、文学史及中国哲学史,每周约计十四时,月薪壹佰捌拾元。如携宝眷至武昌,居住则加送房租二十元。尊意如何,希即赐复为盼,特函奉商本,恕唐突。敬颂
著祺

韦卓民 谨上
1933年4月9日

乃春、贤棣大鉴:

　　广州方面中学毕业生有志升学本校者谅不乏人。兹寄上简章五十份,请烦向青年会李应林先生接洽。以"私立武昌华中大学简章代发处"等字样,榜诸该会门首。遇人领取即代分发,使人明悉本校内容。是所感谢盼。此颂
文祺

　　附简章80另寄

韦卓民 谨上
1933年6月6日

雪艇部长先生钧鉴:

　　查吾国生活程度日见增高,大学教职员待遇自应格外从丰。惟年功加俸,靡有底止,势难持久。尤以私立大学经费来源有限,如敝校者为更甚,然欲增高高等教育效能,非罗致名儒硕彦不为功,是则其待遇必须与

国内公、私立各大学生跻于平衡地位,而不超过学校经济来源所能供应之范围也。如是敝校有鉴于此,爰于本年校董会常会中议决,敦聘国立上海医学院长颜福庆先生为主席委员,中华基督教教育会干事葛德基(E. H. Gressy)先生为文专委员及南京下关姜家园一号陈宗良先生为委员,组织一"调查全国公、私立各大学教职员待遇标准材料委员会",负责搜集国内公、私立各大学教职员待遇标准材料,并拟订敝校各级教职员薪俸标准,交敝校校董会采择施行。又敦聘教育部长王世杰先生、湖南省教育厅厅长朱经农先生及陶知行先生,为该会通讯委员以便咨询在案。相应专函奉达。敬乞俞允,至为感祷,专肃奉聘。顺颂

台绥

私立武昌华中大学校董会书记　韦卓民　谨启
1933 年 11 月 1 日

相青仁弟惠鉴:

　　本校下学期须聘经济学教授一位,资格以曾留学国外研究三四年以上,获有博士学位或至少获有商业管理学硕士学位。在国内著名大学充当教授或副教授三四年以上,确有教学经验,并身为基督徒或最少能照与校环境相安者为合格。留学久而无成绩及有成绩而无教学经验者一概拒绝。待遇当从长计议,惟大致可与国立各大学相仿也。吾弟交游素广,特恳费神代为物色,并早日以成绩见告,俾便议聘至为感祷,专此祗颂

教祺

韦卓民　谨上
1936 年 3 月 6 日

子博先生大鉴:

　　昨承加驾赐教,甚畅。先生学识优良、经验丰富,实一见倾心。下学年拟请担任本校体育指导职务。于教授部定男女学生体育功课之外课外指导及训练事宜,如球艺、田径等等,均当借重。月俸壹佰元,膳宿自理。聘期暂行一年,自本年八月一日起,至二十六年七月三十一日止。谨另具

聘书一纸。随函送达。敬祈浼就见复,至所企祷。专此祗颂

弟　韦卓民　谨上
1936 年

国立武汉大学王校长抚五先生鉴：*

效电敬悉,质廷兄为敝校长期聘任教授,仓促离去,手续发生问题。此例一开,何以应付将来。况时局飘摇,借重质兄甚殷。如果引去,全校震撼,师生责难,尤非弟所能解答。二盼亮察,准其留校,不胜感祷。

弟　韦卓民　叩东

抚五先生道鉴：

十一月二十九日手教拜。悉承曲谅挽留质廷兄之苦衷,感激无既,在时局艰难学校飘摇之会,中流砥柱如质廷兄倚臂方殷,本不能听其接受贵校之聘,惟为顾全历承提携协助之友谊自不能过拂尊意。敝校决更西迁,大约二月初旬可以成行,拟请质廷兄乘敝校起程之隙,束装就道,趋侍左右,惟以一年为期。至民二十九元月底期满,仍须返校。此意质廷兄业经表示赞同,即祈垂察惠按约定期间支配其到后之工作,俾便期满不致爽约是幸。尊意如何,公余尤祈早为赐复为祷！过去一年奔走欧美,虽未能效哭秦廷,亦深得各方对我抗战之同情,尚觉其行不虚,并以附阅专复,祗叩道祺

弟　韦卓民　再拜
一九三九年元月三十日

重庆国民参政会秘书处
转呈蒋议长钧鉴：

参政会第三次会本决意参加,惟学校迁滇,诸待料理,谨电请假并祝精神团结,争取最后胜利！

韦卓民　叩

---

* 此件为一电文。电报原稿及下文函件原稿现均藏武汉大学档案馆。

顷奉贵司本年十二月四日五九零三四号函，以据报校中有不稳分子事谕转嘱众加注意等因，祗悉。查本校教职员，思想尚属纯正，行为亦合轨，则近年维持学校、拥护抗建，尤其一致刻苦奋斗之精神。至于学生训练，本校传统即以养成纯正通达之人才为指针，凡不良分子稍露形迹，无不立予淘汰。

大部秦镜远悬，当已洞察无遗，学校办理情形如此，而竟有所误不稳分子存在之报，臻深惊异。现经会同教务长、各院院长详加研讨，佥信此举如为本校某教员最近所为，盖该员本学期之初对学生演讲，曾因滇省文化落后一语，激起滇籍学生愤慨，事后提出质问，请其答复也。当时本校长得讯，即向滇籍学生多方晓喻。此种误会亦立经永释，乃该员不知此事全出一时语言之误会，而以为学生中有人拨弄是非，以属无事自扰，惟恐杯弓蛇影，有碍视听。特此申复。请烦释注为祷，此复

教育部高等教育司

校长　韦卓民　谨启
民国三十三年一月

凌高校长吾兄惠鉴：

去夏拜别以后，忽尔经年，音问多疏，想念为劳。近惟公私迪吉，为颂为望。敝校僻处滇西，延揽教员极感艰困，经济商业系教席虚悬尤多。反观贵校人材荟萃，力量充实，相形之下，弥深愧怍，不禁妒羡。为调剂偏枯，不得不作挹彼注兹之图。图以与贵校经济研究所之滕茂桐先生有同学之雅，拟请其来此相助为理。爰本去年基督教高等教育会议在蓉开会，关于基督教姊妹大学教员移植，应允先行通知有关学校之决议。函请垂察，务祈俯念通工合作之义，惠准滕先生离职到校，毋任感祷。专函奉恳。祗叩

道祺

诸维爱照不尽

弟　韦卓民　再拜
民国三十三年五月二十四日

萍生处长先生勋鉴：

前承在普海春宠赐盛宴,嘉惠雅教,醉酒饱德,实感激靡已。辞别后因事务烦冗迟未肃谢,更抱歉无以。日作贵处王科长天行先生来校视察,并垂询校中情形甚详,仰见贵处关怀教育之至意。王先生戾止,时以事外出,未能当面请益,仅由敝校男生训导长沈来秋先生延接后转告经过,及应行申报各事,谨分三点为先生一陈之,是否有当尚祈多多指导,匡我不逮是奉。(一)寒假学生人数。刻因距结业放假之期尚有三周,不能确定。惟学生假中留校,照章须办理登记手续。一俟登记人数确定,当即补陈。(二)教职员名单。兹检奉一份备查。惟名单上未列各人性别、年龄、籍贯、资历、等次,不知适用否。如若须较详细之名册,容当缮制。(三)应变准备。敝校员生之思想言行素极纯正。平日只知致力教学、研究,鲜问外事,对于学校,爱护珍惜外观为第二家庭,绝不容外力摧残破坏。此在历次变乱中均有其明确坚定之表现。可以自信不移者,如时局无严重变化,敝校寒假后仍当照常开学。员生生活所需,将按照当前币值及物价,早作确切之预算与充分之准备限期。在学期中可以绝对自给自足不虞缺乏,万一寒假中,发生变故,敝校留校员生已遵照大部指示备有三月之粮,为维持校内秩序,并将由留校员生中之年富力强能刻苦耐劳者,组织护校团应付一切。至于下(学)期能否如期开学,则须视演变情形再作临时计划。

专肃祗叩

政祺

诸维仁照不一

弟　韦卓民
民国三十七年十二月二十三日

为时会艰难拟为远道困苦学生劝募食米二百五石函恳慷慨玉成由

（私立武昌华中大学公函　学字第211号）

窃查大局动荡,民生憔悴已达极点。敝校为维系文化绵延国脉,因备承社会人士之扶植与赞助,上期幸能按照校历于一月二十日结业。本期亦决于二月十四日开学,十七日上课。惟在此艰难之会,校中同人虽愿本牺牲服务之精神与培植后进之决心,坚守岗位支持到底。然在本校学生都计五百余人,真能按照学校规定缴纳学膳宿杂各费者,实寥寥无几,尤以来自川、滇、黔及湘西等远道学生为甚。盖此项学生不惟半途废学情所难甘,即被补言旋亦势有不能,进退失据,实属狼狈。敝校近年鉴于社会经济困窘,对于学生缴费极力减少。本期只收食米五石二斗(膳宿在内),实较一般私立中学所收者为低,为救济远道学(困)苦学生,更经宽筹奖学金额,豁免其学杂各费,然各生食宿费用仍苦无着落者尚有百五十余名。计每人一期至少需食米二石五斗,非另筹食米二百余石,无以渡此难关。素仰贵会同仁热心教育,爱护青年学子无微不至,用敢披沥代为请命,务恳垂察慷慨捐助嘉惠士林,当不仅个人感戴靡既矣。临颍依依,毋任拜祷
此上
汉口市商会理事长程

校长　韦卓民
民国三十八年二月二十四日

武汉警备司令部司令刘勋鉴:

　　三十八年三月十五日迈字第○二七号代电奉悉。武汉各学校学生本日并无假本校开会情事,请释注。本校对于学生管教,向采严格主义。凡行动越轨违反校规者,定依规惩处,从不宽假。至于学生在外触犯国法,则悉听法律制裁,亦从不姑息袒护。盖本校除致力学术研究外,更以崇尚民主法治精神养成健全公民为首务。故本校校风严肃,早为各界所周知。惟近来汉口某报对于本校报道一再失实,不知系该报故意中伤,抑系另有奸人假借本校名义,借该报散布烟幕,以为图谋不轨之隐被。为息止流言,避免误会起见,敢请贵部予以查究。毋任企祷。

私立武昌华中大学校长　韦卓民
1949年寅铣训(237)

英 文

Whither Christian Education?

FRANCIS WEI
Notes of a Statement Made to the Executive Committee of the N. C. C.

Government educators have been telling us that, as far as tendencies of Chinese government educational polices go, it is likely that the Christian forces may have to retire from the field of primary education when the government finds it possible to take care of that field to any considerable extent. Leading Christian educators also feel that the government will strictly enforce its regulations in regard to primary education. The first step has already been taken in the regulations promulgated in December of 1932, in confining normal training to government middle schools and normal schools.

What preparations are the churches making to meet this changing situation? Do we want to continue in primary education or not? If we do, shall we be satisfied to have teachers all trained in non-Christian schools? How many Christian parents would prefer Christian primary schools for their children to non-Christian schools, other things being equal? Would the desire for Christian primary schools for their children be strong enough for them to organize primary schools under Boards of Directors, consisting of Christian men and women?

Take the present situation. Are our primary schools dovetailed with middle schools? How many primary school graduates are going to Christian rather than to non-Christian middle schools? If only a small percentage go to Christian middle schools, is it or is it not a loss to the Christian movement? At the same time is it not a matter of grave concern that the Christian middle schools are not getting a larger proportion of their students from the Christian primary schools so as to secure a longer continuous period for the pupils to be under influence of Christian institution?

Our general impression is that up to the present time parents have been anxious to send their children to Christian middle schools for the better teaching of English and for the better preparation for entrance to the Christian colleges, but, above all, for the better discipline maintained in these schools. Normally, we should expect that the other schools, particularly those of the government, will be improving in all these three aspects. In due course of time, perhaps sooner than we expect, they will teach English more efficiently than is now the case, give better preparation to their pupils for college matriculation, and maintain stricter discipline. When that day comes, how many Christian parents, not to say other parents, will still desire to send their children to Christian middle schools? In other words, what distinct contribution in concrete terms should we expect the Christian middle schools to make to the education of their children? Fifteen years from now, let us say, will there be a strong enough demand for Christian middle schools to insure their continued existence?

What particularly is the place of Christian educational institutions in the Christian movement? What would be the loss to the Christian movement in China if any of our present schools were to be eliminated?

And similarly, one may ask: "Whither are our Christian colleges going?" Two ways are open to us. One is to build such strong universities, regardless of their Christian character, as to insure their ability to stand on their own feet as do Harvard and Columbia in America, no matter what changes may take place in the attitude of the government toward Christian institutions. Would the attainment of such a goal be enough of an advantage to the Christian movement to warrant the heavy expenses of building up such institutions with money from Christian sources, provided always that we are free to have the teaching of the Christian religion tolerated in those institutions?

The other way would be to maintain small Christian colleges with high educational standards and with a strong Christian atmosphere, but with a definitely limited program, hoping in this way to make a distinctly Christian impact upon the educational movement in China. These colleges would take care of the training of Christian leaders up to the university graduation. Research work and post graduate work would have to be done in the government universities. At this stage the student should be mature enough to do his own independent thinking. Might there not be, however, an imminent danger that such small institutions would in the course of time be eliminated by keen competition with the strong government universities? What has led to the gradual elimination of small Christian colleges in the United States? What influence is being exercised by the remaining Christian colleges in America? What has been the tendency in this respect of Christian institutions of higher learning in England? What lessons can we learn from the experience of the West for shaping the policy of Christian institutions of higher learning in China?

The Council's Personnel

The meeting of the General Assembly of the Church of Christ in China at Amoy in October made radical changes in its representation upon the N. C. C. The nucleus of its representation is afforded by appointing its Executive Committee, composed of representatives of sixteen synods, as representatives on the N. C. C., supplementing this with nine cooptions from cooperating missions and the executive staff of the General Assembly.

Following is the list of the new appointees, so far as determined, in alphabetical order: Alexander Baxter, G. S. Bell, Stephen Chen, Chow Shih-kwang, R. C. Coonradt, W. B. Djang, T. C. Fan, J. W. Findlay, Hsu Sheng-yen, Samuel K. Ing, Kang Teh-hsiang, K. T. Kao, A. R. Kepler, Y. S. Lin, G. W. Shepherd, Y. S. Tom, H. F. Wallace, James Watson, Ralph C. Wells, Wu Kuo-wei, with four appointments yet to made.

Two of these appointees, Rev. Chow Shih-kuang and Dr. A. R. Kepler, were previously members of the Council, and three others, Mr. W. B. Djang, Rev. Lin Yu-shu, and Dr. R. C. Wells were alternates, while Rev. K. T. Kao was a coopted member of the Council.

Losses

We note with deep regret the passing of two former members of the council. Rev. Frank B. Turner of the English (formerly United) Methodist Mission in North China, was elected a member of the China Continuation Committee in 1915 and attended its annual meetings in 1916, 1917 and 1918. In 1926 he became a member of the Methodist group on the National Christian Council and attended the Annual Meeting of 1926 and 1929. Upon reorganization of the council in 1929 he became a representative of his own church upon it and so continued until his death, attending the Biennial Meeting of 1931, but was detained in 1933 by the illness which eventuated in his death. He was an enthusiastic supporter of the council and cooperated at every point where his help was called for. His forty-six years of service in China were a notable contribution to the life of the Church.

Rev. H. C. Jett of Yungchun, Fukien, passed away after a brief illness in July. Appointed a representative of the Methodist Episcopal Church on the council, he was never able to attend a Biennial Meeting. His position at the end was a striking illustration of his own ardent desire to promote that effective spirit of cooperation for which the council stands. When reduced resources determined his society to withdraw its personnel and support from South Fukien, he elected to remain with the church which he was serving and to ally himself with the English Presbyterians in that district, while seeking to bring his people to a new loyalty with the church of Christ in China.

New Members of the Executive

Dr. T. C. Fan is one of the Executive Secretaries of the Church of Christ in China, of whose staff he has been a member since his return from study in America in 1929. He attended the Annual Meeting at Hangchow in 1929 and actively assisted in writing the present Constitution of the N. C. C.

Rev. K. T. Kao of the Church of Christ in Moukden, was coopted as a member of the N. C. C. at the Biennial Meeting in May and was elected to the Executive Committee. He now becomes a member representing his church.

Miss Li Kwan-fang, M. A. is one of the staff of the Christian

Literature Society. She has served recently as chairman of the N. C. C. Committee on Christianizing the Home, and as a Volunteer secretary of that Committee during part of the last year.

Mr. S. C. Leung, Acting General Secretary of the National Committee of the Y. M. C. A. has been for the past two years a representative on the Council of the Church of Christ in China, to whose Kwangtung Synod he rendered notable service before coming to his present position. He now becomes a coopted member. He is at present serving as chairman of the Commission on Program and Cooperation. He has served on the Executive Committee from 1922 to 1926 and since 1931. He attended the Biennial Meeting in May 1933.

Dr. Ralpb C. Wells, chairman of the China Council of the Presbyterian Church in the U. S. A. (Northern) served as a member of the Executive Committee from 1929 to 1931, and attended the Biennial Meeting of the N. C. C. at Sungkiang in May 1933.

Church of Christ General Assembly Meets

Some seventy official commissioners of the sixteen synods of the Church of Christ in China met in General Assembly on the island of Kulangsu, Amoy, for the ten days beginning October 20 and ending October 29. This was the third General Assembly of the Church's history, the first having been held in Shanghai six years ago and the second in Canton three years later. Fraternal delegates and official representatives of various missionary societies brought the total regular attendance up to over one hundred persons.

The careful planning which had been done to facilitate prompt and definite action on the many questions which came before the Assembly, the efficiency of the Chinese presiding officers in fulfilling their responsible functions, the absence of all evidence of any racial or sectional prejudices, the spirit of harmony and goodwill which pervaded every session, the esprit de corps evident from the opening sessions, facility in using the *kuo-yü*, these were among the main impressions made by the Assembly on at least one of its fraternal delegates. Three-fourths of the voting commissioners being Chinese, and the non-Chinese delegates failing actually to take their proportionate share in discussions, gave the meeting a distinctly indigenous color from start to finish.

Among matters of general interest to readers of the Bulletin, actions of the Assembly on the following lines may be listed:

Plans were adopted for a continued promotion of the Five-Year-Movement.

Of special importance was held to be the work for youth. All constituent churches were urged to encourage the formation of church youth fellowships, with their four-fold emphasis on worship, fellowships, search for truth and practical service.

Tentative forms were adopted for such special services as those for use at funerals, weddings, baptisms, dedication of infants, celebration of the Lord's Supper and the ordination of ministers. These forms had been worked out by sub-committees and were an attempt to adapt western forms to Chinese habits of thought.

With a view to reducing expenses, it was decided that in the future General Assembly shall meet quadrennials, not triennially, the General Council biennially, and the Ad Interim Committee semi-annually. All standing committees of the church were condensed into one, a Committee on the Life and Work of the Church, with twenty-four members, made up of eight sub-committees of three persons each; the committee as a whole is to meet annually.

Dr. C. Y. Cheng, who for six years has served as the first Moderator of the Church, was unanimously elected to become its General Secretary, while the Rev. Y. S. Tom, General Secretary of the Kwangtung Synod, was chosen to succeed him to the office of Moderator. A fuller statement of the bearing of this action on the work of the National Christian Council will be found elsewhere in this issue.

Hua Chung (Central China) College

PRESIDENT FRANCIS C. M. WEI, PH. D.
Wu Chang, China
Excerpts from the President's Report for the Year 1932—1933

The college has been growing steadily. Our enrolment increased from 80 in the spring of 1932 to 102 in the following fall. It is a small increase, but large enough for the healthy development of the Institution. Forty-seven students in the Freshman Class is the largest entering class in our history. Of the one hundred and two students, thirty-one are women, who fill Yen Hostel, the dormitory for women, to overflowing.

Besides Boone Hostel in Ingle Hall for men students, another hostel for men, taking the name of St. Paul's Hostel, was opened at the beginning of the year, as a hostel for Free Church students, under the control of the Methodist Mission. This latter hostel is a small unit, with only twenty students in residence; but the small number possesses many advantages. It makes possible an intimate hostel life, denied to a larger group. This is originally intended to be one of the features of our Institution. Thus reports the Rev. L. Constantine, Master of St. Paul's Hostel: "So the most noticeable feature of the year has been the comradeship which exists among the students themselves and the faculty members connected with the Hostel. As one senior student expressed it at our farewell dinner: 'We are just like a band of brothers here.' This spirit has shown itself in all the activities of the Hostel, in academic work and in social and religious life."

The Boone Hostel in Ingle Hall, with a larger number of students, but only about fifty in number, has been doing splendid work under the guidance of Mr. John L. Coe, Warden, and the Rev. Charles F. Whiston, Chaplain. As the Boone Hostel is primarily a hostel for the Episcopal men students, Mr. Whiston has been, during the year, devoting most of his time to the pastoral care of the Hostel, together with whatever Episcopal women there are in Yen Hostel. In both of the two hostels for men, as well as in Yen Hostel for women, there is a social room, combined with reading room, which adds to the usefulness of the hostel. Aside from Yen Hostel, however, it is felt that much has yet to be done to improve the social room in each hostel so as to make it of greater use.

Daily morning chapel is in the charge of a committee appointed by the Board of Directors to represent all the cooperating missions. As before, members of the Faculty take turns to lead. They are free to conduct the service in whatever form they feel most congenial. Attendance has been good, varying around 40% of the student body. On Sunday evening, there is a college service, with preachers invited from outside.

Beside these services for the whole college, there have been also a daily prayer meeting, conducted with great success by Mr. Watkins in St. Paul's Hostel, and Holy Communion services on Sunday morning and at mid-week in the College Chapel in Episcopal form, arranged by the Rev. Charles E. Whiston for the Episcopal group. A daily evensong, also in Episcopal form, has been conducted by the Episcopal students at their own initiative but under the guidance of Mr. Whiston at their request. The daily attendance at this evensong is reported to be about one half of the Episcopal students.

It is also encouraging to notice the formation of various discussion groups in the hostels, meeting from time to time with the advice of faculty members.

The pre-term retreats for the Faculty are of significance. Immediately before the opening of each term, members of the Faculty met for half a day of quiet meditation and prayer, to face squarely the great task of working for the spiritual welfare of the college, to exchange experiences in their religious life, and to plan for their personal work with the students during the coming term. On the third Monday evening of each month, there is also a Faculty prayer meeting, held in one of the faculty houses, when members of the Faculty gather for a period of devotion.

Equally of interest is the fact that numerous clubs have been organized among the students during the last year: such as the Education Club, the International Relations Club, the Sociology Club, the Radio Club, the Biology Club, and so on. The students have been turning out a monthly bulletin in Chinese, which is a semi-official organ of the college, and also two other publications, purely as their own enterprises and financed by themselves. The publication of the Annual for 1932 in December was somewhat late, but it was quite a remarkable piece of work, much to the credit of the board of editors, composed entirely of students.

A beginning in inter-collegiate athletics has been made this spring. There have been several matches played between the college and the two sister institutions in the city, namely Wuhan University and Chung Hwa University. This promotes good feeling among the three institutions, which are the only institutions doing university work in the province of Hupeh. In this as well as in other respects, our relations with these two institutions are the most cordial.

Even to the casual observer, our students are most hard-working in their studies. The Government requires a heavy schedule, which means 132 credits for the four years besides Party Principles, Physical Education and Military Training. Every student in each of the three schools in the college has to take a major subject which is to be his field of concentration, and a minor subject, generally recommended by his major department. The major takes about one-third of the four years' time, and the minor, about one-sixth. Then, there are the general requirements of the college in Chinese, English and Philosophy, including Religion as an elective, taking altogether about one-fifth of the four-year total. These three groups of courses, with departmental requirements added, leave only a small margin for free electives. Our laboratory period, each to count one credit, is three hours; and all our lecture courses involve extensive collateral reading. Only conscientious students, with adequate preparation before matriculation, are equal to the amount of work expected of them. At the same time, we have to make due allowance for athletic games and extracurricular activities; and frequently we find the students too busy in their regular duties to develop much that usually goes under the name of college life.

We have done everything possible to keep the students' expenses down. From our study of students' expenses in the universities and colleges in China, we know that the students' budget depends not so much upon the fees charged, which with the exception of the government institutions which charge little tuition or none at all, do not vary so much in the country, but largely upon the habits of spending money on the part of the students themselves. It is our belief that no student in our part of the country is justified in spending more than $300.00 Chinese currency a year, including all fees paid to the college, and, with very few exceptions, this amount represents the annual expenditure of our students here.

Dean Kwei reporting on the development of the Yale-in-China School of Science summarizes the additions during the year to the science teaching equipment as follows:

"The Department of Biology bought, among other things, a kerosene incubator, an air sterilizer, 3 sets of models for development stages of animals, one microscopic projection apparatus, a lecture table and other furniture for the general laboratory. Just to the east of the laboratories, the department is building a small experimental botanical garden with a pond for aquatic animals."

"The Department of Chemistry has been building up a set of important reference books and journals. It now has a complete set of Chemical Abstracts to date and has about 300 volumes of books and bound journals. During the past year, particular emphasis has been laid on the second year course both in respect to equipment and laboratory directions, which Dr. Djang has been trying to standardize as he has already done with the first year course. Some essential pieces of apparatus for physical chemistry have been bought."

"The Department of Physics bought some apparatus for experiments on modern physics, such as electrometers, photoelectric cells and apparatus for measuring the charge of an electron by Millikan's method. Through the generous help of the Rockefeller Foundation, the Department bought a precision wave meter for short waves together with a quartz crystal and accessories for temperature control. The machine shop has made, among other things, an optical bench, a student potentiometer, an experimental condenser for determination of dielectric constant of liquids and a nickel plating outfit."

We are happy to report the appointment of Prof. P'u Hwang, Ph. D., as Dean of the school of Education. Under his leadership, the school is getting properly organized giving facilities for two majors in Education. In his report to the President, he says: "The aim of the school of Education of Hua Chung College is to serve the middle schools of Central China, by giving our students a thorough training in Education, Psychology, and Practice Teaching, which are necessary for their success as teachers and administrators in middle schools. During the current year, we have thoroughly revised our curriculum according to this aim, and we have kept in mind the proper proportion of three important elements in the training of teachers and administrators for middle schools, namely, the content subject which the student has chosen to teach, the study of Education, and Practice Teaching." Negotiations have been going on with the American Church Mission, to take over a junior middle school of that mission, a short distance from the College campus, as a practice school of the School of Education. It is expected that the arrangement will be completed before long, so that better facilities can be provided for the practice teaching of the increasing number to students studying Education.

With a growing faculty, and with the steady increase of the student body, the demand for better library facilities is pressing. As we reported a year ago, greater support has to be found for the development of the College Library. The Library reports a total number of 24,497 English books against 23,705 for the preceding year; and a total of 11,500 Chinese books against 9,800 for the preceding year. We are particularly appreciative of the generous help of the Church Periodical Club of the Episcopal Church in America, which has sent us more than two hundred books during the year, all carefully selected by member of our own Faculty for the use of the different departments in the college. Considerable additions have been made to the departmental collections of technical books in Education, Biology, Chemistry, and Physics. Purchases have also been made to build up collections of books for teaching purposes in the departments of Chinese, Economics, and Sociology; and the departmental collection for English Literature continues to grow.

Our relation with the Christian middle schools in the Central China region has been most happy. Distributed over the three provinces of Hupeh, Hunan and Kiangsi, there are ten senior middle schools at present doing college preparatory work, of which six are for boys and four for girls. They are all affiliated with the college. Besides these, there are twelve junior middle schools, one of which has recently started senior middle school work and two more planning to do so, beginning with the next fall. These, also, are related to us in a most intimate way through secondary education conferences and principals' conferences, which alternate with each other annually. The first secondary education conference of the Central China Christian middle schools was held in the winter of 1931, and that led to the holding of a conference of the principals of Christian middle schools last January in Kiukiang, when the principals of all the middle schools, with only two exceptions, were present. These conferences give an opportunity not only for the college to get acquainted with the middle schools which it wishes to serve, but also to create an *esprit de corps* among those who are engaged in Christian education in this region. We wish to remind one another that we, one and all, are doing the same work of building up the Christian Churches in Central China and of helping the Chinese people to meet the present situation in the social and spiritual reconstruction of the Nation.

The secondary education conference and the principals' conference held during the last two years have borne other fruits which ought to be mentioned in passing. The principals of the Christian middle schools in the Wuhan center, altogether ten in number, are meeting three times a term at dinner with the President of the college, to discuss problems of common interest. To those occasions each institution, the college included, invites also a member of its faculty. It really does one's heart good to see a band of over twenty men and women meeting together with the sole aim of making Christian education count in the Christian movement of the country, and of making it a worthy part of the educational movement of Modern China. Our school of Education has been sponsoring a reading circle for the principals of the Christian middle schools in the Central China region, and has been editing a monthly newsletter containing all the news sent from the different middle schools. In the college, the Department of Pedagogy has been conducting, during the last year, two seminars for the benefit of the local middle school teachers: one for Physics and one for English. Both of these seminars have been quite successful, and next year we expect to expand this work to other subjects if there should be need. The School of Education has constructed three different tests: a special mental test; and with the cooperation of the departments of Chinese and English, tests in Chinese and English. All of these are now in the process of standardization. We look forward to the time when such tests will multiply for the benefit of all the middle schools that may care to use them. Thus Hua Chung College is not an institution standing aloof, but a part of the Christian educational movement in Central China, seeking at all times for the closest cooperation with the other Christian educational institutions, as well as with the educational work of the Government, by the side of which our work is only supplementary, though it has its own distinct contribution to make.

The Role of Scholars in the War

By Dr. Francis C. M. Wei

I am glad to have the opportunity to speak from Chungking, our wartime capital, to my friends in the United States of America. It is two years and a half since I came back from my visit in America. How the world has changed since! When I was in the States, I told my friends there that our war in China was only the vanguard of the world war between totalitarianism and democracy. Facts during the last year and a half have proved my statement. China is still fighting on and is determined to continue her fight until righteousness and international justice are vindicated.

When the war in China broke out in the summer of 1937, I was abroad. In spite of the speculation of many people to the contrary, my own conviction was that the Chinese nation, under the able and inspiring leadership of our Generalissimo, would fight to the bitter end and that the war would be a long drawn-out one. I was not unaware of the unpreparedness of our country for war, but I was confident of our final victory, because I knew the morale of our people and the cause for which we accepted the gauntlet of our enemy. The cause was not ours only.

When I returned from America, the war had been going on for a whole year. My personal observation has borne out my belief. No hardship can daunt the spirit of the people. No adversaries can shake our confidence in our government. One city after another has been lost to the enemy. We cannot for the time being stand their attack by planes and mechanized forces. Our equipment is admittedly inferior. But it has been improving. We are waiting for more and better trained soldiers. We are getting them rapidly into the field. When the opportune time comes, we will counter-attack on a large scale. We are more confident now than ever in the final outcome of the war, just as friends in America are now more confident in our ability to win.

During the last three years and a half, millions of our people, largely of the intelligentsia and the skillful artisan classes have withdrawn from the occupied areas to the interior. Under the protection of high mountains and behind natural barriers the Chinese nation continues to resist the Japanese invasion and has started a remarkable program of national reconstruction. The magnitude of this reconstruction program is so great that it can be believed only by those who see it with their own eyes. The war has made a new nation of the Chinese people. It has given us a new birth.

There are many indications of this. I have time only to dwell briefly on one point, namely, higher education. I know it best, and I can speak from personal experience.

Before the war China was already making rapid progress in higher education. Had this progress been uninterrupted, we would soon be able to catch up with the American universities and colleges. But the war has compelled many of our best institutions of higher learning to retreat into the interior where education has been backward and conditions less favorable.

In 1937 we had 108 universities and colleges. Only 9 of these were originally in what we now call Free China. Half of the rest had to retire from the invading army to the Southwest and the Northwest, one quarter are remaining to operate in Peiping, Tientsin, and Shanghai, where the enemy has not been able to interfere seriously and 22 have been forced to close.

But now many of the colleges closed have been reopened in Free China and new ones have been established by the Government to meet new needs created by the war. The number of universities and colleges at present is 113, more than we had before the war. The total number of university and college students had a drop when war first broke out, but for the last three years it has been increasing steadily. Now, it is approximately the same as in the spring of 1937.

Friends used to ask me in America two and a half years ago, and they may want to ask still, why university students retreat to the interior behind the fighting line instead of joining the defending forces at the front. Some of them have joined the fighting forces and many are continuing to do so. But what China lacks is not man power. Five million of our men are under arms and more are in training. Our government considers it too costly to send all university students to the front. It takes many years to bring them up to the university level, and only one in ten thousand of the total population is a university student. Should they all be massacred in this war, there would be a serious gap in the intellectual life of the nation, when the war is over and when reconstruction work will tax the talents of the nation to its utmost. The great task of modernizing China has just begun and must be completed. This needs men and women of modern training. So this training must continue at any cost. For this reason the government has adopted the policy of maintaining the educational institutions even at the greatest expense, and for this reason institutions of higher learning have moved into the interior, nor running away from the war, not even from the ruthless massacre of the Japanese army, but carrying out a part of the national program of resistance for the sake of national reconstruction.

I have already mentioned the fact that new colleges have been started by the government since the outbreak of the war. The government has also set aside large sums of money for the relief of teachers and students affected by this national struggle. Many of the private middle schools and colleges have moved from the occupied areas into the Province of Szechwan, which is now the seat of the Central Government. The high price of food has worked severe hardship on both the teachers and students. By special action of the Central Government the sum of one million dollars has been appropriated for their relief. Refugee students in other parts of Free China have also been receiving similar aids for the last three years. We were greatly encouraged when we heard just the other day from the Minister of Education himself in his report to the People's Political Council that in spite of serious financial difficulties; the government budget for education had been increased by 30 percent over the budget at the beginning of the war. It is the clearest demonstration of the determination of the government to keep education at the greatest efficiency.

But despite the efforts on the part of the government, the hardship on the students and teachers in the universities is severe. Many students are refugees from the occupied areas, their homes are either destroyed or impoverished and no longer able to pay even their food bills in college. Some of them are entirely cut off from their relatives. Wartime food is always a problem. There is the danger of under-nourishment, and prices are soaring every day. Stationery is expensive. Books are almost impossible to obtain. Several students have to share one copy. The refugee universities have found libraries expensive to move, if at all possible. Scientific equipment is either too heavy or too fragile for long distance truck transportation. Therefore little has been brought out. As the sojourn becomes longer, the lack of books and equipment proves to be more and more a handicap. Chemicals and other supplies are being used up and are difficult to replace. Many experiments become impossible. Teachers have to resort to their ingenuity in overcoming such difficulties.

This has not been, however, without its compensation. It stimulates resourcefulness, and in many cases it turns the attention from remote academic problems to those of immediate local interest. But even of these more practical problems many are insoluble without the minimum required books and equipment. Friends in America may give us invaluable assistance by sending us more books and scientific apparatus.

It is with problems like these the higher education in wartime China is being confronted. But like our soldiers at the front, we carry on with undaunted spirit and strong determination.

Through hard struggle and persistence, higher education in China has not only maintained itself in wartime but has also made noted improvement in some significant respects. Particularly, the migration of many institutions of research and higher learning into the more backward parts of the country has its beneficial effects. It has given opportunities to both students and teachers, more accustomed to conditions in large centers on the coast and along the rivers, to get acquainted with life in the interior. This in itself is an education with far-reaching consequences. Culture is more widely disseminated. Modern ideas are spread. Schools of the lower levels, by contact with universities from the more progressive provinces, are stimulated to raise their standards and to increase their efficiency. As a result, there will be a more evenly educated nation after the war.

There have been many adjustments in higher education necessitated by the war, and there will be many more at its end, but all are for the best interest of the nation.

Semi-Annual Report to Board of Trustees Known as Board of Founders and Board of Directors of Hua Chung College (Wu Chang) in Kweilin, Kwangsi, China

Members of the Board:

I am submitting this semi-annual report of Hua Chung College in a twofold capacity, both as chairman of the Executive Committee of the Board of Directors, appointed here in Kweilin, and as president of the College. Circumstances make it impossible for the Board of meet, and, therefore, I have no way to submit this report for their approval before it is forwarded to the Trustees.

The college had already moved from Wu Chang to Kweilin when I returned from abroad last August to resume my work as president. At that time the Standing Committee of the Board of Directors, anticipating circumstances which have since arisen, appointed Dr. Paul C. T. Kwei (alternate Dr. Richard P. Bien), Dr. Paul V. Taylor, Mr. David F. Anderson, Dr. Hu I, and myself as the Executive Committee of the Board of Directors to function in Kweilin. Because Mr. Anderson had to leave Kweilin in November on account of Mrs. Anderson's health, Miss Margaret Bleakley has been acting for him on the committee. The appointment of this Executive Committee has proved to be most fortunate because since the latter part of October we have been cut off almost completely from communication with Wuhan.

FACULTY AND STAFF

With the exception of one missionary teacher on furlough, two who stayed behind for relief service in Wuhan, one Chinese senior faculty member in service for the wounded soldiers, and another on sabbatical leave, the whole faculty and staff have been accounted for in Kweilin. I had expected to find our faculty greatly depleted upon my return, but those members who had been most eager to serve found that they could serve best by continuing their work in the college. An article written by Mrs. E. P. Miller Jr., Assistant Professor of English Literature, which has been sent to the Trustees and the Missions, gives a vivid description of the adventurous and self-sacrificing spirit in which the missionary members of the faculty and staff have come to join us here in the work of the college in Kweilin. It is the experience of us all that the difficult times have drawn the faculty and the students more closely together when we look forward to the day when hostilities will come to an end, and when the Christian spirit must seek to influence more deeply the leadership of China in the reconstruction of the nation.

Before the severe air-raids, which occurred mainly in December, Kweilin was a crowded city and rent was at least four times the normal rate and twice that of the pre-war rate in Wu Chang. For this reason we had to make special rent allowances to the low salaried members of the faculty and staff; otherwise, they would not have been able to subsist with their families since war prices prevailed.

So far all faculty members have escaped uninjured from the air-raids and other war hazards, but the houses in which three had their quarters were burned in Kweilin.

STUDENTS

In a strange city and with the uncertainty of the future, the Senate decided at the beginning of the term not to take in more than two hundred students, and owing to the limited accommodations in the hostels, we enrolled only one hundred and sixty-three. After the fall of Canton and the evacuation of the Wuhan cities, we had a period of intense nervousness in Kweilin, and on account of financial and family reasons, a number of students withdrew, but we have finished the term with one hundred and twenty-seven. The drop is not as serious as we might have expected.

We have not put any hindrance in the way of any of our students who wanted to join war services, and some have volunteered. It is the policy, however, of the Central Government to encourage students to finish their courses so that they may be better prepared to serve China after the war. We can easily see the wisdom and necessity of such a policy in China. In proportion to the future needs of the country trained men are few. Unless the young men go to the front, for which the government has already sufficient man power and, therefore, is not willing to call upon college students for this purpose, they have only limited opportunities for government service in these war times. Industry has not been developed in China and, consequently, most of our equipment and war materials have been purchased from abroad instead of being manufactured in the country. Also, we are caught so unprepared for this conflict that many kinds of organized activities for civilians, which would naturally be found in another country at war, are not in existence here. These reasons may count for the fact that there are proportionately more students staying in college during this national conflict than we might find in a modern warring country. But "they also serve who only stand and wait."

  The spirit of the students in the college has been the most gratifying. In spite of the difficult circumstances and the destructions of the air-raids and of the war itself, they apply themselves diligently to their studies and are always ready to cooperate with the college authorities to be useful in every way possible to the community and to maintain the good name and the academic standards of the college. Many of them are cut off from their homes in Hupeh, Hunan and Kangsi. Those whose homes were burnt in Changsha find themselves in grave financial difficulties. But they courageously go on with their work and are willing to do anything so as to work their way through college. Opportunities for students' self-help in a place like Kweilin are however limited. The level of wages is low. A number of them have been partially supporting themselves by private tutoring in local families. Others can find no employment. Mrs. Miller's article on "Farewell to Kweilin" describes a few typical cases of students meeting their financial problems in the most undaunted spirit. Many things have been done by students voluntarily whereas in Wu Chang before we would have needed hired labor. The program of the college needs modification to meet the challenges of the new day.

TEMPORARY BUILDINGS

After a great deal of effort and negotiations arrangements were completed in September for the college to use one of the Southern Baptist Mission three storied buildings with a finished attic as the main building of the college. Grounds surrounding it are ample for athletic purposes. The loan includes five matsheds which had been used by the Provincial University of Kangsi before we came, and which proved to be useful to us in arranging for our classrooms and offices. One of the matsheds was used as a chapel and assembly hall, another was used to house a small practice school for our School of Education. These matsheds were torn down in January to reduce the hazard of fire in case of an air-raid. With slight remodeling and improvements we have been using the main building for all the classrooms and offices, turning the attic into a library.

It was impossible to bring with us from Wu Chang any furniture, so very rough wooden desks and benches were bought at the cheapest possible price. Four hostels, two for men and two for women, were set up at the beginning of the term. The Christian and Missionary Alliance allowed us to repair a small house on their property and to erect a temporary building at a cost of twelve hundred dollars Chinese currency. This was our first and the larger hostel for men. For the other men's hostel we rented a house in another section of the town about a fifteen-minute walk from our main building. At first all of our women students were crowded into the Church Missionary Society building used for women refugees. It was very kind of the Bishop of the Diocese of Kangsi-Hunan and the members of the Kweilin station to allow us to use these rooms. Later we rented a house five minutes' distance from the college which was large enough to accommodate forty girls. During the middle of the term the Baptists released another building in which we put all our girls together.

AIR-RAIDS

It is beyond my words to describe the shocking air-raids in Kweilin which, according to those who went through numerous air-raids last year in Wu Chang, have been by far the worst and most devastating ever experienced by a civilian population. Five raids hit five different sections of this populous city. One half of the buildings are now in ruins, but thanks to the numerous and spacious caves in the rocky hillsides just outside the city, the loss of human life has not been heavy.

At first we followed our Wu Chang experience and had two dug-outs constructed near the college main building, another near the larger hostel for men, and another near the Church Missionary Society women refugee' camp where 15 of our girls stayed. These dug-outs were places of refuge for our faculty and students in the earlier air-raids, but later when dug-outs in the city received direct hits, burying people alive, we ordered all our people to resort to the caves whenever the siren sounded, using the dug-outs to store equipment and books not in daily use. In this way we secured the best protection for both people and equipment.

The damage done by numerous air-raids to the college property is comparatively slight. The small hostel for men with the rough equipment in it was completely destroyed, but most of the students' belongings were salvaged. The larger hostel for men had a narrow escape. Its kitchen was demolished, and the hostel had to be abandoned because the whole section of the city surrounding it was in ruins. The very day that the incendiary bombs caused the destruction to the small hostel for men on November 29, the fire almost spread to the girls' rooms in the Church Missionary Society refugee building. The fifteen girls housed there have since then been placed with the other women's group.

FUTURE PLANS: MOVING AGAIN!

In spite of these circumstances and in spite of the difficulties of bringing in either equipment or books from abroad for our work, we would still be willing to carry on here. But we have to face the danger of being cut off from the world if the enemy should push hard their Southern China campaign. Besides, there is the greater danger that the "scorched earth policy", coupled with guerrilla tactics, both necessary for effective defense on the part of the nation, might compel us to leave Kweilin when leaving would be too late. It is in view of these possibilities that we have been seriously thinking for the last six weeks of moving the college farther west. Yunnan seems to be the most logical place; next would be Szechwan. There is little choice between the two as far as war hazards, local peace and order, climate and health conditions, and food supply go; but Yunnan holds out greater hope of communications with the outside world. Some of us have some knowledge of conditions in Szechwan, but Yunnan remains comparatively unknown to us. Mr. Anderson, who has been staying in Hongkong, writes that as far as information in Hongkong is concerned, to move the College is necessary, and he gives us the impression that the Rt. Rev. R. O. Hall would favor our move to Yunnan which is a part of his large Diocese. There is Church Missionary Society work and Methodist Missionary Society in Kunming, but Kunming being the capital of the Province is not so attractive to us. We would rather go to a smaller town away from the railway and highways in order that our experience here of air-raids may not be repeated. We realize that in time of war no place is safe in China, but we must look for a place to continue our work quietly and to experiment in Christian higher education in these troublesome times. We have heard of two places north of Kunming with Methodist Mission stations, but we are inclined to go west of Kunming and thirty kilometers north of the Burma-Yunnan route, appears to be the best for our purpose.

There are two ways to reach Yunnan. One is the southern route by way of Nanning, Lungchow, and the Indo-China railway. The other is the northern way through Kweiyang in Kweichow. The cost is about the same by the one route or the other. With the recent developments in southern China, there is an element of risk of our trucks getting stopping at the other end of the southern route, but the northern trip would take more time for trucks to drive.

After the approval of the Executive Committee of the Board Directors to move the college away from Kweilin, the Senate appointed Dr. Richard P. Bien and Dr. T. W. Zee to go to Yunnan to investigate conditions there, with the purpose of locating some possible sites for the college. The preliminary report has now reached us by our own radio station here in the Physics Department from Dr. Bien in Kunming saying that conditions in Yunnan are favorable and the Senate has taken action, with the approval of the Board of Directors, to move the college to Kunming first where we may stay with the help of the Church Missionary Society and the Methodist Mission until most of the members of the Senate have arrived, and then steps will be taken to determine a definite site. The moving of the whole group with equipment, books, and baggage may take a long time, and will certainly mean a great deal of effort, but the whole trip has been carefully planned, both economically and with due regard to safety. The Senate is drawing up a budget for this move.

FUTURE PLAN: CURRICULUM MODIFICATIONS

Ever since I returned from abroad I have been thinking about modifying the curriculum of the college, and even of taking a bolder step in recommending a new policy which may be more appropriate for the China after the war. One of my weaknesses is to be prepared for the worst even though I work and hope for the best. It is very difficult to visualize the conditions in China when the present hostilities come to an end, but I have been informally discussing with groups of the faculty various ideas and plans for the future. We hope in Yunnan to make a careful study of conditions there and make some preliminary experiments. I shall then be in a position to recommend to the Trustees and the Directors a modification of the policy and the curriculum in order to train our students more definitely to take a lead in improving isolated rural communities with the religious spirit and intellectual stimulus they have gained from the college. We shall not lower the Hua Chung standards, but our men and women students may spend a part of their time learning to be productive members of a self-sustaining community while they are being educated along the most up-to-date lines. This is still in the visionary stage, but something may come out of it when it has been tested by my colleagues, many of whom are wiser and more practical-minded than I am. Whatever we may do we will remember the purpose for which the college has been founded and carried on. Our problem is how to fulfill that purpose in the most effective manner in the present crisis in China and in view of the future that the younger generation may have to meet.

In no other time do we realize the importance and the far-reaching significance of Christian Higher Education in China. The future is still obscure. But one thing is certain. China is being truly reborn. What the nation will be depends upon her leadership after the war. Shall we leave it entirely to the forces of the world or is Christianity going to have a determining share in it? The Christian colleges are our answer.

I shall continue my monthly reports to the Trustees and to the Cooperating Missions so as to keep you well informed about the college. We are hopefully carrying on the work which you have entrusted to us, and you may be certain that we shall remain ever faithfully your co-workers in the great enterprise of helping to establish His Kingdom in a world sin-sick and war-torn. We are confident of China's ultimate victory and we are even more confident that no labor in His Name shall be in vain.

Respectfully submitted,
Francis C. M. Wei
President of Hua Chung College and
Chairman of the Executive Committee
in Kweilin of the Board of Directors
Kweilin, Kwangsi
February 14, 1939

Three Years of Chinese Education in War Time

Francis C. M. Wei, M. A., Ph. D., D. C. L.
President, Hua Chung College
Hsichow, Yunnan

China is a country with an age-long tradition of education. Her people have been taught for centuries by her sages to believe that men live not by bread alone, but must, for the existence of the nation, maintain at any cost the accumulated experience of the past generations. They have learned to look to an educated leadership, which would serve the nation with their learning and by that service bring glory to the family and to the community from which it has sprung. It is largely due to this tradition that the torch of learning has never lacked its bearer and the work of education never stops, whatever the fortunes of the nation.

This proud educational tradition of the Chinese goes as far back as the millennium before the Christian era. When life was simpler and when an education could be acquired by reading the books of one's father, educational activities could go on uninterrupted even in time of war in the country. A tutor and a few books were all that would be necessary to carry on the work of educating the rising generation. But for almost half a century, China's educational system has been modeled after that of the modern nations in the west. Education has ceased to be a simple business. School buildings are more elaborate. Equipment needs to be more expensive and less movable. Instead of a single tutor with a handful of pupils, we have a sizable staff and a considerable number of young people under its care. Such an educational machinery can easily be disrupted and its work is liable to be interfered with by any serious social or political disturbance in the locality. Hence, when the Japanese invasion began in 1937 and when China adopted the policy of long resistance, one of the problems confronting the government was how to carry on the educational program in face of a major war fought within its own territory.

The fighting is Shanghai in 1932 and still more the bitter experience of our people in Manchuria since 1931 are enough to teach us that the enemy has no particular love for our educational institutions. As soon as they have a chance, schools are the first to be attacked and destroyed. This being the case, the problem of conserving our educational strength is a stupendous one. As the war continues and as our troops are drawing the enemy more and more into the interior, educational activities could not possibly stop and wait until the end of the war. There is also the more serious problem of planning for the education of the people behind the enemy's lines. The enemy would certainly attempt to exploit the young minds among the Chinese population in the occupied areas, but exploitation is no education. In face of such circumstances, should we move the schools and the school population with them? Or should we close the schools and send the youth of school age to the front line? China is not a wealthy nation. Every cent at the disposal of the government in time of war ought to go to support the prosecution of the war which is fought for the very existence of the nation. Should we allow the young minds to remain fallow as long as the war lasts, or should we by hook or by crook endeavor to continue our educational work under the most difficult and most baffling conditions? The story of Chinese education for the last three years in time of war is nothing short of an epic which the Chinese people will remember and sing for generations to come, and which the world will undoubtedly admire and treasure.

Much has to be attributed to the mellowness of the Chinese civilization, the far-sighted policy of the Chinese Government and the genuine peace-loving character of the Chinese people for what has been happening in Chinese education in war time since the summer of 1937. To take the institutions of higher education alone, only fourteen of the one hundred and eight universities and colleges which were in existence in the country before the war have been able to keep open either in foreign concessions, still not openly interfered with by the Japanese army, or in cities already occupied by enemy troops like Peiping, where the institutions are able to continue their operation under the auspices of foreign missions of the Christian Church from abroad. Seventy-seven of the original number of these institutions have moved to the interior and are operating as refugee colleges. These include the national, private and Christian colleges and universities.

For anyone who has had the unpleasant experience of having moved an institution, it is no fun whatever. Buildings are of course unmovable, all the furniture has to be left behind, scientific apparatus and equipment are mostly too fragile or too clumsy to move, books have to be packed and they are heavy. In time of war transport is difficult, and where it is possible, the expenses involved in moving a library or even a small part of it are almost prohibitive, yet to move a college or a university without its books and its teaching equipment may just as well not to move. Their replacement in the interior, when the enemy has blockaded most of the seaports, is costly, if it is possible. Then, the moving of faculty, staff, families and students. Each of the seventy-seven institutions has on average a hundred faculty and staff members. Each has a family of the size of four or five. The average student body moving with the institution is about three hundred. This rough, low estimate, and we can only estimate, as actual statistics are unavailable, was the moving of 38,500 faculty and staff members and their families and the same number of students, making a total of U. S. $77,000. And we have not yet counted the lower schools.

Why should we have moved at all? Certainly not for the sake of property, most of which is unmovable anyway. But the experience of Shanghai, Soochow, Nanking, and other places during the early months of the war had given sufficient demonstration that Chinese women and children were not safe behind the enemy lines. The Japanese army has no love for the intellectual and student classes. The mental agony, not to say the physical suffering, would be unbearable, if these people should remain after the city has been occupied. To sacrifice human life and still more to sacrifice human personality for no great purpose is indefensible.

Friends abroad often ask why those students do no join the fighting line or other kinds of war work in defense of the country instead of migrating to the interior for their education. Does the government not need the technical knowledge of the university professors in time of war? Yes and no. Before 1937, China was not highly organized for war, having only a few industries and those only on small scales. It is not easy to turn our productive efforts overnight into preparation for war. Most of our ammunition and war equipment are imported. University professors do not readily turn into specialists in factories to produce for the army and its auxiliaries. Many professors have joined the war services and large numbers of students have enlisted in the army and the air forces. But one thing China does not lack is man power. The government considers it too costly in the long run to send all the students to the front line, it takes years to bring them up to the university level and only 0.01 of one percent of the population are university students. Should they all be massacred in this cruel war, there would be a serious gap in the intellectual life of the country after war, when construction will tax the talents of the nation to its utmost, as experience in England and France after the last European war has sufficiently told us. Our watchword at present is "resistance to make the reconstruction of the nation possible." If reconstruction is lost sight of in our resistance, we would be defeating our own purpose. The great task of the modernizing China began not long before the war must be completed after the fighting and this will need men and women of modern training, training which requires years and which must not be suspended or too seriously interrupted, if the war is to be of a long duration. For this reason mainly institutions of higher learning have moved into the interior, not running away from the war, but carrying out a part of the national program of resistance for the sake of national reconstruction. The cost is heavy and the suffering great, but it is only a part of the cost of the war for self-defence and self-preservation.

In the spring of 1937, before the war broke out, there were one hundred and eight institutions of higher learning. Of these, forty-two were universities, each at least with three faculties, thirty-four colleges and thirty-two professional schools. They were supported as follows:

	National	Provincial	Private incl. Chris.	Total
Universities	16	7	19	42
Colleges	5	8	21	34

	National	Provin. & Municipal	Private incl. Chris.	Total
Professional Schools	6	16	10	32

As soon as the war broke out, those institutions in the coast provinces and in the lower and mid Yangtze Valley were threatened. Even before the cities were actually occupied by enemy troops, bombing from the air with absolutely no regard for civilian population or civilian property, it was difficult to attempt any educational work when the siren was sounded almost everyday and when air-raids happened frequently day and night. Yet some of the institutions continued to operate under those circumstances until moving became imperative.

As a consequence of the ruthless air-raids and of the atrocities of the enemy troops after the occupation of the cities on the coast and the lower and mid Yangtze Valley, the loss in educational buildings and teaching equipment is inestimable. Records and manuscripts are destroyed, buildings burnt and some of the precious, rare books became a part of the enemy's loot. Unfortunately, forty per cent of the colleges and universities, tax-supported and otherwise, were in the cities of Shanghai, Peiping, Nanking and Canton, which within a year and a half from the outbreak of hostilities were all occupied and forty-two institutes had to choose between moving into the interior or operating under foreign protection and serious handicaps. It is difficult to estimate whether the suffering in choosing the former alternative is greater than the agony involved in choosing the latter.

But the moving of the institutions of the higher learning into the interior is not a pure misfortune. They have moved into areas which were formerly undeveloped in culture. The diffusion of learning and technical ideas help to hasten the modernization of the country. Educational standards and efficiency of the lower schools of those areas are bound to be improved by the coming of the higher institutions.

College and university students, as well as their professors and lecturers, mostly brought up in large cities along the coast, come into contact with life in the backward parts of the country and learn to appreciate from first-hand experience the problems confronting the Chinese nation. Many of the professors are forced by the new circumstances to tackle problems, the solution of which are not to be found in books written for western consumption or to be gathered from lecture notes brought back from classrooms in American or European universities. Their ingenuity and creative ability are taxed to the utmost, all to the benefit of the nation. Simpler and less adequate equipment may not be a pure disadvantage. Teaching may become more interesting and more fruitful on its account, and not in spite of it.

But after the government has done all it can to mitigate the difficulties of students struggling to carry on their studies in time of war, the situation still remains serious and become increasingly so as the war continues. Many of the young people have to run away from death, leaving behind them their parents and elder relatives in occupied areas. They are sent away for their safety. Their families have lost their income and they are therefore cut off from their support. Prices keep on rising. The food-bill alone in many places is prohibitive. It is remarkable that even under these circumstances, the total enrollment in ninety-one institutions of higher learning in the spring of 1938 was seventy-four percent of the total enrollment of one hundred and eight institutions immediately before the outbreak of hostilities. During the year 1938, six more institutions were reopened and the total enrollment in ninety-seven institutions increased to ninety-five percent of the pre-war enrollment. There were one hundred and two institutions under operation in 1939, but statistics are still unavailable for this year. This is the best demonstration of the undaunted spirit of Chinese higher education and of the indefeasible determination of the both the Chinese government and the Chinese people not to allow the enemy to break through their cultural front. Our resistance is stern and we are confident that the ultimate victory will be ours. We keep on training our youth so that when the war comes to an end, we may be in a position to carry out our program of reconstruction. While the war goes on and while the government needs more and more trained men for its various activities, our desire is to try to supply the demand by keeping our educational home-fire burning.

The problem is not simple, of course, in spite of all the efforts made by the government and by private groups which are interested in education, a few of the institutions had been forced to close and those which are able to operate have to reduce staff and expenses. Large numbers of college and university teachers have to join the ranks of the unemployed. The government started to face this problem shortly after the autumn of 1937. The Ministry of Education have all the unemployed teachers registered and they were given work to do as (1) Editors of Mass Movement or Youth Movement Literature, (2) Translators of books in the National Translation and Editorial Bureau, (3) Temporary teachers in institutions continuing in operation, with salaries paid by the Ministry, (4) District Directors of activities to promote education in the backward places. Teachers who formerly held the ranks of college professors were given the subsidy of $100 to $120 a month according to living conditions in different localities, and those who were formerly college lecturers or teachers in professional schools were given the subsidy of $80 a month. College assistants were given the subsidy of $50 a month. Reports up to July 1938, a year after the outbreak of the war, show that four hundred and forty-seven of such college and university teachers were receiving this help from the government.

There is also the problem of the refugee students, those who escaped from the invading army and had neither work nor money to support themselves in strange places far away from home. The government, through the Ministry of Education, came to their rescue. Some of them have been placed in different kinds of war work according to their age and previous training. Others are paid their travelling expenses to go to the institutions to which they originally belonged, but from which they have become separated by long distances. Still others are sent to institutions nearby as refugee or "guest" students.

These refugee students, however, and many others have to get financial aid to stay in school, since their families are either cut off from them in occupied areas or unable to give them full support in war time. The government gives them loans to pay for their food, varying from seven to fourteen dollars a month according to the cost of the living in the various localities where the institutions are. In the academic year of 1937—1938, 4,256 students received these loans. The number increased to 5,372 in the year 1938—1939, and to 6,384 in 1939—1940. This means approximately 13.5% of the students in colleges and universities are being thus helped by the government.

The government has in mind also the students studying abroad. Naturally they, too, have been affected by the war in the income they used to receive from home. Many of them got actually stranded financially in foreign countries. In the year 1938—1939, there were in North America alone 1872 Chinese students in 313 institutions. Many of these students were privately supported and their income from China was affected both by the unfavorable exchange for the Chinese dollar and by the reduced financial strength of their families in the war-torn country. The government gave them $700 currency, either for travelling expenses to come home or to tide over their difficulties for three months before they could make the necessary readjustments. Three hundred of the students abroad received such financial aids from the government.

Since 1938 Chinese students are not permitted to go abroad for their studies. The government issues student passports only to those students who go to foreign universities for military science, medicine or engineering. Several years before the war, the Ministry of Education had already issued order that students should go abroad only for postgraduate work. With the marked improvement of colleges in China in almost every line of university study, it is really a financial waste and quite inadvisable from the point of view of cultural education for young students to go abroad for undergraduate studies. They ought to have their university training first in China and go to foreign countries for special studies when they have already made up their minds what their special interests are and where they may get the best training for the work they want to do afterwards. To go abroad for the sake of the prestige of having been abroad is sheer folly, and in time of war it ought to be stopped, especially when that prestige is rapidly evaporating. Even under the present war conditions many of our colleges and universities are still able to give to our young people as good an education in many lines as may be expected from the average universities in the West. The loss of Chinese cultural background for a student going abroad before his intellectual maturity more than counter-balances whatever advantages he may get from travel and contact with another civilization. The war has brought afresh to the attention of our government the necessity of rethinking our policy of sending students abroad in large numbers.

Another effect of the war on higher education is the combination of colleges and universities under government auspices and on government support. Peking University, Tsing Hua University, formerly in Peiping and Nankai University, formerly in Tientsin, were combined and moved from the north, first to Changsha and, as the war continued and as the Central China region was being threatened, they moved again to Kunming and are now operating as a combined institution under the name of the National Southwest Union University. Similarly, other national universities moved to Shensi in Northwest China from Peiping and combined to form the present National Northwest Union University. A new engineering college has come into existence as the result of the amalgamation of three engineering schools. So also have three medical schools combined to operate in the interior, remote from the war front. These combinations, all for the good of higher education in China, would have never been thought of, still less brought about, if not for the war.

It is during this period of military activities and tension that six new teachers' colleges have been inaugurated in the national system of education. In former years there were five higher normal schools, which trained teachers for the secondary schools. Later, these higher normal schools, except the one in Peiping, were either closed or turned into a part of a university. The Peiping higher normal school continued to exist before the war under the name of Peiping Higher Normal School. Secondary school teachers have been trained by colleges and universities. Shortly before the war, the Ministry of Education ordered that to qualify as teachers in secondary schools, students must have a certain amount of work in educational subjects in the universities. In 1938, a new plan for the training of secondary school teachers was introduced by the Ministry of Education and has been enforced throughout the country since that time. According to this plan, the training of secondary school teachers is to be the responsibility and right of the government alone. Of the six new teachers' colleges, five are attached to national universities and the sixth to be an independent institution in Hunan. All the schools of education and department of education in the universities or colleges, tax-supported or otherwise, with but two exceptions in private universities and one of a provincial normal school, have all been closed down. This indicates the policy of the government to keep in its own hand as far as possible all education below the university level. It is more than an attempt at the standardizing of secondary education and the raising of the standard thereof, which is necessary and desirable; it is really a step towards the regimentation of secondary schools and can be put over on the country only in time of war, when the people in general and the educators in particular are willing to support the government in all its efforts in bringing about a united front in our resistance to a foreign invasion. Nothing shows more conclusively than this, that the intelligentia in the country is solidly behind the government in the war.

It is during this war also that the government has been able to promulgate and enforce prescribed curricula for all the departments in colleges and universities. Formerly the institutions of higher learning were practically free to teach whatever they wanted, except that there must be a lecture a week for one year in the Party Principals of the Kuomintang, physical and health education throughout the four years for all students, one year of military training for two hours a week for men and an equivalent amount of first-aid for women before graduation. No matter how one may regard these requirements, they did not interfere with the liberty of the universities in their experimentation with university courses. There had been, of course, abuses of this privilege, but for institutions which aimed at high standards and good training for the students and did their work honestly, this freedom was the best that could be desired. The new prescribed curricula leave the institutions little room for freedom and experiment. Practically all the lectures in the first year in the universities in all their departments are uniformly prescribed throughout the country. More lectures in the upper classes are elective, but they are elective within the limits of courses previously approved by the government and as a rule it is next to impossible to get approval for a course not listed in the prescribed government curriculum. Prescribed lectures except at the very minimum are odious. To have all courses leading to the degree in a college or university prescribed throughout the country tends to reduce higher education to a dead level, but these new prescribed curricula are being effectively enforced. It is another indication that in war time educators in China are supporting the government whole-heartedly.

There is a definite determination on the part of the government to maintain the high standards of higher education during these times of war and even to raise the standards wherever possible. For many years there have been government examinations, which students must pass before they are qualified for the certificate of middle school graduation. These examinations, more than anything else, have been instrumental in bringing about an approximately uniform standard for the middle schools throughout the country and have been conductive to the improvement of secondary education.

It can hardly be doubted that hither to the standards in the colleges and universities are far from uniform. The government has been wanting for years to effect some improvements. But not until a year ago did the college and university courses have anything like a recognized standard. This year the government is encouraging students to participate in competitive examinations in the various subjects taught in the colleges and universities, and students from institutions of higher learning in the same region compete for honors and prizes. It will be interesting to watch how this works out. It is beyond doubt that these examinations, if properly conducted, will produce wholesome effects upon higher education in the country. What we hope is that there may be standardization without regimentation, for regimentation in higher education is deadening. There must be room for variation and experimentation, especially when the whole program of modern education is still so new in China and much has to be adapted by experience. Only be a long process of trial and error can the right policy and method be found for higher education in this country with its age-long culture and its special and varied needs.

Another innovation in the educational field during the war is the introduction of the tutorial system for middle and higher schools as promulgated by the Ministry of Education in the spring of 1939. The following is a translation of some of the regulations governing the tutorial work:

1. In order to improve the present system of education which has been stressing too much the teaching of knowledge and neglecting to conduct any moral discipline, as well as to avoid mechanical or remote relationships between teachers and students becoming more commercialized, the Ministry of Education intends to adopt the old tutorial system of our country and to follow the regulations of Oxford and Cambridge Universities to be enforced in middle and higher schools.

2. Every class in a school be divided into certain groups. Each group should be composed of 5 to 10 students with a full time teacher appointed by the principle to take charge of it. The principle should also designate either the head of the tutorial department or the disciplinary department to be in charge of the tutorial and disciplinary business of the whole school.

3. The tutor should see to the thinking, character, progress in learning, mental and physical development of the individual students and give strict instruction and advice so as to ensure proper development and to cultivate wholesome character.

4. The method of the tutorial instruction is not only of one kind. Besides individual instruction, the tutor should avail himself of leisure

hours and holidays to gather his own group of students to hold conference and discussion meetings of picnics, etc, for a group life instruction.

The war has certainly directed the attention of the educational authorities to the importance of vocational training which has perhaps been the weakest feature of modern education in China. During the last three years, however, nine vocational schools on the support of the Central Government and directly under the control of the Ministry of Education have been started and are known as the national vocational schools. They give training along such lines as paper-manufacturing, tanning, dying, agriculture, electric-communication, automobile engineering, husbandry and agricultural economics. Subjects like accounting, veterinary science and sanitary administration are also taught. This is intended to promote the light industries and to develop more rapidly the interior in order to meet the demands created by the war.

The professional schools are to have longer courses without, however, taking more of the students' time. Formerly, courses of the professional schools, being of "junior college" standard, to use an American expression, were of two or three years, and they admitted graduates from the senior middle school, which meant twelve years of schooling before professional training began. Since 1938, the Ministry of Education has introduced a new scheme, by which the professional schools may take graduates from the junior middle schools after six years of primary and three years of the secondary education, and have on top of that five years of vocational training, taking the students to the same level as before. This longer training ought to be all for the better. One difficulty, however, is to expect pupils to decide so early as the fifteen year of natural age on the special line of training to take. By giving more time in the five years in the vocational school to the fundamental subjects and by increasing only slowly the special training, we may hope this difficulty will be obviated.

According to the Chinese system of educational administration, schools of the secondary grade are to be financed and administered locally, either by the provincial or municipal or district governments, although still under the Ministry of Education of the Central Government through the Provincial Commissioner of Education appointed by the Ministry. When the war spread into the province, the provincial, or municipal, or district secondary schools moved behind the Chinese lines and tried to operate there. These have been able to take care of a number of pupils, but many families migrate from the occupied areas to the interior provinces which are beyond the reach of the enemy but which have not been developed educationally. Thousands of boys and girls of secondary school age have migrated to the inland cities and towns without their families. They have been sent to "free China" by their parents for safety and for the continuance of their education. Secondary schools in the occupied areas, particularly in cities and towns only a short distance behind the Chinese lines, are therefore overcrowded with these refugee students. A few of the schools supported by the private sources, especially the Christian middle schools, have found it possible to move to the interior and are able to meet a great demand created by the situation. But such schools are few and the demand is increasing. There are also places where the private schools choose not to go. The Central Government, to meet this crying need of large numbers of secondary school students finding no schools to enter, had opened thirteen national middle schools in various localities in the provinces of Honan, Szechwan, Shensi, Kansu, West Hunan, Kweichow and Kiangsi. The total enrollment of these national middle schools is 30,000, according to the latest available report.

  The migration of the Chinese population before the invading army is a phenomenon not unknown in Chinese history, but certainly unprecedented in magnitude in the present war. The great bulk of people, however, has to remain in the occupied areas. Many are unable to move because of various reasons, of which economic necessity is only one. Some of the children of secondary school age may be fortunate enough to find their way to schools a short distance behind the Chinese lines and thus continue their education. In spite of the restrictions put on the movement of the people from the occupied areas by the enemy, nothing can prevent the ingenious and resourceful Chinese from finding ways and means to overcome the obstacles put in their way and send the young people out. Yet the fact remains that many boys and girls, particularly those of the elementary school age, too young to leave their families and get out, are forced to go without education as long as the occupation lasts. Some of them may receive private instruction from their own parents at home. The old method of a tutor taking only a few pupils in the home may be received. If this could be done effectively without molestation by the enemy, we may mark time in this way in the education of our young in occupied areas until the war comes to an end and the enemy is ejected from the country. There seems to be no alternative. It is inconceivable to have organized education under the influence and control of a hostile force, the whole intent and purpose of which is to destroy the national spirit of the Chinese people. We may deplore the fact that Children do not have the opportunity even to learn to read and write. But to learn to read and write is in itself no education, nor is it education merely to acquire the ability to earn a livelihood. Centuries ago our sages taught us better. We must try to prevent at any cost the exploitation of the minds of our young people by the enemy, in the good name of education. Exploitation of human minds is contrary to the fundamental principle of education. The only way in the occupied areas then is not to attempt any organized education but try to teach the young in the home and keep the national ideals alive there. When the children are older, old enough to get into "free China" and breathe the fresh air again, the government will take care of them and give opportunities for them to continue their education. For this reason, the Ministry of Education has modified a regulation of old standing governing the admission into schools by examinations of students without the ordinarily required graduation certificate from the lower school. If this scheme is properly administered and if the people compelled by circumstances to remain in the occupied areas cooperate with the government, as we are sure they will, a whole generation of school children will be spared the deadening influence of the enemy, whose aim is to break up the national life of the Chinese people by poisoning its citizenry at the root.

The education of the Chinese people during this heroic struggle for the existence of the nation is, indeed, the cultural front of our resistance to a foreign invasion. Space does not permit any lengthy account of the social education or of the mass education which is sweeping over the country. The wall newspapers, the war pictures, the news cartoons, the broadcasting of war news, the teaching of the populace of war songs—all this is of the nature of patriotic education and has its telling effect for years to come. The present article deals exclusively with formal education in war-time China, and it is significant that during the three years of war so much has been accomplished in face of such baffling and overwhelming difficulties.

Education in Wartime China

BY Francis C. M. Wei
August, 1940
Published by China Information Publishing Co.
P. O. Box 107, Chungking, China

Francis C. M. Wei, M. A. (Harvard), Ph. D. (London), and D. C. L. (University of the South), has been president of Central China College since 1929.

A noted educator, he is well known in England as well as in America for his lectures and writings on Chinese philosophy. The college, of which he is president, has been compelled by the war to move first to Kweilin, Kwangsi, and then to Hsichow in the heart of Yunnan Province.

The present pamphlet embodies Dr. Wei's personal observations and experiences during the last three years of war.

For centuries the people of China have been taught by their sages to believe that men live not by bread alone, but must, for the existence of the nation, retain at all costs the accumulated experiences of the past. They have learned to look to an educated leadership, which would serve the nation with its learning, and by that service bring glory to the family and the community from which it had sprung. It is largely due to this tradition that the torch of learning has never lacked a bearer and the work of education has never stopped, whatever the fortunes of the nation.

This proud educational tradition of the Chinese goes as far back as the millennium before the Christian era. When life was simpler and education could be acquired by reading the books of one's father, educational activities could go on uninterruptedly even in time of war.

Then a tutor and a few books were all that was necessary to carry on the task of educating the rising generation. But for the last half a century, China's educational system has been modelled on that of the West. Education has now ceased to be a simple business. School buildings are more elaborate. Equipment is more expensive and less movable. Instead of a single tutor with a handful of pupils, we have a sizable staff with a considerable number of young people under its care. Such an educational machinery and its work can easily be disrupted or interfered with by any serious social or political disturbance. Hence, when the Japanese invasion began in 1937 and China adopted the policy of resistance, one of the problems confronting the government was how to carry on its educational program in face of a major war.

The fighting in Shanghai in 1932 and still more the bitter experiences of our people in Manchuria since 1931 are enough to teach us that the enemy has no particular love for our educational institutions. Whenever he has a chance, schools are the first objects he attacks and destroys. This being the case, the problem of conserving our educational strength is a stupendous one. As the war continues and as our troops are drawing the enemy more and more into the interior, educational activities cannot possibly stop and wait until the end of the war. There is also the more serious problem of planning for the education of the people behind the enemy lines. The enemy would certainly attempt to exploit the young minds in the occupied areas. In face of this possibility, should we move the schools and the school population with them? Or should we close the schools and send the youth of school age to the front line? China is not a wealthy nation. Every cent at the disposal of the government ought to be used in the prosecution of the war which is being fought for the very existence of the nation. Should we allow the young minds to remain fallow as long as the war lasts, or should we by hook or by crook endeavour to continue our educational work under the most difficult and most baffling conditions? The story of Chinese education for the last three years of war is an epic which the Chinese people will remember for generations to come.

Migration of Colleges

For what has happened to Chinese education since the summer of 1937 much is to be attributed to the mellowness of Chinese civilization, the far-sighted policy of the Chinese Government and the genuine peace-loving character of the Chinese people. To take the institutions of higher education alone, out of 108 universities and colleges which were in existence before that year, only 14 have been able to keep open either in foreign concessions or in cities already occupied by enemy troops like Peiping, where the institutions are able to continue operation under the auspices of foreign missions. Seventy-seven of the original number of these institutions have moved to the interior and are operating as refugee colleges, which include national, private and Christian colleges and universities.

For anyone who has had the unpleasant experience of having to move an institution, it is no fun at all. Buildings are of course immovable, all the furniture has to be left behind, scientific apparatus and equipment are mostly too fragile or too clumsy to be moved, books have to be packed and they are heavy. In time of war, transport is difficult and where it is possible, the cost involved in moving a whole library or even a small part of it is almost prohibitive. Yet to move a college or a university without its books and its teaching equipment would be useless. Their replacement in the interior, when the enemy has blockaded most of the seaports, is costly, even if it is possible. Then, there is the question of moving the staff, their families and students. Each of the 77 institutions has on average 100 faculty and staff members, and each member has a family of four or five. The average student body moving with the institution numbers about 300. This rough, low estimate (and we can only give an estimate, as actual statistics are not available) means the moving of 38,500 faculty and staff members and their families and the same number of students, making a total of 77,000. This figure does not include the elementary schools.

Why should we have moved at all? Certainly not for the sake of college property, most of which is immovable anyway. But the experiences in Shanghai, Soochow, Nanking and other places during the early months of the war had sufficiently shown that Chinese women and children were not safe behind the enemy lines. The Japanese army has no love for the intellectual and student classes. The mental agony, not to say the physical suffering, would be unbearable, if these people should remain after a city had been occupied. To sacrifice human life and still more to sacrifice human personality for no great purpose is indefensible.

Friends abroad often ask why these students do not join the army or do other kinds of war work in defense of the country instead of migrating to the interior for education. Does the government not need the technical knowledge of the university professors in time of war? Yes and no. Before 1937, China was not highly organized for war. It is not easy to turn our productive efforts overnight into preparation for war. Most of our ammunition and war equipment is imported. University professors do not readily turn into specialists in factories. Yet many have joined war service groups and large numbers of students have enlisted in the army and the air force. But one thing China does not lack is man power. The government considers it too costly in the long run to send all the students to the front line; it takes years to bring them up the university level and only 0.01 of one percent of the total population are university students. Should they all be massacred in this war, there would be a serious gap in the intellectual life of the country after the war, when reconstruction work will tax the talents of the nation to its utmost, as experience in England and France after the last European War has sufficiently shown. Our watchword at present is "resistance to make the reconstruction of the nation possible." If reconstruction is lost sight of in our resistance, we would be defeating our own purpose. The great task of modernizing China, which was begun not long before the war, must be completed after the fighting, and this needs men and women of modern training, training which requires years and which must not be suspended or too seriously interrupted. Mainly for this reason institutions of higher learning have moved into the interior, not running away from the war but carrying out a part of the national program of resistance for the sake of national reconstruction. The cost is heavy and the suffering great, but it is only part of the cost of the war for self-defense and self-preservation.

Just before the war broke out, there were 108 institutions of higher learning. Of these, 42 were universities (each with at least 3 faculties), 34 colleges and 32 vocational schools. They may be classified as follows:

	National	Provincial	Private	Total
Universities	16	7	19	42
Colleges	5	8	21	34
Vocational Schools	6	16	10	32

As soon as the war broke out, the institutions in the coastal provinces and in the lower and mid-Yangtze Valley were threatened. Even before the cities in those areas were actually occupied by enemy troops, it was difficult to carry on any educational work when air raids happened frequently day and night. Yet some of the institutions continued to operate under those trying conditions until removal became imperative.

As a consequence of the ruthless air raids and atrocities committed by enemy troops after the occupation of the cities on the coast and the lower and mid-Yangtze Valley, the loss in educational buildings and teaching equipment is incalculable. Records and manuscripts were destroyed, buildings burnt and some of the precious, rare books became a part of the enemy's loot. Unfortunately, 40% of the colleges and universities, tax-supported and otherwise, were in the cities of Shanghai, Peiping, Nanking and Canton, which within a year and a half after the outbreak of hostilities were all occupied; and 42 institutions had to choose between moving into the interior or operating under foreign protection and serious handicaps. It is difficult to judge whether the suffering in choosing the former alternative was greater than the agony involved in choosing the latter.

But the moving of the institutions of higher learning into the interior is not a misfortune. They have moved into areas which were culturally backward. The diffusion of learning and technical ideas has helped to hasten the modernization of the interior. Educational standards and efficiency of the lower schools in those areas are bound to improve with the coming of the higher institutions. College and university students, as well as their professors and lecturers, mostly brought up in large cities along the coast, come into contact with life in the backward parts of the country and learn to appreciate from first-hand experience the problems confronting the Chinese nation. Many of the professors are forced by their environment to tackle new problems, the solutions to which are not to be found in books written for Western consumption or to be gathered from lecture notes brought back from class-rooms in American or European universities. Simpler and less adequate equipment is not a total disadvantage for, because of this, teaching may become more interesting and more fruitful.

But although the government has done everything possible to mitigate the difficulties of students struggling to carry on their studies in time of war, the situation still remains serious and will become increasingly so as the war continues. Many of the young people have had to migrate to Free China leaving behind them their parents and older relatives in the occupied areas. Their families have lost their incomes and are therefore unable to support them. Prices keep on rising. The food-bill alone in many places is prohibitive. It is remarkable that even under these circumstances, the total enrolment in 91 institutions of higher learning in the spring of 1938 was 74 per cent of the total enrolment of 108 institutions immediately before the outbreak of hostilities. During the year 1938, six more institutions were reopened and the total enrolment in 97 institutions increased to 95 per cent of the pre-war enrolment. There were 102 institutions under operation in 1939, but statistics are still not available for this year. This best illustrates the undaunted spirit of Chinese higher education and the determination of both the Chinese Government and the Chinese people not to allow the enemy to break through their cultural front. Our resistance is stern and we are confident that ultimate victory will be ours. We keep on training our youth so that when the war is over, we may be in a position to carry out our program of reconstruction. As the war goes on and the government needs more and more trained men for its various activities, our desire is to try to supply the demand by keeping our educational home-fires burning.

Use of Unemployed Teachers

However, in spite of all the efforts made by the government and private groups interested in education, a few institutions have been forced to close down, while those able to operate have had to reduce their staff and expenses. Large numbers of college and university teachers have had to join the ranks of the unemployed. The government first faced this problem shortly after the autumn of 1937. The Ministry of Education has all unemployed teachers registered and they are given work to do as: (1) Editors of the Mass Movement or the Youth Literature Movement. (2) Translators of books in the National Translation and Editorial Bureau. (3) Temporary teachers in institutions continuing to operate, with salaries paid by the Ministry, and (4) District Directors of activities to promote education in backward places. Teachers who formerly held the rank of college professors are given a subsidy of $100 to $120 a month, according to local living conditions, while those who were formerly college lecturers or teachers in vocational schools are given a subsidy of $50 a month. Reports up to July 1938, a year after the outbreak of the war, showed that 447 of college and university teachers were receiving such help from the government.

There is also the problem of the refugee students who have fled from the invading army and have had neither work nor money to support themselves in strange places far away from home. The government, through the Ministry of Education, has come to their rescue. Some of them have been placed in different kinds of war work, according to their age and previous training. Others are paid their traveling expenses to go to the institutions to which they originally belonged, but from which they have become separated by long distance. Still others are being sent to institutions nearby as refugee or "guest" students.

These refugee students, however, and many others have to get financial support to stay in school, since their families are either cut off from them in occupied areas or unable to give them full support in wartime. The government gives them loans to pay for their food, varying from seven to fourteen dollars a month. In the academic year of 1937—1938, 4,256 students received these loans. The number increased to 5,372 in the year 1938—1939, and to 6,384 in 1939—1940. This means that approximately 13.5% of the students in colleges and universities are being helped by the government.

Assistance to Students Abroad

The government also has in mind the students studying abroad. Naturally they, too, have been affected by the war in the income they used to receive from home. Many of them were actually stranded financially in foreign countries. In the year 1938—1939, there were in North America alone 1,872 Chinese students in 313 institutions. Many of these students were privately supported and their income from China was affected both by the unfavourable exchange and by the reduced financial strength of their families. The government gave them $700 Chinese currency each, either for traveling expenses to come home or to tide over their difficulties for three months until they could make the necessary readjustments. Three hundred of the students abroad have received such financial aid from the government.

Since 1938 Chinese students have not been permitted to go abroad for study. The government issues student passports only to those who go to foreign universities for military science, medicine or engineering. Several years before the war, the Ministry of Education had already issued an order that students should go abroad only for post-graduate work. With the marked improvement of colleges in China in almost every line of university study, it is really throwing money away to send young students abroad for undergraduate studies. They ought to have their university training first in China and go to foreign countries only for special studies when they have already made up their minds what their special interests are and where they may get the best training for the work they want to do afterwards. To go abroad for the sake of the prestige of having been abroad is sheer folly, and in time of war it ought to be stopped, especially when that prestige is rapidly evaporating. Even under present war conditions, many of our colleges and universities are still able to give our young people as good an education in many lines as may be expected from the average university in the West. The loss of Chinese cultural background for a student going abroad before his intellectual maturity more than counter-balances whatever advantages he may get from travel and contact with another civilization. The war has brought afresh to the attention of our government the necessity of altering our policy of sending students abroad in large numbers.

Another effect of the war on higher education is the combination of colleges and universities under government auspices and with government support. Peking University, Tsing Hua University, formerly in Peiping, and Nankai University, formerly in Tientsin, were combined and moved from the North, first to Changsha; and, as the war continued and as the Central China region was being threatened, they moved again to Kunming and are now operating as a combined institution under the name of the National Southwest Union University. Similarly, other national universities moved to Shensi in Northwest China from Peiping and combined to form the present National Northwest Union University. A new engineering college has come into existence as the result of the amalgamation of three engineering schools. So also have three medical schools combined to operate in the interior, remote from the war front. These combinations, all for the good of higher education in China, would never have been thought of, still less brought about, if not for the war.

It is during this period of military activities and tension that six new teachers' colleges have been established. In former years there were five higher normal schools, which trained teachers for the secondary schools. Later, these higher normal schools, except the one in Peiping, were either closed or turned into a department of a university. Secondary school teachers have been trained by colleges and universities. Shortly before the war, the Ministry of Education ordered that to qualify as teachers in secondary schools, students must have done a certain amount of work in educational subjects in the universities. In 1938, a new plan for the training of secondary school teachers was introduced by the Ministry of Education. According to this plan, the training of secondary school teachers is to be the responsibility and right of the government alone. Of the six new teachers' colleges, five are attached to national universities and the sixth is to be an independent institution in Hunan. All the schools of education and departments of education in the universities or colleges (government supported or otherwise) have been closed down except two in private universities and one in a provincial normal school. This indicates the policy of the government to keep, as far as possible, all education below university level in its own hands. It is more than an attempt at the standardization of secondary education and raising of the standard thereof, which is necessary and desirable: it is really a step towards centralized control of secondary schools. This is possible only in time of war, when the people in general and the educators in particular are willing to support the government in its efforts to create a united front in our war of resistance. Nothing shows more conclusively than this, that China's intelligentsia is solidly behind the government in the war.

New Curricula

It is during this war also that the government has been able to promulgate and enforce prescribed curricula for all the departments in colleges and universities. Formerly the institutions of higher learning were practically free to teach whatever they liked, except that there must be a lecture a week throughout the year in the Party Principles of the Kuomintang, physical and health education throughout the four years for all students, one year of military training for two hours a week for men and an equivalent number of hours for first-aid classes for women before graduation. No matter how one may regard these requirements, they have not interfered with the liberty of the universities in their experimentation with university courses. There have been, of course, abuses of this liberty, but for institutions which aimed at high standards and good training for the students and did their work honestly, this freedom was the best that could be desired.

The government is determined to maintain a high standard in higher education and even to raise the standard wherever possible. For many years there have been government examinations, which students must pass before they can graduate from middle schools. These examinations, more than anything else, have been instrumental in bringing about an approximately uniform standard for the middle schools throughout the country and have been conducive to the improvement of secondary education.

Hitherto, the standards in the colleges and universities have been far from uniform. The government has been wanting for years to effect some improvements. But not until a year ago had the college and university courses anything like a recognized standard. This year the government is encouraging students to participate in competitive examinations in the various subjects taught in the colleges and universities, and students from institutions of higher learning in the same region compete for honor and prizes. It is interesting to watch how this will work out. It is beyond doubt that these examinations, if properly conducted, will produce wholesome effect upon higher education in the country. What we hope is that there may be standardization without regimentation, for regimentation in higher education is deadening. There must be room for variation and experimentation, especially when the whole program of modern education is still so new in China. Only by a long process of trial error can the right policy and method be found for higher education in this country with its age-long culture and its special and varied needs.

Tutorial System

Another wartime innovation in the educational field is the introduction of the tutorial system for middle and higher schools as promulgated by the Ministry of Education in the spring of 1939. The following is a translation of some of the regulations governing tutorial work:

1. In order to improve the present system of education, which has

over-emphasized the imparting of mere knowledge, and to bring about a more intimate relationship between teachers and students the Ministry of Education intends to adopt the old tutorial system and follow the practice of Oxford and Cambridge Universities in our middle and higher schools.

2. Every class in a school is to be divided into certain groups. Each group should be composed of 5 to 10 students, with a full-time teacher appointed by the principal to take charge of it. The principal should also designate either the head of the tutorial department or the disciplinary department to be in charge of the tutorial and disciplinary business of the whole school.

3. The tutor should see to the mind, character, progress in learning, mental and physical development of the individual student and give instruction and advice to each student so as to ensure his proper development and to cultivate a wholesome character.

4. Beside individual instruction, the tutor should avail himself of leisure hours and holidays to gather his own group of students to hold meeting or picnics, etc. for group life instruction.

Emphasis on Vocational Training

The war has certainly focused the attention of educational authorities on the importance of vocational training, which has perhaps been weakest feature of modern education in China. During the last three years, however, nine vocational schools supported by the Central Government and directly under the control of the Ministry of Education have been started. The subjects taught include paper-manufacturing, tanning, dyeing, sericulture, electro-communication, automobile engineering, husbandry and agricultural economics. Accounting, veterinary science and sanitary administration are also taught. This is intended to promote light industries and to develop national resources to meet the demands created by the war.

The vocational schools are to have longer courses without, however, taking more of the students' time. Formerly, courses of the vocational schools, being of "junior college" standard, to use an

American expression, were of two or three years, and they only admitted graduates from senior middle schools, which meant twelve years of schooling before vocational training began. In 1938, the Ministry of Education introduced a new scheme by which vocational schools may take in graduates from junior middle schools after six years of primary and three years of secondary education. They then have five years of vocational training. This longer specialized training ought to produce better results. One difficulty, however, is to expect pupils of fifteen years of age to decide on the special line of training they wish to take. By giving more time to fundamental subjects in the five years spent in vocational schools and by gradually increasing the special training, we hope this difficulty may be obviated.

According to the Chinese system of educational administration, schools of secondary grade are financed and administered locally (either by the provincial, municipal or district government), although they are under the general supervision of the Ministry of Education of the Central Government through the Provincial Commissioner of Education appointed by the Ministry. When war hits a province, the provincial, municipal or district secondary schools move behind the Chinese lines and try to resume activities. These have been able to take care of a number of pupils, but many families migrate from the occupied areas to the interior provinces, which are beyond the reach of the enemy but which have not been developed educationally. Thousands of boys and girls of secondary schools age have migrated to inland cities and towns without their families. They have been sent to Free China by their parents for safety and for the continuance of their education. Secondary schools in Free China, particularly in cities and towns only a short distance behind the Chinese lines, are therefore overcrowded with these refugee students. A few of the schools supported by private sources, especially the Christian middle schools, have found it possible to move to the interior and are partly able to meet the great demand created by the situation. But such schools are few and the demand is increasing. To meet this crying need, the Central Government has opened thirteen National Middle Schools in various localities in Honan, Szechwan,

Shensi, Kansu, West Hunan, Kweichow and Kiangsi. The total enrolment of these national middle schools is 30,000, according to the latest available report.

Education in Occupied Areas

Mass migration of the Chinese people before an invading army is a phenomenon not unknown in Chinese history, but the present one is unprecedented in magnitude. The great bulk of the people, however, have to remain in the occupied areas. Many are unable to move for various reasons, economic necessity being only one of them. Some children of secondary school age may be fortunate enough to find schools a short distance behind the Chinese lines and thus continue their education. In spite of enemy restrictions put on the movement of the people from the occupied areas, nothing can prevent the ingenious and resourceful Chinese from finding ways and means to overcome these obstacles and to send the young people away. Yet the fact remains that many boys and girls, particularly those of elementary school age, too young to leave their families, are forced to go without education as long as enemy occupation lasts. Some of them may receive private instruction from their own parents at home. The old method of a tutor taking only a few pupils in the home may be revived. If this could be done effectively without molestation by the enemy, we may mark time in this way in the education of our young in occupied areas until the war comes to an end. There seems to be no alternative. It is inconceivable to have organized education under the influence and control of a hostile force, the whole intent and purpose of which is to destroy the national spirit of the Chinese people. We may deplore the fact that children do not have the opportunity even to learn to read and write. But to learn to read and write is in itself no education, nor is it education merely to acquire the ability to earn a livelihood. Centuries ago our sages taught us better. We must try to prevent at any cost the exploitation of the minds of our young people by the enemy, under the name of education. Exploitation of human minds is contrary to the fundamental principles of education. The only way in the occupied areas then is not to attempt any organized education but to try to teach the young in the home and keep the national ideals alive there. When the children are older, old enough to get into Free China and breathe fresh air again, the government will care for and give them opportunities to continue their education. For this reason, the Ministry of Education has modified a regulation of old standing governing the admission of students into schools by examination without the graduation certificate customarily required from the lower schools. If this scheme is properly carried out and the people compelled by circumstances to remain in the occupied areas cooperate with the government, as we are sure they will, a whole generation of school children will be spared the poisonous influence of the enemy, whose aim is to break up the national life of the Chinese people by infecting them at the root.

The education of the Chinese people during this life-and-death struggle is, indeed, the cultural front of our resistance against foreign invasion. Space does not permit any lengthy account of the social and mass education which is sweeping over the country. The wall newspapers, the war pictures, the news cartoons, the broadcasting of war news, the teaching of war songs—all this is of the nature of patriotic education and has its beneficial effects. The present article deals exclusively with formal education in wartime China, and it is significant that during three years of war so much has been accomplished in face of baffling and overwhelming difficulties.

What Makes a College Christian[*]

FRANCIS C. M. WEI

THIS is a problem of paramount importance for our college and this present paper deals with it from the point of view of college administration.

As stated for many years in our college catalog and as it was presented to the Ministry of Education for the registration of the college, the purpose of the college is "to provide for the youth of China a college education of high standards with a view to developing character and intellectual capacity in the students in order that they may be loyal and useful citizens of China and may be prepared to aid in building up and strengthening their respective communities along moral, intellectual, physical and humanitarian lines, and to promote the general purpose had in mind by each of the several missionary societies which founded the Institution." This statement was formulated by the Board of Founders in New York with legal advice and was translated literally into Chinese for presentation to the government for recognition, and it was with this statement of our purpose that the college has been registered as a university under the Chinese Ministry of Education.

Before the question of the registration with the government was raised fifteen years ago, no one ever asked explicitly about the purpose of the college, which was a Christian college founded as part of the Christian movement in China. As far as the government is concerned the college is an educational institution and its educational efficiency and

---

[*] Last term the Hua Chung Faculty Christian Fellowship held its first meeting of the year in the form of an afternoon conference on the general topic "What makes a college Christian?" Three short papers by President Wei, Professor Anderson and Dean Hwang, introduced the subject from the points of view of administration, religious activities, and general educational results respectively, and these papers are presented herewith.

standards that concern the government. Along this line we comply entirely with government regulations. But let us note particularly the last clause in the statement of our purpose which reads:"to promote the general purpose had in mind by each of the several missionary societies. " What does this imply?

It implies that the college is founded as a part of the Christian movement in China to spread Christianity among the Chinese, to supply the churches with clerical and lay leadership for the various departments of church activities, to help to formulate an intelligent and reasonable policy for the program of Christianizing life in China, both individual and social, as an integral part of the promotion of Christian culture in the world, and to try to think through problems confronting Christendom in the present day world. Our function is both ministerial and prophetic. We have to help to carry on the work of the churches in China and to lead Christian thinking in the country.

In fulfilling this function we have many difficulties, of which government regulations for educational institutions on private support are not the most serious one. Indeed, according to these regulations, religious exercises may be held in the college, through attendance must be voluntary, and religious subjects may be taught on the elective basis. Before we received the order from the government to enforce the new curricula for the different departments in the college, our difficulties were slight, except for those few people who believe in compulsory worship, which is almost a contradiction in terms, and in required courses in religious instruction for every student. Government regulation or no, we would not have these for the sake of genuine worship and honest learning. But the new curricula, uniform for all colleges and universities in the country, leave little room for even elective religious courses. This certainly curtails our academic liberty. Yet, even with these limitations we can still carry on a full-fledged Christian college and fulfill our religious function. Our Christian character should not be seriously affected so long as we have a faculty which will be willing to make the necessary efforts in presenting the subject matter from the Christian point of view, and this we believe will not interfere at all with the efficiency of our teaching or with our academic standards. When the question of government regulations for the registration of private Christian educational institutions was under discussion fifteen years ago, my personal feeling was that as long as we were free to select our faculty and staff, we would be able still to carry on our work in Christian education. Give me a Christian faculty, competent for the work in teaching and in research, and let government regulations come as they may. We have nothing to fear.

But this is the very crux of the situation. We have at present in China as many as twelve Christian colleges, not to mention the many theological seminaries and other professional schools under Christian auspices. If we should try to maintain a high academic standard, do we have enough Christian scholars in the several lines of learning to staff these institutions? Only people who are ignorant of the situation in the country or indifferent to academic standards would answer in the affirmative.

NEED FOR MISSIONARIES

For this reason we must, for many years to come, appeal to the older churches abroad to send us an adequate number of missionaries to teach in the Christian colleges in China. We need missionaries as teachers because we are not able to find a sufficient number of mature scholars among the Chinese Christians, but we need missionaries who are well trained in their subjects and who are coming to teach not only for the sake of teaching but with a distinct Christian and missionary purpose. In various statements that I have made, I put it dogmatically that a Christian college needs to have approximately one-third of its faculty missionaries, and the rest ought to be, as far as possible, Christian scholars.

We are not unmindful of the fact that in some cases it is entirely a matter of name whether a man is Christian or not, but it means something if a man should call himself a Christian. He could not openly oppose Christianity so long as he is calling himself a member of the church and in that way identifying himself with the Christian movement.

Under the present circumstances it is of course impossible to have the faculty of any college entirely Christian, perhaps it is in some ways undesirable. Some non-Christian members with an earnest purpose and an exemplary personality may serve as a challenge to those who call themselves Christians. As a college administrator, I have no hesitation and a clear conscience in appointing non-Christian scholars to our teaching positions with the only proviso that they are not against us in our efforts to make the Institution Christian. This is of course a negative statement. The positive side of it is that every Christian member of the faculty and staff must be conscious of his duty to do everything possible to maintain the Christian character of our work. I sometimes find it difficult to make the choice in appointment between a Christian man who is a poor scholar and a good scholar who is not a professed Christian. We have to bear constantly in mind that our Christian influence is limited if we should make a poor show in the classroom in an educational institution. We have to be good teachers before we can exert any Christian influence on the students. There are of course exceptions, but this is a good working rule.

FINANCIAL SUPPORT

Another problem that confronts the Christian college at present and will do so in the future is its financial support. Higher education is an expensive enterprise and will become more so as time goes by. Standards have to be raised and efficiency has to be increased, the faculties have to be strengthened and the library and equipment in other lines have to be improved. All these cost money. It is futile to mention any figure as an adequate budget for a college with three faculties and even a limited program under each faculty, as in our own case. In my personal reckoning based upon administrative experience, a college of our size and scope needs at least $300,000 national currency before its depreciation, and this is a large sum of money, quite beyond the financial ability of the churches in China. And no one knows how long the churches abroad will be able to give us the necessary subventions, especially when the world is going through a trying period as it is at the present moment.

No far-sighted administrator of a Christian college can fail to worry about this. Where are we going to get the support if some of our present resources should dry up? Institutions of higher learning cannot depend upon fees taken from the students. A Christian educational institution that is self-supporting has to be looked into carefully. There must be something wrong with it. Some of the self-supporting Christian institutions ought to be closed. Shall we look to the government for larger and larger subsidies? If we should follow this path, we should end by becoming entirely a government institution, and certainly that is not our desire. There may be foundations in China and abroad from which we could get financial aids, but he who controls the purse strings controls the policy. Many an educational institution founded originally with a Christian purpose has become secularized when it depended mainly upon secular money for its maintenance and expansion. We have many examples, particularly in America and they are not to be imitated. Of course it may be asked what constitutes secular money. My answer is, secular money is money given and spent for a purpose in which God is left out. Even a Christian college like our own may use government money as we have been doing for many years, provided the receiving of it will not interfere with our Christian character; we may use any kind of money if it does not carry with it the condition that we should modify our Christian program in receiving it. Even alumni support is not always an unmixed blessing for a Christian college. Universities in England and in continental Europe do not depend upon alumni support. A graduate of a university in those lands gives to an educational institution not because it is his Alma Master but because it is an enterprise worth supporting. That spirit ought to be encouraged and commended. We hope that our graduates will support the college more and more in the future, but we hope at the same time that they will support it as a Christian institution worthy of their generosity, not only because of its educational efficiency but also because of its Christian influence.

It will be a long time, however, before we can begin to depend upon contributions and donations from our graduates to maintain the college. An endowment fund seems to be the logical solution, but in raising such a fund we have to see it that no string is attached to make the Institution and its work less Christian.

With these difficulties in view our policy must be a limited program with high standards and a limited enrolment to assure on the one hand that our work will be adequately supported financially and on the other hand that we can touch every individual student before he leaves the walls of the college to represent us in the wild world.

Before I come to a close in this paper I must mention one more problem which deserves our close attention and that is student supply. It seems almost absurd that here in China we have Christian primary schools and Christian middle schools and Christian colleges, and that they are not working together for the same aim in the same program. We need statistics to show how many of the children finishing the course in the Christian primary schools are going to the Christian middle schools, what percentage of the Christian middle school population is Christian and what percentage of their graduates go to the Christian colleges. We cannot have a Christian college unless a majority of the students have previously received some kind of Christian training. Four years in the college are not long enough for us to cultivate Christian attitudes. It would be a waste of time and energy for the Christian middle schools to have their graduates go to non-Christian colleges and for Christian colleges to get the majority of their students from non-Christian middle schools. The two must work together if the result of the Christian training of the one is to be conserved and the work of the other to be efficient. The whole program of Christian education must be thought through and revised.

I am not going to anticipate the papers that are to follow, but I must add one brief word before I am through. Teaching and research, in a Christian college like ours, must go hand in hand, and our teachers in every subject ought to bear in mind the Christian purpose. In some cases we ought to have research professorship to tackle problems of which the world needs Christian solutions.

The Future of Christian Education in China

(An article by Dr. Francis C. M. Wei in August, 1943, and subsequently published in Szechwan, China)

No apology for Christian education is now needed. Take Christianity where it is strong, where it exerts an influence upon the life and thinking of the people in China, and one will find invariably a group of men and women who have been through Christian schools and who are now serving as church ministers, teachers, doctors or church wardens. These people have learned their ideals, their devotion to the church and their love of God in their school days. Look casually into China's "Who's Who", unreliable as that test may be, and the thing that strikes one's eye is the number of men who have been one time or another under the influence of Christian education; or talk to any unbiased intelligent person in the government, in the industries, or in business in the country and see whether there is any adverse criticism of the educational work of the churches, by-and-large. The present crisis is an acid test for Christian education. Wherever a church is strong in any important centre, wherever Christianity is able to weather the storm and look with any measure of confidence and optimism into the future, there the church has for the last generation invested personnel and money in Christian education of all grades. The strength of a church in China is in direct proportion to its faith in its educational work for the last thirty years.

There is no space in a short article to recount the history of Christian education for the last century. It had a humble beginning. Starting as a feeble attempt to meet the needs of the time, it has steadily grown to its present magnitude. The interpretative Statistical Survey of the World Mission of the Christian Church, published in 1938, gives under Table IV the following figures for China (Manchuria included):

Table IV pp. 24-28

Elementary Schools	2,887	Colleges	14
		Total students	6,151
Total pupils	182,110	Med. Colleges	7
Middle Schools	270	Total students	666
Total pupils	45,482		
Special Schools	118	Kindergartens	113
Total pupils	4,348	Total pupils	5,815
Bible Tr. Schools	141	Teacher Tr. Schools	58
Total pupils	4,440	Total students	2,639
Theological Schools	32		
Total students	1,032		

These are no insignificant figures. They represent the impact of Christian education upon the changing China whose fate is still in the balance. They represent what Christians in China and abroad try to contribute to this old nation trying to become young again. As one writer has aptly put it:

"And human lives behind the figures show
The Master moving in His Church below."

But when we turn from the past and look beyond the present into the future can we be sure that all has been well with Christian education in China? Christian educators are now groaning under government curricula and government regulations. For the moment leave alone the question whether such complaints are warranted or not. But there was a time, and it was not too brief nor too far remote, when Christian schools and colleges were absolutely free, free to follow any education policy, to adopt any system, to have any curriculum, and to enforce any discipline, or to have none of these at all. From this period of experimentation, or rather of hit-and-miss, have we inherited any teaching methods adapted to the needs of the Chinese, any new curriculum rooted in the soil, any new ideals that can stand the test of time? We had perhaps a little better discipline than some of the schools in the same city. Our English was better taught, perhaps at the expense of some other subjects equally as important from the education point of view. Many of our schools at present would still rest content with such achievements. A primary school is deemed flourishing if its pupils fill the classrooms during weekdays and the adjacent church on Sunday. Any other consideration seems immaterial. The middle schools charge high fees and pay low salaries to the teaching staff. Enrolments are rushed up as far as conditions allow, regardless of educational efficiency, for self-support is the dominating criterion of success. Formerly the colleges imitated their prototypes in the United States. Now their ambition is to be like a national university. There is the cry for vocational education, for that is the fashion of the day. Whether we have the resources or the personnel for this type of school is not seriously considered, and why vocational education under Christian auspices at all has been hardly thought through. There is an apparent lack of consistent policy for Christian education in the new day. We can no longer hit-and-miss, and so we blindly follow.

We can hear the impatient rejoinder that from the very first the aim of Christian education has been evangelistic, and it remains so still. Agreed, but we need a broader view of evangelism and must explore its implications. Do we measure the success of evangelism by the number of baptisms recorded or by the total impact of Christianity upon the life and thought of the people? Is the Christian religion to become a creative force in China by merely increasing the number of Chinese Christian from year to year, or by transforming the culture of the nation? Is our educational work instrumental in furnishing the Chinese society with a new leaven? Is the Christian spirit penetrating Chinese life through its Christian schools and colleges, penetrating it deeply and effectively enough as to become a power working from within? Christian education must have such aims.

With these aims in view, have we been making scholarly studies of Chinese life in the rural districts as well as in the cities, Chinese social, political and economic institutions, Chinese philosophical ideas and religious aspirations, the Chinese conception of the good life, and the

Chinese conviction of human destiny? If instead of doing these things we have been in the Christian colleges busy in turning out more technicians to grow more grain and raise bigger hogs, to build wider roads and to construct stronger bridges, to keep more readable accounts, and to compile more impressive statistics, even to manufacture more indelible ink and more hygienic soap, then, important as these activities may be to the welfare of the community and of the nation, Christian education has missed its mark, which is to re-make human life by the light of truth from the source of the Christian religion. It is not advocated here that Christian education should be exclusively concerned with only those activities, which come directly under the auspices of the church. As the present writer wrote in 1938 for the Interpretative Statistical Survey of the World Mission:

> "Social workers with a Christian motive, journalists with a Christian standard, and writers with a Christian vision can do wonders, and the church must have a share in training them. We desire to see Christian principles applied to business, industry, and politics. Let there be those institutions in which economics, history, and political science are approached from the Christian point of view. Does the modern world suspect that Christianity and science can ever keep house together? Let the Christian church take a real interest in scientific investigation and encourage her promising young men and women to apply themselves earnestly to the pursuit of the various sciences."

But let us not fail to see the wood for the trees or lose sight of the end because of the alluring means. Christian education can achieve success only by fixing its eyes steadfastly and with a singleness of heart upon its ultimate goal.

And it must sit down to count the cost, lest it should have laid the foundation and find itself unable to finish the building. Christians are to lend their helping hand to every good work, but it is undoubtedly beyond the ability of the Christian church to meet all the educational needs of the nation. We should do only those things which we can do best and which are essential to our cause. In education we are not to duplicate the government efforts, not even to supplement them. We have our definite, vital duty which if not performed by ourselves will not be done by others. We must teach our children our Christian faith and help other children as far as possible to catch a glimpse of it. We want to prepare our youth for a courageous, robust, and dynamic Christian life and for the propagation of the same in the community in which they live. We desire our young men and young women to search unflinchingly for God's truth and to interpret it wisely and unfeignedly into the language of the modern world. This we must seek to do in Christian education for otherwise it will not be done. It is our bounden duty. Upon its proper performance hangs the success of Christian education in the future. In doing it we shall bear witness to our Master, witness far more worthwhile than vaunting our own petty personal experiences, and in doing it we may if need be have to accept even martyrdom, and not the martyrdom of people who stumble into prison for irresponsible remarks on current events which they themselves regret later. This should be the guiding principle of our Christian education in China for the future. But how is it to be carried out with or limited resources both in money and in energy?

Let us first take the Christian primary schools. Should we endeavour to maintain the 2,887 schools with the total enrolment of 182,110 pupils as reported in 1938? Undoubtedly everything that the churches can do towards meeting the overwhelming need of primary education in China is a noble contribution. Three-quarters of the Chinese children between the ages of six and twelve who ought to be in school and are required by law to attend school are not in school. There are not enough schools in this country for them all. And three-quarters of these children is approximately 30,000,000 children. Imagine, every year 5,000,000 children miss the chance of starting in school and lose the opportunity of a school education. In ten years the number of Chinese illiterates from this one cause alone would equal in number the population of Great Britain and in twenty-five years that of the United States.

But in Japan there have been no Christian primary schools for a number of years. In Turkey and Mexico government regulations have ruled Christian primary schools out of existence. A tidal wave of nationalism is surging all over the world. Unless the present war leaves the nations with an entirely new educational outlook, we may well expect that what has already happened in Japan, Turkey, and Mexico will come to pass soon in China. The ideal of universal education of all children in a uniform public school system makes a strong appeal to the national sentiment. The government will spare no effort in realizing it.

It may, however, be some years before this ideal is realized. In the meantime groups of private citizens may be permitted to operate primary schools under strict government regulations and supervision. It would then be one form of Christian service. The local Christian community ought to rise to the challenge. But whatever may be the case, whether there be Christian primary schools or not, the local churches must give more-and-more attention to the religious education of their children. Sunday schools and other forms of church educational activities can be made attractive and effective enough to do the work of Christian education without any conflict with government regulations, unless religious teaching to children even outside of the school is prohibited, which is not likely in China.

The question of Christian secondary education presents a rather different appearance. Statistics of the Roman Catholic Church in China are not available to the writer at the moment. We have to take the non-Roman churches alone. There are approximately six hundred thousand baptized Chinese Christians, less than two-tenths of one percent of the whole population. These churches take care of only about one and five-tenths percent of all the primary school children in the country, already ten times their proportional share in primary education, but nine percent of the secondary students are in Christian middle schools, proportionally six times as strong as Christian primary education in the country.

Neither the Chinese educators nor the Chinese authorities can ignore this fact or take it lightly. If the Christian middle school should go out of existence, there would be a serious gap in the Chinese educational system, perhaps not to be filled for a long time. In the secondary field, too, there is less plausibility for a strictly uniform public school system, and it will be much longer before the government will be in a position to provide for all children who desire or need a secondary education, when the number finishing the primary school is increasing annually. There is therefore likely to be a more permanent place for private schools of this grade.

But the middle school has been the weakest link in the educational system in China, Christian or non-Christian. There was a time when some of the Christian middle schools enjoyed a reputation for the better discipline of their students, but that is rapidly becoming less true. Spurred on by the desire of a greater income from students' fees in order to achieve early self-support, the enrolment is steadily being pushed up and up until the school becomes entirely unwieldy. Teaching deteriorates, discipline slackens, and standards drop. In some of the schools Christian education becomes a mere name. They attract young spendthrifts from the rich families, and because their fees go to support the school, they determine the general tone of the school life.

We may have to bend our efforts, therefore, not necessarily to maintain all the 270 Christian middle schools in existence before 1938, but to have a few more schools better staffed, better supported, and more Christian. Self-support may be a good thing for a school to aim at, but it is a danger to secure it at the expense of the Christian character of the school and of educational efficiency. Before the war the average number of Christian students in a Christian middle school was about thirty percent of the total enrolment. Is that enough to maintain the Christian atmosphere of the school? What percentage of the graduates from the Christian middle schools go to the Christian colleges so as to conserve the Christian work done for them while in school instead of having it dissipated when these graduates drift away from Christian influence? There ought to be a more organic relation between Christian secondary education and Christian higher education if the best results are to be attained.

By-and-large, the Christian forces have not succeeded well in vocational education in China. With the present development of industry

在 the country vocational schools are difficult to run. Vocational education must be practical education, taught by men of practical experience from the industries. Such men are few and difficult to find for teaching. From the experience of other countries the best way to maintain vocational schools seems to be in connection with factories. There ought to be first Christian industries before there can be Christian vocational schools.

But the problem demands our immediate attention. Many of the Church's youth need vocational training. The very fact that in 1938 there were 45,482 pupils in the 270 Christian middle schools of whom only thirty percent were Christian, whereas there ought to be easily as many Christian boys and girls to fill all those middle schools, shows that a large number of Christian children of secondary school age were not in the Christian middle schools. One of the reasons, and perhaps the chief one, was that their families could not afford it. Vocational schools would meet their needs. As the field is new and difficult, only a few of such schools should be attempted on an experimental basis. When these prove successful, more may follow later.

As to Christian higher education, the greatest need is a clearer vision of its future. Are we building privately-endowed universities like Oxford and Cambridge in England or Harvard and Yale in the United States? If so, can we have thirteen of such in China? What is the prospect of adequate resources? Or, perhaps we are less ambitious and would be content with some thing like the denominational colleges in American. Would this be a worthwhile attempt? What surviving value would such institutions have in china, especially when our limited resources would have to be distributed among thirteen of them?

What after all is the ideal of Christian higher education? Have this clearly defined. Then, formulate our policy and devise a reasonable plan for its prosecution. Our present method of trying to muddle though is very costly, to say the least. Certainly we should not rest content to continue preparing technicians, because it is not particularly our business. Our money and energy could find better use. We seek to influence the destiny of the changing nation and of its teeming millions.

Shall we succeed by slightly improving the livelihood of a few hundreds a year? We do not want to minimize the value of the Christian colleges even as they are now. Neither the country nor the church can afford to see them disappear. But have we in Christian higher education in China achieved the greatest effectiveness with the resource available? Should we not aim at the highest possible standards in every department of university education we attempt and not be satisfied with any second best? To meet an immediate need in a given locality is not good enough. Only in this way can Christian higher education hope to be of permanent value. But above all, let us not forget our special contribution which is the Christian attitude in approaching any problem. Unless that is inculcated into our students we miss the aim for which the Christian college exists. To accomplish this we need not only better equipment for teaching and for research, not only more adequate funds to maintain our work at the highest level of efficiency, but more than anything else, a stronger faculty mainly of Chinese Christian scholarship, who know what Christian higher education is for, and who are dedicated to the great work of building God's Kingdom on earth. Given such a band of Chinese scholars, all other problems of Christian higher education will solve themselves.

The cap-stone of Christian higher education is of course, theological education. Whatever may go in Christian education, this must remain. Upon it depends the very vitality of the Christian movement in China. But it is easily the last developed part of Christian education in the country. Its teaching staff is the least indigenous; its curriculum least rooted in the Chinese soil; its standards least comparable to those in Europe and America. In how many theological colleges in the country is the Bible taught by scholars who can refer their students to the original texts and criticize these texts with original views of their own? In how many theological colleges are the courses on the interpretation of Christian teachings, generally known as systematic theology, presided over by professors who are versed not only in western Christian and philosophical thought, but are also steeped in the knowledge of Chinese philosophy and of the history and phenomenology of the Chinese religions? We need such teachers to lead and inspire the Chinese students of theology in the scientific study of the Christian religion and in its interpretation and presentation to the Chinese people. But we are still far from this goal, farther perhaps than the Chinese professors are from their own goals in Chemistry or Physics, in History or Philosophy. The goal in theological teaching is more difficult to attain, but that is no excuse for less effort on our part. To reach it, China must produce her own Christian theology. The church will be richer when this is done. Christian education in China will have missed its mark unless this is done.

Francis Cho-min Wei
Hua Chung College
August, 1943

Development of Hua Chung College after the War

PREAMBLE

While it is uncertain when the war is to come to a close, victory seems to be within sight and it may not be premature for those concerned with the future of the college to start planning now for its development after moving back to Wu Chang. For the duration of the war many of the faculty members have accepted hardships and stood loyally by the college with their eyes fixed upon the future as their only consolation. This alone is the reward they have expected and they must not be disappointed. They realize that a strong Christian college in Central China should be the part of the strategy of the Christian Movement in China. We owe it to our constituencies in China and abroad and plan for the future development of the college. We feel our responsibility in this work to those who have labored in the past in building up so far Hua Chung College and the former Christian colleges in the Central China region which have been amalgamated into it; We own to the missions and churches which have supported Christian education in the provinces of Hupeh, Hunan, Kiangsi, Western Anhwei, and Southern Honan with a population of nearly one hundred million and have been looking to us for Christian intellectual leadership; and we owe it to the whole country which we shall seek to serve in Christian Higher Education and in Christian thinking and planning in the development of the nation. We cannot shrink this responsibility.

For more than a year the Executive Committee Pro tem of the Board of Directors of the college has been considering such plans both in meetings of the committee and in their private individual thinking. The plans are now being submitted to the committee and the Senate of the college meeting together. These two bodies, one representing the Board of Directors and, through it, the Cooperating Missions, and the other the highest authorities of the college for internal administration, are, after careful deliberation, jointly presenting the plan to the Board of Founders, known as Trustees, of the college and, through it, to the Cooperating Missions, for their approval. The membership of this joint group consists of faculty members who have, every one of them spent more than ten years, some twenty, and some over thirty years, in the service of the college and they feel solemnly the responsibility laid upon them in the drawing up, and in the submitting of, this plan.

HISTORY OF THE COLLEGE

Before 1924 there were in the Central China region five Christian colleges. These were Boone University under the America Church Mission (Protestant Episcopal Church in the U. S. A.) in Wu Chang; the Lutheran College in Yiyang; Huping College, under the China Mission of the Reformed Church in the U. S. A., in Yokchow, in Wu Chang; and the College of Yale-in-China, under the Yale-in-China Association, in Changsha. At that time the London Missionary Society was also contemplating the developing of Griffith John College (Middle School for some time with a normal department) into a college.

Shortly after the Revolution in 1911, a movement was on foot to establish in the Wu Han center a private Christian university. It was initiated by a group of university men in Great Britain with Lord William Cecil as the prime mover. This was to bring into cooperation with it all the Christian forces interested in higher education in the Central China region, and the Wuhan cities were selected for its site not only because of its strategic position as one of the most important political, educational, industrial and commercial centers in the country, but also because it was foreseen even then that with the trunk lines of the railways meeting there from Peiping (then Peking) through Changsha to Canton and from Szechuen through Nanking to Shanghai and with two of the most important navigable rivers connecting with Han Kou the most prosperous ports in the country, this metropolis was destined to be the Chicago of China. Han Kou is one of the ports first opened to international trade. Its long river front and its board hinterland allow unlimited development. Across the Han river in the city of the Han Yang where Viceroy Chan Tze-tung in the last years of the 19th century chose to build the Government Iron Works and Arsenal. Opposite to Han Kou and Han Yang across the Yangtze river is Wu Chang, the capital city of the province of Hupeh where Chang Tze-tung in the first decade of the present century built the first system of modern schools and trained the first modern armies. It was in Wu Chang that the first shot of the Revolution of 1911 was fired. It was in the capture of Wu Chang in 1926 that General Chiang Kai-shek saw the beginning of his final victory in the Northern Expedition against the Tuchuens before the establishment of the present National Government. Wu Chang holds a key position in policies as well as in education and culture and its importance will be more marked in the future. Wu Chang was therefore the chosen site of the British University Movement in China.

This movement was, however, frustrated on account of the last European War, although it had reached the stage of electing Professor Soothill of Oxford as the first President and sending out to China three lectures two of whom stayed for some years to teach in Boone University and Griffith John College on the American Church Mission and London Mission support respectively.

After the war in 1921 the Mission Boards in America and Great Britain sent out to China a commission to study Christian education in the country. It was under the chairmanship of Professor Burton of Chicago University and its report published in 1922 under the titles of "Christian Education in China" made the recommendation among others that Christian higher education in the five regions of North, West, East, South, and Central China ought to be strengthened by consolidation and by the amalgamation of the existing colleges in the respective regions. This carried the conviction of all interested in Christian Higher Education in China, but its only substantial result was the establishment of Central China University in Wu Chang in 1924, Central China being the English translation of Hua Chung.

In 1924 Hua Chung had only three cooperating units. The America Church Mission placed at the disposal of the new Christian College the whole establishment of Boone University. The Wesleyan Mission closed Wealey College and sent to the Union, or federated, institution a lecturer and a small contingent of students and appropriated a sum of money for the erection of a faculty residence on the Boone campus and for the allocation to it by the American Church Mission of a building for a non-episcope hostel. The London Mission made no contribution in personal or in money but pledged its support. Thus Hua Chung was formally organized.

The Northern Expedition was started from the South in the summer of 1926. It swept through the province of Hunan in early autumn and reached Wu Chang in September. By Charismas the radical element gained control of the army and the revolutionary government. All the Christian schools and colleges in Hunan and most of them in Hupeh were closed. In March after the "Nanking incident" the missionary members of the Hua Chung staff were evacuated, but the College was carried on by a handful of Chinese faculty members. It was not until May of 1927 that Hua Chung as the solitary Christian educational institution in the whole region of Central China was finally suspended when Christian principles of education were at stake and it remained closed until the autumn of 1929.

In September 1929 the college was re-opened. Besides Boone University, Griffith John College, and Wesley College, it had now two more cooperating units in Huping College and the College of Yale-in-China. The Lutheran College decided not to participate as an active unit, but chose to remain permanently closed, sending all its former students to Hua Chung. On this new basis Hua Chung has been operating ever since. Practically all the important missions in the Central China region have been looking to Hua Chung as their center of higher education. Efforts have been made to secure the participation of both the Lutheran and the Presbyterian Missions, both very active in the province of Hunan, but owning to the financial policy of those missions such participation has not materialized. Both missions, however, have officially acted to give Hua Chung their good-will and moral support. We covet the active cooperation of the Presbyterian

Mission for its educational zeal as shown by its strong secondary schools in Hunan and elsewhere and we desire the participation in our work of the Lutheran Mission because of the possible contribution to Christian Higher Education in China of the continental tradition from Europe. We were partially compensated, however, during the few years before the war in Wu Chang by the semi-official cooperation of the Swedish Mission in the college when one of its most scholarly missionaries taught the courses in French and German. We had hoped that this connection might develop further, and this it certainly would have done if not for the war.

Even after 1929 Hua Chung had a loose organization. To bring five missions together in a Christian higher Education institution was no simple task. Representatives of three, nay, more than three nationalities and of several church groups had to learn to work together and to appreciate each other's good points and weaknesses. Only American optimism, British fair play and Chinese good humor plus Christian charity could make the enterprise a success. We were sure of these and were moreover sure of the worthwhileness of the undertaking. If Christians from the different countries could not work together, who else could? In this spirit we went through successfully the first experimental period of five years.

After 1934 everybody realized that Hua Chung was a going-concern. The faculty was being strengthened, the student body steadily increased, plans for a new campus adjacent to the old were made and Hua Chung after its registration with the Ministry of Education of the National Government in 1931 as a university had its future assured. Then the war came. After a year remaining in Wu Chang the college moved hurriedly to Kweilin with a full staff, but only ten percent of its books and one third of its scientific equipment. In the summer of the 1938 its life as a refugee institution began. The severe bombing of Kweilin in the winter sent the college still further into the isolated southwest and there it has been for five years, and will probably remain for the duration of the war. We had chosen a quiet spot with two possible back-doors into the wide world, but these back-doors have been closed and we are left only with the monotonous quietness. But it is war and we must accept our lot.

THE AIMS OF THE COLLEGE AND HOW FAR THEY HAVE BEEN ATTAINED

This quiet isolated life has given us opportunity to reflect on our past and evaluate our achievements.

Our task as one of the Christian colleges operating in the Central China region is to supply the churches with an educated leadership; to bring together a number of Christian scholars in the various fields for thinking through the problems confronting the country and the world, and for finding their solutions from the Christian standpoint; to train men and women for the great task of interpreting the Christian religion to the Chinese and bringing to the altar of God the genius and culture of the Chinese nation; to bring about a better understanding of the West by the East and of the East by the West, and to hasten the day when the whole of mankind regardless of racial or national differences will live together as God's great family on earth. The education we give to our students must be scientifically sound but Christian in its emphasis, rooted in the cultural past of the people but abreast with the modern achievements and discoveries of the world, of real service to the country but international in its outlook. We do not deprecate practical results in helping to meet through our graduates the immediate needs of society, but our more important aim is to make forceful and lasting impact upon the life and thought of the nation as a whole, to make our Christian contribution to the reconstruction of China, this oldest country seeking to become young again. Should we lose sight of these objectives, we would soon be content with a college of inferior standards and of questionable value. But the achievement of our aim will require the rethinking of our policy and the re-formulation of our plans. Our first experiment from 1924 to 1927 has taught us many lessons, our experience after the re-organization of the college and before the war had confirmed them, and our reflection during our sojourn in the Southwest has shown us their real value. These lessons are: (1) that to accomplish what is set before us we ought to see clearly what courses of instruction the college must have, what else it should not attempt, and that what it has to offer must be well balanced and well rounded out; (2) that we must have a well selected and well balanced teaching staff consisting of the best scholars, the great majority of whom should be Chinese Christians and missionaries from abroad, who cherish a genuine pride in the work and are willing to devote their lives to it; (3) that we must increase our enrollment and at the same time endeavors to draw into our student body more men and women from Chinese families with a better social and cultural background; (4) that adequate facilities must be given for both faculty and post-graduate research so as to attract the better scholars and keep them for the teaching staff and to train the younger generation for the work; and (5) that there must be a closer relation and a better articulation with the Christian middle school so that the college may build its training on theirs, in religious and character discipline as well as in intellectual development.

Let us dwell in detail on these points.

FACULTIES AND DEPARTMENTS OF INSTITUTION

By faculty we mean what is ordinarily called a school in American universities and what is called a college in the Chinese system of education, and by department we mean a group of courses of instruction in a particular field to prepare the students for a government recognized bachelor's degree:

We have at present the following Faculties and Departments:

Arts: Chinese Literature, Foreign Languages and Literature (mainly English), History-Sociology, Economics-Commerce

Science: Biology, Chemistry, Physics

Education: Education (with emphasis on training of secondary school teachers)

Besides these eight departments under the three faculties, we have courses in Philosophy, Psychology and Religion under Arts, Mathematics under Science, and Music under Education. These courses are for students who have to meet certain requirements, or they may be chosen as content subject in preparation for teaching, or taken as pure electives.

The present departments must be kept and developed.

In registering with the Ministry of Education in 1931, it was reported that as soon as possible the college would develop its Economics-Commerce Department into a School of Commerce. Such a school will have an important role to play in higher education in a center like Wu Han, the economic and commercial importance of which is bound to be greater and greater immediately after the return of peace. We shall seek to train not only practical business men, bankers, accountants, statisticians and personal directors in factories. These are important and by all means we ought to get them prepared for the new China in her future development. But this must be in its proper proportion. The more solemn task for the School of Commerce will be sent into the various economic activities of the nation an increasingly large number of men imbued with Christian ideals so that such ideals may be upheld in the national and international economic policy. The expectation of more support for the college in the future from alumni engaged in business is only a secondary consideration.

The government has already required that History and Sociology be treated as two separate sections under History-Sociology. Sociology, for some years at least, ought to be dropped and History be further developed by adding to the Department courses in Political Science. When resources permit and the men with proper qualifications available, a research chair or chairs in Chinese Sociology ought to be established to supply the necessary material for the teaching of Sociology in China.

Philosophy ought to be strengthened and out of it a department, experimental in character, be developed similar to the Modern Greats in Oxford by combing courses in History, Political Science, Economics and Philosophy with emphasis on the Chinese cultural heritage and a world outlook. The need of men and women trained in this way will be more and more felt in the Government and in Chinese society. Government permission can be secured for such an experiment.

Mathematics under the Faculty of Science ought to be developed into a Department to prepare students for the Science degree. This is not only because of the importance of the subject in the country and its present under-development in most of the Christian college but because also there would be a great demand for teachers of mathematics in colleges and in special types of middle schools preparing for technical studies which require a good mathematical grounding.

In the Department of Biology, Chemistry, and Physics the present policy of emphasising the pursuit of the basic principles will be continued. When this is properly done and adequately developed, one of the natural results will be the application to many practical problems arising from the development and needs of the country. We envisage in this respect our cooperation and connection with government and private industrial establishments and with the Christian Missions in their medical and public health work.

Music is to be developed into a full-fledged Department as soon as possible, and later even into a Conservatory. It is the Fine Art which has been least developed in China in spite of the proud tradition of Music which lives now only in memory. The Evangelical and Reformed Church in the U. S. A. has undertaken to find the necessary support for this work and a separate plan for it has already been submitted with all the details regarding courses of instruction, personnel, equipment and budget, calling for the operating expenses of U. S. $7,000 for the first year which will increase to U. S. $10,500 for the third year and thereafter.

In the School of Education there should be two departments: a teacher-training department and an education department. The former will have the task of training teachers for middle schools, especially for our affiliated Christian middle schools in the Central China region, of which there were twenty-one before the war. The latter should be dedicated to the work of training administrators and research workers in the field of secondary education and Christian education in China. We shall have to train teachers for all the main subjects in the secondary schools such as Chinese, English, Mathematics, Sciences, History and

Geography, and Music. Very soon we ought to train teachers also for Home Economics and Fine Arts which are being neglected in the national system of Education. All these will need specialists as lectures in special methods, although for the content courses we may have the advantage of courses in the School of Arts and the School of Science. Research in education, particularly in Christian education in China, is a comparatively new field in the country, and we ought to seek to make our contribution. By such research we wish to assist the Christian middle schools in their improvement and future development and to bring about a closer integration and coordination of all the Christian educational institutions in the Central China region. China has to cease copying the West in education and build up a system of middle schools against her own cultural background and to meet her own needs. Particularly Christian education in China must be rooted in the Chinese soil, and yet there has been no well-thought-out and consistent policy for implementing this. To contribute to the formulation of such a policy should certainly be one of the duties Hua Chung School of Education which is now the only School of Education among the Christian colleges in China. Of course, the present tempo of the government may not permit the School to continue after the war, but should not the Christian forces in the whole country labor to save its future? One way to save it is by strengthening its teaching staff so that the value of its contribution cannot be ignored by the authorities. Whatever the future policy of the government may be, the staff assembled for the School of Education will serve as a nucleus for the Institute for Research in Christian Education recommended by the Burton Commission in 1922.

For experiments in secondary education in all its aspects, the school feels the necessity of a complete middle school of six years, possibly with two departments, one for boys and the other for girls, both partially boarding, entirely under its management. This attached school should serve also as a model Christian middle school as well as an experimental and practising school. With the masters of methods and practising students from the School of Education this attached middle school may operate with a comparatively reasonable budget of its own.

If the government should permit the charging of fees as before the war, U. S. $5,000 may suffice. This should be outside of the college budget.

The Department of Theological Training and Research must be established and developed with vigor and earnestness, if Hua Chung is to make its best contribution to the churches in China. A well educated ministry, properly trained directors of religious education and other qualified church workers are the greatest and most urgent needs. The college ought to help to train them, and to give them their training in theological and technical studies against the Chinese social and cultural background. Such a department in the college will be helpful also in setting a more distinctively Christian tone to the faculty and in holding before the students the ministry and direct religious work as professions for them to aim at.

The department will admit two grades of students to be called the "B" grade and the "A" grade. The "B" grade will admit students who will take a combined Arts and Theological course of five years with a year of "internship" during the sixth year. This training is intended for ministers, student pastors, religious directors, translators and writers. The "A" grade will admit to a three-year course students who have had for their preparation a college Arts course mainly pre-theological in character and have obtained their B. A. degree. They are to be trained as teachers of theological subjects, research scholars and writers in the religious and theological fields, and ministers of the more important churches in the great centres.

Five full-time lectures are necessary to launch this department. Later when, besides teaching, the work of translation and editing has developed, when refresher courses for ministers in service have become a regular feature, and when there is a greater demand from church workers and ministers for directed systematic reading by correspondence in the theological and relative fields, there must be two full-time lectures for each of the five theological disciplines, which are Old Testament, New Testament, Church History, Systematic and Moral Theology, and Practical Theology and Religious Education. The non-theological lectures required by this department may be taken in the School of Arts and the School of Education. Some of the practical theological work such as Church Polity, Parish Administration and Homiletics, will be taught by experienced ministers of the church outside the college, from which the theological students have come. Well-organized and well-staffed churches, schools with good religious programmers, Christian literature societies, and centers of other types of Christian work will be asked to take the students during their intern year.

FACULTY NEEDED

If this policy outlined above should be approved and the plan for development of the college adopted, the following teaching staff will be needed.

	Arts	Sci	Ed	Com	Theo	Music	Total
First four years	19	14	5	4	5	6	53
Fifth to ninth years	20	17	7	5	7	7	63
Tenth year and thereafter	22	18	8	7	10	7	72

These figures are tentatively arrived at by allowing during the first period six recognized teachers each for the two Departments of Chinese Literature and Foreign Literature, four each for the four departments of History-Political Science, Biology, Chemistry, and Physics, three for Philosophy, Psychology, and Religion, two for Mathematics, and the other departments according to the table above. In course of time the number is to be increased as indicated to meet the increased number of students and to strengthen certain departments according to development. While the need of the total number is pretty certain, there may be necessity of readjusting the distribution over the various departments according to their development. A recognized teacher is a faculty member of at least the lecturer's rank. According to government regulations fresh graduates from a university without adequate teaching experience may serve only as assistants and may not teach independent courses.

Then we must have at least one physical director at the beginning. With a larger enrollment there ought to be two. There has to be an administrative staff. Some of the responsible offices requiring no great amount of time and energy but only planning and supervision may be held concurrently by members of the teaching staff as it is being done at present. But others consuming more time and energy and various types of clerical work require full-time appointees, such as librarians, business manager, registrar, and warden of the women's hostel. It is estimated that an administrative staff of ten full-time officers will be needed during the first period of four years, fourteen during the second period and sixteen thereafter. Hence we have the following for the whole college:

	Teaching	Administration	total
First four tears	53	10	63
Fifth-ninth years	63	14	77
After the ninth year	72	16	88

From 25% to one third of the whole administrative and teaching staff ought to be missionaries and 80% Christians including the missionaries.

As this teaching staff includes only those who can be responsible for independent courses, assistants will have to be added when the enrollment gets beyond a certain point according to the nature and needs of the departments. Their salaries will have to be found from the increased student fees.

Such a staff has been planned for a student body of 300 in the first four years, 500 for the second five years, and 800 for thereafter.

ENROLLMENT

But why should we plan for a larger enrollment? It will be recalled that shortly after the reorganization of the college in 1929 the Directors adopted the policy of fixing the maximum enrollment of the college at 240 students and of limiting the scope of its offering to three schools, viz., Arts, Science, and Education, with eight or nine, major departments altogether, each offering sufficient courses to qualify the students for the bachelor's degree at the end of four years, according to the regulations of the Ministry of Education of the National Government.

This was a wise policy. The resources of the college were known to be limited. It was felt that whatever we attempted to do ought to be maintained at the highest possible educational standards, emphasizing adequate contact between teachers and students for religious work and character formation, as well as for intellectual development.

The maximum enrollment was later increased by action of the Directors to 300, but this has never been reached. Our highest enrollment was 244, plus 98 refugee students from other colleges in the first year of the war while the college was still in Wu Chang. The move to Kweilin and later to the present site in Hsichow has meant practically the entire cutting off of the main supply of students from the affiliated Christian middle schools, and the low standards of the students coming from schools of inferior teaching, seriously affected by the war, have kept the college enrollment low, in spite of all our efforts to raise it.

But experience during the last thirteen years, particularly during the last five years and a half during our sojourn in the southwest, has led us to believe it advisable to aim at a higher maximum after the war.

In the first place, the elimination of students from the first two years has been unexpectedly high. That is partly due to our comparatively strict standards which many of the students are not able to maintain, but chiefly due to the fact that many students, especially in the Central China region before the war, were unable financially to finish the four years of college and yet were eager to have some college education and some experience of college life. For the last thirteen years the two upper classes, i. e., the juniors and seniors, constituted only about 25% of the total enrollment, sometimes even less, whereas we ought to have some 35%. We acknowledge the value of the service rendered by the college in having under influence students even for a year or two, but from the point of view of Chinese society our contribution as well as our reputation as a college depends largely upon the number of graduates we are able to turn out from year to year.

Secondly, when the upper classes are small and when these are again divided into the various departments, the number of students in each group is naturally even smaller. It is not economical to have small groups. Besides, it does not furnish sufficient stimulus to the teachers or sufficient competition to the students.

In the third place, when our number is small, the chance of having among them outstanding students is small too. It is debatable whether our contribution would be greater by having a smaller class all attaining to a set standard, but not many above it, or by having a larger class with many of rather commonplace achievements, but with a few of outstanding abilities. There is, of course, no necessary dichotomy between the two. With effort we may be able to maintain a high level for many and yet at the same time turn out more graduates of high achievements. This is certainly to be preferred if at all possible, and we believe it is possible.

In the fourth place, a small enrollment means also a less diversified program for reasons of economic efficiency. It is more difficult to attract good students when the college offering is too limited. It is even more difficult to attract good scholars for the faculty. There is more stimulus for study and thinking when one is in contact with men in allied fields, as well as in one's own field.

Finally, the teaching staff is apt to be on a precarious basis in any department when the limited enrollment necessitates a small number of professors in the department. It is more difficult to get good professors in China than in Great Britain or in America. When there are only three teaching in a department, and probably only one or two who are good teachers and good scholars at the same time, the losing of one may mean a serious handicap to the department for a long time. Good standards cannot be maintained under such circumstances, and academic traditions are slow to build.

For those reasons it is recommended that the enrollment of the college be increased to 500 at first, and then to 800, and the number of faculties and departments be increased as well.

It is not the sense of this proposal to increase the college enrollment to 500 as soon as the college moves back to Wu Chang after the war. But plans ought to be made at once for this number and a reasonable schedule adopted to reach the first maximum inside of a period of, say, four years according to the circumstances at the time, taking care at the same time not to impair the established traditions or the reasonably high standards of the college while the number of students is being increased from year to year.

HOSTELS AND TUTORIAL SYSTEM

To take care of such number of students, indeed to take care of any number above 150, and to give them a good college education, we must house them in separate hostels under well chosen hostel heads.

From the inception of Hua Chung the hostel system has been intended to be one of the distinctive features. This, however, has not been fully developed, for even before the war in Wu Chang it was difficult to find among the faculty sufficient men acquainted with the operation of a hostel. During our sojourn in the southwest the difficulty has been increased. But for work among students, particularly for religious work and for the inculcation of social culture, the hostels must be properly established.

The women students will naturally be in their own hostels grouped together under one management with a Dean of Women and on a separate campus. For this we have a good site in Wu Chang. The men will live in hostels each with the capacity of fifty students and not more. At each end of the hostel building, oblong in shape, will be a faculty residence, semi-detached with its own doors and garden. It would be ideal to have a Chinese faculty family in one end and a missionary family in the other, charged with the responsibility of the religious and social education of the students in that particular hostel. These two faculty members will be Master and Associated Master of the hostel. Thus, each group of students in a hostel will have their own separate life, but through certain college regulations undue separation will be prevented and life on the whole college campus and joint activities of the students will still preserve the esprit de corps of the college.

From the beginning, too, we have been wanting to install the tutorial system. In many ways it is the best method of university education. It is a method indigenous to the Chinese and is especially suitable to a small institution. But it is costly, as every good thing is. Tutorial work requires also tutors who understand how it is done. Perhaps, our purpose will be answered, if in the two lower classes students have only advisers, and only in the upper two years they are assigned to tutors who have charge of them in their major field of study.

SABBATICAL LEAVES AND FELLOWSHIPS FOR STUDY ABROAD

Before the war sabbatical leaves were granted to professors and assistant professors after six years of service, if the college intended to keep such professors for long terms of service. Such an arrangement was deemed necessary for our men to keep in touch with the advancement of modern learning in the world and to maintain the international connection with the scholars in similar fields abroad. But since the war this privilege has been suspended. It ought to be reintroduced when peace returns. It is one of the ways to keep the best scholars for the faculty by keeping them intellectually alive and alert. When the faculty is in full swing, out of, say, sixty members of the teaching staff probably fifteen will be missionaries for whom furloughs are provided by the missions. Of the remaining forty-five, there will be probably twenty-five professors and assistant professors eligible for sabbatical leaves. Not more than three will be entitled to the sabbatical leaves in any one year. For this the college ought to budget U. S. $3,600 annually.

Nothing is more important than the training of the young men on the faculty for advanced teaching and for more responsible positions. Only people imbued with the Hua Chung spirit and tradition will have the loyalty to stand by for better or for worse. The younger men must be given advanced training abroad, to have the advantages of a larger university for study and for research, to come into contact with the Older Churches and their leaders, to understand how missions are supported and carried on, and to see Western civilization at first-hand with all its merits and weaknesses. Two fellowships of an annual stipend of U. S. $1,200 each should be provided. We are confident that after the first year aboard our younger men will be able to win fellowships in Western universities to continue their post-graduate studies. The method of selecting candidates for these fellowships is a detail to be worked out by the Directors of the college.

The two items just mentioned will mean an annual expenditure of U. S. $6,000.

RELATIONS TO THE CHRISTIAN SCHOOLS

Reference has already been made to the necessity of a closer relation and a better articulation with the Christian middle schools, at least with those in the Central China region operating under the missions cooperating in the college. It is the duty of the college to help them to become the best private schools in their Christian character, in administration and in teaching by supplying them with better trained teachers, by assisting them in technical matters, and by emphasizing with the supporting missions the formulation of a sounder and more consistent policy. Efforts ought to be made to attract more of their graduates to come to Hua Chung for their college education. This may be done by a wiser administration of scholarships at the disposal of the missions or of the college and by a better distribution of funds secured for the purpose of improving Christian secondary education. New funds will be needed for such purposes as subsidizing the salaries of full-time religious directors in the middle schools, and bringing scientific equipment and libraries up to the minimum standard for teaching efficiency and the provision of leaves for middle school teachers to secure further training either in the Christian colleges or abroad. Such strengthening of the Christian middle schools is essential to provide a sound foundation for work of real university standards in the Christian colleges.

ESTIMATES OF ANNUAL CURRENT BUDGET

To formulate a budget for the college after the war is practically impossible. What will be the currency in this country or in any other country? What will be the standards of living for the salaried professional men? What will be the general level of prices? These questions we cannot answer. But we must have something to go by as we look into the future. As a basis let us assume that exchange between the Chinese dollar and the American dollar resume its pre-war rate and that prices in China and abroad be nearing normality again. This is a big assumption, but we must make it in order to do our figuring.

We ought, then, to allow U. S. $1,200 as the average annual salary for one full-time recognized teacher. A full professor will need more than this, but a man of the lecturer's rank will need less. For the purposes of reckoning we allow U. S. $1,200 also for a member of the administrative staff. Most of these men will be given less, some more, and when we reckon a man of U. S. $1,200 in the office, we may have only two or three men of smaller caliber there for his work and together get less than this amount. We arbitrarily call U. S. $1,200 the "replacement value" of a missionary on the College staff, merely for the purpose of budgeting.

For the first period, the administrative offices will need ten salaries, for the second period fourteen, and thereafter sixteen. Besides salaries we must reckon under administration such items as wages, lighting, heating, repairs, insurance, medicine, sanitation, etc. U. S. $12,000—$15,000 will be needed for these items, and then we need U. S. $20,000 annually for equipment, books and periodicals.

For the first period we insert the item of U. S. $2,000 a year for research and thereafter U. S. $4,000 a year. Our hope is that new resources may be tapped for this worthy purpose. Thus, referring to our last table of faculty and administrative officers, our estimates for the whole college are as follows:

	Instruction		Administration		Research & Fellowship	Total
	Salaries	Equipment	Salaries	Maintenance		
First period	$63,000	$20,000	$12,000	$12,000	$8,000	$115,600
Second period	$75,000	$20,000	$16,800	$15,000	$10,000	$137,400
Thereafter	$86,000	$20,000	$19,200	$15,000	$10,000	$150,600

Would our resources warrant this?

The income from the cooperating units, the Harvard-Yenching Board, and the Associated Boards for 1943—1944 is U. S. $55,000 exclusive of missionary salaries. This total is approximately the same as the income of the College in 1937—1938.

But take this amount of present income from abroad, and add to it twelve missionary salaries which the Cooperating Missions used to allow us before the war, Reckoning it now at U. S. $12,000 each for budgeting all through, we have then U. S. $69,400. We are expecting from the Evangelical and Reformed Church Mission for the Music Department, included in this plan, U. S. $10,500 a year. The Harvard-Yenching Board may increase its subvention for our Chinese Department by U. S. $5,000 annually. The Theological Project would need U. S. $7,500 for the first period, U. S. $10,000 for the second period, and U. S. $14,000 thereafter. This will have to be raised by missions or individuals interested in the new work.

In 1937—1938 before the war we expected 220 students to bring to the College fees amounting to N. C. $26,280 or U. S. $9,000 approximately. When the enrolment is increased, this item of income ought to be larger.

At present the National Government is granting the college N. C. $30,000 a year. Assume this grant to continue and the Chinese dollar to become of normal per-war value again, it would mean U. S. $10,000 annually for the income of the college.

For the first period, then, assuming a student body of 220 the expected income for the college may be U. S. $111,400 which would be only U. S. $4,200 short of our estimated expenditure.

This of course includes U. S. $28,000 from the U. C. R. in America through the Associated Boards. But the war has cut the Yale-in-China subvention from U. S. $12,000 to U. S. $5,000, which may be expected to go back to its former amount, the highest figure being U. S. $14,000 annually. The remaining U. S. $25,000 would have to be raised abroad every year for the first few years after the war. A portion of this, however, may come from Foundations in China and local contributions as before the war.

Such are our rough estimates. It is unnecessary to venture still further into the future. The uncertainties are too great for us to see clearly. With the increase of enrolment of every hundred students, fees ought to be increased, from our former experience, by about U. S. $3,500 annually. This would add to our income, if our plan should work out.

The Board of Founders and the Cooperating Missions may be willing to raise the possible deficit of U. S. $25,000 a year after the war, either through the Associated Board or otherwise. But the time may have come when the Board should think of ways and means of raising an endowment fund so as to put an end to worry involved in the annual raising of money to cover deficits, which the college will always have with its present financial organization.

Old men dream dreams and young men see visions. It is visions that we see in planning for the future of the college. What we see is a Christian institution of higher learning, internationally supported as an expression of international goodwill for the Christian faith and for a world cause, working in a world not rolling in prosperity perhaps but enjoying the liberties won with costly sacrifices, serving a nation comprising one-quarter the population of the earth—a nation after a real renaissance and now reaching forth for a new destiny, yet its fate still in the balance, and its advancing steps still at the cross-roads! The work will be worth our while. Many of us are investing our lives and our all in this adventure of faith and we desire to inspire more to follow us. Will all who share this vision help us to realize it?

Francis C. M. Wei
President of Hua Chung College and Chairman
of Executive Committee pro tem of the Board
of Directors and of the Senate

Secretary, Executive Committee pro tem
(Signed) Richard P. Bien Secretary, Senate
Hua Chung College
Hsichow, Yunnan, China
February 15, 1944

President's Report to the Board of Directors, Hua Chung College, Hsichow, Yunnan, for the Year 1943—1944

The president takes pleasure in submitting the following report to the Board of Directors of the college. Accompanying this report are copies of the annual reports to the President of Dean Leonard Constantine for the General Faculty, Dean John C. F. Lo for the School of Arts, Dean P'u Hwang for the School of Education, and Professor David F. Anderson secretary of the Chapel Committee. The statistical report from the Registrar for the year is attached herewith. As the fiscal year is not yet closed at the time of writing this report, the treasurer's financial report will not be ready until the end of the July, and it will be sent separately to the directors and the Founders by the treasurer, Professor John L. Coe. As the president has been for the past year again concurrently acting as Dean of the School of Science, there is no separate report for that school.

GENERAL CONDITIONS

<u>The General Situation.</u> With the close of the present academic year we have finished the seventh year of war in China, and it is the sixth year of our moving out from Wu Chang, five and a half years of which have been spent in this rural town of Hsichow in Western Yunnan.

This year, as was the last, has been a comparatively uneventful year, as far as the college is concerned. The war on the Pacific has taken a more encouraging turn, and the attack into Burma has been in progress. But so far we are still blockaded and completely isolated from the wider world. Communications between Hsichow and the other parts of the country have not improved, but it is still possible for people to move about if they are willing to pay the expense. Our monotony has been more-or-less broken by the coming and going of some of our allied officers and men, who find our international community, and particularly our missionary member of the staff, a relief and a comfort. It has taxed the hospitality of our British and American families to the utmost, but it is taken as a privilege and a part of our war effort. Our radio has been working all the year, so that we are able to get news before newspapers and publications reach us from the bigger centers. We are watching impatiently every day for the return of peace, but we have to mark time, realizing how our allies as well as our own troops are doing their best with sacrifices beyond imagination to bring the war to an end.

<u>College Finance.</u> While the treasurer is not able to close his accounts until the end of the month, we know enough to say that we may expect to balance our budget again this year. For the last twelve months we have been fortunate in receiving unexpected gifts from organizations and individual friends to add to our regular income from the cooperating missions, the Associated Boards, the Harvard-Yenching Board, the united committee for Christian Universities in Great Britain, and the Chinese Government. We have been benefited by gifts from the British United Relief through Madame Chiang, by an anonymous gift from Great Britain earmarked for the college, and by the Committee on Professional Relief in Chungking with money coming from the United China Relief in the United States. We have received six special gifts from such private friends as Mr. Li Jui in Chungking, Mr. Li Tse-hu, Commissioner of Civil Affairs of the Provincial Government of Yunnan in Kunming; Mr. Tung Chen-ning, and Mr. Yen Hsieh-chen of Hsing chow, and groups of the college alumni. All these gifts will appear in the treasurer's report. Such gifts have gone to the current support of the college. Mr. Nathanial Holmes II has made a gift to the college, which has been sent to the Board of the Founders for a scholarship Endowment and is being held in American currency in New York. A number of friends in American have continued to send the President money either for his discretionary use in the college or for scholarship grants. We wish to recognize all these gifts with gratitude.

It has been necessary to increase the faculty subsidies three times during the year. In early September subsidies were increased by approximately one-third. In December it was necessary to make another increase to take effect in January, and this increase was approximately one-third of the salaries and subsidies in effect at that time. At the beginning of the June a review of the subsidy scheme was made, and a very substantial increase was put into effect, which on average practically doubled the income of the faculty and staff members. As a result of these increases members of the faculty and staff are receiving on average four times the amount they were receiving a year ago. This is about in pace with the rising prices.

In addition to this, three special gifts were received and divided among the faculty and staff members. In November, a gift of U. S. $2,000 from the Associated Boards for a commodity grant was divided among the faculty and staff, so that each received N. C. $1,600. In April, a gift of U. S. $300 from the British Aid to China Fund, equivalent to N. C. $126,000 was distributed among the faculty and staff in varying amounts, according to rank and length of service, the minimum payment being N. C. $2,500 and the maximum N. C. $4,500. In May, a special gift of N. C. $50,000 from Mr. Li Jui was divided equally among the faculty and staff, so that each received N. C. $1,492. The grant from the Chungking Committee on Professional Subsidies in N. C. $40,000, but only N. C. $14,000 has been received so far, and this amount will go to a large number of faculty and staff members according to applications for relief, as proved by a committee appointed be the Senate. Any other undesignated special gifts have gone to help meet the increase of subsidies.

<u>The Faculty</u>. The faculty during this year has been at its lowest ebb. Just a year ago six members of the Faculty of Science and one member of the Faculty of Arts declined reappointment, and most of the vacancies have not been filled during the year. The Department of Chemistry is completely depleted, and the Department of Economics-Commerce greatly weakened. The Department of Physics has been fortunate enough through the efforts of its head, Professor Richard Bien, to secure the service of three of our own graduates who have helped Dr. Bien not only to carry in full swing the work in the

department, but also to help give courses in Chemistry so as to keep that department going in a way. Professor Sindey Hsiac has been most courageous in teaching two extra courses in Chemistry, in addition to his own load already heavy. As it will appear in Dean Constantine's report, most of the senior numbers of the faculty, including the chief administrative officers, carry extra loads in order to keep the work going, and the president would want to ask for special recognition for these people. It just happens that whenever there is extra work to do, it is always the senior people who are more capable of doing it, and this explains why some of the junior people have lighter loads. There are also specialists on the faculty who are not so ready to venture into any field and do the extra work that has to be done there. We must not give the impression, however, that by lecturing in fields outside of their own, some of our faculty members are lowering academic standards. No one has taken on a course unless he or she is competent to do so. Thus with extra efforts the emergency has been met, and the college is able to finish the academic year without any great mishap. Even with reduced strength and extra work the faculty has shown splendid spirit.

<u>Student Body.</u> Comparing the registrar's statistical report for this year with that of last year, it will be seen that our enrollment for the present year is 150 against 152 in the previous year. The enrollment would have been much greater if the administrative officers had not clamped down on the late admission. Some of the students came late, and the dean of the General Faculty refused to admit them. At least a dozen of them had to go home without getting into the college because of their late coming. While it was hard to do such a thing in times like these, yet discipline of the college must be maintained.

The number of students from Christian middle school has dropped, as well as the number of Christian students. Our Christian students in the college in 1942—1943 was approximately 40%, whereas in the present year it has been 32%. This is to be expected in view of our isolated position and our remoteness from most of the Christian middle school. The President would wish to point out again that by staying in Western Yunnan the college is really making a contribution to education in this part of the country. It will surely be a source of gratification after the war for us to look back upon the number of students whom we have left in Western Yunnan with the kind of education and training we have been able to give them. This is the first year what we graduated a student who is a local product, and he is by far one of the best students we have ever had.

The number of Yunnan students is on the increase, 91 in the present year, as against 73 in the previous year. We regret particularly that the number of students from Central China has decreased. So also has the number of students from the province of Kwantung, from which we would expect to draw more students after our return to Central China. The distribution of students among the different major departments remained about the same except that there is a one-third drop in the School of Education. As a whole, the student body has behaved well and worked hard to keep up with the college standards. The whole senior class received their degrees, and of the 32 students who took the intermediate examinations, no one absolutely failed, although there are five who received a condition in one subject and will have to take their supplementary examinations in September before they can go up to the junior class.

The students are getting very much worked up over the expected celebration of the Twentieth Anniversary of the founding of the college. Yunnan students particularly have gotten themselves organized to launch a financial campaign for the raising of an endowment for the college so as to link up Hua Chung permanently with the students of Western Yunnan, even when we move back to our original site. One group of these students is going to Kunming, and another is remaining in the Tali district for the purpose of money-raising. Students from other provinces are also doing their best to help.

SCHOOLS

<u>The School of Arts.</u> This school has again the largest enrollment because, chiefly, of the popularity of Economics-Commerce and English Literature. The Chinese department has regained its normalcy with the

return of Assist. Professor Fu Mou-chi from Sikong where he had been doing research in the tribal languages, and he assumed the duties of the head of the department at the beginning of the second term. The research in that department goes on as before with Professor Pau Lu-ping as director of research in Chinese studies. The Department of History has been strengthened by the appointment of Asst. Professor Wong Ru-che, M. A. to teach Ancient and Medieval Chinese History, thus bringing the teaching staff of the department up to our normal size of three full-time faculty members.

The Department of English Literature continues to feel its short handedness. Mrs. Coe and Mrs. Constantine have been impressed into the teaching of English. At the end of the year Mr. Walter Allen joined the American Army in China, the Mrs. Lo had to leave even before Commencement to go back to America for medical treatment of her baby. But the work has been carried on with extra effort on the part of all the members of the teaching staff in the department. We have been hoping against hope during the year to have at least one new teacher for the department from England or America, but so far our hope has not been realized. However, Miss Leona Lloyd Burr, M. A. was evacuated from Fukien, and she has now been appointed assistant professor of English Literature beginning with July 1.

The department of Economics-Commerce could not find any qualified teacher to fill the vacancy left by Asst. Professor P. L. Tang, M. Sc. (Econ.) who declined reappointment at the end of the last year. Two part-time teachers and an assistant managed to carry on the courses necessary with assistance from the President and Dean of the General Faculty, who each give a course in the department to meet the government requirements.

The School of Science. This school was greatly weakened by the departure of six members who declined reappointment at the end of last year. Three of them were in the Department of Chemistry, two in the Department of Physics, and one in the Department of Biology, all alumni of the college. The vacancies in the Department of Physics have been filled with comparatively junior men, but the work goes on with efficiency under Professor Richard Bien. Professor Sidney Hsiao worked like a Trojan to carry on his department with only one assistant during the first term, and she left during the winter vocation, leaving Dr. Hsiao therefore entirely alone. In spite of such conditions Dr. Hsiao was willing to teach extra courses in the Chemistry Department, which department also received assistance from Dr. Bien and Mr. Ling Chin-yu of the Physics Department. Dr. Bien and Mr. Ling each gave one course in Chemistry in order to keep the work in the Department of Chemistry going.

For the second year the School of Science, known as the Yale-in-China School of Science, had no dean, and the President has had to act concurrently as dean of the School. It is fortunate that before Commencement Professor Richard Bien of the Department of Physics, who served for several years as dean of Science before 1939, was persuaded to accept the appointment as dean of Science again, and he has gone into that very difficult work with a shout and with a determination to bring it up again.

Mathematics, which is a minor department, has been taken care of by Professor John L. Coe, who has to give the greater part of his attention to his work as treasurer of the college. A treasurer in times like these finds his work most taxing, and Mr. Coe has the assistance of Asst. Professor Shen only to carry on all the necessary courses required by the college and particularly by the science departments.

The School of Education. The School of Education maintains its efficiency as in the previous year. The vacancies of neither Professor P. V. Taylor nor of Professor Hu I have been filled, however, for the last two years. The minor Department of Music, which supplies content courses for some of the Education students and cultural courses for students in the other schools in the college, labors vigorously with Mrs. Walter Allen teaching piano and Mrs. David F. Anderson teaching vocal music. With the departure of Mrs. Walter Allen at the end of the year there is only Mrs. Anderson to carry on both vocal music and piano lessons to keep the work in the department going. All efforts have been made to secure a good piano teacher to strengthen the department and to fill the vacancy left now by Mrs. Allen, but we have had no success.

In spite of all these difficulties research work is still going on among the faculty. Dr. Hsiao had two of his research reports sent to the Ministry of Education, and for these he has received an award from the government of N. C. $8,000. Dr. Richard Bien has been carrying on his research work with the assistance of Mr. John P. N. Wei. Dr. P'u Hwang continues his investigation of Secondary Education in China, and Mr. Anderson has been continuing his experiment in English teaching in middle school. Research work in Chinese studies goes on as before in the Department of Chinese Literature under the direction of Professor Pao. A separate report for this will be sent to the Harvard-Yenching Board under whose support both our Chinese department and research in Chinese studies have been going on for the last seven years.

It is regrettable that due to the weakness of our Economics-Commerce Department very little research of scientific study of the economic and financial situation in China during these years offer has been done. It is a great opportunity missed. We hope that next year we may have a strong teaching staff in the department and get some of the work done, which surely would be of great interest in the future.

RELIGIOUS LIFE

To save space very little will be said here. Professor David F. Anderson, secretary of the Chanel Committee, has sent in a splendid report on the religious activities in the college during one year, a copy of which is accompanying this report. The president would like to endorse Professor Anderson's opinion that with the increasing number of non-Christian students in the college, there is a greater challenge to direct evangelism among the students, many of whom still stay in this province and should serve as a foundation upon which the churches in this apt of the country will build. As a whole the non-Christian students in the college during these years of war have been taking a greater interest in Christianity than they did before the war in Wu Chang. We would not have chosen to have a small percentage of Christian students in the college, but that being the situation we ought to make the best of it.

The fact pointed out by Professor Anderson in his report that the junior and senior students are at taking advantage of the courses offered to them as elective in the English Bible and in Christian Teaching is to be regretted. The course, however, of this is not simple. Students are overloaded because the government requirements for the degree are heavy. In our courses we insist on high standards. It is natural that department heads think first of all of their own department work. Especially during their last two years the students are very cautious in correcting their courses, favoring only those which are required for the degree. They are afraid to fail in their courses, since that might mean their staying in the college for an extra year, a thing students cannot very well afford in times like these.

With the smaller number of Christian students the chapel attendance has naturally been not so good as in former years, but the number of non-Christian students in chapel service is encouraging. The President is particularly gratified to see so many of the faculty members taking such an interest in the personal religious work among the students.

HOSTELS

During the year the college has maintained the same women's hostel and four hostels for men. Living conditions for students are not so comfortable as they were in Wu Chang, but this is not to be expected in wartime. The students continue to manage their own board, which is simple, but as far as food value is concerned, it is as good as it is in any other college in Free China at the present time. For students who come from occupied areas the government loan is just about sufficient to cover the expenses of the food. With the college helping by storing in rice at the beginning of the year the men students, who require simpler food than the girls, have been able to have a small balance on their board money returned to them at the end of the year. Beginning with the current year the government has stopped loans to students in the School of Arts and in the School of Education, giving full scholarships to Science students only to cover their complete board and lodging. This works hardship on the non-Science students, but it is government policy against which our protest is entirely ineffective. At the beginning of the year four such students were caught by the new government regulation. Mr. Li Jui was generous enough to send N. C. $20,000 as financial aid for them.

MEDICAL CARE

Dr. Logan H. Roots, M. D. of the American Church Mission carried on the medical care as in previous years until the end of the May when he has to take his family back to America, mainly for the schooling of his two daughters. He expects to return to the college as soon as possible when he gets his family settled in the United States, but with the present difficult conditions of passage from America we cannot possibly count on his return to Hsichow until at least next Spring. In the meantime we have arranged with the local Hsichow Hospital to take care of our community with reduced rates for outpatients only. Their charge for drugs is simply exorbitant. Fortunately we have some of our own which may last for sometime.

On the recommendation of the Medical Committee, appointed by the Senate, a trained nurse has been appointed beginning with July 1, in order to see patients before they go to the hospital so as to insure better and quicker medical care for both faculty and students.

VISITORS

We have been fortunate in having distinguished visitors during the year. The Rt. Rev. R. C. Hall, Bishop of Victoria in South China, came and spent a whole week here last July. The Rt. Rev. A. A. Gilman, S. T. D, Bishop of Hankow, visited us in September. Dr. William Fenn, representative in China of the Associated Boards, was able to come and make a short stay in the college early in December. Dr. Robert Brank Fulton, representative in China of the Yale-in China trustees, arrived in China late in May and came at once to the college, making a stay here of three weeks. We were all so glad that Dr. Fulton was able to stay so long in order to get a really first-hand knowledge of our work here to get acquainted with our faculty. He has agreed to accept appointment as assistant professor in Economics and Social Ethics to teach whenever circumstance permit for one term in the college every year until we are able to go back to our original site, when we expect he will take up his residence in the college.

All these guests have given us valuable suggestions and put us in touch with movements in the wider world. For their visits we are most grateful.

LOOKING INTO THE FUTURE

During the year we have been busy planning for the future in spite of the uncertainties. A proposed plan for a major department in music has been sent to the Board of Foreign Missions of the Evangelical and Reformed Church in the United States, asking that mission to sponsor the development of this work. A complete plan for the future development of the college after the war has been drawn up and submitted to the Board of Founders acting concurrently as Board of Directors and through it to the cooperating missions. We are happy to report that the Reformed Church Mission has shown great interest in our plan for the development of Music in the college and that the Board of Founders has approved in principle our plan for the future development, pending financial developments.

Suggestion has come to us from time to time as to the advisability of moving the college to a greater center possibly nearer to our original site. Careful study has been made of this problem, and our conclusion is that under the circumstances such a move would neither be wise nor possible. Transportation is not the most serious consideration, although it would certainly be very expensive. But more so would be the expense of getting up the college again in a new site when any town of considerable size with good communications is already overcrowded in Free China.

The question has also been raised and studied by a committee appointed by the Executive Committee pro tem to start a freshman class in another center, preferably in the Central China Region, not remote from some of our affiliated Christian middle schools. The report brought back by this committee is unfavorable. It seems impossible to start a freshman class in another place and carry it on unless the college is able to move back to Central China inside of a year after such a class is started, or else it would mean either having another branch of the college in a second site, which is out of the question, or splitting the faculty and equipment which is again impractical. It is, therefore, the considered policy of the college to stay in Hsichow until it is time for us to move back to Central China with the return of peace.

We are looking forward to the new academic year with great optimism, as far as the college is concerned, than we felt at this time a year ago. Dean and Mrs. Constantine are going only on furlough back to England. Mr. Constantine expects to return to the college after a year in Great Britain, Mr. and Mrs. Walter Allen are leaving the college, Mr. Allen to join the American army in China, and Mrs. Allen to return to America on health grounds. Professor Bleakley and Professor and Mrs. Anderson have decided to stay on one more year in the college before they take their furloughs, and the decision has added to the morale of both the faculty and students. All the other members of the faculty and staff have accepted reappointment.

Mr. Gorge Bien, Ph. D., Brown, for many years a professor of Chemistry in government universities and now a chemist in government service, has accepted our call to become professor of Chemistry and head of the Chemistry Department. Professor Teng Mo-tung, who did his postgraduate work in the London School of Economics, has accepted appointment as professor and head of the Department of Economics-Commerce. Mr. Daniel Chen, B. S. Hua Chung 1936, who has been teaching in middle schools for the last eight years is returning to be lecturer in Biology, and Mr. Sun Chang-hsi, B. A. Peking University, has accepted appointment as lecturer in Chinese Literature. Miss Leona Lloyd Burr, M. A. Wisconsin, who has been evacuated by the American government from Fukien, has come to join us as assistant professor of English Literature. She has accepted two-years' appointment, leaving the question open at the end of that period. We are in negotiation with three or four other prospective teachers, as we are still badly in need of strengthening the departments of Biology, Chemistry, English, Economics, and Music. It is an ill wind that blows no good to anyone, and we hope that the disturbed conditions in the southeastern provinces of China may make it easier for us to get teachers to fill more of our vacancies.

Francis C. M. Wei
Hsichow, Yunnan, China
July 7, 1944

A Memorandum on the Planning of the Christian Colleges in China After the War

The Minutes of the meeting of the Planning Committee of the Associated Boards for Christian Colleges in China on May 5, 6, and 7, 1944 and those of the Twelfth Annual Meeting of the Associated Boards on May 8 and 9, 1944, together with the Preliminary Report of the Planning Committee to the Associated Boards on May 8, 1944, are significant documents. No one can read them without being deeply impressed by the genuine concern of the members of the Associated Boards and of all its committee about the present situation of the Christian colleges in China and their future development after the war. There was clearly manifest in the meeting much consecrated thinking. All the recommendations made and the actions taken showed wisdom, statesmanship, and a balanced outlook. Even if one may not wholeheartedly agree with all the decisions, one must admire the foresight and the courage embodied in those decisions, which it must be remembered are only preliminary.

Those of us in Hua Chung College who have considered carefully the Preliminary Report of the Planning Committee to the Associated Boards on May 8, 1944, as recorded in the Minutes of the Twelfth Annual Meeting of the Associated Boards, feel impelled to agree in general with the Principles to guide the future development of the Christian colleges in China after the war. The report recommends that there should be only six centers of Christian Higher Education—in North China, West China, South China, Central China, East China, and the National Capital—to meet the needs of the Christian movement in China and those of the nation as far as the personnel and the financial resources available for Christian Higher Education will permit, taking fully into consideration the educational policy of the Chinese National Government. This is entirely in accord with the recommendation of the Council of Higher Education of the China Christian Educational

American meeting in Chengdu and Chungking in May 1943, advocating "concentration in a limited number of strong institutions carrying on Christian liberal education, each with such professional training as the Christian movement in China warrants, but with special care to avoid duplication."The recommendation of the Council of Higher Education is found mentally sound, although its working requires explanation and amplification. We agree also with the Preliminary Report of the Planning Committee that for the postwar planning of the Christian colleges in China the program for Christian Higher Education in North China, East China, Nanking, and Foochow must be thoroughly re-examined. Such re-examination should be objective, realistic, and take into consideration the experience of university education in Europe as well as that in America. The Planning Committee enumerates five different ways which the colleges in the four locations mentioned above may follow in order to achieve cooperation in each of the areas. It takes the cautious position of not urging organic amalgamation, but declares that "cooperation based merely on friendly consultation will not suffice to meet postwar needs," and recommends "Academic Consolidation," "Federation," or "Coordination" as defined in its Preliminary Report, believing that at least "Coordination" should be effected in each of the areas mentioned, although the past has clearly shown that "amalgamations have resulted in great gains and no significant losses." The committee could not have chosen a milder language in expressing its convictions. But is there not a very marked distinction between the situation in North China and East China on the one hand and Nanking and Foochow on the other? In the former two areas there used to be strong colleges with government recognized "university" standing, whereas in the latter two areas the question has always been coeducation or a separate and entirely independent college for women. In the discussion recorded in the minutes of the Planning Committee, as well as in those of the Associated Boards, reference is made more than once to the "Oxford and Cambridge Plan." What better suggestion could be made than that the college for women in Nanking or Foochow become an Oxford or Cambridge college in its own area? We have yet to find an argument for independent women colleges that is a compliment to womanhood, but that may be only a confession of ignorance on our part. This is, however, a detail which will be solved in due course of time. For the present let us keep our attention to the main issues.

First, six centres for Christian Higher Education in China is the very maximum.

It is readily admitted, as it has been eloquently argued, that reduction in the number of colleges does not guarantee improvement in quality and that money should not be the only consideration. But adequate funds constitute one of the essentials for the proper conducting of Christian Higher Education in China. Whether we like it or not, experience has shown that adequate financial support is necessary to educational efficiency in this modern world of ours. What would six Christian universities "of highest standards, firm Christian purpose, and vigorous and growing effectiveness" cost in personnel and finance?

We envisage six strong institutions "carrying on Christian liberal education." But "liberal education" must not be given an American interpretation. According to the present educational policy of the government, it can not be done by "the breaking down of department walls"; it has to be done, and we believe it can be done, by keeping within the framework of the government educational program, but with internal modification, provided the scope of offering in each institution is wide enough to make such modifications possible, into these details we do not propose to go in this connection. A "strong" institution ought to be qualified to be a "university" (ta hsueh) with the Ministry of Education. At least three colleges are called for in each institution. These three "colleges" should be Arts including Theology, Science, and Education. Theology at present is not recognized by the government as a separate faculty, but in our own budgeting it should be so reckoned. There will be six times four or twenty-four "colleges". If it is deemed wise to have not one single strong medical college, but five of the B, or at least of the C grade in the Christian Higher Education program, and only one college of commerce, one of agriculture, one of political science and law, and one of engineering, the last being entirely doubtful to the mind of the present writer, this adds nine colleges to our whole scheme, making a total of thirty-three "colleges" (Hsueh Yuen) in the six institutions altogether.

According to the latest report of the Ministry of Education, published in 1943, giving the most up-to-date statistics which are for the year 1940, there were in that year 192 "colleges" in the whole country. This number is not likely to increase rapidly, for the policy of the government as far as we can ascertain, is to strengthen the existing institutions of higher education, not to increase their number. With 33 "colleges" Christian Higher Education would have more than one-sixth of the "colleges" in the entire country.

We would be doing well, if we could maintain all these thirty-three "colleges" in "highest standards, firm Christian purpose, and vigorous and growing effectiveness." Of course, "highest standards" is a relative term. Naturally, we have in mind and we ought to keep in mind, the international standards of the highest kind. Nothing else would be worthy of China or of the Christian name. At least we must keep our institutions of Christian Higher Education at par with the national university or else we may not attract the students of the highest caliber as we would want to do. In 1935 one of our Japanese colleagues in Christian Higher Education in Tokyo told the present writer that the Christian "university" in which he was dean could get only the Japanese students of the third or fourth grade, because the better ones chose to go to the imperial universities or government professional schools. It was a pitiable predicament. May we in China keep ourselves out of it? Let us assure ourselves and rejoice that the national universities and professional schools will improve in personnel, equipment, and general financial support, yet also, in instruction and research, in discipline, and character-formation of the students as well in other words, in all round educational efficiency. This must be the case or else China has no hope in higher education. The Christian colleges can never meet all the educational needs of this vast country with its increasing demands for trained men and women. We must not be under the illusion that we shall lead in higher education, particularly in its more technical branches. But we should never rest content to be too far behind in whatever line of university education we may attempt. Our duty is not to do all that may be needed, but to do that which our resource will warrant that we can do the best.

What then, would be the cost of thirty-three "colleges" in our program?

According to the prewar regulations of the Ministry of Education governing universities, a college of Arts, Law, Commerce, or Education should have the minimum annual current budget of N. C. $80,000 and a college of Science, Medicine, or Agriculture should have the minimum annual current budget of N. C. $150,000. While this minimum budget was not in every case maintained before the war, although some colleges had more, it will not be adequate after the war, even assuming prices will after a period return to the prewar normality. We must budget N. C. $150,000 for each of the colleges of Arts, Education, Law, or Commerce, and N. C. $200,000 for a college of science or a college of Agriculture. In the estimate of the government, Engineering is the most expensive, N. C. $200,000 a year before the war. We may have to allow at least N. C. $300,000 after the war. Certainly, N. C. $150,000 will not be enough for a college of Medicine. Even before the war the minimum annual current budget for a medical college of the "B" grade, as rated by the China Medical Association, ought to be in the estimate of the Association at least N. C. $400,000. Theology in the Christian program has to be reckoned to cost as much as Arts or Commerce.

Six colleges of the Arts, six of Theology, six of Education, one of Commerce, and one of Law would call for the minimum annual current budget of N. C. $3,000,000; six colleges of Science N. C. $1,200,000; and one college of Agriculture and one of Engineering, N. C. $500,000; and five colleges of Medicine, N. C. $2,000,000. The thirty-three colleges, at this reckoning, would cost Christian Higher Education in China after the war at least N. C. $6,700,000. But imagine an annual budget of N. C. $200,000 for a college of Agriculture, or N. C. $150,000 for a college of Law. Such a budget would certainly not insure "highest standards" and "vigorous and growing effectiveness." And all along we have been thinking of only six centres of Christian Higher Education. Can we eventually count on N.C. $6,700,000 for the support of six "strong institutions" of Christian Higher Education in the postwar China? A study of the total prewar financial resources of the Christian colleges in China will throw some light on this problem.

In several of the Christian colleges before the war income from tuition and other student charges was a considerable item. With flourishing national universities in all of the six centres of Christian Higher Education, charging no tuition fees, with the greater prestige of those national universities, and with government restrictions to the amount of tuition and other fees which private colleges will be allowed to charge, how much could the Christian universities still count on as income from student fees in postwar China? Undoubtedly the Chinese government will continue its grants to the Christian universities and probably increase them. Would these grants counterbalance the reduced income from fees? What would be the maximum grant that a private college may receive in terms of percentage of the whole college budget without jeopardizing its private character? Appropriations by the Missions abroad for Christian colleges in prewar China, not to mention these last seven years of war, have never been adequate. If not for the extra support derived from the United China Relief through the Associated Boards and the British Aids to China, how many of the Christian colleges would have been able to maintain themselves since 1937? The goodwill of the American and British peoples for China for the last five or six years has been overwhelming, and the Christian colleges have profited by it. But we must not remain under the illusion that goodwill always manifest itself in money gifts. In the postwar world money may not be over-abundant everywhere. There will be for years many calls for whatever money there is for relief, for rehabilitation, and reconstruction. Besides, goodwill is a sentiment, and sentiments are evanescent.

On Christian Higher Education finance is, of course, not the sole consideration. Personnel is equally important, if not more so. Our experience in the Christian colleges in China has taught us that the faculty-student ration is at least 1:10, not counting assistants, technicians, and clerks. If there should be 1,000 students in each of the six centres, when the Christian universities are in full swing in a few years after the return of peace, there would be a total enrollment of 6,000 students. There must be 600 faculty and staff members. The Christian character of a college depends largely upon the men and women who make up the faculty and staff of the college. For a Christian college we believe that at least 75% of these men and women would be practicing Christians. Let us assume that 25% of these are missionaries and that every missionary is a practicing Christian, we still have to find three hundred Chinese Christian scholars qualified to be university teachers with an international outlook and dedicated on Christian Higher Education, before the six Christian universities can be strong institutions of "highest standards, firm Christian purpose, and vigorous and growing effectiveness." Are these three hundred Chinese Christian scholars to be easily found? The president of every Christian college in China will say it is not easy, and it will not be easy after the war. Unless the Christian scholars are found, the Christian universities will suffer in standards in Christian purpose.

In 1922 after the National Christian Conference in Shanghai one of the leading missionaries with the widest experience in China remarked that there were at that time in the whole country more than fifty Chinese Christians who were able to think in terms of the whole Christian movement. But in each of our proposed six Christian universities we must have a number of such Chinese Christian leaders. It must be extravagant to imagine that their number has been increased six times during the last two decades. Suppose that has been the case. There are 300 of them then. Not all of them have the peculiar stuff of which university professors are made. Neither should all of them be roped into university teaching and administration. The Christian movement in China has other activities, and some of our most highly educated Christians ought to be engaged in the various departments of national and social life. Assume, then, that only one-third of the 300 Chinese Christian leaders of the highest intellectual qualifications, a number entirely conjectural and problematic, only one hundred of them are devoting themselves to Christian Higher Education. We could on an average count on only sixteen of them in each of the six Christian universities. When the butter is spread too wide, it naturally becomes too thin! We dare not make it thinner.

Then we have the number of Christian students to consider. Without a sufficient number of Christian students the universities still lack a Christian atmosphere. But how many of such students should there be in each college? Generally and arbitrarily speaking, we say there should be 60% of Christian students in a university before it can effectively maintain its Christian atmosphere. The percentage of Christian students in the Christian middle schools has been, to be sure, only about 30%. We do not propose to discuss here whether 30% is good enough for a Christian middle school. Let it be pointed out, however, that university students are as a whole more independent in their thinking and not so easily led as a class by their teachers. Unless we have a good majority of the student body Christian, the tendency is for the student activities to be dominated by the non-Christian element. And 60% of 6,000 students gives us the number of 3,600 Christian students in the six Christian universities. Are we sure to have that many? Before 1925 the percentage of Christian students in all the Christian colleges in China was high, but once then it has been dropping in many of the colleges. This may have serious effects, and we ought to take steps to check the tendency.

The Christian population in China now is approximately 500,000, outside the Roman Catholic Church. The Roman Catholic Christians are not considered in this connection because we are thinking only of the non-Roman Christian Higher Education, and so far very few of our students in the Christian universities are Roman Catholic. Assume, and it is a big assumption, that in thirty years the non-Roman Christian population in China grows to one million. 9% of this population or 90,000 children would be in the primary schools. That would mean universal education for all Christian children of primary school age of 6 to 12, whereas at present only between 1/4 and 1/3 of the Chinese children of primary school age are in the primary schools. Assume, further, that 20% of the Christian primary children will go on to the secondary schools. (For the whole of China at present the secondary school population is less than 5% of the primary school population.) Assume also that 20% of the secondary school children will, after graduation, come to the Christian universities. (At present the college population is only approximately 10% of the secondary school population.) On such liberal assumptions, our calculation gives us only 3,600 Christian university students. Some of these are bound to go to the national and other non-Christian institutions of higher education. We would not have, then 3,600 Christian students in our six Christian universities. We should count the number of converts in the Christian middle schools and colleges, but they will not counterbalance the loss to non-Christian schools and colleges. Therefore, on every count, six Christian universities of 1,000 students each is the very maximum for which we may do our postwar planning.

Would it be wise, then, to reduce the enrollment in the Christian universities? Hardly, because in the first place, it is not economical. To have strong institutions to attract the best students the range of offering must be reasonably wide. A large offering requires a large faculty and this is expensive. Secondly, when the faculty is not sufficiently large to assure in adequate number of professors in each department, the teaching staff in the departments will be easily upset, as experience in the smaller colleges during the war years has taught us. Thirdly, when the enrollment is too limited, the classes in the upper years when divided into departments, for specialization, as required by the government, will be too small to be stimulating. Fourthly, the students in China have the tendency to flock to universities where there is a large number. There is the mistake in the student's mind and in the unenlightened public mind to judge a university by its size. This mistake may take years to correct. Fifthly, then the number of students is too small, the chance of having those of the highest caliber is proportionately small, until the small universities have proved their quality after a long period of years and have built up their prestige. Now the Christian universities are fighting against time while the national universities are forging ahead full steam. An enrollment of 1,000 students may be too large, but we are planning for future decades. If the maximum of 1,000 or 800 is reached by a gradual growth of twenty years, we may not be overwhelmed by numbers, and then the principle of more strict selection may be applied. What must be borne in mind from the beginning is not to build Rome in a day. Our calculation above of the maximum enrollment of 6,000 for the six centres of Christian Higher Education is based on a period of gradual development. This implies that the present enrollment of some of the Christian colleges is too large for effective Christian Higher Education. What it should be in any Christian college is a question to be answered by the authorities of the college concerned.

The above consideration lead us to agree with the thinking of the Planning Committee in its Preliminary Report to the Associated Boards on May 8, 1944, that there should be "six major centres of Christian Higher Education," except that we would like to suggest the deletion of the word "major," which must have been inserted by a cautious member of the committee to avoid over-lengthy discussion on a controversial, delicate subject.

Secondly, what are the courses to be included in our program of Christian Higher Education?

We are impelled also to agree in general with the Preliminary Report of the Planning Committee on the question of the courses to be included in the program of Christian Higher Education in the postwar China. The Minutes of the meeting of the committee on May 5, 1944, report "a wide range of views." Undoubtedly, "in view of the population and needs of China, no limit can be set to the opportunity for Christian Higher Education in the future," but we seek to develop "the type of education which Christian institutions at their best can most effectively provide within the limitations of resources in personnel and finance which can be made available in China and the West." The range of views on the courses to be included in the Christian Higher Educational program can be narrowed only by a "far-visioned, statesmanlike, and united action" in emphasizing above everything else "the fulfillment by the colleges of the high mission to which God is clearly calling them in the years ahead." Obviously we are called not to meet all the needs of China in higher education. This we cannot do and therefore it is not our duty to do it. It is clearly not our paramount duty to seek to improve tea culture or the porcelain industry by diverting to the task a portion of our limited resources, although China may increase its tea exports and revive one of its famous practical arts by our efforts, because we have other calls in higher education more pressing and because industrialists will take care of them without our cooperation. Surely we will not be allowed by the present government policy, not likely to change, to have a hand as private institutions in military education and aeronautics. Outside these and other similar fields, our resources in personnel and finance will confine our endeavour to even a smaller area which is determined by the needs of the Christian movement in China and by our desire to help shape by our Christian influence the cultural development of the Chinese people and the social, economic, and political trends of the Chinese nation in the generations to come. This is already a huge order. We are compelled to make a further distinction, the distinction between our influence in contact with the physical element and our influence in contact with the human element. Without any idea of divorcing the two too sharply and without any intention of minimizing unduly the physical element, we want to emphasize the importance of touching the human element. Whether a Christian or not, an engineer has to build a good bridge or else a better engineer will take his job from him. But from our point of view a good teacher ought to have the right outlook on life, besides being well trained in pedagogy. The scientist helps to shape the weltanschauung, and we want to see to it that he seeks not only "knowledge for knowledge sake," but knowledge for revealing the unity and majesty of truth underlying the universe. In between we have shades of difference. But such a principle guides us in placing our emphasis on where it should be greater and where to stop at the end of our rope. Hence, we propose to classify the courses under four categories in the order of their relative importance from the Christian point of view in developing our private Christian institutions.

A. Theology, Arts, Education, Science

B. Medicine, Commerce (including Economics)

C. Political Science and Law, Agriculture

D. Engineering

Arguments for Class "A" need no further laboring. We consider Theology, Arts, Education, and Science to be essential to the Christian universities in all the six centres with proper coordination between East China and the national capital (assuming it to remain in Nanking) in Theology, Education, and whatever "colleges" to be developed in that region.

We desire to register our dissent from the argument advanced for a single medical college of the top-notch grade in the whole Christian Higher Education program. Such an attempt would consume our entire financial resource, if this one medical college is to be really top-notch. It was wisely and eloquently pointed out in the meeting of the Twelfth Annual meeting of the Associated Boards on May 8, 1944, as recorded in the Minutes, that "medicine has been traditional one of the three great enterprises of the Christian Mission and today there are hundreds of Christian hospitals scattered all over China," which must "maintain their Christian character," not necessarily by specialists of "the highest standards of the Rockefeller Foundation and Harvard University," but mostly by general practitioners of sound training as may be graduated by medical colleges of the high C or B grades at the prewar rating of the China Medical Association. But we must see to it that these doctors "should be Christians approaching their task with the insight of their faith." It would be wise and within the resources of the Christian movement in China to have one medical college of the type we have in mind in each of the five centres, counting East China and national capital as one.

It may seem strange if we should attach greater importance to economics and commerce than to political science and law. We are inclined to do so not only because "China can get along without 10,000 lawyers," (We may need 10,000 lawyers, but we may leave their training safely to other institutions,) but because we believe that the economists will have much to do in shaping the national economic policy which is of vital importance for the welfare of the people and for the permanent peace of the world, and also because of the penetrating influence of the 10,000 business men, big and small, scattered all over China and coming into daily contact with Chinese society and with other nations. Besides, we know that while good officials may not have any training in political sciences or law, a knowledge of economics helps all people engaged in modern business.

It is not essential for all the Christian universities to have a college of commerce or a college of political science and law. North China may by tradition find the latter advisable, but can get along without the former. South China and Central China will need a college of commerce because of their location, and East China in the Shanghai area may deem both political science and law and commerce necessary. But nothing should prevent all the six centres from teaching some economics and political science in one of the departments, although when the Christian university is in a big commercial centre a college of commerce will be necessary.

We agree with the Planning Committee that there should be only one college of Agriculture under Christian auspices, but we wish to add our own reasons for this conclusion. China is an agricultural country, and therefore the science and art of agriculture are of paramount importance to its development. But for the Christian movement it will be of vastly greater value for the Christian forces to devote their energy to the training of agriculturists to help the farmers than to devote it to scientific research in agriculture which is expensive and will be taken care of by government institutions. The agriculture training required for our purpose can all be done in vocational schools at the secondary level. In the Christian Higher Education program only one front rank college of agriculture needs to be included. This will train teachers for some ten or twelve vocational schools of agriculture of senior middle standards under Christian auspices and distributed over the five main regions of Christian education. Besides this, it may carry on scientific research in agriculture to only a limited extent according to the resources available.

Indeed, the relation of the Christian universities to the Christian middle school is one of the problems to which the Planning Committee has not given adequate attention. Without taking carefully into consideration Christian education at the secondary level in all its aspects, our picture of Christian Higher Education is confused. China, according to the Generalissimo's estimation, will need within the first ten years of reconstruction, approximately two million four hundred and forty thousand trained people in all the branches of science and technology. Only less than one half a million, or less that 1/5 of the number required, are to be graduates from universities and technical schools of junior college grade. Over 4/5 will need education of the secondary grade. The agriculturists we propose to train in vocational schools come under his category. Vocational training along other lines in many of our Christian middle schools should also be attempted. Business schools, and schools of mechanics or other technicians, may come within our purview.

This leads us to the question of engineering. A college of engineering will be a most expensive undertaking for Christian Higher Education. We would not say that "nothing less than the absolute best can be tolerated," in our Christian Higher Education program. Certainly the absolutely best college of engineering would be beyond our reach. But a course of civil engineering or one of mechanics or electricity does not make an engineering school worthy of the Christian name. What resources will be available for the college of engineering in any of the centres of Christian Higher Education to keep up with the rapid development of the modern science of engineering, the latest inventions and the most up-to-date processes? Shall we teach our students in engineering with engines shed by the engineering firms from their showrooms in Shanghai or Hongkong? Will the manufacturers of machines and tools send their models for advertisement to our mediocre college of engineering or to the more flourishing and better supported government universities? Many students in China will wish to study engineering, but they may go to the government institutions. We do not pretend to meet all the educational needs of China, and we might just as well admit our limitations. If our resources are ample, we may attempt everything. But if our resources are limited, let us do those things we must do and can do best. We recommend that we take the courses or faculties classified under the four headings above, and according to the best policy for the mobilization of our total resources eliminate, it need be, from the bottom up. To our mind engineering would have to be the first to be eliminated.

One word more must be added before we are through with the subject of special courses to be included in the Christian Higher Education program. The Ministry of Education has proclaimed the policy of concentrating all the training of both primary and secondary school teachers in the government normal schools and national teachers' colleges. Only one of our colleges is at present allowed to keep its school of Education, and that permission may be withdrawn after the war. What about the faculty of education proposed for all the centres in our scheme? In the eventuality of the government persisting in its policy of eliminating all privately-supported schools or even departments of education, the Christian universities ought to endeavor at least to secure permission to maintain the so-called Second Part of teachers training. This would enable the Christian universities to give a one-year course of pedagogy to qualify as secondary school teachers graduates from the colleges of Arts or the colleges of Science. In that eventuality, however, one research institute of Education with emphasis on research in Christian education ought to be maintained in our nation-wide program of Christian Higher Education.

Before we conclude this memorandum a word must be said about the distribution of the total resources available, both personnel and finances. Certainly we should not return to the prewar status. But what should be the guiding principle for the distribution of our resources? It is a wise, broad principle that there should be "no single pattern, as respects size or program, which is applicable to all Christian institutions of higher education." However, "each institution should regard itself as part of an organized cooperative enterprise." The character and the needs for higher education vary from region to region. This should not be determined by the courses already established and the number of students enrolled in the past, but gauged according to the potential possibilities in the future to the best of our knowledge. Consideration ought to be given to the geographical and cultural conditions in each of the five main regions, the government policy for its economic development, the number and character of the tax-supported and other institutions of higher education movement to be met there by the Christian university. Each region, as a region, not the Christian institutions of higher education in it, ought to be taken as a unit so as to ensure the even and proper development of the whole country for the future. This is mainly a financial matter, but it concerns also the problem of planning.

Francis C. M. Wei

Hsichow, Yunnan, China

September 9, 1944

Annual Report on the Work of the Department of Chinese Literature and History in Hua Chung College for the Year 1944—1945

July 5, 1945
To the Board of the Harvard-Yenching Institute
Professor Serge Elisseeff, Director
17 Boylston Hall, Cambridge, Massachusetts, U. S. A.

Dear sirs:

I have the honor of submitting to you, on behalf of our department of Chinese Literature and History, the report on the work of the department for the year 1944—1945.

As in previous years, the committee appointed by the Executive Committee Pro tem of our Board of Directors, consisting of five members, administers the funds received from the Harvard-Yenching Board through the treasurer's office in the college, and decides on the research work to be done by the various members of the department. For the last year the members of the committee were: the President of the college ex-officio, as chairman; Dean P'u Hwang of the School of Education; Dean John C. F. Lo of the School of Arts; Dean Richard P. Bien of the Yale-in-China School of Science; and Assistant Professor Fu Mau-chi, head of the Department of Chinese Literature and History as Secretary. The committee meets regularly twice a term and at other times when necessary.

Professor John L. Coe, treasurer of the college, will send you on behalf of the committee the financial statement for the year ending July 31, 1945, sometime early in August. I enclose a copy of the 1945—1946 Budget for the Department of Chinese Literature and History, as prepared by the committee on the administration of the Harvard-Yenching Funds, approved for recommendation by the Executive

Committee Pro tem of the Board of Directors, and finally approved by the Board of Founders now acting concurrently as the Board of Directors with its office in New York. I am sending you also a list of the teaching staff in the college for Chinese Literature and History with qualifications and experience, a list of the students who have been majoring in the Department of Chinese Literature, a list of the courses which have been offered in Chinese Literature and History during the past year, and also a list of the courses to be offered for the next year.

As you will see from our budget, as well as from our financial statement, the grant from your Board for our Department of Chinese Literature and History is not sufficient to meet the expenditures with rising prices, owing to inflation in the country, and the expenditures for next year will be even higher. We are, however, thankful that the blocked dollar is having a higher rate of exchange, or else the deficit would be still greater. But the rate of exchange of the blocked dollar can never catch up with the soaring prices. Whatever deficit there is will be met from the reserve fund accumulated from your annual grants during the past year. It is my hope that the balance from the reserve fund at the end of this year will be sufficient to meet our deficit at the end of next year.

In previous years members of our Department of Chinese Literature and History were greatly benefited by the criticisms which members of your Board had made on the papers we sent to you. For one reason or another we have during the last year received no criticism from you on the papers we sent a year ago. All members of the department who have been doing research work have asked me from time to time whether I had received any work from you about their research papers, and I have had to disappoint them by saying no criticism had been received.

A. THE TEACHING STAFF, COURSES, AND FINANCES

1. We started the current year with the hope that we might have a full staff for the Department of Chinese Literature and History, but unfortunately Professor L. P. Pao, the senior professor in the department, passed away early in August. Because of the fact that he

left a widow and two children here in Hsichow and three children in his native province of Kiangsi, all of whom depended upon his income for a livelihood, particularly during these war years, the college authorities decided to accept the recommendation of the committee on the administration of the Harvard-Yenching Fund to continue the payment of salary and subsidies to the Pao family for the whole year, so that there might be time for family and the college to make some adjustment for their support. This was necessary because the family has been cut off from their native province on account of the war, and therefore it was impossible for them to return to their native home until at least after the end of the war. For this reason the department did not fill Professor Pao's vacancy, and adjustments were made to take care of his courses. We have been, however, fortunate in securing the services of Mr. Sun Chang-hsi, B. A. Peking University, to give the courses on Modern Chinese Literature. All of the other members in Chinese Literature, viz. , Assistant Professor Fu Mou-chi, Chinese Linguistics; Assistant Professor Tung Chung-peh, Chinese Poetry; Assistant Professor Yin Fa-lu, Chinese Literature; Assistant Professor Lin Chih-t'ang,Chinese Literature; have been carrying on their courses as in the previous year. Mr. Che Chung-chih, instructor, has been teaching the make-up courses in Chinese, and he has been doing some research in Chinese Philosophy, largely under my own direction.

Mr. Ma Feng-sheu, Professor of Chinese History, and Mr. Wang Yu-tse, Assistant Professor of Chinese History, have been taking care of the courses in History. Because of Professor Constantine's absence from the college on furlough in England during the year, Mr. Ma was asked to teach a course in European History, which was handed over to Mr. Hsi Yen-liang in the second term when he arrived from Chengtu.

2. All the courses in Chinese Literature and History given during the year were necessary to meet government requirements, both for students majoring in Chinese Literature of History, as well as for the requirements in Chinese and History for students in other departments in the college. We are proud to report that so far we have been able to meet all the government requirements, as well as the needs of other

students in the college who may wish to take selective courses in these subjects.

3. It is not necessary for me to make any comments, except what I have just said, about the rising prices and the ensuing deficit both for this year and probably for the next, as these matters will be cared for in Professor Coe's financial report for this academic year and in the budget for the department for the next year.

B. RESEARCH WORK

We are sending under separate cover by air to Egypt, and thence by surface means to your office, five research papers as follow:

(1) The Origin and Structure of the Chinese Suite of the T'ang and Sung dynasties. ( ) This paper has been prepared by Assistant Professor Yin Fa-lu ( ). It is a part of the result of this study on the Ta Ch'u ( ), which was developed particularly during the T'ang and Sung dynasties. Mr. Yin has consulted carefully the studies on the same subject by the late Professor Wong Kuo-wei( ), and he feels that there are certain supplements which he ought to make to Professor Wong's research. The paper represents only two chapters of a larger manuscript which he has written.

(2) A Study on the Change of the Concepts Yung ( ) and Ti ( ). This paper has been prepared by Assistant Professor Wang Yu-tse ( ). According to Mr. Wang's research, the conception of Yung and Ti has been changing greatly in the course of Chinese History, leading to misunderstanding frequently in the study of Chinese History. His study intends to bring out the different changes so as to fix the meaning of these two terms in different periods of Chinese History.

(3) A study on Chin Wen Kung ( ). This historical paper has also been prepared by Mr. Wang Yu-tse. It is intended to bring out various facts which are not always clearly understood concerning the period under review.

(4) A Study of the Lolo Manuscript, Sii-zeu-bo-p'a, form the Ta-liang Mountains (in English), by Assistant Professor Fu Mou-chi( ). While Mr. Fu was doing his field work in linguistic studies in the Ta-

liang Mountains a year and a half ago, he was able to procure this manuscript, which according to his study contains many interesting myths of the gods worshiped by the tribes people in the mountains, references to tribal organization, and folk lore. He has transliterated the Lolo language in the manuscript into sounds, giving the meaning of each word and then the meaning of each sentence. It is chiefly a linguistic study.

(5) The Lolo Proverbs (l-pii) in and near the Ta-Liang Mountains (in English). Also by Mr. Fu Mou-chi. These proverbs were collected by Mr. Fu when he was doing his field work a year and a half ago in the Ta-liang Mountains, and he has treated these proverbs in the same as he did the manuscript in the his first paper. By his linguistic study he is able to bring out many interesting characteristics of the social organization of the tribes.

While we realize that our main work is not to do research in Chinese Literature, History, Linguistics, and Sociology, yet it has always been our feeling that unless a certain amount of research work is done, it would not be possible to keep up the academic standards of our teaching staff or to inspire our younger students in the college. Hence the committee has been encouraging the Department of Chinese Literature and History, as the college encourages the other departments in the college, to carry on as much research work as time and facilities permit. Members of the Department of Chinese Literature and History have projected following research:

1. It is Mr. Fu Mou-chi's intention to spend the greater part of his summer vacation on a trip to Likiang in order to study the Mosu( ) language. It is Mr. Fu's judgment that this tribal language has two forms: one is the pictorial writing; the other is the phonetic writing. He feels that the phonetic writing has probably some connection with the Lolo language. Studies done by other specialists have emphasized more the pictorial writing to the neglect of the phonetic writing. It is his intention to investigate the latter during his visit to Likiang this summer.

2. Mr. Yin Fa-lu will continue his research in the History of

Chinese Literature.

3. Mr. Wang Yu-tse will continue his research in Ancient Chinese History.

It is our feeling that before very long the college will be able to move back to Wu Chang when peace returns. Therefore, our research work will be done more along the lines which bear on the Central China Region. Mr. Fu will, of course, continue his research in the tribal languages in Southwest China, as far as facilities will permit, but he will extent his linguistic studies to the languages of the Miaos in Hunan and the Chinese dialects in the Central China Region.

It is our ambition that our Department of Chinese Literature and History may be able to cooperate with students in Archeology to investigate the ancient culture of the Central China Region. We hope that we may be able to get an archeologist appointed to the college faculty so that we may have constant cooperation with him. We have now in mind an archaeologist who has done postgraduate work in England and has had experience as a research fellow of the Academica Sinica. His interest is especially in field work, and it is field work that will help the exploration by excavation of the ancient culture in the Central China Region.

After our return to Central China we would want to make a collection of the folk songs and folk lore current among the people in that region. Assistants may have to be trained to make the collection in different parts of the vast region of Central China for the proper study by senior members of our department.

Furthermore, we realize the importance of a careful study of the local history of the Central China Region. As soon as we have a chance, we shall make a complete collection of the Hsien Tsz (　) of the different districts in Central China Provinces and make a sociological study of them.

There is an urgent need for a more popular commentary on the Chinese Classics, to be compiled on the model of such commentary on the Bible as Peake's Commentary. Such a work is necessary to enable the students in the senior middle schools and in the colleges to understand the ancient classics, which are getting to be more-and-more a closed book to most Chinese youth. To accomplish such an objective it will be necessary to have at least two scholars on the Classics and two or three assistants to get the Classics properly punctuated and annotated.

All these projects may seem ambitious, but with the end of the war getting so near we cannot help looking into the future and planning for what we may be able to do in order to make our work in Chinese Literature and History more of a help to the students in the college, as well as in the country as a whole.

Respectfully submitted for the
Committee on the Administration of the
Harvard-Yenching Funds, and for the
Department of Chinese Literature and History
Francis C. M. Wei
President
Hua Chung College

Report Regarding Hua Chung College Given at the Yale-in-China Trustees' Meeting in New Haven on January 26, 1946 by President Francis C. M. Wei

<u>Present Conditions of Hua Chung College.</u> The college is still operating in Hsichow. The first term was finished before Christmas and the second term has just started, beginning on the third of January. They expect to finish the academic year by the end of March, shortening the year considerably in order to allow time for the college to start its moving back to Wu Chang as early as possible in April. This is done in order to avoid the rainy season in Yunnan which will set in towards the end of May and also to get back to Central China early enough so as to get our people, both faculty and students, re-acclimated for the hot climate in the summer.

For the current year we have a stronger faculty in all departments except in the three major departments of the Yale-in-China School of Science, namely, biology, chemistry and physics. In each of these three departments we have had only one senior man with a number of junior men of instructor and lecturer rank to help out. In the minor department of mathematics, which we expect to develop as soon as possible into a major department, we have two full professors, Mr. John L. Coe and Mr. C. S. Shen, but Mr. Shen has been away during the greater part of the years, and so the Physics Department has had to help out by giving some of the courses in mathematics.

The enrollment for the first term was 286 students. This dropped down to 250 in the second term which is a drop to be expected every year in the college in Wu Chang as well as in Hsichow. Owing to poor work or other reasons about 15% of the students in the first term usually drop out in the second term.

The budget for the current year is approximately U. S. $60,000. About one-half of this has to come from the Associated Boards

Sustaining Fund and the other half from the cooperating missions.

I am very happy to report that according to letters recently received from Hsichow the college has been able to weather the storm of nationwide student agitation very well. There has been no strike of students or suspension of classes during the recent months of political turmoil in China as there has been student difficulties in almost every college in the country.

<u>The moving back of the College to Wu Chang.</u> As has been indicated, the college is fully planning to start its trek back to Wu Chang in April. A committee has been appointed by the Executive Committee Pro tem of the Board of Directors to make all the necessary arrangements. It is proposed that the route be from Hsichow to Kunming by truck, from Kunming to Chutsin by rail, from Chutsin to Kweilin by truck, from Kweilin to Hang Yang and from Hang Yang to Wu Chang by rail.

Writing under date of January 1, 1946 from Wu Chang, Dr. Taylor reported that the college buildings in Wu Chang were practically intact, including the Yale-in-China houses, one of which was only slightly damaged. But all the buildings have been stripped which means that two-thirds of the science equipment of the Yale-in-China School of Science is lost. All the books, except about 15% of them carried out in the summer of 1938, are lost and this includes about one-half of the science books in the Yale-in-China School of Science.

Dr. Taylor's letter indicates that if labor and material should be available it would take only about two months to put most of the buildings back in working condition.

Mr. Lyford has prepared the following estimates for the rehabilitation and reconstruction of the college, estimates which have not yet been finally approved by the Hua Chung College Board of Founders as the Board has not yet met since December.

Moving of the college from Hsichow to Wu Chang	U. S $60,000
Repair of the buildings	$80,000
Furniture and fixtures	$50,000

Replacement of books (for first year, the total being $180,000)	$80,000
Replacement of science equipment	$48,000
Subsidies for families on the road and for family rehabilitation in Wu Chang and other items	$60,000
	$378,000

Ten-Year Plan for the development of Hua Chung after the war.

I have with me here today a copy of the Ten-Year Plan known as the Development of Hua Chung College after the war, and I have asked Mr. Fowler to send you thirty copies as soon as they are ready. I hope you will have this document sent to all the members of the Yale-in-China Board of Trustees, except those who are in New York because they have received them.

This Ten-Year Plan has been approved tentatively by the Hua Chung Board of Founders and everything indicates that it is necessary for us to put into effect the Ten-Year Plan immediately when the college moves back to Wu Chang. You will see from the plan that the first of the ten years will call for a budget of U. S. $115,000 for annual current expenditures. Judging by the present trend of things, it looks as if in five years we would have to increase the budget up to U. S. $165,000 for the annual current expenditures. If Hua Chung is going to hold its important position as the only Christian college in the Central China region, we must keep in mind the necessity of increasing the annual budget eventually to U. S. $300,000.

Yale-in-China Association used to take a leading part in the maintenance and development of Hua Chung before the war. Its highest appropriation to Hua Chung before the war was U. S. $14,000. Shortly after the outlook of hostilities in China, it was cut down to $5,000. We did not make a very strong protest to this cut because it was our impression in Hsichow when communication was difficult that the cut was due to the reduced income of the Association at this end. While we were able to receive subsidies from the Associated Boards to meet our deficit from year to year, we did not consider it right to urge Yale-in-China Association to maintain its high-water mark appropriation for Hua Chung or even to increase it. It is our hope, however, that the Yale-in-China Association will at least double its maximum appropriation so as to make an appropriation of U. S. $30,000 towards the Hua Chung annual budget for the next academic year 1946—1947.

It is at present uncertain how much Hua Chung will be able to get from the Associated Boards to meet the needs of rehabilitation and reconstruction which according to the estimates given above will amount to U. S. $378,000. We hope that the Yale-in-China Association will at least do its share besides making a substantial contribution towards the annual budget of the college for the next academic year and thereafter.

The Ten-Year Plan will call for a new set of buildings to be erected on the present Boone campus which is entirely above the highest flood level. It has been reported to the National Council of the Episcopal Church of the United States that the Boone Middle School is definitely planning to move out and build its own campus outside the old city wall so as to leave all the land inside the Boone campus to the college. We are taking steps to buy more land adjacent to the Boone campus inside the old city wall and you will remember that land was purchased outside the old city wall amounting to approximately 25 acres. Together with the old Boone campus and several lots of land to be purchased, the land for the college will be more than fifty acres (American). According to a letter from Dr. Taylor, referred to above, land outside the old city wall and adjacent to our new property is now also in the market. The officers of the Board of Founders are taking steps to give proper authorization to Bishop Gilman, representing the Board of Founders in China, and Dr. Taylor, representing the faculty in Wu Chang, to make those purchases so as to increase the total amount of land for the college to about seventy-five acres in order to meet all future needs.

While I am raising these questions with regard to the financial support that the Yale-in-China Association may give to Hua Chung, please do not forget the necessity of Yale-in-China Association appointing some American Yale graduates to the Hua Chung faculty so as to strengthen the personal connection between the Association and the college. As I pointed out at the last meeting of the Yale-in-China

Trustees in New Haven, there is every possibility for the National Council of the Episcopal Church in the United States to appoint American Yale graduates as missionaries under the support of the National Council to teach in Hua Chung. We hope that you and members of the Yale-in-China Association and other friends will keep this in mind so as to increase the number of American Yale graduates on the Hua Chung faculty.

But over and above all these helps which the Yale-in-China Association may give to Hua Chung as one of its cooperating unites, the most valuable contribution which it can make for the future development of Hua Chung will be the possible association that Hua Chung may have with Yale University through Yale-in-China. This would give us not only academic prestige but also all the possibilities of educational and cultural cooperation between Yale University in New Haven and Hua Chung in Wu Chang, by way of exchange of visiting professors, exchange of students and cooperation in investigation and research to mention just a few of the things that may be done towards this important end.

Francis C. M. Wei

New Haven

January 26, 1946

Training Educated Leadership for the Church in China

An Address given at the Mid-Winter Quiet Day of the Alumni of the Episcopal Theological School Cambridge, Mass., Feb. 27, 1946

There is always the need of educated leadership in the church in China, and the need is particularly urgent in this new day after the war.

We need more men for the ministry, better educated men and as many of them as possible in the shortest time. They must be trained; the need must be met.

The Chinese have their traditional respect for their educated leaders. Only men who are really educated can ever lead in China. There have been a few exceptions, but those are born geniuses. They are too few to be depended upon. We must educate the others.

Leaders of the church in China must not be just practical men, men of affairs. These are valuable and necessary, but we must have real leaders, if the church in China is to command the respect of the people. After all, the church is still new in China. It is not quite understood yet. People are waiting to see what it is all about. They will watch its life and the life of its members. But they will want to know whether those who are most active in working for the maintenance and expansion of the church are people who have any other way of making a living, and whether their zeal comes from convictions reached after careful study and thinking and religious experience. Emotional appeals touch only a few in China. By and large, the Chinese are not emotional. Their culture has trained them to control their emotions. Speakers or preachers who can make only an emotional appeal are apt to put their audience on its guard. The Chinese will listen to close reasoning. They are reasonable people, even those who lack book knowledge. Church leaders must, therefore, know pretty well what they are talking about and be able to make a balanced presentation of their case. In other words, they must be well educated, at least as well educated as leaders in the other walks of life in China. Even the Chinese peasant reasons cool-headedly, although he may not be able to read or write. He may be illiterate, but he thinks and thinks shrewdly.

And the church in China is confronted with some very complicated problems, family and social problems, problems of the economic and political structure and policy, educational moral, religious and international problems, and problems concerning directly the future and the strategy of the Christian church itself and the whole Christian movement in the world as well as in China. We need the best Christian leaders in China to face these problems which will tax them to their full mental and spiritual capacity. Christian higher education in China must help to prepare them, and Hua Chung has its share.

This raises at once another question. When all the people have been prepared for leadership in the church, with the best opportunities of education, to reach the highest possible standards (and there will be so many of them if we are successful in our educational undertaking), how are they to be supported? The church is still young, numerically weak and financially feeble. Would not highly educated leadership defeat our purpose of getting the church to be self-supporting? This is a question of mission policy and I have had it put bluntly to me, because I have always been advocating educated leadership for the church in China. What is the answer to it?

Many years ago my answer was: we expect our Chinese Christians to have the sacrificial spirit and be willing to serve the church for a salary considerably lower than they could get elsewhere. This is a sound principle and ever since I assumed responsibility as college president almost twenty years I have wanted to realize this high ideal, but I have found it difficult to work.

It is difficult to work, because, in the first place, income for the professional classes in China is as a rule low; not low, of course, when compared with the wages of the coolie or day laborer in China. Before the war a professor in a government university or a government employee with equal training and ability would get a salary about fifteen times the income of, any, a man who pulled a rickshaw for a living. In the pre-war period in Hua Chung we aimed at paying our professors about 80 percent of the salary of a professor in the government, i. e. the tax supported university. It worked with some Christians but not with all. The rickshaw coolie was pitifully underpaid, due to the social conditions and economic development of the country. China was going through a transitional period in her economic development even before the war. You would find in the same community in the urban areas some people who belonged economically to the 18th century, some to the 19th, and some to the 20th. The university graduate belonged to the last mentioned group which consisted of men and women with economic requirements of the 20th century, perhaps of the 4th decade of the 20th century. But the economic development of China before the war, and therefore her social structure, was of the early 19th century even in the city. For instance, there were little or no public library facilities and therefore the professor or the man in the other professions would have to buy their own books and subscribe to their own special periodicals to keep themselves intellectually alive and to keep reasonably abreast with the 20th century world, because he realized that he belonged to it. But at the same time the 18th century village from which he could not set himself loose and the 19th century urban community in which he lived had other demands on his income and put him under social obligations which the 20th century man in American would not have to meet. As illustrations I may cite the support of a blood-kin even of the third degree, contribution to the funeral or wedding of a distant relative or friend, an occasional feast he returns for the many feasts to which one had been invited; and much business had to be transacted over the feasting table in China. It is bad to be caught between two worlds like that, the old and the new. It is costly. That was the fate of the Christian leader in China before the war, and that of the Chinese educated clergyman was even worse. He had a lower income still. One of my Christian colleagues in Hua Chung said this to me one day: "It is all right to expect the Chinese Christians to sacrifice for the church; they ought to do it. But there is a limit. One cannot sacrifice the education of one's children or the health of one's family." His remarks were very sobering to me as administrator, for I knew what it meant for I had my own family budget to look after. That is one reason why the principle of self-sacrifice alone does not always work, and I have had to elaborate it somewhat because of the peculiar social conditions in China which may be difficult for you to understand from a distance.

The second reason is that to put the self-support of the church before a church that is worthy of support is putting the cart before the horse. The cart simply wouldn't go. For self-support we get a poorly educated minister for the church or a poor educated teacher for the school. People are not attracted to it, still less willing to support it. At the most they would give it a poor support. A university or even a good secondary school can't be self-supporting in any community in the world. It is an investment, not a profit-making enterprise. I am notorious for making strong statements, but I sometimes do it when I am faced with a desperate situation in order to call attention to it. I have said it more than once both in writing and in speaking in China that if we should find a Christian university or Christian school self-supporting from student fees, the best thing would be to close it down. There must be something wrong in it educationally, and I wouldn't labor on this point.

A church can become self-supporting. But we must begin by getting for it a good minister first and give him time. A poorly educated ministry only delays the process of getting the church to be self-supporting. Would you think a drug store selling stale and inferior drugs would ever get any business even though the Public Health Bureau of the city would not interfere?

I envisage the work in the church in China will develop more rapidly than its financial strength. Even financial aids and aids in personnel from the church abroad would not be able to keep pace with it, if we should be successful in our work in the church in China.

To meet such a situation I would venture the suggestion of unpaid church ministers. I would experiment with the project of giving the minimum theological training to as many students in Hua Chung, both men and women, as there are students willing to receive it, and I would combine this theological training with an arts, or education, or science course leading to the B. A. degree or equivalent by spreading the four-year college course over five years. The extra time is for the students to take courses in theological subjects, some of which may be counted towards the college degree within the regulations of the government, for even private institutions of education when registered with the government have to operate under government regulations, but some of these theological courses will have to be taken care of by the extra time in a prolonged college course. It will work, for it has worked in the past. The bulk of our modern educated clergy, graduates of St. John's or Boone, have been trained in this way, and you know quite a number of them who have come to this country for further studies. They are not such a bad lot. One of such men, our own graduate from a combined Arts and Theological course, came to the E. T. S. and in three years he got his Ph. D. from Harvard. Several of our Chinese bishops are products of such a course of training. We call this type of training the "B" grade. It gives adequate training for the ministry, but not for the specialist in sacred learning.

To train specialists for theological teaching and research, for writing, translation, and original work we must have a three-year course of theology, on the top of a four-year college course, mainly pre-theological in character. I say "pre-theological", because we would want the candidates seeking admission to this "A" grade course of theology to have sufficient preparation in the Chinese culture in the languages in Chinese and English, which are two of the most difficult languages in the world, in a second modern European language and a Biblical language in history and philosophy. Such a course of studies in the college will give him the cultural background as well as some of the tools for his theological studies. We can train only a few of these each year, but we need them in the church in China. Please do not misunderstand me here. I do not mean to say only men of this "A" type of training can do the work we have in mind for them. Some of the men with the "B" type of training may also do it. They are the exceptions and we cannot depend upon exceptions to get the work done. I am here discussing plans and we can only plan as our human reasoning leads us.

There are churches in China, even within the Anglican Communion, which would employ preachers with a much lower educational standard. It is not my concern here to comment on this policy. We have had in China preachers and church workers whose training measured by educational standards is very inadequate, being equivalent to high school standard or at most junior college. These people meet a great need in the church and will perhaps continue to do so for some time to come. Some of them do very creditable work. It would be a grave mistake as well as gross injustice to minimize the value of their service. As long as we cannot have a sufficient number of candidates with better educational preparation to take the more advanced training, we shall have to continue to train the lower standard men in order that the work of the church may be carried on. But men with such training would find it hard to reach the educated Chinese such as university students and professors, government officials, the more intelligent business men, the professional classes. They would not have the self-confidence if they are given the work which we would give to the men with the more advanced training with such men. The church may be carried on, but not developed.

But there will be for some years to come theological seminaries even in the city of Wu Chang to train these men of lower grade. We shall seek to cooperate with them. We shall cooperate with them by throwing open to their faculties our library facilities. Some of our theological professors and lecturers may teach some of their courses or give some special lectures. Their students may have the fellowship of our students. They may come over to our university for some of the public lectures in all the departments. To accomplish such aims we would do everything possible to help these seminaries to locate in our neighborhood, so that cooperation may be easier. In this way Hua Chung will become a center of theological learning and training in the Central China region. We would not be satisfied with anything less than that.

All our theological courses are open to men and women alike. The churches in China need women leadership as well. They need church workers among the women. They need women as Sunday school directors. They need particularly women for woman's adult religious education and religious directors in the schools for girls. These workers must be trained and our theological training is intended for them, too. The combined course of Arts and Theology or Education and Theology will suit particularly their needs.

Our theological courses, particularly the combined course of five years in the college, which we call that of "B" grade, are taken not only by those students who are candidates for the ministry. We would encourage as many students in the college to take them and get as much theological training as the candidates for the ministry get. Those students who have had the combined course of Arts and Theology or of Education and Theology or even of Economics and Theology may go out after graduation to teach, to serve in government offices, to do business, or to be engaged in other lines of service in society. With their regular college course they can make their living as the other college graduates can make their living. But with their theological training they may serve the church better. It is our hope that with the theological training they would want to serve the church as lay teachers. Some of them may even seek ordination but will not depend upon the church for a living. They can carry on their secular work and continue to receive their income from that. We don't see any reason why they should not do that and give their spare time to serving the church. We are aware of the objection that the ministry is a full-time job and therefore ministers have to devote their whole time to it. Of course they ought to do so, if they are paid to do it. But the young struggling church in China with 99% non-Christian of the population of China to reach would not be able to do its job and fulfill its tremendous mission if it had to depend entirely on paid ministers, especially when a religious teacher with a regular salary paid by the community is totally a new institution in the country. Many voluntary non-salaried church ministers will have to be enlisted, and we believe that when many laymen properly trained for the ministry will seek orders and serve as voluntary ministers by giving a part of their time to ministerial work while they earn their livelihood in some other way. Our minister's work in a parish may have to be divided among two or three of such voluntary unsalaried part-time ministers. We would keep the parish small, not only to make it more effective as a parish but also to make it possible for the voluntary ministers to administer it efficiently.

We envisage, therefore, a considerable number of students taking the combined course of theology if our project should prove a success, perhaps 20 or 25, if not more in each class. Then, there ought to be a few of the post B. A. theological students who will take the "A" grade theological course, very similar in nature to the course in the Episcopal Theological School here in Cambridge, with one half of the three years given to required course, in the five main theological disciplines and the other half of the time devoted to concentrated study in one field. Only students of honor caliber will be admitted to this course. They are trained not just for a "job", but for scholarship. In China we are poor economically. Particularly the church is so and will remain so for many years to come, poor financially at least, for no matter how liberally the Christians may give and how generally the church abroad may help, our work is bound to outstrip our available resources. We would not be able to afford the academic luxury of "post-graduate" work, especially in theology, as the "A" grade theological course requires 19 years of formal education, that is, six years in elementary school, six in secondary school, four in college, and three in theology. To our mind that is enough. If a student is not prepared for scholarship by that time, additional training can do little more for him. Our "A" grade theological course should do the work of the post B. D. course in this country. I am inclined to think that our "A" grade course when properly planned will be sufficient. Circumstances will compel us in China to do it anyway. At least we believe it a worth while experiment to try. We must make this course efficient to prepare competent translators of the Bible and of the Christian classics into the Chinese language, theological teachers, Christian writers and thinkers, not only on church and religious problems but also, and equally as important, on all the problems confronting China so as to bring the Christian point of view to bear on the solution of all problems.

This is an ambitious problem and we must have an adequate and well-trained teaching staff to implement it. We need two specialists as professors in each of the five main theological disciplines, and in due course of time we shall have to appoint teaching fellows or assistants to share a part of their routine in teaching and research and writing and editing. The "B" grade combined course has to be taught, the "A" grade students need tutorial training besides instruction and tutorials, if properly done take time.

But we expect our theological faculty not only to teach students, but also to do other jobs. Whether we like it or not, it is a fact we cannot hide and still less deny that in the church in China ministers ten years out of the theological school may get into a rut and become stale, if not intellectually dead. They have to be kept alive by refresher courses and other devices to be mentioned later. The church ought to cooperate with the theological training centre to make this possible. Ministers and other church workers must be given the opportunity to return to the university from time to time, at least after every seven years of active service, and be refreshed by taking short courses of six weeks in some theological subjects by coming into contact with scholars whose business is to keep abreast with world scholarship in their own friends, by browsing about in the university library, particularly among those stacks which should interest the church minister most. Of course, if they are expected to run high-class social clubs called the church, to keep their parishioners amused and in good humor, or just to marry people, to baptize babies and to bury the dead, they could have learned all that is to be learned, once for all, in the seminary. But if they are to lead their people, old and young, in thinking as well as in enlightened devotion in a rapidly changing world. They dare not to be left too far behind the thinking world. They ought to know the latest ideas and the latest movements which have something to do with religion in general and Christian life and work in particular.

To enable our church ministers and Christian workers to do this, occasional refresher course, valuable as they may be and necessary for many, are not sufficient. The group of theological scholars in a Christian university like Hua Chung owe to their brothers working year in and year out in the rural churches, particularly those at the far-flung out-posts, the duty of relaying to them in popularized from the most up-to-date religious thinking and thinking in other areas related to the religious field. This can be done by a theological periodical combining in purpose such magazines as the Journal of Biblical Literature, *Theology Today*, *the Anglican Theological Review*, *Christendom*, etc., to mention only a few published in this country with which you may be familiar. Through such a publication we would attempt to keep our church workers posted as to the current theological thinking and the world Christian movement, introducing to them from time to time the best literature in the theological fields and hoping that through a lending library of books in Chinese, and at least in English also, they may keep up in a measure their reading and thinking. Through such an organ they may share with one another their experience and maintain their fellowship in thinking and in service.

Furthermore, there is the lay people to train, men and women who have not had the opportunity of even a high school education and who must be taught so that they may help to teach the other church members still less privileged. We see the possibility of a team of younger men under the leadership of a more mature theological professor touring the country and stopping at various centers to conduct short courses of study on the Bible, the history, the work, and the teachings of the church. We need better educated preachers, but we need also more enlightened and better informed people to fill the pews. We need more effective ministers, but their work can be more effective when the laity has been trained to cooperate with them in all their undertakings.

All these enterprises will consume time and energy. You should not wonder then, that we would need at least ten full-time theological professors. They will be kept frightfully busy, but we must see to it that they will not be too busy to do research and original thinking. They ought to have adequate facilities and adequate clerical assistance. No one should be idle, of which there is little danger in the mission field, but none should over-work which is the real temptation.

But can we find the professors we need to implement such a program, a program both elaborate and difficult? Not among the Chinese Christian scholars alone, for the next fifteen or twenty years at least. Very few Chinese Christians have been adequately trained to teach the Old or the New Testament. They have not had sufficient training in the language essential to the teaching in these fields with any originality and authority. The Chinese language is not an easy one to master and it is the language which every Chinese scholar must master just for the sake of commanding the respect of his fellow countrymen, if for no other reason. Then, he must learn his English, his German, and French, and the Biblical languages. This is no easy task. It takes time. When a Chinese student starts college with the knowledge of only Chinese and English it is a pretty hopeless job for him to master at least two more languages and acquire the use of at least three more even for reading alone. Hence, we shall have to depend upon Western scholars to teach O. T. and N. T. for some years to come. These two subjects require four western Biblical scholars for our theological work.

Of the two professors of Church History we would like to have one Chinese and the other a missionary. They cooperate to supply the Western scholarship and the Chinese interpretation, both of which are necessary.

Systematic Theology, Christian Ethics, Religious Education, and Pastoral Theology ought to be taught by Chinese scholars, because in these subjects the Chinese background is of paramount importance. Our theological faculty will be lined up with one half Chinese and the other half missionaries, i. e. five in each group, altogether ten.

Government regulations do not permit us as a registered institution to have a theological school or even a theological department. To obviate this difficulty we propose to distribute our theological professors over the different departments in the university, literature, history, philosophy, education, and what not. For certain course of instruction we draw upon the university faculty, such as philosophy, psychology, social studies, and most of the languages.

Our theological training is not denominational, because in our institution several churches are cooperating in all the other departments. Nor would we have it on the union basis.

The churches work together but each is given full opportunity to keep its own tradition and to teach its own students in some special subjects on portions of certain subjects particularly in devotional practices according to the desire of the church concerned. In this way we hope to have the maximum inter-church cooperation with the minimum compromise.

After the student has finished his five years of combined course or the three years of post B. A. theology, he takes a year of internship. We expect to arrange with certain city churches, certain churches in middle-size towns, certain rural churches, certain schools with a good religious program under an experienced chaplain or religious director, certain social centres, certain Christian literature societies, etc. to take our students as "interns". Every student after the academic theological training is assigned to one or two of these places as an apprentice to get his practical training according to the type of church or Christian work he proposes to do after graduation. During this year he spends half of his time in practical work under an experienced man. By this he will be able to pay his way through the year. The other half of his time must be devoted to reading under the direction of the theological faculty to round out the academic side of his training for the type of work to which he proposes to devote his life. Besides a satisfactory report from the man he works under for a year he is required to pass his comprehensive examinations on his whole theological course including his practical work and his directed reading during his year of internship.

Perhaps you may say that we are expecting too much from our theological students. That may be true. The usual danger, however, is to expect too little from them. The theological course should be at least as rigorous and as exacting as the medical course. The physician or the surgeon holds in his hand the life and death of his patient. But we entrust to the church minister the spiritual welfare of his parishioners, and he is to be confronted with problems different in nature from those confronting the medical man but more important and sometimes far more complicated and delicate. I wish I could be assured that the ministry as a profession has improved as much as the medical profession during the last half century and that the church as an institution has advanced into society for its uplifting as the hospital has. In China church traditions are still in the making. Perhaps it will be easier for us than for you in the West to blaze some new paths. We must create good traditions before it is too late.

  Another objection may be raised, and that is academic learning alone is not enough to make good ministers. A rich devotional life, spiritual experience, and a keen insight into the nature of man are more important. We are not unaware of this in our program of theological education, and we seek to emphasize devotional practice and spiritual discipline in our hostels. In our whole university we intend to house our students of all departments in separate hostels of fifty students each. Each hostel has a house master and an assistant house master whose business is to look after the social cultural and spiritual welfare of the students in their own hostel. The hostels are under the auspices of the different church groups which cooperate in our university. Each church group has the right to conduct the hostels under its care in its own way and according to its own traditions, as long as it conforms to the broad principles governing the life of the hostels as laid down by the universities' authorities which represent all the church groups. On our university campus we maintain the principle of diversity in unity. As to religious life in the hostels, the church groups have absolute liberty to do what they desire. It is our hope that all the traditions and practices of devotion may be maintained and kept at the highest level possible. Perhaps with a variety of traditions we may test out what is really most congenial to the spiritual nature of the Chinese people and enrich it by new experience.

  In theological education devotion and scholarship must receive equal emphasis. The neglect of either would be disastrous. But while the university can determine the scholastic standards of the one, the church groups in charge of the hostels must use their resources to promote the other, and the devotional spirit can be festered only by professors who have it themselves. Scholarship and devotion are not incompatible. On the contrary, we believe that the one promotes the other, if both are wholesome.

Francis C. M. Wei
Cambridge, Massachusetts
February 27, 1946

The President's Annual Report for the Academic Year 1946—1947 Hua Chung University, Wu Chang, China

The President has pleasure in submitting the following report of the year 1946—1947 to the Board of Directors:

Accompanying this report are the reports to the President from the Dean of the General Faculty, the Dean of Yale-in-China, School of Science, the Dean of School of Education, and the Registrar's statistical report. As the President was the Acting Dean of the School of Arts concurrently during the year, there is no report from the Arts Faculty. The Acting Treasure's report is being sent separately.

At the request of the Board of Trustees, known as the Board of Founders, in the City of New York, acting concurrently since the war years as the Board of Directors, and with the concurrence of the Executive Committee pro tem and of the Senate of the University in Hsichow, the President was granted a year of leave from the University as his sabbatical year in order to accept the appointment as the first incumbent of the newly established Henry Luce Visiting Professorship of World Christianity in Union Theological Seminary in the City of New York and as Lecturer on the Hewitt Foundation.

He left Hsichow early in July 1945, but owing to long procedure of securing passport and owing still more to the difficulty of getting transportation by air from Kunming to the United States, he was unable to leave China until early September. He was, however, able to make use of the time in Kunming to direct the affairs of the University from Kunming concerning which the Acting President frequently sought his advice from Hsichow, particularly after the surrender of the Japanese in August when the general situation in China became rather unsettled. Plans for the University for 1945—1946 were finally made before the President flew from Kunming to Calcutta, India, on September 13, arriving by air at New York City on September 21, just in time for the beginning of the term in Union Theological Seminary.

At the end of May 1946, he went to England from New York on the invitation of the China Christian Universities Association in London and visited various cities in England in the interest of the Association and for the various British missionary societies and Christian organizations until the middle of August 1946, when he flew back to Wu Chang.

Upon his return to Wu Chang, he had the pleasure of finding the university faculty, staff, families, and a certain number of students, many of whom were natives of Yunnan, already arrived at the original campus from Hsichow, together with all the library books, taken out in 1938(only about 15 per cent of the pre-war library), and part of the laboratory equipment taken out in 1938, part having been worn out and part disposed of in Yunnan owing to difficulties in transportation. Eighty-five per cent of the pre-war library and over two-thirds of the scientific equipment left behind in Wu Chang and in the warehouses of the British shipping companies in Han Kou when the university evacuated from Wu Chang in July 1938, were completely lost, and no trace could be found of them except about 300 bottles of biological specimens which have been subsequently recovered. All the furniture in the university buildings and hostels and all the personal belongings of the faculty members left behind in 1938 were also completely lost.

Before the President left China in September 1945, he had appointed in August, immediately after the surrender of the Japanese, Dr. Paul V. Taylor of the China Mission of the Evangelical and Reformed Church, a member of the faculty, but at that time still serving under the Church Committee for Relief in Asia, to get back to the university campus in Wu Chang as early as he could and to take charge of the buildings and start their repairs. Dr. Taylor reached Wu Chang from Kweilin on December 4, 1945. With the assistance of friends he was able to get the buildings gradually evacuated by the occupying Chinese troops. He found the buildings totally stript and badly ravaged, and the grounds covered with debris and dirt, some parts almost knee-deep. On the campus were found everywhere Japanese slit trenches and machine-gun pits, which had to be filled, and the ground leveled off. We had, however, in Dr. Taylor, a resourceful and indefatigable worker, just the man for the job. By May 1946, the faculty and staff members, their families and almost a hundred students, men and women, who arrived from Hsichow, were given their living quarters in university buildings. Hostels were repaired and furniture was made by local carpenters under Dr. Taylor's own supervision, so that by September, the university campus was in working condition again.

Over 10,000 volumes of books in English had considerable quantities of office supplies and laboratory equipment had been ordered by Dr. Paul Ward, working since April 1946 in New York and Washington; but these were slow in coming on account of shipping difficulties. However, the university was reopened on its original campus on September 30, after eight years of refugeeing in the Southwest.

STUDENT ENROLLMENT

Entrance examinations were held in August. Nearly 4,000 students sat for them in three centers, namely, Wu Chang, Changsha, and Kunming. In Wu Chang registration had to close earlier than the date previously announced in order to cut down the number of applicants. Of the 4,000 candidates only 300 could be admitted. As the Dean of the General Faculty has reported, "It was our hope that after our return to Wu Chang, when we could again receive students from our own affiliated schools, standards would rise, and that is being proved true." In September 1945, our last year in Hsichow, only 15 per cent of the whole student body were graduates from Christian middle schools, but in September 1946, the first term after our return to Wu Chang, it rose to 29 per cent when our student body was almost double that of the previous year.

The university was reopened with a record enrollment of 447 students. Of this number 177 were Christians, and 270 non-Christians;

英 文

and of this number 307 were men and 140 women. Seventeen provinces were represented, with the highest number, 169, from the Province of Hunan, next 109, from Hupeh, and next 68, from Yunnan, owing to the fact that many old Yunnan students had come with the university from Hsichow. Other statistics are shown in the Registrar's report accompanying the President's report.

FACULTY

We are happy to report a much stronger faculty after our return to Wu Chang. Of the missionary members, Prof. and Mrs. John Coe returned from Hsichow where they had been since 1941; Rev. John Chamberlayne and his family came back also from Hsichow; Dr. Taylor has been mentioned in connection with the work of rehabilitation; Mrs. Constantine came back from England to join her husband, Dean Constantine, who had returned to Hsichow the year before; and Miss Venetia Cox was transferred by the American Church Mission to take charge of the Music Department which had been left by the war without a senior member. The American Church Mission appointed also Miss Lilian Weidenhammer, Ph. D. , Prof. of Chemistry; Miss Edith M. Hutton, M. A. , and Miss Margaret Sheets, M. A. , both Assistant Prof. of English Literature. These ladies arrived from America in October. From this mission came in January 1947, also Prof. Paul Ward, Ph. D. , with his family to join the Department of History; the Rev. G. Francis S. Gray, M. A. and family, and the Rev. Alfred B. Starratt, B. A. , B. D. , arriving in April 1947 to teach Theological subjects as Assistant Prof. and Lecturer respectively. In November, Prof. T. R. Tregear, Ph. D. , and family arrived from the Methodist Missionary Society in London to teach Geography. Mrs. Tregear, M. B. , B. S. , serves voluntarily as Resident Physician. Prof. Margaret Bleakley, M. A. , of the London Missionary Society, returned from furlough in England after the winter vacation to resume her post as Head of the Department of Western Literature and Registrar.

Nine new Chinese faculty members have been appointed in Wu Chang. They are Prof. Chien Chi-po, Prof. Hsu China-juei, Asst.

Prof. Shao Tse-feng and Mr. Shin Sheng-hwei, lecturer, of the Chinese Department; Prof. Li Chung-chi, Ph. D., and Prof. Tseng Sheng-tse, D. Sc., (part time) of the Department of Biology; Prof. Ho Chun-chiao, Ph. D., of the Department of Chemistry; and Asst. Prof. Hu Lo-teh, of the Department of Mathematics; Asst. Prof. Ta Yun-sen of the Department of Economics-Commerce.

Dean John C. F. Lo took his sabbatical leave to be Visiting Professor in Franklin and Marshall College, Lancaster, Pa., U. S. A. and Prof. Sidney C. Hsiao of the Biology Department has been granted indefinite leave of absence for research work in Yale University.

We lost by death a promising young lecturer, Mr. Che Chung-chi, B. A., Hua Chung 1942, who had been trained by the President to teach philosophy. He died near Changsha on his way from Hsichow to Wu Chang. Miss Tai Hsun-chin, Miss Hwang Hsien-yuin, and Mr. John Wei left for post-graduate studies in the United States of America.

For the year 1946—1947, our faculty and staff are as follows:

	First Term	Second Term
Chinese	8	7
English	6½	7½
Economics-Commerce	4½	4½
History-Sociology	4	5
Philosophy	¼	¼
Theology	½	2½
Biology	3½	3½
Chemistry	5	5
Physics	4	4
Mathematics	2½	1½
Education	4	4
Music	2	2
Total:	44¾	46¾
Administration	14¾	18¾
Grand Total:	59½	65½

Of the total teaching administrative staff of 65 ½ in the second term, only 70 per cent are Christians; but if we should take the teaching staff alone, i. e. 46¾, 77 per cent are Christians. The difference is due to the number of clerks in the offices who are mostly non-Christians.

It is also to be noted that of the 65 ½ (the half is given by a missionary wife), only 15 were members of the staff in Wu Chang before the war, and 43 came back with the university from Hsichow.

THE PHYSICAL CONDITIONS to which we returned after eight years of absence were better than we had dared to expect.

Wu Chang as a city had about the same external appearance as when we left it in July 1938. So also had the other two cities, Han Kou and Han Yang, which really belong to the same metropolis of Wu Han. The streets in Wu Chang were in much better condition than those in Han Kou and Han Yang. But 40 percent of the houses were gone—torn down, not bombed out. It was therefore fortunate that the university still had its buildings and faculty residences, ravaged as they were, with only the roof and the four walls left. Repairs had been costly, but not so expensive as to rebuild. Foodstuff was available in quantity, and there were more goods in the market than we had expected.

The women students occupied, as before the war, the two buildings of the Yen Hostel. Po Yu Hostel for men was divided by temporary partitions into eight apartments for faculty and staff families. The main portion of Ingle Hall was used as a hostel for men, just as before the war, and the two wings as the Physics and Biology Departments. The Administration Building was restored to its pre-war condition, with offices and classrooms downstairs and the Chemistry Department upstairs. St. Paul's Hostel was occupied by the single men teachers or men teachers who did not have their families in Wu Chang. To accommodate all the students, the women's hospital building of the London Missionary Society, about three minute's walk from our campus and on the same street, was remodelled at our cost into a hostel for men with capacity for 96 students. Even by using all double-decker beds, the two hostels for men were not enough. A semi-permanent hostel for men was built on university land newly acquired next to the lot on which is the Practice School of the School of Education. For the first time, we had permission from the authorities of the American Church Mission to use the whole library building. Slowly but most gratifyingly, the university library was rehabilitated and opened to student use again. The library's holdings are as follows:

Western books approximately 20,000 volumes, including

    periodicals: New Accessions   14,000

                Old Accessions   6,000

Chinese books approximately 20,000 volumes, including

    periodicals: New Accessions   5,470

                Old Accessions   14,530

A larger library staff had to be employed to catalogue the many new books and magazines in both Chinese and English coming in by the hundreds every week, and also to re-catalogue the old books and magazines brought from Hsichow, many of which had to be rebound after years of rough handing during the war.

In every way we feel thankful for the reopening of the university on its original site. But it must be pointed out that hardly any of the buildings are really fit for use. The hostels, expect the new Yen Hostel, which is only half finished, are all make-shifts. They are impossible if we should attempt to run the hostels as centers of social and religious life of the students with proper care given by house masters with their own residence nearby. The Administration Building was built seventy years ago for a small school for girls. The library has no reading space, certainly not enough for an enrollment of over 400 students. It has not been constructed for proper lighting or heating. Nor can we install in it any facilities for research or serious study. We have to share the chapel with the local parish and Boone Middle School which has over 800 students, and this chapel was condemned by the architect twenty years ago as unfit for use. The small chapel in St. Paul's Hostel, with a seating capacity of only about 80, is so ridden with white ants that the rooms above it are totally unfit for occupancy. But to meet our various religious needs, we had to put it into repair during the second term in the spring of 1947, and it is now being used almost every day.

The old piano rooms formerly between the two women's hostels had to be turned over to the women students for other purposes. Six small piano rooms and a studio were built at the far southwestern corner of the campus on a piece of land bought by the university two years before the war, adjacent to the land bought known as Lambeth Field on which five faculty residences had already been erected. The Lambeth Field was bought with funds raised by the church of England to enable the former Boone University to render wider service to the Anglican Communion in China.

In anticipation of the necessity of releasing half of the Po Yu Hostel for men students in 1947—1948, thus depriving four faculty families of their apartments in that hostel, and on account of the expiration of the lease of the property of the Christian and Missionary Alliance, which we used during the year for the housing of another four staff families, we had to build during the summer of 1947 twelve simple dwelling units with an appropriation voted for housing purposes by the Board of Founders. This solves a very pressing problem and is an economic proposition, because the scarcity of houses in Wu Chang has forced up the rent on every house available, and as a rule, houses rented are unsatisfactory.

THE SCHOOLS OF ARTS

The Dean of the School, Dr. John C. F. Lo, was absent in America taking his sabbatical. The President acted concurrently as Dean of the Faculty of Arts. Professor Lo's courses in psychology were suspended, except the essential ones which were divided between Prof. Wai-king Taai and Prof. Wen-min Hsiung of the Faculty of Education.

The Department of Chinese Literature has been much strengthened, not only with a larger teaching staff but also with more experienced teachers.

But the Department of Western Literature, mainly English Literature, is still short-handed, even with the addition of some very competent teachers. Hua Chung has a reputation for its good English teaching and standard. With the poor preparation of students in middle schools during the war and with our increased enrollment, particularly in the freshman class in the year, it was difficult to maintain standards. Good teaching in English would mean small classes or sections of the same class. This has become impossible with our present staff Standards suffer. Improvement must wait for better prepared students in the middle schools as the after effect of the war is decreasingly felt.

History-Sociology and Economics-Commerce need further strengthening, which we hoped would be feasible in 1947—1948. Especially the Department of Economics-Commerce required additional appointments. It has the largest number of students, 133 in the first term and 110 in the second term, approximately 30 per cent of the total enrollment. In this department we aim at the training of not just ordinary government employees and business people, as is sometimes assumed, but the education of men who may make some impact upon the economic policy of China and her economic-relations with other nations for the promotion of better international understanding and eventually of a more lasting peace in the world. The department has two sections, Economics and Commerce. It is significant that the former is far more popular.

The Chinese student has much to learn from history, not only of his own country, but of other nations. It is regrettable that the department remains small. But during 1946—1947 it had 24 students. We must make it more attractive. In due course of time the Chinese are bound to regain their historic sense. Our duty is to hasten the process.

Philosophy under Arts is not a department. That is to say, it does not offer sufficient courses to lead to a degree. The President, for whatever time he can find for teaching, teaches all the three subjects in philosophy, viz. Logic, Ethics, and Introduction to Philosophy, required by the government, amounting to 9 hours a week. It seems that Philosophy in China as in the West at present has fallen into disrepute. It is more difficult to find competent Chinese to teach Philosophy than to teach almost any of the ordinary subjects in a college. Perhaps, the Christian universities are to blame for not having given the subject more attention in the past. We must do better in the future.

In 1945 while the university was still in Hsichow, the Theological course was started with Dr. Wai-king Taai teaching Biblical Literature and Religious Education, and the Rev. Leonard Constantine teaching church History. It is a course combined with any other major course in the university, requiring five years for the degree for which the other students not taking the theological course required ordinarily only four years. This is to meet a crying need of the churches for more and better trained ministers and other church workers, both men and women. With the arrival of the Rev. G. Francis S. Gray and the Rev. Alfred B. Starratt, the theological course has two more teachers, but it needs two more, one for Systematic Theology and one for Old Testament. The day is gone when a man can teach with confidence in more than one of the main fields of theology, and we would like to have specialists to give our students as good a theological training as circumstances permit. While we are raising the standards in the study of every other subject, we should not leave the Queen of Science behind.

THE YALE-IN-CHINA SCHOOL OF SCIENCE

Under this Faculty there are three departments offering the degree of Bachelor of Science. They are Biology, Chemistry, and Physics. Mathematics remains a minor department as before the war. It needs more emphasis, for it is the foundation of every physical science.

So far we have been laying stress on the basic training in the pure sciences, whereas the trend in the country is to emphasize the applied sciences. Our conviction, however, is that the pure sciences ought to come first, and we believe the tide will turn some day. In the meantime our enrollment in the school suffers. It is only 25 per cent of the total enrollment, whereas before the war it was 50 per cent in some years.

As Dean Richard P. Bien of the School points out in his report, "It is far from the intention of the School to offer graduate work," although Dean Bien believes that we are in a position to do post-graduate, " if standards obtaining in a number of graduate schools in this country are to be compared with ours. " But, Dr. Bien continues, "more intensive research work according to a definite long term program should be encouraged so that real serious contributions may be made to the scientific world. For this purpose a number of assistants or teaching fellows should be appointed and funds for such appointments found within the nearest future." Besides this, Dean Bien makes several other recommendations for the improvement of the School which can be read in his report.

THE SCHOOL OF EDUCATION

Ours is still the only School of Education not only among the Christian colleges but among all privately supported college in China. It serves primarily the Christian middle schools in the Central China region in supplying them with trained teachers and in assisting them in administrative problems.

Since our return to Wu Chang the local Wuhan Association of the Principals of the Christian middle schools has been revived. This brings together once a month all the principals from these schools in the Wuhan cities to meet with the President of the University and the Dean of the School of Education. From time to time other administrative officers of the middle schools are also invited when school problems concerning them are discussed. Meetings are held in the different schools in rotation. This organization promotes the sense of fellowship and solidarity among the eight Christian middle schools in the Wuhan cities, which are affiliated with Hua Chung.

A conference of the principals of the Christian middle schools in the Provinces of Hupeh, Hunan, Kiangsi, and Anhwei was held on our campus under the auspices of the School of Education from January 28 to January 31, 1947. In spite of travel difficulties, seventeen of the twenty-three principals attended and many important administrative problems were discussed in a most helpful way.

Another way by which our School of Education seeks to help the local Christian middle schools is to encourage their teachers to attend the courses offered by the school, free of tuition fees. About a dozen of the teachers made use of this privilege during the fall term in 1946.

At Eastertide, a whole day retreat of the staff members of the university and the Wuhan Christian middle schools was held in Boone Middle School with one hundred teachers attending. One of the results was bringing to the attention of all present the importance of the religious program in the Christian middle school. The need of more teachers trained to tackle the religious problems of the adolescent boy or girl was more strongly felt. Hua Chung was asked to organize a special training class for the middle school teachers, meeting for two hours one afternoon a week. This plan has been adopted by Hua Chung to begin in the fall of 1947 and the lectures are to be given by the theological staff, President Wei and Dr. Taai in the first term, and Dr. Taai and Mr. Starratt in the second term.

During the first rehabilitation year, the Practice School, which before the war served as the laboratory of the School of Education, was not reopened. The Education students did their practice teaching in Boone Middle School and St. Hilda's School for girls, both nearby. It is planned to reopen our own practice school as a junior middle school in the fall of 1947.

EXTRAMURAL ACTIVITIES

During the first year after the return of the university to Wu Chang, as well as while we were sojourning in Hsichow, the senior professors were the ones more heavily loaded for the simple reason that their longer experience had equipped them to undertake more readily those courses required by government regulations or by the needs of the students. But upon the time of these senior professors are many calls from outside the university.

Dean P'u Hwang has to serve on the Board of Directors of several Christian middle schools affiliated with Hua Chung, because he is our outstanding educational expert. Dean Richard Bien as a physicist is frequently consulted by the Provincial Government and he always renders his service freely and cheerfully. So also does Prof. Shen Lai-chiu, Head of our Department of Economic-Commerce. Prof. Wai-king Taai, Dean of Women and Professor of Religious Education, has been appointed by the Hupeh Christian Council on several committees because of her experience and keen interest in adolescent psychology and Christian education. Once a week she goes to Han Kou to conduct a training class for the Bible women of the Han Kou Diocese of the Sheng Kung Hui (Episcopal Church in China). Every Sunday afternoon, she runs a Sunday school for the faculty children and other children from our neighborhood.

So we multiply such instances of voluntary extra-mural services rendered by members of our faculty. One more type of work of significance, must however, be mentioned. New missionaries from America, Great Britain and other European counties used to go in the pre-war years to Peiping (Peking) or Nanking for their study of the Chinese language. It is well-known that our local dialect is not the same as that in Peiping or Nanking. For an alien it is sometimes painful to learn one dialect and then change to another later. Further, it is of obvious advantage to get acquainted with the local conditions of the district and of the church in the district in which one has to serve, while one is spending a year or so in the study of the language. But there had been no language school in the Central China area to which many new missionaries come every year from abroad. There is certainly the need of a language school in Wu Chang for Central China. Hua Chung helps the Lutheran Mission, with headquarters in Han Kou, in the organization of such a school. Prof. Paul V. Taylor was appointed the first director and he acquitted himself well in that office. Beginning with the autumn term of 1947—1948, we shall have our own language school on the university campus, so as to make it easier to draw upon our faculty for lectures on various libraries which are acquiring once more, gradually, a good collection of important books on China, her history and culture, in the European languages, mainly in English. Dr. Taylor will continue to serve as director. But he is concurrently professor of education and superintendent of university buildings and grounds.

FINANCIAL CONDITIONS

Financially the year 1946—1947 was comparatively a happy one.

We had many rehabilitation problems to face. Repairs had to be done and they were expensive. Consequently some still remain undone. It was impossible to replace all the library books and laboratory equipment lost during the war. This would call for U. S. $300,000. So far we have been able to find only a quarter of this amount.

For the operation budget we had an income of approximately U. S. $55,000 besides the "replacing value" of U. S. $19,625 for 18¾ missionary salaried and voluntary workers, of the operative budget exclusive of missionary salaries, more than 2/3 went to Chinese salaries. For details the Acting Treasurer is sending a separate financial report for the year.

During the first half of the fiscal year, August 1, 1946 to January 31, 1947, particularly during the first three months, exchange was very unfavorable. As a consequence we had a deficit of U. S. $5,123.03. After January exchange became more favorable and so in spite of steep increases of subsidies following the government scheme our deficit for the second half year was only about U. S. $500.

The cooperating Missions as a whole have been generous in their appropriations. Special mention ought to be made of the British Missions cooperating in the university. Great Britain has been undergoing a trying time economically, but the Missions have spared no efforts in supporting their missionary work and Hua Chung has been in the forefront of their mission consciousness.

We are happy to report the formal decision of the Evangelical United Brethren Church in the Thirty-ninth Annual Session of its China Mission held in April, 1947, in Liling, Hunan, to have an active share in our work in Hua Chung. It is so significant that we quote in toto the action of the Mission as follows:

Thirty-ninth Annual Session of the China Mission of the Evangelical United Brethren Church.

April 17th—24th, held at Liling, Hunan.

Whereas a request has come to us from Dr. Wei, President of Hua Chung University, for us to appoint a representative to their Board of

Directors: Resolved: That a member of the Mission be appointed annually, and that this shall be a standing rule of the Mission.

Closer Cooperation with Hua Chung University

Whereas it is desired by the Mission that our cooperation with Hua Chung University become more active, Resolved: That we put the following plan into effect as soon as practicable:

1. The appointment of one of our missionaries by the Mission to serve on the university faculty, as our denominational representative, and as the Hostel Housemaster and Advisor to our own students.

2. The providing of an Evangelical United Brethren Hostel for our own students, and a residence for our missionary representative on the Hua Chung Faculty.

Singed: F. W. Brandauer,
Yuanling, Hunan

It is to be pointed out here that this was the year when Yale-in-China Association would give Hua Chung a money grant. Beginning from 1947—1948 its contribution will be only in personnel, thus reducing our income for the operation budget by U. S. $5,000 a year. Further the appropriation by the Evangelical United Brethren Church is U. S. $1,000 annually. But for the year under review, it was U. S. $1,500, because the church follows the calendar year and our fiscal year crosses two years.

Grants by the Ministry of Education for the fiscal year under review were small, only N. C. $3,500,000, but before the university returned to Wu Chang, the Ministry made a Rehabilitation grant of N. C. $100,000,000 in April, 1946, when the Chinese dollar was still worth one-tenth of half an American cent. Later in June, 1947, upon our application, the ministry made another special grant of NC $20,000,000, eighty per cent of which was for rehabilitation purposes. But by that time the Chinese currency had depreciated much more.

Income from student fees was also small. We had to bear in mind the general economic conditions in China, particularly in our region.

The paying ability of the Chinese family was extremely limited. The great majority of the professional classes could hardly support more than one child in school, and usually they have more than one of school or college age.

But before the war, student fees paid into the University Treasury totaled about 150 per cent of the cost of the student's board. During the later years of the war, we charged no fees in Hsichow. In the first year of our return to Wu Chang, the fees charged were equivalent to 60 per cent of the student's board. In 1947—1948 we shall charge more, but the increase must be gradual lest we should make the university a university for only those who could afford the expenses, and lose sight of the aim for which we maintain the institution. As our fees go higher, we intend to increase the number of scholarships with proportionately higher stipends to keep pace with the rising cost of living and consequently the cost of the student's board.

Of the special grants by the cooperating Missions we wish to mention with gratitude particularly U. S. $200,000 made by the National Council of the Protestant Episcopal Church in the U. S. A. for new buildings. This was from funds raised by the church in its Reconstruction and Advance Campaign, and it was in addition to the Rehabilitation grant of U. S. $105,000 made earlier to Hua Chung.

There were during the year also contributions by individuals. The most significant single contribution was that of N. C. $10,000,000 by a Christian friend of the university who had been very generous to us before and during the war. (By the time of the writing of this report, the same friend has sent another contribution of N. C. $20,000,000).

RELIGIOUS ACTIVITIES

Hua Chung takes pride in its religious program. As before the war, we have our morning worship in the chapel every weekday except Monday when we use the period of twenty minutes 9:50—10:10 for the Weekly Assembly. Chapel attendance is free and as a whole it is good. On Sunday evening there is the Sunday Evening Service. Members of the faculty and staff are chosen by the Chapel Committee, appointed by the Board of Directors or its Executive Committee, to lead this service as well as the morning chapel. Occasionally we have a local minister or a visitor from outside of Wu Chang as preacher. As we wish to encourage the Christian students to attend services in the local city church of their own religious affiliation, we do not have any service of our own on Sunday morning.

The Chapel Committee, representing all the churches in the university, has change also of the religious program on Friday evening for five to six weeks in the first term of the year for the first-year and second-year students, among whom there are comparatively more non-Christian students. In the year under review the program consisted of six meetings. At each meeting there was a subject, such as "Why Do We Need Religion?" It was introduced by a speaker for about 20 minutes, and then the meetings broke into small groups for discussion. Many of the new students were thus given the opportunity to get acquainted in an intellectual as well as a religious atmosphere with some of the problems which lead to the understanding and perhaps the acceptance of the Christian Faith.

Each of the main denominations represented in the University has its own "Fellowship." Its membership includes both the faculty and students members of that particular church. In order of the size of membership, are Sheng Kung Hui (Episcopal Church in China), the church of Christ in China, and the Methodist Church. Besides these three fellowships the Lutheran students are planning to organize a fellowship of their own to make the fourth. It is the policy of the university to encourage all the churches cooperating in it to retain their identity and its tradition while they cooperate with each others as far as feasible in the religious program of the university as a whole, particularly in presenting a united front to the non-Christian members of the university and to the vast non-Christian community surrounding us.

We are thankful for the cooperation and harmonious spirit prevailing in the whole university, between the Westerners and the Chinese faculty members, and between the faculty and students. This may be attributed to the wonderful way in which the different religious groups work together. It is a good example of unity in diversity. One of the results was thirty university students baptized during the year into the church, and another was the growing missionary spirit among the students which must be further promoted and strengthened until Hua Chung becomes a center of missionary activities for the extension of God's Kingdom in China and in the world.

CONCLUSION

To conclude this report, the president wishes to use the words of Dean Constantine in his own report. The year under review is indeed "a year of achievement and steady progress." The year was completed according to schedule with commencement on June 28 in the midst of festivities and much rejoicing.

But we have had many problems. Some of these problems are the aftermath of the war, so to speak, and others are perennial. The enrollment has been practically doubled since we left Hsichow. But in Hsichow, the supply of students who could approach our admission standards was limited. In Wu Chang we are in close touch again with our affiliated Christian middle schools, graduates from which should always be the basis of our student body. It was only after the first term that we were reasonably sure to have properly assimilated the large number of new students. With our good traditions jealously maintained during the war years we had the confidence that we could take care of a goodly number and our faith has been justified. The happy day we went through a very difficult period of student disturbances in May and June without losing a single hour of teaching and without any ill feeling between faculty and students was our witness. But the congestion in the hostels must be relieved and the student life ought to be restored to normality as quickly as possible. The erection of two or three hostels on a permanent basis with proper facilities would be development along that direction.

Our faculty and staff members, particularly those of the higher ranks, have been sadly underpaid in terms of price index or in terms of the American currency as compared with our salary scale before the war. The suggestion of 40 per cent pre-war purchasing power is still far from our reach. And it has to be borne in mind that our faculty and staff observe strictly the principle of giving their whole time to the work in the university, and in this respect we are at present one of the very few exceptions among colleges and universities in China. For this reason we must find ways and means to give recognition to the loyalty and devotion of our faculty and staff members.

Reference has already been made to the heavy loads carried by most of our senior professors. This can be remedied by the appointment of a few more assistants or teaching fellows or by giving the senior professors more clerical help as many of them have administrative duties besides their teaching and research. Our present system is really uneconomical, for we use highly trained people for much routine work.

And research is not to be entirely neglected. Without it, teaching would become more uninteresting and even deadening. A seat of learning without vigorous and creative intellectual activities does not deserve its name. Our ambition is not to compete with the tax-supported national universities. We are aware of the danger of being elaborate and then secularized. But unless we keep up with the march of time our place as a Christian university in the educational system in the country cannot be sustained. We constantly remind ourselves and our colleagues that during the next few years of hard times, we would do well if we could hold our own, but on the other hand we dare not forget that this is also the time to lay the foundation for our work in the future, or else the future may not be ours. We ought to be modest, but under God's grace, we must be daring.

Respectfully submitted,
Francis C. M. Wei
President
October 30, 1947

The President's Annual Report for the Academic Year 1947—1948

The president takes pleasure in submitting the following report for the 1947—1948 to the Board of Directors:

Accompany this report are copies of reports to the President from the administrative officers of the university. The treasure's financial report will be submitted at a later date when the fiscal year is closed at the end of July.

......

Enrollment and Standards

The year started in September, 1947, with 537 students, of whom 192 were women and 345 were men, filling practically all the six hostels. Owing to the heavy elimination referred to in Dean Constantine's report quoted above, the enrollment dropped down to 470 in February when the second term of the year began. Some students withdrew early in the autumn to go to national universities which reopened much later than we did, because there they would receive a free education and virtually the guarantee of a degree at the end of the four years. Others realized their physical or scholastic unfitness for the work and life in Hua Chung and dropped out, and still others were required to withdraw at the first term on account of poor academic previous years the drop has been usually 15%.

Of the 470 students in the second term, 174 were women and 296 men. In the first term 41.1% of the student body was Christian, and this rose to 47.4% in the second term on account of the many baptisms during the year. In the first term there were students from 17 provinces, but only 16 in the second term. The only solitary students from the Province of Kweichow did not return in the second term. Hunan and Hupeh had the largest number of students in the university, 172 and 155 respectively in the first term and 145 and 139 respectively in the second term. Kwantung and Yunnan came next, and then Kiangsi, Kiangsu, and Chekiang. The contingent from each of the other provinces was small.

The following were the most popular departments in descending order during the year: Economics, Education, English, Chemistry, Physics, and Chinese. The figures are shown in the Registrar's Statistical Report.

In this year, the enrollment was 90 students more than that of the previous year. The demand for admission was certainly great last September. Some 3,000 students took the entrance examination in August, and from this number we did not dare to select more than 6 to 7 per cent, allowing for only two-thirds of these to enter, for over 100 had already been recommended to enter college without examination by the affiliated Christian middle schools from the highest quarter of the graduating class of each school.

In the coming year the demand for admission is apt to be greater. There may be fewer candidates for our entrance examinations in July. The university has been back in Wu Chang for two years. It is better known now that our standards are high, and middle school graduates with inferior preparation will be scared away. On the other hand, Dean Constantine reports that "More schools are applying for recognition as affiliated schools." The General Faculty has rejected such applications from several schools. But since the Christian middle schools already recognized "prize this link with Hua Chung, it has been decided to continue the system (of recommended students on condition that the regulations are strictly observed and that schools whose students fail to reach a certain standard will lose the privilege of recommending students)."

Faculty

Dean Constantine reports that "The distribution of Faculty among the different departments is fairly balanced, and it has been possible to offer all the courses required by the Ministry of Education."

The requirement of the Ministry of Education has necessitated the comparatively large teaching staff in many of the departments, particularly in those under the Faculty of Arts. A student to be qualified for the degree has to take almost three times as many courses in his own department as in an American college, and the courses prescribed are so specialized that experts have to teach them.

The following shows the teaching staff and the number of courses offered during the First Term 1947—1948.

	number of courses	teachers full-time	teachers part-time	on leave
Arts				
Chinese	28	8	—	—
Foreign Languages	29	7	2	1
History	16	5	—	—
Economics-Commerce	14	6	—	—
Philosophy, Psychology, and Religion (Theology)	7	4	—	—
Total of teachers	—	30	2	1
Science				
Biology	12	4	—	—
Chemistry	10	5	—	—
Physics	11	3	—	1
Mathematics	4	2	—	1
Total of teachers	—	14	0	2
Education				
Education	12	5	—	1
Music	2	2	3	—
Total of teachers	—	7	3	1
Physical Education	—	1	—	—
Total of 4 departments' teachers		52	5	4

Of the 61 engaged in teaching, 22 are Christian missionaries (some being wives teaching part-time), 24 Chinese Christians, and 15 Chinese non-Christians. The Christians represent 74.4% of teaching staff. There are 18 devoting their whole time to administrative work, including office clerks and assistants. Only 11 of these are Christians, 2 being missionaries and 9 Chinese Christians. These constitute only 61% of the whole-time administrative staff, but the heads of the administrative departments are all Christians. Taking the teaching and administrative staff together, we have 72% Christians. Most of the leading members of the Faculty give a part of their time to administrative duties, as deans, heads of departments, or chairmen of important committees, carrying concurrently a heavy teaching load. But the dean is able to report that "The teaching staff has shown enthusiasm and loyalty in its work." Since the return of the university to Wu Chang academic standards have been steadily going up in spite of all the adverse circumstances.

19 of the teaching staff hold the Ph. D degree, 12 the Master's degree, and 30 the Bachelor's degree. Of the last group one-fourth belongs to the Chinese department in which an advanced degree is rare, and experience in teaching and writing counts for more.

It is, however, the Department of Chinese which has done more research work. This is particularly due to the Facilities furnished by the Harvard-Yenching. Institute in Cambridge, Mass., U. S. A., whose annual grant makes possible the appointment of specialists in the several fields of Chinese studies and the purchase of certain necessary books. A limited amount of research is being carried on in the College of Science as Acting Dean George Bien's report to the President shows. But, as Dean Bien says, "due to the heavy teaching duties of the faculty members, hardly any far-reaching research project has been under way."

Members of the university staff have various joint activities for mutual intellectual stimulation. There is the Poetry Club meeting periodically. The Faculty Club, which was originally a social organization, sponsors also meetings to hear and discuss papers by its members on topics chosen from time to time. A group of about 15 senior faculty members meet every month to discuss an original paper presented by one of themselves on a subject in the field of special interest to the writer.

Extra-Curricular Activities of the Faculty

Such activities are many and various. Faculty members take active part in the life of the church with which they are affiliated, both inside and outside the university. Some of them occupy important ecclesiastical or mission position. The fellowship of the church groups, preaching at the daily Chapel and Sunday services, the work as advisers of the numerous academic clubs organized by the students, duties as wardens of hostels, Senate and Faculty committee —all these and others too many to enumerate, demand who are already overloaded with teaching.

Special mention must be made of the University Choir, the Glee Glub, the Weekly Musical Evening, and the recitals and concerts sponsored by members of the Department of Music. They add to the interest and edification of the university community.

The Language School for new missionaries and other westerners from abroad is a new feature of the university program. From the point of view of the university, it is an extension activity. It seeks to serve mainly the churches and missions in the Central China region by giving their new recruits an opportunity to learn the Chinese spoken in the district where it is to be used. Professor Paul V. Taylor of the College of Education has been serving as Director of the school. The American Church Mission, the Swedish missions, the Methodist Mission, and the Christian and Missionary Alliance made financial contributions to the capital fund, which has enabled the rebuilding of some partially demolished small buildings and the erecting of new classroom buildings for the school. All on the site obtained by the country of Boone Middle School and of the American Church Mission.

The school has been self-supporting. Fees are charged to maintain 22 teachers who give class instruction and individual tutoring to 64 students from 11 missions. The Director's report to the President gives the number of students from each of the missions as follows: 14 from the Christian and Missionary Alliance, 10 from the Roman Catholic Mission, 9 each from the Swedish Missionary Society and the Methodist Mission, 8 from the American Church Mission, etc. During the year special courses of lectures have been given on Chinese Culture, Chinese Education, and Chinese Geography by Dr. Francis C. M. Wei, Dr. P'u Hwang, and Dr. Thomas R. Tregear of the University Faculty.

Faculty and Departments

There are three colleges in the university with eight departments as before the war, and they are as follows:

 College of Arts:
  Chinese Literature and Language
  Foreign Languages and Literature (mainly English),
  History and Sociology
  Economics-Commerce
 College of Science:
  Biology
  Chemistry
  Physics
 College of Education:
  Education

Philosophy, Psychology, and Theology are taught under Arts. They are not listed as departments, for a "department" in the Chinese official educational terminology means a groups of courses following the curriculum of the Ministry of Education which will enable students to get a government recognized degree in four years.

Similarly, Mathematics is taught under Science and Music under Education, but not listed as departments.

Beginning with the next academic year there will be two "departments" in the College of Education, and they are (1) Education and (2) Teacher Training. The policy of this division is to offer opportunities for students to emphasize more the scientific study of education or to get more practical training as middle-school teachers in specific fields.

According to the Ten-Year Plan for the Development of Hua Chung University after the war, already approved in principle by the Board of Founders, acting at the time concurrently as the Board of Directors,

Philosophy and Psychology under Arts, Mathematics under Science, and Music under Education are to be developed into departments for reasons clearly stated in the Plan, and we are working towards its realization. Those are fields sadly neglected by the Christian colleges in China with deplorable consequences. Take Philosophy as an instance. Courses in Philosophy are required by the Ministry of Education in all universities and colleges, and yet there are less than half a dozen Chinese in all the thirteen Christian colleges qualified by any standards to teach the subject, and Philosophy and Religion are closely allied. Perhaps to a lesser extent the same may be said of Mathematics and Music.

Hua Chung wishes to stress the importance of its Department of Economics-Commerce, not to train clerks, accountants, and the ordinary businessmen, although they too have their roles to play in modern China, but to have a share in supplying the country with men and women steeped in sound economic thinking and fired with the enthusiasm for international cooperation so that in due course of time they may influence the economic policy of the nation as a part of the economic development of the world. The present popularity of the department is due perhaps to a different motivation, but it is our golden opportunity for Christian education, our friends and supporters in America, because of their different environment, may not share our feeling, but those in Great Britain with their recent political experience ought to be more sympathetic to our aspiration.

Sociology has not received sufficient attention in Hua Chung, but as a rule it has not been properly taught in other universities and colleges. Sociologists are few in the country. Research in the Field is still in its early stage. Until more Chinese data are available, Sociology can hardly be handled as a university subject. But we ought to make our own contribution to its development, because we are more-or-less responsible for the Central China area, rich in sociological materials and fraught with great possibilities for social studies.

Theological training in the university has been going on for three years, the class every year is small, and our plan of combining Theology with Arts, Education, or Science makes a heavy load for the students. At present there are only thirteen students in the three classes. Our intention, however, are not to make Theology easy, but to make it respectable as a university discipline. The Church in China needs leaders. While intellectual equipment is not the sole factor of leadership, it is nevertheless essential in this new and perplexing world. We are happy that after three years students in the university have come to realize that Theology is not for those who cannot make a success in other subjects. They can now believe that only those who are of the caliber to succeed in other walks of life will make good church ministers. We have a group of specialists to teach the Theological subjects, but we still need a professor of Old Testament and one of Systematic Theology to complete our teaching staff. At present these subjects are being taken care of temporarily by the other members of the staff.

The Library and Scientific Equipment

The University Library and the laboratory equipment of the College of Science suffered heavy losses during the war. Since our return to Wu Chang the library has acquired by purchase and gifts many books which are now adequate for instructional purposes and some limited research. In number of titles and volumes it is still not up to the pre-war high watermark, but in quality it is judged by experts to be superior.

The library has a staff of three trained librarians and four clerks. It is still unable to keep pace with continuing acquisitions. The books brought back from Yunnan, as well as the new ones, have to be processed during the year, 2,656 (8,215 volumes) of Chinese books and 7,530 western books have been processed. There are 257 Chinese and 346 western periodicals, making a total of 603 periodicals. Files of 6 newspapers are kept in bound volumes. The number of books circulated, according to the Librarian's report, is about 2,700 each month when the university is in session, except during the examination periods. Many books, of course, are only consulted and used in the Library. Many books and magazines are kept in the department collections outside the Library. These are not included in the figures given.

For instructional purpose, the three departments in the college of Science have brought their laboratory equipment up to the pre-war standard. But with the increased enrollment more duplicate sets have to be added for the first year laboratories. There is no limit to the research equipment. We attempt, however, only those problems for which our resources give adequate facilities. In the re-equipment of our science laboratories we owe much to the generous gifts which have come to the university from many individual firms in Great Britain through the Association of Christian Universities in China with its office in London.

The Physical Plant

The main buildings of the university remain the same as before the war. During the two years after its return to Wu Chang the university has added no academic building, not entirely because of the lack of funds, of which there is a small amount, but largely because of the unsettled conditions in the country and the scarcity of building materials. Classrooms are therefore crowded, students continue to sleep in double-decker beds, the hostels can give the students only inadequate space for social and reading rooms, and many administrative officers of the university have to share offices. Such conditions are not conducive to efficiency or the creation of a wholesome university atmosphere, not to mention personal comfort.

Our first step has been to build sufficient houses for the faculty and staff. Rented quarters are neither economical nor satisfactory. Twelve small houses were completed early last autumn, and the Evangelical and Reformed Church Mission built a house for its appointee on the faculty, but the housing problem remains pressing. Families occupying a part of a hostel for men will have to be evacuated in order to make room for students next term, and faculty members are returning from leave of absence and their families must be housed. Ten houses must be erected before the re-opening of the university in September, but that will solve only one of the problems arising from the physical plant.

With the completion of the hostel for women students, half-finished just at the outbreak of the war in 1937, dormitory space for women may be sufficient for the next three years, but the Library and a new building for the administrative offices ought to be constructed in the near future. The university is fortunate to have received a generous donation of £45,000 for the Library building, and the Project and Johnston Building Fund is sufficient for the new administration hall. When these two buildings are completed, the problem of teaching space will find a temporary solution, and when Boone Middle School moves out to its new site, the College of Science will have its quarters in the present school quadrangle with four buildings and some side houses, all of which, however, will need remodeling at some considerable cost.

The master plan for the development of all the land available for university use is at present under consideration. It is difficult to anticipate how much land will be needed by the university in the twenty-five years. Some people are of opinion that there is enough land, but in this opinion the President cannot share. There is Boone Compound, divided now about evenly between the university and Boone Middle School, each occupying approximately 75 Chinese mou or $12\frac{1}{2}$ English acres. When the school moves out, the entire 25 acres or 150 mou will be used by the university.

Twenty-five years ago the Rt. Rev. Alfred A. Gilman, S. T. D., then President of Boone University, started to acquire more land for university development outside the city to the east of the Boone Compound, and 50 mou or 8 acres were bought, with the City Wall dividing it and the land inside. This was a strategic purchase. It turned the attention of the university extension to that direction. Since 1935 more land has been bought contiguous to that piece acquired by Bishop Gilman, and it has been paid for with money contributed by Mrs. Procter and Miss Johnston through the National Council of the Protestant Episcopal Church in the United States. The City Wall was torn down by the government in 1928, and the section of the City Wall land along the new property was bought in 1937 from the Provincial Government after a great deal of official red tape, ending only with a special administrative order issued by the Executive Yuan in Nanking. These purchases have added 160 mou or 27 acres to the University property.

On June 23, 1948, the deal was closed with the official representatives of the Chekiang Guild in Wu Chang for the purchase by the university, in the name of its Board of Directors of the land on which the guild building used to stand, but is now demolished. The area of the land is 504 fong or 8.4 mou or 1.4 acres at the price of 42 silver dollars, or equivalent in National Currency, per fong . The total cost of the purchase, when all expenses are paid, is estimated at about U. S. $ 16,000. Together with a few small lots acquired inside the city and in the vicinity of the university there are approximately 400 mou or 66 2/3 acres of land for university use. The shape of the new land outside the old City Wall is such that more purchases must be made in order to round out its contour. When this is done, the total area will be about 70 acres or 420 mou or 25,000 fong, a fong being 100 Chinese square feet.

The proposed general plan for the university is to have most of the main buildings on the Boone land, and the faculty residences, men's hostels, and playing fields on the new land outside, reserving, however, sufficient space for expansion beyond the present maximum of 800 students. This reservation is deemed wise, for, although the Ten-Year Plan calls for only those projected buildings inside the Boone Compound, experience tells us that in university planning what is wisdom now may be folly twenty-five years hence. The new city of Wu Chang will grow up around us, and we should leave no serious handicaps to posterity as far as space for reasonable development concerned.

Financial Conditions

The Treasurer will present his preliminary financial report later. His final report is possible only when the books are closed at the end of the fiscal year on July 31. He has had his instructions to make the report in two parts, the first consisting of capital and rehabilitation funds and the other, the current operating budget.

As far as we can estimate, the accounts for the year will be balanced. When the budget was presented a year ago, it was approved for recommendation by the Provisional Board of Directors with a deficit of U. S. $11,000. Thanks are due to the United Board in New York and the Association for Christian Universities in China in London for having secured sufficient funds to cover this deficit. But the budget was by no means extravagant. Besides the twenty missionary salaries (including three missionary wives counted as full-time workers, or else only 17), the budget amounts to U. S. $56,200. Reckoning U. S. $1,200 for every missionary members for budgetary purposes in China, the total is only U. S. $80,200. As far as the student enrollment and the size of the faculty are concerned, we have already completed the fifth year of the Ten-Year Plan. But the budget is still U. S. $35,000 short of the estimated expenditure of the First Year of the Plan. One-third of this shortage has been borne by the Library and scientific equipment items, which have, however, not felt the effect so seriously, because the rehabilitation funds have made up this shortage for the last two years, but the other two-thirds taken from the salary items has had grave consequences. Chinese members of the teaching and administrative staffs have been inadequately paid. Had U. S. $24,000 been added to the salary items in the budget, the present remuneration of the faculty and administrative members would be increased by 60%.

The income of the University is now suffering from the low fees charged to students, low compared with those of the pre-war years in real value, although the present figures are astronomical. The income loses also from the decreased government subsidies on account of the inflated Chinese currency, and grants formerly from various foundations in China have ceased since the outbreak of the war. It is our hope that some day conditions may become more normal, and income from these sources will be received or substantially increased.

During the year under review, the university has received grants from both the National and Provincial Government. There have also been gifts from friends and alumni in China. The Joint Campaign for the Christian Colleges in China has yield huge amounts in Chinese currency, but the real value is very small. Hua Chung was asked by the Joint Campaign Committee to raise N. C. ＄3,000,000,000. When we closed our local campaign, the book figures showed that we had raised more than four times this amount. When pledges were paid in from time to time, and some of them were rather slow in coming, we did our best to keep the value of the money received from serious depreciation. The Treasurer will report that from the Joint Campaign alone we he in the books over N. C. ＄5,000,000,000, but this is now worth about U. S. ＄2,400.

From this Joint Campaign, government grants and gifts, except a few earmarked for students aid, we have about U. S. ＄10,000. The Hua Chung Committee has decided to put this amount into building fund.

Reference has been made to the University Building Fund held abroad in foreign currencies. There is approximately U. S. ＄500,000 or equivalent in this fund. Recently, the Hua Chung Committee had secured the released of U. S. ＄100,000 from this amount for the erection of some of the most urgently needed buildings which will be 9 or 10 faculty houses and the completion of the new women's hostel to cost altogether about U. S. ＄70,000. As soon as the political and economic situation in the country permits, the donation of £45,000 sterling from Great Britain will be spent on the new library building. By that time the construction of the men's hostels ought to be also under way.

The Hostel System

Until the proper hostels for men are erected, our long-cherished hostel system cannot very well be realized. At present only the Dean of women has her apartment attached to Yen Hostel for women students. This has made it possible for her to give the attention due to the guidance of her students. The wardens of the men's hostels do not have such facilities, and it has proved a great handicap to their work, but every effort is being made to bring about a closer contact between the wardens and his students in the hostels.

According to the Constitution of the University, the hostel is the social and religious centre, in which any one of the cooperating missions may choose to take a special interest. Questions have recently been raised as to the possibility of realizing this idea. The directors may wish to reconsider it and bring the problem to the missions, which originally had the principle written into the Constitution. Whether the hostels for men are to be the special interest of the several missions or not, their erection ought to be completed at the earliest possible date for the comfort of the students and for a wholesome university atmosphere.

The Religious Life

Hua Chung feels proud of its religious heritage. There are several churches cooperating in it, different in church policy and in tradition. We have been working on the principle of freedom and cooperation, unity in variety. We believe in comity and mutual respect, and we have achieved the goal of comradeship in the great common cause of Christian higher education, and while we may differ in minor points we are all one in the great issues.

Morning chapel is held from Tuesday through Saturday, and the usual Sunday Evening Service continues. The Board of Directors or its Executive Committee appoints the Chapel Committee, consisting of faculty members and student representatives to make arrangements for all the religious services except those which are under the auspices of the several cooperating churches for their own respective members, and even these latter are open to all of the university community qualified to attend.

Each of the churches has its own Fellowship with its membership including all the faculty and staff members, as well as the students affiliated with that particular church. The Fellowship are at present four in number viz, the Seng Hung Huei, the Methodist, the Church of Christ in China, and the Lutheran, and they have programs and activities of their own. Occasionally they join together for some common cause.

The result of this religious work is indicated not only by the encouraging number of baptisms during the year, but especially by the general attitude of all the students towards Christianity and by the loyalty of the church members.

The General Morale

Improvement in the general morale during the year has been quite noticeable. The latter part of May and early June were anxious weeks for the administration. Student disturbances usually occur in that period. We are thankful that another year has passed peacefully with such a pleasant time at commencement on June 25. Conditions have not been easy, but our students seem to have understood much better the policy of the university and the genuine interest of their teachers in their welfare. They consult the President and other officers of the university about almost everything they do. We make allowances for their inexperience and youthful enthusiasm and are not afraid of their occasional mistakes. We are confident that from mistakes they will learn, but we lose no opportunity to put in a word of advice and warning whenever possible, and they are appreciative of that. If this spirit and general attitude should continue through the difficult time still ahead of us, we would be building up a greater tradition unknown yet in the long history of the university. It is worth all our effort and our patience.

The General Situation

But will the political situation permit this? We are hopeful, for to be Christian is to be optimistic. Yet, realism is also a Christian duty. In case of emergency it would be the function of the Board of Directors to decide upon the method of meeting the crisis, the form of which cannot now be anticipated.

There may not be time for the Board to convene, perhaps not even for its Executive Committee to meet. What would be the authority then to determine the fate of the university? The president asks for your instructions.

Before closing this report the President wishes also to remind the directors that he is passing the age of 60, and soon his successor must be appointed. Since 1939 he has been holding his office only at the pleasure of the directors or as his strength permits without any term of appointment. Thirty-eight years continuously in one institution is a long period. It may not be a compliment for one to be told that one is fit for only one type of service, especially when that service is not of one's own choice. The university has entered a new stage of development, and it needs a new leadership. The directors are asked to give this matter their early attention.

Respectfully submitted,
Wu Chang (signed) Francis C. M. Wei
President
June 28, 1948

Comments on the Report of the Committee to Study the Progress of the Ten-Year Plan for Hua Chung University

Shortly after the opening of the new term in September, I felt that it would be necessary at this juncture for a committee to study the development of the Ten-Year Plan, which was drafted and approved by a joint meeting of the Executive Committee of the Board of Directors and the University Senate while we were still in Hsichow before the end of the war. The report was submitted to the Board of Founders, which acted concurrently during the war as the Board of Directors, and it received the tentative approval of that Board. Later the administration of Hua Chung University was given permission to start the Ten-Year Plan only in the autumn of 1946 when the institution moved back to Wu Chang from Hsichow. Counting from that time, this is the third year of the Ten-Year Plan, and therefore towards the end of the first period of that plan.

The committee consisted of Dean Leonard Constantine, Chairman; Dean P'u Huang of the College of Education, several time acting president during my absence; Dean Richard Bien of the College of Science, who acted for me in 1945—1946; Dean John C. F. Lo of the College of Arts; and Professor John L. Coe, treasurer of the University. The report submitted by this committee has been approved by the Senate, and it is now being mimeographed for people interested in our work. I am, therefore, sending out this report for the information of the Hua Chung Committee of the cooperating mission and of others who are interested in our work here.

As president, I would like to make a few comments which do not affect the report as a whole.

First, in the first paragraph of the report it is stated that "in fact students are no longer able to take a degree in commerce." This is because so few of our faculty members in the Department of Economics-Commerce under the Faculty of Arts are able to teach effectively the courses required by the Department of Commerce. They are all interested in subjects in the Department of Economics. Our Department of Economics-Commerce is a combined department with two sections: one emphasizing Economics; and the other commerce. Because of the shortage of teachers for the commercial subjects, students are no longer able to take a degree in commerce, not because of government regulations, but because of our actual situation in the university.

This, however, should not interfere with our plan to develop the Department of Economics-Commerce into a School of Commerce. Speaking in the United States and in Great Britain during my last visit in those countries in 1945—1946, I tried to make clear that we should develop our Department of Economics-Commerce into a College of Commerce, it would not mean that we would have just a Commercial School. Our interest would continue to be in the teaching of Economics, which is such an important subject in China and in our relation to other counties, as well as in the whole world. Even at the present time the Department of Economics-Commerce, with practically all the students taking their degree in Economics, is the largest department in the whole university. The enrollment for this year is 160. This shows the general trend of the interest of the students.

Secondly, it has been our desire to develop Philosophy and Psychology into a major department, which means that we ought to have sufficient courses for a student to take a degree in that department under the Faculty of Arts. So far we have been able to give only elective courses in Psychology and Logic and Ethics, and Introduction to Philosophy as required by the government. Dean John C. F. Lo is professor of Psychology, and Professor Edith Wal-king Taai has been teaching Educational Psychology. But I am the only person who has been teaching all the Philosophy courses, in addition to my administrative duties. It is almost imperative that a teacher of Philosophy should be found not only to release me from the teaching of the required courses, which I always enjoy in spite of my heavy administrative duties, but a younger person ought to be secured to take the courses over, which I cannot teach for many more years.

Furthermore, I have other interests even in teaching, such as History of Religions, other Theological courses, and Advanced Philosophy.

With the Theological course functioning with four classes now, we ought to have a good Philosophy major course, which could be combined with Theology, according to our present plan of combining the Theological course with one of the other major courses in the university. Philosophy ought to be the most natural one, if there should be adequate preparation for the study of Theology. This would be more necessary if and when there should be students who would like to finish the four-year college courses first before starting their studies in Theology. Philosophy and Religion are alike subjects for university study. There have been very few graduates from the Christian colleges in China who are prepared to teach Philosophy. In many of the Christian colleges today there is no one to teach Philosophy, and that is deplorable. We ought at least to do our share in preparing a few students to teach that subject.

Thirdly, towards the end of the report when it refers to the importance of securing around U. S. $125,000 at the present prices for the Procter Memorial Building, it ought to be pointed out as a supplement to the report that "the rest of the other gifts from Mrs. Procter and Miss Johnston" are being rapidly used up or allocated for other buildings in the general plan. Therefore, if we should have to put up a building to cost about U. S. $125,000, U. S. $95,000 would have to be found to supplement the original gift of U. S. $30,000 for the Procter Memorial Building. How we are going to find this U. S. $95,000 required is a question which the Hua Chung Committee and the Board of Directors ought to decide, and certainly the attention of Mrs. Procter and Miss Johnston ought to be called to it.

Aside from these few comments, the report in my opinion is a good one, representing the present situation in Hua Chung University as all of us see it, and we hope that all our supporters and friends will give it due attention.

Francis C. M. Wei, President
October 26, 1948

英文通信 175 通

1. To F. E. Hawkins (December 2, 1929)

Dear Mr. Hawkins:

······

Your good letter of Oct. 31st, with enclosure, was received on Saturday, Nov. 30th. I am very glad to have the full description of Mr. Anderson's qualifications. He fits in splendidly with our staff. According to government requirements, we have to organize our college in three Schools. The first school required of every college is that of science. We have made plans for the Yale Unit to establish and maintain it as a Yale School of Science in Central China College, which is quite within the financial limits of the Yale Mission. We are counting on five professors and instructors of science, and an annual allowance of G. \$6,000.00 for equipment from Yale for the next period of four or five years. By the end of that period, the science department will be fairly well-equipped and more money will be released for the salaries of additional teachers. In this work, Yale will have the assistance of the Huping Unit, which has been asked to send a man for mathematics and one for biology. In this way, we have a rather good prospect for a first-class school of science in Central China.

The second school that we are organizing in the college is that of arts, which will include such courses as commences, and library training. All the general arts subjects such as history, languages, economics, sociology and religion will be taught in the School of Arts. The corresponding English term is "faculty," but the terms "school" is better known here in China.

The third school is that of education. It is very essential for us to be able to train teachers for the secondary schools in the churches in this region of Central China, as well as for private and government schools, who will look to us for teachers with good character and reliability, as well as with training in the teaching of English and science particularly. We are counting on the School of Education as one of the means to extend our Christian influence through our graduates. Plans are under consideration to ask one of the units to be a sort of sponsor to this School, but it is our hope that we shall always maintain in it a Griffith John chair, as well as a Wesley chair, of education, so as to keep the international outlook and to make all the units feel that they have (root) shares in the work.

…… ……

Yours very sincerely,
FRANCIS C. M. WEI
Acting President

2. To Mr. Hutchins (April 2, 1930)

Dear Mr. Hutchins:

…… ……

In order to get the college in shape for registration with the Chinese Government, we are organizing our college work into three faculties, viz., the Faculty of Science, which is required by the Ministry of Education, the Faculty of Arts, and the Faculty of Education. In the Faculty of Science, we offer courses for students to concentrate in Physics, Biology or Chemistry, so that they may be prepared to do post-graduate work in their special line after graduation either in China or abroad, or to pursue professional studies for which a good scientific training is essential. This Faculty undertakes also to run a pre-medical course which will be up to the standard of the best medical college in this country.

The Faculty of Arts has four departments in which we propose to offer major work to the students. These are Chinese Literature, English Literature, Philosophy including Religion, and the social sciences. Besides, this Faculty has two vocational courses, viz., Library Science and Commerce.

The Faculty of Education will begin to offer courses next fall. Its chief aim is to train teachers for middle schools, which is such a great need in Central China at the present time.

It is our plan to divide the college courses into two parts, the first part covering a period of three semesters (four semesters at the present time on account of the poor preparation of the students) at the end of which time every student will be required to take intermediate examinations in six subjects, including Chinese, English and Philosophy and/or Religion. To qualify for these examinations, the students must have had intensive study in at least two of the six subjects so as to assure a scholarly attitude as well as adequate preparation for advanced work. After the intermediate examinations, every student will have to choose a major or a professional course, which will take at least one half of his time, the remaining time being spent on some subsidiary to assure a broad outlook and a better professional training.

Our policy is to limit the enrollment in the college to 240. This is necessary to assure a thorough training, as well as intimate contact between the students and staff, and a real community spirit in the college. According to the present regulations of the Ministry of Education, religious exercises and instruction must be on a voluntary basis; but we are confident that the winning power of the Christian religion will be strong enough for us to bear effective witness to our faith just by living with our students and studying with them.

…… ……

If Yale should support five teachers of science, three senior men and two junior, the salaries will amount to about $15,000.00, Chinese Currency, which at the present favorable gold exchange rate is equivalent to approximately $6,000.00 Gold, but normally it will be $7,000.00 Gold. With two additional senior teachers, however, we shall need $4,000.00 Gold more for salaries. As the science work develops, a science building will become necessary. At the present time, we are having the laboratories in two separate buildings, originally not designed for this purpose. This can be only a temporary measure of course. The science building is a big financial item, but this need has to be met sooner or later. It ought to be counted as one of the first items in our capital expenditure. Then the building is erected, operating expenses, approximately $1,000.00 Gold, will have to be reckoned in. After the first period of five years, we may not have to put in large sums for equipment every year, but replacement and reasonable addition ought to have a yearly, budget of $4,000.00 Gold at the least. This of course, does not make it possible to encourage any research work on the park of the science professors, a certain amount of which, within reasonable limits, is necessary to keep the best men on our staff. The three items, via., salaries laboratories, and operating expenses of the science building have to be reckoned at approximately $18,500.00. These are rough estimates, leaving very little margin and making no provisions for special investigation. If Yale should find it possible to increase its present subvention by 50%, it would be quite within its financial reach to maintain a Yale School of Science.

....

Yours sincerely,
Francis C. M. Wei
Acting President

3. To Dr. E. H. Hume (July 17, 1930)

Dear Dr. Hume:

....

It has been our aim that Yale Unit will develop and maintain a Yale-in-China School of Science at Hua Chung. This has been the policy approved already by the Board of Directors and, as I have outlined the scheme in one of my letters to Mr. Hutchins, it is quite within the financial limits of the Yale Mission even during the initial years. We feel that only by keeping the Yale the identity of Yale in the college, so that be able to have unity in diversity which, to believe, is one of the best mottoes for the modern world.

....

Yours sincerely,
Francis C. M. Wei
Acting President

4. To Dr. Edward H. Hume (November 10, 1930)

My dear Dr. Hume:

……

  Exactly four weeks ago, Bishop Gilman received a cable from Bishop Roots, saying that the registration issue had been satisfactorily settled. Since that was after the date of the New York meeting of the Episcopal Church Board of Missions, we took it for granted that you people had succeeded in persuading the Episcopal Board to allow us to go ahead with registration without any serious impediment attached to the sanction. We have been waiting for letter from Dr. John Wood, but that letter has not yet arrived. We are hoping to have it almost every moment. The Board of Directors is going to meet next Saturday. It is our desire that we shall be able to have official instructions from the Board to apply for the registration of the college. Preliminary preparations have been made, although no official step has been taken along this line. It is certainly a great encouragement to us all here that you are backing us up and that the Yale Mission particularly is in sympathy with our policy in China. I am sending you, under separate cover, a copy of my report on the opening of this term. The college still remains small, but everybody feels that the spirit of students has improved tremendously to the gratification of the members of the staff, and that the college has certainly grown in every way since its reopening a year ago. It is now a pleasure to see the splendid equipment in the laboratories for biology, chemistry and physics, built up with the money granted by Yale last year and this year. It is only a start of course, but if Yale should continue its generous grant for the next four or five years, we shall have a very efficient equipment for the study of science in China, with a small student body. The Christian spirit is encouraging, but the most gratifying thing is that the staff has a wonderful spirit of fellowship and cooperation.

……

Yours affectionately,
Francis C. M. Wei

5. To Canon Anson Phelps Stokes (February 2, 1931)

My dear Canon Stokes:

… …

It is cheering that Dr. Wood is going to consult the different cooperating groups over the question of registration. You mentioned in your letter to Mr. Dixon, that the committee may be formally organized in a few months, but I wish to point out that it is simply impossible for us to wait very later than the early spring before sending in our application for registration. The order issued by the Ministry of Education in Nanking last August, is that all private schools in the provinces must register before the opening of the fall term 1931. We take the liberal interpretation that the papers for registration must be sent in by that time, and not that the institution must be officially registered. The earlier, however, we send in the papers, the more consideration we may have from the government. We must bear in mind that our institution at the present time has only a fighting chance. Both in equipment and in the staff we are below standard. Our current budget is far below what the government requires and our enrollment is small. Our greatest difficulty caused by failing to get registered earlier is that our students begin to feel restless and well trained Chinese, even Christian Chinese, hesitate to join our staff here in account of our non-registration.

… …

Yours sincerely,
Francis C. M. Wei
Acting President

6. To Mr. E. Fay Campbell (February 26, 1931)

Dear Mr. Campbell:

I am writing to endorse the opinions of Dr. Kwei in his letter to you, concerning the advisability of appointing Mr. and Mrs. Powell by the Yale Mission for Hua Chung College. When I was talking with Mr. Eutchins in Han Kou about this proposition, we came to the conclusion that their appointment must be outside of the present Yale budget of $12,000.00 Gold a year. During the last two years, half of the money, $6,000.00 Gold, has been devoted each year to the building up of the necessary science equipment; and the remaining $6,000.00 Gold to paying the salaries of Chinese science teachers. We are having Dr. Kwei at present in the Physics Department, and we are counting on another physicist, trained also in America. Then, we are negotiating to get a professor of biology on Yale support, and it is the opinion of both Paul Kwei and Frank Eutchins that while the coming of Mrs. Powell as a chemist will certainly be a valuable addition to our staff, we do not want, however, to dispense with a good Chinese chemist in the college, so as to hold up the scientific side of our work in the eyes of Chinese educators in this country. On the other hand, we feel that Mrs. Powell's coming will solve immediately the very urgent proposition of securing a well-trained chemist for the college, so that we may take the time to pick and choose a good Chinese chemist without having to come to any hasty decision. All these Chinese science teachers, therefore, will need the full amount of $6,000.00 Gold, even when the exchange is so favorable. Mr. Powell being so well-known to the Yale alumni, I hope you have no difficulty in raising his support and will have him appointed for the college before September of this year. The valuable services which he will be able to render to the college have already been fully described in Paul Kwei's letter to you.

…… ……

Yours sincerely,
Francis C. M. Wei
Acting President

7. To Dr. Edward H. Hume (November 30, 1931)

Excerpt from a letter of Francis Wei to Dr. Hume

... ...

One more thing to stabilize the minds of the Yale men here, as well as others associated with Yale in the college, is for Yale to invest some money in buildings. It is very well to talk about a new site for Hua Chung. I used to be rather visionary myself. But hard facts require me to settle down with what is immediately practicable. A new site would mean a million dollars gold at least, and that is not the horizon yet. In the meantime, we must make the best use of our buildings and make necessary additions to them. In the first place, the Yale staff must be housed. At present, Dr. Kwei and Dr. Djang are living in Boone houses by paying a rent. They are comfortable in their present quarters, but we would like to see some Yale houses built for the staff, so that teachers appointed by the other units may have the advantage of them as Yale members of the staff are having advantage of Boone houses at the present time. A reasonable and modest asking will be for the Yale unit to build at least three houses next summer, with the total cost of $15,000.00 Mex.

Furthermore, a science building is becoming necessary. We have Chemistry at present occupying the upper floor of the Administration on Building, crowding Arts entirely out of the pace; and Biology occupying one wing of Ingle Hall, intended to be a men's dormitory; and Physics occupying the other wing. This, under the circumstances, is the most satisfactory arrangement, but it is far from being ideal. The minimum is to erect at once a chemistry building, to cost fifty to sixty thousand dollars Mexican at the present rate of exchange. I wish to remind you that we do not want to be extravagant, and extravagance is one of the evils that this college would always avoid. But it is human psychology to see some buildings going up on a new institution in order to have the impression of permanency and of a going concern. What we have asked for is only the very minimum for the immediate future.

... ...

8. To Rev. A. P. Stokes (December 4, 1931)

Dear Canon Stokes:

… …

Our science work is developing in a very encouraging manner. We have two senior men and one junior man in physics; and one senior man and two junior men in chemistry. At the present time, we are still negotiating to have a senior man for our biology, but we have two splendid young men to handle the courses called for this year. Equipment in all the departments is being improved upon from year to year, although at present we are able to handle adequately only the first two years' work, with some apparatus for the advanced courses. In course of time, while the Yale appropriation is gradually increased, we hope to have a fine Yale School of Science at Hua Chung inside of three or four years.

… …

$17,000 Gold as our budget for the next year would be just enough to pay all salaries and to supply the additional equipment for the science. We earnestly hope that the Trustees in New Haven will see their way clear to grant this request, as presented by the Yale representative Mr. Hutchins. Now that our registration is going through and the question of site is settled, we hope all the units will support the college more wholeheartedly than ever.

… …

Yours sincerely,
Francis C. M. Wei
President

9. To Mr. E. Fay Campbell (January 5, 1933)

Dear Mr. Campbell:

I am sending to you, for your Mission Board, a copy of the Hua

Chung College Annual, 1932, edited and published by the students here.

The Annual is largely in Chinese, but the pictures may be of interest to members of the Board. I hope you will find it interesting enough to keep in the Library for exhibition.

Yours sincerely,
FRANCIS C. M. WEI

10. To Dr. Edward H. Hume (February 1, 1933)

Dear Dr. Hume:

……

In principle, it is not ideal to have a middle school on the same campus with college. The difficulty is not so great when we are able later to readjust the buildings so as to have the entire upper level of the campus for the college, leaving the lower level to the school to which scheme all parties concerned seem to agree.

As you wrote to Frank Hutchins there are advantages to a city college. There is always the danger of the students losing touch of the community life and growing up, so to speak in a green-house.

I agree entirely with you that financial investment in a large piece of property at the present moment is unwise and impossible. It has been our policy to devote all revenues received at present to current educational expenses. We want to build up faculty and teaching equipment first before we turn our attention seriously to a physical plant. Of course, in doing this, we must not forget that it is essential to have the necessary buildings presentable enough as not to make a shabby appearance. It is our belief that if we should develop along the present line for ten more years, we shall have made a place for us in the sun as an institution of higher learning, and by that time it will be comparatively easier to secure funds for a new site, if that should be our best judgement. All that is invested in the present site will not be money wasted either, especially when it is our conviction that, properly developed and improved, the present site may turn out to be the ideal one. At any rate, we must not sacrifice too much the immediate future for a distant ideal.

……

Yours sincerely,
FRANCIS C. M. WEI
President

11. To Mr. E. Fay Campbell (February 8, 1933)

Dear Mr. Campbell:

……

The college reopened its second term on February 1, and classes have been going on since February 3. With about the same enrollment as last term, i. e., 101. There is a possibility for students to seek to transfer to our college from Peiping and Tientsin if the situation in the North should become more serious, but we have only limited space to accommodate such transfer students and in any circumstance we do not anticipate more than one hundred and fifteen students this term, about one-third of whom will be girls.

Yours sincerely,
FRANCIS C. M. WEI
President

12. To Mr. Francis S. Hutchins (May 9, 1933)

Dear Frank:

We are desperately in need of a teacher of English Literature since Mr. Turner, formerly of the Y. M. C. A., who has substituted for one year here, is going to join the staff of Kuling American School after the summer. At the suggestion of my colleagues in the Department of English here, I have approached Mr. Rugh in Changsha to see whether the Yale Mission would be willing to loan us Mr. Rogers for a year, with the hope that he would stay another year after next before he goes home for post-graduate work. I am doing this with Bishop Gilman's concurrence, but unless you are coming back this summer to stay in Changsha and do work in English in the Middle School, there is very little chance for Mr. Rogers to come to us in the fall. Hence I am writing and urge you to comb the country in order to find a well-qualified teacher of English literature who may be acceptable to Dr. John Wood and his Mission, and be appointed to come out definitely before our fall term begins. We shall be in a bad lurch if such a teacher could not be found at once. At the same time, a teacher of economics is needed. Bishop Gilman is writing to urge his Mission to appoint these two teachers for Hua Chung.

While I am writing, I wish to suggest for your consideration an idea which you may take on its own merits. If you should find some undergraduate in the Junior Class of Yale College, who is willing to do athletic work or students work, and/or anxious to study Chinese philosophy and religion under myself or somebody else on the faculty, it may be good to get one at a time to come out to Hua Chung at his own expenses, so as to establish a link between the student body in New Haven and the College here, as well as to promote interest in the college after graduation of such students from Yale.

…… ……

Yours sincerely,
FRANCIS C. M. WEI

13. To Prof. S. M. Gunn (December 18, 1933)

Dear Professor Gunn:

…… ……

After your observation of our work here, you will probably agree that the Hua Chung College is attempting to do a unique piece of work to meet the needs in a vast territory which is at present not given sufficient facilities for the training of leaders in the various fields of service. As a private institution, we are aware of the limitations of our resources. For this reason, our policy is to confine our efforts to a few selected fields in which we may expect to do efficient work at the highest possible standards.

Firstly, our work is unique, in that we are practically the only private institution of higher learning in the Central China region, comprising the provinces of Hupeh, Hunan, Kiangsi and southern Honan.

Secondly, we are experimenting on a line which has not been explored by any other institution in this country. We are not imitating British or Continental European methods any more than we are copying American institutions. We are adapting the best of Western countries in university education to the needs of the Chinese. By limiting our enrollment, by regulating the growth of our student body, and by our hostel system-under which small groups of students are taken care of by members of the faculty through the tutorial system, we wish to assure the building up of good traditions and the closest possible personal contracts between teachers and students. By strict matriculation, by requiring the passing of intermediate examinations at the end of the sophomore year, and by comprehensive examinations in the major and minor subjects to qualify for the degree, we aim at giving a university education only to those few who deserve it and are able to profit by it, and not to more students than our staff and equipment can adequately handle.

Thirdly, the loyal support of our cooperating missions, even during the present period of economic depression in America and in England, and our limited budget in accordance with our guaranteed income—without, however, serious sacrifice in educational efficiency—have demonstrated the stability of an institution of our type.

Fourthly, we believe in scholarship, but we also believe in training for practical life in Chinese society. A careful study of our major courses, as outlined in our catalogue, will amply show that we aim at equipping our students for practical service to meet the needs of such a large industrial and commercial center as the Wu Han cities at the very heart of the nation on the one hand, and, on the other, the educational and social needs of the many Christian middle schools and church communities which look to us for leadership and for the training of teachers and workers.

………

Yours sincerely,
FRANCIS C. M. WEI
PRESIDENT

14. To Dean Wallace B. Donham (November 6, 1934)

My dear Dean Donham:

………

The college was first organized in the year 1924 in accordance with recommendations of the Burton Commission which was sent by the missions interested in Chinese education in China and which made its report in the year 1922. When Hua Chung College was organized in 1924, three colleges then operating in the Central China region under Christian auspices were united in college work in Wu Chang. Owing to political disturbances in the Central China region the college was closed from 1927 to 1929. When we re-opened in the fall of 1929, two other missions, namely, Yale-in-China and the Reformed Church in the United States joined in and co-operated with the three other missions— the American Church Mission which formerly supported Boone College, the Wesleyan Methodist Mission Society which supported Wesleyan-in-Wu Chang, and the London Missionary Society which supported Griffith John College in Han Kou.

During the last five years, therefore, we have had in the college five co-operating units with Yale-in-China sponsoring largely the School of Science; the Reformed Church Mission sponsoring the School of Education; the American Church Mission sponsoring the School of Arts; and the remaining two Missions, that is, the England Methodist Mission and the London Missionary Society contributing to all three schools in the colleges.

The college now is the only Christian institution of higher learning in the whole region of Central China comprising the Provinces of

Hupeh, Hunan, Kiangsi, Western Anhui and Southern Honan, with its site in the Wu Han centre which is the very heart of the country, at a junction of the trunk lines of the Chinese Railways and on the bank of the Yangtze River. The college has been registered since 1931 with the ministry of Education in Nanking.

In 1930 I sent a memorandum to you through Bishop Roots raising the question of the applying at that time to the Board of Trustees of Harvard-Yenching Institute for financial aid in developing our Department of Chinese Studies. You told me in your answer to wait for a better time to bring up this question. We are very anxious to receive any financial aid from your Board for the development of our Department of Chinese Studies in Central China College. It is hardly necessary for me to emphasize the importance of the study of Chinese culture in the Central China region. It has been my main interest in my own research for many years, and it is only on account of lack of funds that this department in Hua Chung College has not been developed as I desired it to be.

Any financial aid from the Harvard-Yenching Institute will be a great help. At any rate, we would wish to be placed on the list of your affiliated institutions in China, since we are one of the Union of Christian Institutions in the country and are registered with the government; serving a large population in a vast area at the very centre of the country; fully correlated according to the recommendations of the Burton Commission; being practically the only result of the work and recommendations of the Commission on the correlation of Christian College in China.

…… ……

Yours faithfully,
Francis C. M. Wei

15. To the Directors, Alumni, Parents of Students, and Friends of Hua Chung College (1935)

It is my duty to report on what has happened during the past three weeks.

The college has been closed for the winter vacation earlier than the scheduled time, as all the educational institutions in the Wu Han centre above primary school grade have done, by government order in order to avoid further complications which might arise from the Student Patriotic Movement. This period has been one of great anxiety but so far our students have not caused any disturbances to the college or government authorities.

On December 14th, Saturday, our students, meeting as the Students Association in the college, decided to send telegrams in the name of the student body to the Central Government in Nanking and to the generals at the head of the Provincial Government in Peiping supporting them in their policy of maintaining the territorial integrity and sovereignty of China with regard to the recent events in North China. They decided also to send a telegram to the Student Union in Peiping and Tientsin, which had been protesting against the situation in North China, so as to express their sympathy concerning the difficulties of the present political circumstances. A manifesto to the public was also drafted and issued, stating that the students in the college would do their best to support the Central Government as far as their efforts would not cause at the present time further international complications and would not interfere with their ordinary college studies.

When the students showed such a strong patriotic sentiment and with motives which appeared to be pure and unselfish, the college authorities did not deem it wise to discourage their simple expressions of feelings which must find an outlet.

Two days afterwards students in many schools in the Wu Han centre responded to the declaration issued by the students in the college, and the students' union was formed in this center, based on the principles which the students in the college had adopted. This students union, assuming the title of "The Students Patriotic Association," decided to have a demonstration in the city of Wu Chang to call the attention of the public to the grave situation in North China. All the educational institutions above primary grades participated in the demonstration on December 20th, which took the form of a procession in the streets. The students in the college were allowed to ask leave of absence individually by signing their names in the president's office, in order to join the demonstration. All except twenty students obtained leave of absence for this purpose, and left the college in procession at nine o'clock Friday morning, December 20th, after an address by the president, who pointed out to them the dangers they were confronting and the necessity of orderly action. The president personally inspected all the handbills and paper banners carried in the students' hands while going out to join the procession, so as to be sure that there was nothing contrary to the original principles of their organization.

The students had agreed that as soon as they reached the office of the Police Commissioner in the city, which is at the most important crossroads in the city, they would return to their respective schools. The procession reached that point about one o'clock that day, and our students courageously left the procession and came back, while other students remained there and surrounded the Provincial Government demanding permission to cross the river although the ferry had been stopped by government order. As far as the college was concerned, nothing happened on Friday afternoon nor on Friday evening December 20th, and the students were all in classes Saturday, December 21st.

Hundreds of students slept in the streets on Friday night continuing to urge the Provincial Government to resume the ferry service so that they might go to Han Kou and make a demonstration there. Early in the afternoon of December 21st permission was given by the Provincial Government, and the students in Wu Chang were to go in two large groups to Han Kou for the purpose of demonstrations on December 22nd and 23rd. The students from the college, who joined the first group on the 22nd, went to Han Kou under the supervision of some of the Chinese members of the college staff, and the procession in Han Kou turned out to be an orderly affair. When the second group went to Han Kou, however, on Monday, the 23rd, there was some difficulty near the Customs House in Han Kou and also a little riot in the Bureau of Public Works, caused by the students from one provincial school on their way from the ferry back to their school. Fortunately our students were not involved in any of these disturbances.

16. To Mr. Richard D. Weigle (September 19, 1935)

Dear Mr. Weigle:

I have the pleasure to report to you and through you to the Yale-in-China Association the opening of the new academic year in Hua Chung College.

Registration of old students was on September 9th and of new students on September 10th. On separate sheets enclosed herewith please find statistics of our student body this semester totaling 161 with two more old students to come who are now on special leave of absence.

We have according to this figure an increase of 23 students over the enrollment a year ago. Owing to our strict standards many of the new students, particularly those from the non-Christian middle schools, usually find our work too heavy and consequently the elimination at the end of the first semester and then again at the end of the freshman year is heavy. Of the 68 freshman students enrolled a year ago, only 40 have returned this year. We can meet this difficulty only by helping to build up still further the Christian middle schools now affiliated with the college so as to increase our enrollment from this source.

On a separate sheet you will please find a list of new teachers with detailed information concerning them. All the departments are now in good working order except that we still feel the need of strengthening the teaching staff for Chinese, Economics-Commerce, and Sociology-History, all in the School of Arts.

…… ……

The Procter Memorial Building to be built with the gift of U. S. $30,000 has not yet been started. Mr. Bergamini, the A. C. M. architect who was with us before 1927 and has been the architect of St. Luck's Medical Centre in Tokyo, paid us a visit a fortnight ago and is going to recommend plans to the Directors for approval and submission to the Founders. Some further slight remodeling, however, in one or two places has been effected to accommodate the increased enrollment and the additional demand for class room space.

The Practice School has been started with a new appropriation of U. S. $1,250 from the Woman's Missionary Society of the Reformed Church Mission. This gives the School of Education the much needed laboratory. Dean P'u Hwang is in charge of it and Assistant Professor D. F. Anderson acts as supervisor of practice teaching. The school occupies a site of about an acre with three buildings allocated to college use by the A. C. M. The site is about four minutes' walk from the college.

This year the Central Government has made us a grant of C. $16,873 for science equipment and two chairs, one of Chemistry and the other of Psychology. The China Foundation has granted us C. $5,000 for science equipment, and the Provincial Government is considering a grant for an additional chair in the Chinese department.

…… ……

Yours sincerely,
Francis C. M. Wei
President

17. To Mr. R. D. Weigle (November 6, 1935)

My dear Mr. Weigle:

…… ……

Shortly after the opening of the term I send you full statistics of the college. The enrollment has increased, but there is a noticeable drop in the percentage of Christian students in the first-year class. This is largely due to the fact that mission appropriations for scholarships for Christian students have been reduced, and I would urge you to do everything possible to restore and increase those appropriations, so as to enable more Christian students, graduated from the Christian middle schools, to come to the college here.

Yours sincerely,
Francis C. M. Wei
President

18. To Mr. Richard D. Weigle (March 11, 1936)

Dear Dick:

…… ……

I have learned from Frank that you have changed your field of study in Yale University and that you are now working for your doctorate in History instead of taking a theological degree in the Divinity school. It is of special interest to me to know that you are taking European History as your major and the orient as your minor. This leads me to think that after your doctorate three or four years from now you may be willing to come to Hua Chung and teach Western History, doing at the same time, further research in the history of the orient. It is still too early for us to decide whether you are going out for a regular missionary term or to stay for only a shorter period, but I would like to raise this question with you even as early as this, so that you may think it over in your mind and possibly make it a part of your program of study in Yale. Nothing will make us happier than to strengthen the tie between New Haven and Hua Chung by such a visit from you when you have finished your post-graduate studies.

There is another thing that I want to consult with you about. Charles Whiston has been talking to me about a scheme of bringing some of the professors in the Cambridge Theological School to Hua Chung during their sabbatical year for a semester each, as visiting professor in their own respective fields. Their expense will not be much. We are figuring that U. S. $300 currency for travel subsidy, and Board and Lodging here in Wu Chang for five months amounting to U. S. $150 at the present rate of exchange. If the man should bring his wife along he ought to look after her expenses himself. If we should have one visiting professor every year we would have to raise U. S. $450 every year, which could be done from among the theological students in the two or three seminaries of the Episcopal Church in the U. S. within the help of some special gifts from other friends. I am writing to ask whether it be possible for Yale University or Yale-in-

China Association to participate in this scheme, and to arrange to send to Hua Chung one visiting professor on the basis I have mentioned, once every three years if not more frequently. We have to budget, therefore, $150 Gold every year. Some interested friends may give this to us a special gift.

You will see the advantage of such a scheme. We would have in the first place a number of experienced professors to teach in the college all the time in their own fields. Secondly, it would be good publicity for the college both in China as well as in America. Before their coming to Wu Chang and after their return to America they would naturally talk about Hua Chung and be actively interested in our work, thus inspiring enthusiasm in the students they come into contact with. Thirdly, the scheme will establish a strong link between Hua Chung and two or three seminaries of the Episcopal Church in the U.S. as well as Yale University and possibly one of the Reformed Church Colleges in the States. As a whole, I think it is a good scheme, and whatever money we invest in it will prove to be productive. I would like you to give this proposal careful consideration and think of ways and means of participating in it for the Yale-in-China Association interest.

…… ……

The students have all made up their lost work from the last term and finished their examinations and have been doing their work as usual for the second term since February 19. We have to make up only nine days on account of the Student Patriotic Movement after Christmas, and this can be done by cutting short the spring holidays and postponing Commencement for four days until June 28, which is not bad at all. Enclosed I am sending you a copy of my letter to Dr. Wood which embodies some very important information with regard to the site of the new buildings.

…… ……

Yours sincerely,
Francis C. M. Wei

19. To Mr. Richard D. Weigle (March 16, 1936)

Dear Dick:

…… ……

With the gift from Miss Johnston to strengthen the Liberal Arts School here in the college we are planning to get an additional man for English. Miss Bleakley, the head of the department, has been thinking of asking you to get a Yale bachelor at the same rate that you have been paying the bachelors this year, but we want someone who is trained to do the work and has had some experience, and unless you happen to find a man especially qualified he may not be able to do the work here. After further consultation with Miss Bleakley I may write to you again on this matter.

…… ……

This library is a special problem by itself. The feeling of some of the clergy, who are members, of the Diocesan Council, is to make it an independent institution on the support of the American Church Mission, and as an independent institution the college would have the use of it in the same way as the Boone Middle School and other educational institutions in the neighborhood may have use of it. If that should be the decision of the National Council of the Episcopal Church in America, the college would not count the Boone Library as a college library any longer and would not consider giving it any kind of support financially or otherwise, and look ahead to building up our own library facilities in the new buildings to be erected. It may not be best thing for the college if that should be the case, but that must be our last resort unless the Boone Library is definitely contributed by the American Church Mission as college library on the support of the mission or of the college. If the library should become independent its future would not be very great, and that would naturally be a handicap also to the Library School which, as you know, has been for the last six years an independent institution without any connection or affiliation with the college except that the librarian of the college, who is an A. C. M. appointee, serves also by Bishop Gilman's order as director of the Library School, an arrangement which has proved to be not entirely satisfactory. I am telling you all this so that you may know what problem we are facing in connection with the proposed lease and the library. Whenever there is an opportunity I hope you will raise this question in the meeting of the Founders.

……

Yours sincerely,
Francis C. M. Wei

20. To Mr. Richard D. Weigle (April 27, 1936)

Dear Dick:

……

It is Frank's opinion, as well as mine, that we ought to keep within the limits of the Five-Year Plan at the rate of three to one for the next year and do the same as far as possible, no matter what the exchange may be, until it comes to a point when we must get more subvention to meet the budget of the year. You will be pleased to know that the China Foundation has recently granted $6,000 Chinese currency for science equipment for us for 1936—1937. This is less than we had expected, but the University of Nanking gets only $6,000, Lingnan $5,000, and Yenching $15,000. The institutions which have medical schools seem to receive greater favors. West China gets $25,000, Cheloo $14,000, and Shanghai Medical College $30,000.

……

Yours sincerely,
Francis C. M. Wei

21. To Mr. Richard D. Weigle (June 1, 1936)

Dear Dick:

……

The question of exchange students is very interesting. Under the circumstances we cannot even take care of six foreign students until more hostels are built, but we ought to encourage some few, say two or three, to come and take one year here as they do in Lingnan and Yenching. I hope you will work out some details and send the scheme to me in concrete for submission to the Senate.

… …

Yours sincerely,
Francis C. M. Wei

22. To Rev. Edwin C. Lobenstine (August 28, 1936)

Dear Mr. Lobenstine:

… …

U. S. $10,000 was given to the college by Miss Johnston and Mrs. Prooter a year ago while they were visiting here explicitly for the purchase of the new land and the whole own has been paid over and kept here in China for several months. As we have to buy more land than this money can pay for we have written to the ladies asking for their permission to spend part of the U. S. $100,000 also for land. It is wise to get enough land for future development before we start the buildings.

The land that we have just bought is full of graves, which can be removed only with the help of the Provincial Government, or else it would mean a great deal of trouble, expenditure and delay. This land amounts to about seven acres, and with the help of the Government we have got the graves practically all removed at a rate almost unknown in this part of the world. The government is helping because they have the understanding that we have bought the land for a college which is registered with the Ministry of Education in Nanking and is operating under the law of the land conforming to all regulations.

… …

Yours sincerely,
Francis C. M. Wei

23. To Mr. Richard D. Weigle (September 12, 1936)

Dear Dick:

… …

The college reopened on the 7th with a record enrollment, and we expect to begin classes on the 14th. An unusually large number of candidates tried our entrance examinations this last summer. In May we qualified a large number of students by special entrance examinations for only affiliated middle school students. Then in August we held our regular entrance examinations for everybody; 160 tried and 30 were qualified. In September the examinations were given again as usual; 216 tried, and we qualified only 11. We could have passed more if there had been more space, particularly for the men students. 74 men and 37 women have registered, with one rejected by the doctor since then, making therefore a freshman class of 110. 94 old students have returned, and the total enrollment is 204, 60 women and 144 men. 51 of the freshmen have registered in the School of Science, 37 in Arts, and 21 in Education. 90% of these students are from our affiliated Christian middle schools. As a whole, they are much better prepared students than the freshmen during the last three years.

The faculty has been much strengthened, particularly in the School of Arts, which for the first time is able to hold up its head alongside the School of Science and the School of Education. This is largely due to the generous special gift of Miss Johnston designated for the strengthening of the Faculty of Arts.

With 204 students all our hostels are filled to capacity. There may be a few more spaces in Yen Hostel, but if those should be filled the girls would feel uncomfortable. There is absolutely not a single space left in the men's hostels. When the college grows at this rate it is essential that Church of Christ in China Hostel to accommodate forty-eight men be completed before next September. The London Mission has already arranged with the Reformed Church Mission to turn over the London Mission Women's Hospital property to be used as the site of the new hostel. The London Mission Society has gotten its funds ready for one-half of the hostel, but the Reformed Church is still raising its share. I have written both to Dr. Casselman and Dr. Taylor that money should be raised as soon as possible only ＄3,000 or ＄4,000 American currency, so that we may push ahead the erection of the hostel. Yen Hostel too must have an annex if not a second unit, and as soon as Mr. Bergamini comes back in four-weeks' time we shall take the matter up with him.

....

Yours sincerely,
Francis C. M. Wei

24. To Dr. John W. Wood (September 12, 1936)

Dear Dr. Wood:

....

  I have written to Miss Johnston about the U. S. ＄5,000 for the strengthening of the Arts School in Hua Chung College, which she has pledged for the next three years. The money has been budgeted and certain teachers appointed on its support. We hope that Miss Johnston will be able to send the money out to us or through your department as soon as possible.

  The college reopened on the 7th and classes will begin next Monday, the 1st. We have had an unusually large number of candidates at our entrance examinations. Over five hundred tried, and about one hundred eighty were qualified. Many of those candidates had also tried examinations for admission into other colleges and only varsities, but one hundred ten of the successful candidates registered in this college, thirty-seven women and seventy-three men, 20 of whom are from Christian middle schools affiliated with the college.

....

Yours sincerely,
Francis C. M. Wei

25. To Mr. Richard D. Weigle (November 20, 1936)

Dear Dick:

... ...

We have already had the permission of the Provincial Government to buy the City Wall land and moat, and it has been surveyed. We may get something like ten acres out of it. We also are taking steps to buy the cultivated land intervening between the moat and the grave land already bought. When these purchases are completed we shall have together with land bought by Bishop Gilman some years ago for the college, something like twenty-six acres outsides the City Wall. You will remember that I wrote you sometimes ago about the possibility of getting the provincial first middle school across the street, which would cost us around $150,000 Mex. and which is considered by Bergamini to be the ideal site for part of Hua Chung campus. I have just written to Dr. Wood about it, hoping that he may take an interest in the proposition.

... ...

Yours sincerely,
Francis C. M. Wei

26. To Dr. Sherman (January, 1937)

Dear Dr. Sherman:

I believe I have already written you about the general conditions in the college after the opening of the fall term. We started the term with an enrollment of 205, 60 women and 145 men. During the last two months and a half some had to withdraw on account of ill health and others for other reasons. At the present time we have 197 students in the college, which is still the highest enrollment we have ever had. The freshman class is particularly encouraging. They have been doing very well, and all the teachers are pleased with them for their preparation as well as for their general conduct.

I am very happy to report to you that we have closed our deal with the Government on the City Wall land and moat. Upon the advice of Mr. Bergamini, the architect, we are buying nine acres of this land, which stretches from the northern edge of the old land bought by Bishop Gilman to the Hsun Tao Lin extension. You will remember that Hsun Tao Lin is the street on which the Church of the Resurrection stands. It is a big stretch of land costing us $55,000 Chinese currency, but in Mr. Bergamini's opinion it is very essential for our future development.

…… ……

Yours sincerely,

Francis C. M. Wei

27. To Mr. Richard D. Weigle (May 3, 1937)

Dear Dick:

…… ……

I would like you to begin to think vigorously about our aims in our campaign next fall. We must keep two things in view. One is to raise enough money, as you say, for at least two or three new buildings, which ought to be the Physics Building $65,000 Chinese, the Chemistry Building $85,000 Chinese, the Biology Building $55,000 Chinese. The Yale-in-China School of Science Lecture Room and Power Room will be $30,000 Chinese, and the Mathematics and Surveying unit $20,000 Chinese, making a total of $255,000 Chinese according to Mr. Bergamini's estimate. This, however, does not include electric fixtures, furniture, etc., for which I am asking the different departments to make detailed estimates before I leave. Then further, prices are going up on account of the new taxes on such things as iron steal, and other kinds of building material, so I would venture to suggest U. S. $100,000 currency as our objective for the School of Science building project. You will remember that the three buildings, together with the library, will make the main court in Bergamini's plan. All the buildings will be connected by a corridor, and the enclosed court will be fitted up as a Chinese Garden. We could name the court as Yali

Court and get the different units as memorials of different donors.

For a college every new building is a liability unless we have an endowment to operate it and to maintain it. We have been worrying on the increased budget of the college when it is working in full swing. Mr. John Coe is getting ready an itemized estimated budget of such a nature. I feel the only sane thing to do is to begin to think about an endowment. I would not mention figures, but we ought to aim at U. S. $500,000 to begin with. That may take two or three years to raise, but with your energetic working we may be able to get the project under way before you leave the office. It is really one of the most important stabilizing forces for the college that we can think of.

······

Yours sincerely,
Francis C. M. Wei

28. To Mr. Richard D. Weigle (March 3, 1937)

Dear Dick:

······

Frank has also written about it, and when he was here for the Directors' meeting last week he mentioned it to me in person. I told him at the time that if the money should be given to me outright I would spend it to buy books for the library, which is at the present time the most poorly supported department in the college. As a matter of fact, it is very difficult for me to decide how to use this money unless I know what conditions are attached to the gift and what is the particular interest of the donor. I am therefore submitting to you a project from each of the Science departments which can always make the best use of any amount of money for equipment or some project, with the fourth alternative that the money be given for books in the English Department or the Chinese Department or both. Will you please use your discretion to decide what particular purpose you would choose to spend the money for, keeping in view the interest of the giver and the nature of the gift. We ought to spend the money in such a way that we may encourage the giver to give again. Of course, we are struggling now to raise money to pay the salaries in the Department of Chinese, as we are struggling to raise the budget for the whole college. I do not suppose you would like this gift to merge in a big pool.

Yours sincerely,
Francis C. M. Wei

29. To Dr. P'u Hwang (January 4, 1938)

Dear Dr. Hwang:

... ...

I hope you will consider carefully the re-appointment of the faculty. Those who are not of vital importance to the institution in your judgment need not be re-appointed. Our policy ought to be to strengthen our departments so as to make our work even more worthwhile. Possibly one of the departments in the School of Arts could be eliminated in order to reinforce the Departments of Economics and Commerce. The Harvard-Yenching grant of U. S. $4,000 for the year 1938—1939 ought to be enough to strengthen the Department of Chinese. I am hoping that I may receive a report from you with regard to the professors who are going to occupy the two chairs on Harvard-Yenching support in Chinese Literature and Chinese History. The Board in Cambridge wants to know their qualifications, the courses they are going to offer, and whatever research work they may undertake. The department also wants to know what books we would propose to buy with the $1,000 American currency and what research work our Department of Chinese Literature and History will undertake with the $1,000 grant.

... ...

Yours very sincerely,
Francis C. M. Wei

30. To Dr. P'u Hwang (January 17, 1938)

Dear Dr. Hwang:

……

I hope it may be possible for the college to re-open on February 14th for the second semester, even though the enrollment may be very small, provided circumstances at that time warrant. Of course you will be able to judge better on the spot and so I don't dare to venture any suggestion from such a distance. I cannot help feeling, however, that it may be the best for our work if we could hold out the hope of re-opening even as late March or April. In case re-opening should have to be postponed to such a late date, it would be better to try to carry on with a modified program and perhaps a somewhat reduced staff. I will suggest this even if there may be students already in the college opening in February. What I mean is, in case the situation should considerably improve, take another batch of students later in term and carry them on with a modified program and wind up the work for these students in the middle of the summer. This is what Lingnan has been doing this last term and found it encouraging.

No matter what happens we must do our level best to take care of our permanent staff and faculty. You may assure every one of them that we want to hold together and we feel sure that we would not do anything worse for them than any other educational institution under similar circumstances as ours in the country would be able to do. We owe this to them for their faithful work in the past as well as our desire to retain their services for the future.

……

Of course there is always our resource to take into account. The cooperating missions, I am sure, would back us up in everything that is reasonable. Unless there should be serious international complications our mission budgets will continue as they have been. For the current academic year we have received U.S. $4,703 from the Associated Boards for Christian College in China Emergency Fund. We may appoint this money to balance our budget as well as to meet emergency needs this year. There are certain expenses that we are responsible for in getting this money raised through the Associated Boards and so you may count on an appropriation of only U. S. $4,000 at present. Richard D. Weigle, as Associate Secretary of our Board of Founders, is taking steps to have this amount remitted to the college treasurer. More could be raised in case of need. Please be sure to send me as soon as possible itemized estimates of your finance needs (1) in case we re-open for the second semester with say an enrollment of 100 students, and (2) we are unable to re-open for the balance of the year. It would be of great help to us at this end if later in the spring you should send me another itemized estimate as to our financial needs, if we should look forward to re-opening the college in September under such conditions as we may anticipate.

…… ……

Yours sincerely,
Francis C. M. Wei

31. To Professor David Hsiung (January 19, 1938)

Dear Dr. Hsiung:

…… ……

I have written to the Acting President expressing my hope that the college may find it possible to re-open on February 14th, but circumstances may not warrant that, and in that case I wish plans could still be made, and have it made known to the public, that we still hope to reopen later in the spring, say in April when the situation begins to clear up a bit. Under any circumstances, let us try to keep our faculty together and get in touch with our students. I agree with Dr. Djang with whom I have been talking about the college these last few days, that as soon as the war is over our college will have a great future. We are better known now, and a great deal of interest has been aroused in China. As soon as normal times return we ought to be able to reap a good harvest from the seeds we have been sowing all these last few months in talking about China and our work. I constantly think about my colleagues in Wu Chang as to how to keep them together for services in the college after the war. Of course, even if we could open in February many students may find it difficult to find the fees. I am sure the Acting President and the Senate will find ways and means to meet the difficulties of such students.

......

Yours sincerely,
Francis C. M. Wei

32. To Professor Paul C. T. Kwei (January 19, 1938)

Dear Paul:

......

  I have written at length to Dr. Hwang about my hopes for the college under these very difficult circumstances. I have told him that you people on the spot have to make the decisions according to the changing circumstances from time to time, but as far as circumstances warrant I wish the college could be reopened for the second semester, even though we may have to postpone the reopening until March or April. Some kind of modification of the program will have to be made under these abnormal circumstances so as to maintain our continuity and to keep the faculty and the students together.

  I think of the financial problems of the students during the war and immediately after it. We may have to reduce fees or allow many of them to postpone the payment. It would not be very difficult for us to appeal for funds in this country in order to help us to do that. I have already written to Dr. Hwang about the sum of $4,703 from the Emergency Funds of the Associated Boards for Christian Colleges in China, which is to help us to balance our budget or to meet emergency needs. If itemized estimates could be sent to us at this end showing in a convincing way our needs in this emergency situation it would not be difficult for us to raise some more money. We must do everything possible to keep our senior men, and to do adequate justice even to those of our staff and faculty members who are appointed from year to year. Of course, all of us shall have to share the hardship brought to the country by this terrible war, but we must do everything possible for our men in order to show that we are really interested in their welfare. I am sure we are able to do as well in this respect as any other educational institution in the country. Unless there should be serious international complications the Mission Boards will be solidly behind us and many friends will be willing to give a helping hand.

... ...

Yours as ever,
Francis C. M. Wei

33. To Rt. Rev. Logan Roots (February 4, 1938)

Dear Bishop:

... ...

The salaries schedule recommended by the college to go into effect in case the college should fail to re-open in February must have been drawn up before the Acting President had heard anything about the $4,700 American currency for our college from the Associated Boards. With this money and the unexpected larger income from fees last term, we ought to be able to give better treatment to our faculty and staff members, even though we should have no income whatever from fees next term. This Associated Boards' money will not be available if we did not have to use it. Certainly it would not seem right if there should be a credit balance in the bank at the end of the year when the salaries have been considerably reduced, on the ground that our budget could not be met.

... ...

Ever affectionately yours,
Francis C. M. Wei

34. To Dr. P'u Hwang (February 4, 1938)

Dear Dr. Hwang:

... ...

John Coe has written me in detail about the salary scale and cuts to be applied to our faculty and staff members in case the college is not able to re-open for the second semester. I agree with you in principle and have absolute trust in the judgment of the committee who has made the recommendation to the Standing Committee of the Boards of Directors, but there are one or two considerations to which I would like to call your attention. (1) There ought to be, of course, some difference in our treatment between those who are going to continue working for the college, even though the college fails to re-open, and those who go away without any work. (2) There ought to be also a difference in our treatment between the permanent members of the faculty and staff and those who are appointed from year to year. (3) By this time you must have heard from me and Francis Hutchins that we have allotted to us, by the time you must have, a sum of U. S. $4,700 from the Associated Boards' Emergency Funds for the Christian College in China. Unless we should make use of this money, we have no legitimate reason to receive it, and it may not be given to us at all. (4) Richard Weigle has expressed his opinion that unless the Yale-in-China fund of U. S. $14,000. Currency is needed to meet expenses in the college he would hesitate to send the whole amount out. It would mean that part of it would be kept in the bank while the medical unit in Changsha would be able to use every cent available for good purposes. (5) In view of the conditions in the country and the salary cuts in other institutions, it may be perfectly reasonable for us to make cuts say 15 to 20 per cent, for all salaries, making the suggestion to everybody, however, that if they should want to contribution part of their reduced salaries to the National Emergency Fund or to relief funds or to the medical work in Changsha, or to any other similar cause he is free to do so. In other words, I feel that ours are justifiable under the present circumstances only when our income does not balance our budget. Many of our faculty and staff members have heavier and unexpected expenses and they should not suffer more than is necessary. Please take these suggestions only on their merits. Richard Weigle is very emphatic that we should not have cuts and leave a greater balance at the end of the year in the bank.

…… ……

Sincerely yours,
Francis C. M. Wei

英　文

35. To Mr. Richard D. Weigle (May 3, 1938)

Dear Dick:

　　　…… ……

　　The cooperating missions here are very much encouraged to hear that we have been able to get as much as £30,000 from the other cooperating units in America. The Yale-in-China Board has voted to do its share in the building scheme, which will mean undertaking the three science units amounting to approximately U. S. 100,000 dollars, which is equivalent to £200,000, and Dr. Casselman has said that his mission would undertake to raise U. S. 55,000 dollars, approximately £11,000. Our estimate is that the total cost of the buildings and land is about £65,000 and we must have £10,000 to endow the buildings for upkeep, making a grand total of £75,000. After careful consultation with Mr. Rattenbury of the M. M. S. and Mr. Cocker-Brown of the L. M. S. we are appealing for £16,000 in this country, £10,000 for the Library building and £6,000 for the Social Science unit, at the right hand side of the Library building and adjacent to the Physics building. The two missions here are not going to raise the money for us but they have taken official action in their respective Boards to give me the liberty to appeal for the money among their constituencies. There is, of course, no telling whether we shall be able to get any money at all, but the enthusiasm of the two missions for our building scheme and the willingness to back us up are quite encouraging.

　　　…… ……

Yours sincerely,
Francis C. M. Wei

36. To Rev. A. M. Sherman (September 13, 1938)

Dear Dr. Sherman:

　　　…… ……

　　Two thirds of our faculty, mostly with families, are already here and about 100 of our students, two thirds men and one third women, are at present living in our rented hostels, although we are not going to begin our term until October 1st. We have set 200 as our maximum enrollment, but we may have to beyond that limit. There will be probably four hostels for men and two for women. It is quite a problem how to take care of all the students quartered in such a way. It is essential that under the circumstances at least one man must devote his whole time to religious work among the students. Charles Whiston is on leave in America. His substitute, young Higgins, fresh graduate from Virginia, is being kept by Bishop Oilman for work in Han Kou. Park Lee is acting Principal of the United Middle School of the Han Kou Diocese, which is now going to function in Ch'uenchow, on this side of the Kwangsi border from Yungchow in Hunan, about half a day by bus from here. C. M. S. is rather short-handed and Bishop Stevens finds it difficult to assign any of his clergymen for student work in the college. It is my hope that the Rev. Quentin Huang who, you will remember, is a St. John's graduate, with post graduate theological training in Philadelphia about ten years ago, and who is priest in the Diocese of Anking, doing student work in Nanchang with Craighi ever since his return from America. He is now refugeeing, with his family, in Kweilin, and may come to our help as chaplain of the students with the permission of Bishops Huntington, Gilman and Stevens. You will remember further that Mrs. Huang was Grace Sung, who graduated from St. Hilda's and taught there for a while. She may be able to help in work among the women students.

It is quite a job to get the college organized in a new place, but the faculty and the students who are here keep up a very good spirit, and with a few exceptions we are expecting all our foreign members of the staff to join us here. So you see we are going to have a full instructional program and we shall carry on the best we can under the circumstances. I am confident that what we may lack in equipment and facilities will be made up by the experience of our students will have. They are all sleeping in double decker beds. All the hostels will be crowded with limited space for recreation; books will be a few here, and our laboratories will have to get along with limited apparatus, but it will be a challenge to our ingenuity, patience and willingness to work under strained circumstances.

…… ……

Yours sincerely,
Francis C. M. Wei

37. To Members of the Board of Founders (December 5, 1938)

Dear Sirs:

…… ……

Even before I went to Chungking, towards the end of October and particularly after my arrival there and my return to Kweilin I have been exploring possibilities of moving the college to a safer place, if there is a safer place these days in China. Another question is how to move 300 people since means of transport is so difficult. Thousands of people are waiting for seats on the buses to get away, but they have not been able to do any booking. There seems to be little danger yet of Kweilin becoming involved in the fighting zone since the enemy has many other more important objectives than the capital of the Kwangsi Province, but we have to look ahead and take whatever precautions are necessary.

The alternatives facing us now are (1) go to westward, (2) to move to a smaller town nearby, say fifty miles from the highway, (3) to stay where we are, (4) to send the women and children to Hong Kong, keeping the men where they are until it is absolutely necessary for us to move on just one hundred miles ahead of the fighting. The first alternative is difficult on account of lack of means of transportation, and I have already mentioned the question of finding a place safer than Kweilin. If we should adopt the second alternative we have to consider health conditions, safety from bandits if the situation should become worse, and the possibility of communicating with the outside world. If we should stay where we are until we have to move the waste of time from running to the caves two or three mornings a week, and the exposing of women and children to serious dangers would be important considerations. We may have to think more seriously of the last alternative, as soon as we could secure means of transportation for the women folk.

Please do not get the impression that our work is being paralyzed. The students have wonderful confidence in us and very few of them are willing to go away for safety even when we throw out gentle hints that they should do so. So far we have still 147 students, 53 of them are women. Our enrollment at the beginning of the term was 163. Aside from the interruptions of air raid alarms the work of the college is going on regularly. More students are using the Library which has only 10% of the books from the college Library in Wu Chang, and laboratory work is being carried on as usual although we have brought here about one third of our equipment. We are one of the few colleges in the country operating as nearly normally as possible. We feel that it is worthwhile to try to keep the continuity of the institution and try and keep the faculty together. A better day may be ahead of us. While we prepare for the worst we are still hoping and praying for the best. I feel the responsibility very heavy on my shoulders in a time like this but it is a joy to bear hardships and particularly to remember that all of you are with us in spirit and in your prayers.

…… ……

Yours sincerely,
Francis C. M. Wei

38. To Dr. E. C. Lobenstine (January 19, 1939)

Dear Dr. Lobenstine:

…… ……

Probably when we actually start moving west 120 students will follow us, but of this number at least 50, being entirely cut off from their homes in the occupied areas, will have to depend upon scholarships for their entire support. If we should have an emergency fund of not less than $10,000, I would recommend to the Executive Committee to allocate $10,000 for the relief of our own students.

We started the term with 164 students, and up to date 35 have withdrawn, and of this 35 only 7 were originally from the college in Wu Chang, the remaining 28 being new students admitted in Kweilin.

... ...

Yours sincerely,
FRANCIS C. M. WEI

39. To Rev. A. M. Sherman (January 21, 1939)

Dear Dr. Sherman:

... ...

We started the term with 164 students, about one third of them are women. Up to date 35 students have withdrawn from the college owing to the situation, and of these 27 are new students, having been admitted into the college here in Kweilin. Practically all have left due to family reasons. There is no group of college students with a greater spirit and loyalty to the institution than ours. Even with all the air raids and with all the uncertainty of the future, and with the destruction around us, the faculty feel that the students have been able to maintain at least 75% of our Wu Chang pre-war efficiency. We are completing the first semester after 16 weeks of lectures and one week of term examinations. Laboratory work has been going on, and the reading room in the library is full every day. Everybody is touched by the family spirit of the Hua Chung group. Our experiences in this war have not only drawn us nearer to God, but have also drawn the faculty and students even more closely together. For this we feel that we ought to continue the college as long as we can, aside from the fact that the college morale and the educational standards of our institution ought to be a contribution, not only to the Church, but also to higher education in China after the war. We are one of the few colleges, outside of those in Szechuan, able to carry on almost normally during these war days.

We are thinking of Yunnan instead of Szechuan, although both are of equal distance from us here, because we believe that Szechuan may be facing isolation from the outside world; in Yunnan it would be easier for us to get books and other educational supplies from the outside.

……

Yours sincerely,
FRANCIS C. M. WEI
PRESIDENT

40. To Mr. Robert A. Smith (August 12, 1939)

Dear Mr. Smith:

……

On July 29 we graduated seventeen students. Three were not able to graduate on that day owing to illness. One was my daughter Anna who had an attack of scarlet fever during my absence in Hong Kong. She is recuperating now in the college infirmary and will be able to take her examinations before November 1. Another student will do the same. But a third has got to wait a whole year. A fourth died at the end of June while I was away. Most of the graduates have got jobs, and only a few are still uncertain.

……

The college closed for the summer on July 29. A summer program is going on keeping all the students and faculty busy. The autumn term will begin on September 7. We have many applicants for admission, but owing to lack of hostel space we can take only about one in ten. Many new students are coming from Christian Middle Schools affiliated with the college by recommendation. We expect a freshman class of about 70, half being girls.

……

As a whole the college has been going along well except the short period when both faculty and students were very nervous about epidemics just a month ago. Part of our equipment is still on the way from Kweilin. The temporary science buildings, altogether costing C. $4,500, are about ready for use. It was only yesterday that we were able to have radio news at our radio station which is not quite complete as we have yet no electricity.

... ...

The co-operation with the Canton Union Theological College here in Hsichow as our guest institution has been very happy so far. We expect three or four of our own students taking the combined theological course next year, which is very encouraging. Even in the summer program, going on now for five weeks before the term begins again, there are two theological courses given and they are taken by our own students as well as by the seminary students. The seminary is also co-educational. They have only about 25 students altogether, and they have six on their faculty.

... ...

Yours sincerely,
Francis C. M. Wei

41. To O. S. Lyford (November 8, 1939)

Extracts from letter of President Francis Wei to O. S. Lyford

The college re-opened on September 7 and lectures have been going on since September 12. There are at present in the college 117 students, a rather reduced number but still encouraging under the present circumstances. The number would have been enlarged by at least 30, if not for the fact that the highway traffic was interrupted owing to the damage to the road by heavy rainfall just at the time of our registration and therefore students were not able to come until it was too late.

... ...

The cooperation between the Canton Union Theological Seminary and Hua Chung has been a most happy one. Five of their students have registered in the college taking a combined course leading to a college degree and therefore they are counted as fully Hua Chung students. Twenty-four of the seminarians are taking some courses in the college and only three, owing to inadequate knowledge of the English, are taking no course in the college whatever. All their students are living in our hostels and participating fully in our college life. We have joint chapel service every day including Sunday and all our undertakings outside of curricular work are joint enterprises. It is really a pleasure to have such a close cooperation with the seminary. Among the happy consequences is the fact that two of the Hua Chung graduates and two undergraduates, incidentally all Anglicans, are taking theological work. We hope this means only a small beginning of greater things to come.

Yours sincerely,
Francis C. M. Wei

42. To Mr. Robert A. Smith (November 9, 1939)

Dear Mr. Smith:

……

I hope that our students might have caught some of the spirit which we endeavor to demonstrate in our work. Our college motto is "Christian sacrifice and service, universal brotherhood and love." The graduates of the last year prefer positions with higher salaries to those of greater service to the nation in time of war. I felt I must accept my defeat, but young men have their own problems and in these war days they have to find more money to support families and relatives who have lost all they had. I am willing to excuse them and to sympathize with them, but I do hope that our education with so much self-sacrifice behind the work both in America and England on the part of the Founders and friends, and in the college among some of the teachers will turn out students with a genuine self-sacrifice spirit. Rome, of course, was not built in a day, but it may have been due to my shortcomings and weaknesses. If a better man could be found for the position, I am at any time prepared to step out from the administrative office. My letter sent to the Executive Committee of the Board of Directors expressing my preference to accept re-appointment only from year to year is no protest against anything that the Directors or Founders have done to me or to the college, as a matter of the fact I feel they have been the most generous and thoughtful in every way, but as a gesture that I am not here to block the way of a more competent man who may be able to bring about a fuller realization of my own ideals for

Christian higher education.

　　……

　　As I have already reported to Mr. Lyford, the college re-opened on September 7 and lectures have been going on since September 12. On account of the interrupted traffic on the Indo-China railway as well as on the Burma highway, many of the new students arrived here late and others failed to arrive entirely. Consequently our enrollment is much reduced. The total to date is 117, consisting of the 29 seniors (14 men and 15 women), 16 juniors (9 men and 7 women), 26 sophomores (18 men and 8 women) and 46 freshmen (26 men and 20 women). Therefore 67 men and 50 women. Of this 77 are Christian and 40 non-Christian. 100 have come from Christian middle schools and 17 from non-Christian middle schools. The Province of Kwantung leads with 46 students, then comes Hupeh with 30 and then Hunan with 20. The rest are distributed among 8 different provinces, namely, Anhui, Kiangsu, Kiangsi, Chekiang, Fu Jian, Shang Dong, Shensi and Yunnan. Only two students are from Yunnan and they are being admitted on probation, more or less as a courtesy to the local community. Secondary education in this province is rather backward.

　　It distresses me that owing to some misunderstanding, very few Yali or Fuhsiang students from their graduating classes have come to the college. Distance is another reason. None of the Boone or St. Hilda graduates have entered the college this year. In their moving they all stayed in Kunming and went to national institutions where they thought they will get more financial support and have greater securities which experience will surely teach them to be untrue.

　　　　　　　　……

Yours sincerely,
Francis C. M. Wei

43. To Mr. Oliver S. Lyford (November 16, 1939)

Dear Mr. Lyford:

　　　　……

　　This year marks the 15th Anniversary of the Founding of Hua

Chung College and 10th Anniversary of its reorganization with Yale-in-China Association and the Reformed Church Mission joining in as cooperating units in 1929. Every year November 1 is our Founders' Day and it has been our custom to have a holiday to celebrate the occasion and to have the Matriculation Exercise on that day. The Senate of the college has acted this year to postpone the celebration of the Founders' Day for one month so as to give more adequate time for preparation and we are going to have the week-end of December 1—3 for the celebration of the 15th and 10th anniversaries. The first day, Friday, is to be devoted largely to celebration, the second day, Saturday, to student festivities and games with a college meal on Saturday evening when the whole faculty and student body together with the faculty and students of the Theological Seminary, will have a communal dinner in one of the hostels, and then the last day, Sunday, the celebration will end with a thanksgiving service. The whole celebration will cost N. C. $300.00 or U. S. $25.00, at the present rate of exchange. The Executive Committee will communicate with you concerning this expenditure.

…… ……

Yours sincerely,
Francis C. M. Wei

44. To Francis S. Hutchins (November 20, 1939)

…… ……

The enrollment this year is small because we have a small freshman class. Many new students came to Kunming, but because just at the time of our registration, the highway between Kunming and here was flooded out by heavy rain falls and buses were not able to run for almost a month. The new students who had come from Hong Kong and Macao got tired of waiting at Kunming and went to other colleges. We have 48 freshmen instead of 80 as I had expected.

…… ……

Yours sincerely,
Francis C. M. Wei

45. To Mr. Robert A. Smith (January 8, 1940)

Dear Mr. Smith:

…　…

The term examinations begin today and will be all finished by the 16th of this month. The winter vacation will commence on the 18th and the second term will start on February 18 with classes to resume February 22.

…　…

One woman student died at the end of the last term and a man student passed away in the middle of September, both during my absence. It was decided that a piece of land be bought for cemetery purpose as it was felt that a Christian cemetery ought to be started here.

…　…

During the winter vacation of a month, laboratory work in the School of Science will have to continue in order to make up the lost time. For the other students there would be some activities in the form of public lectures and conferences in order to occupy part of their time, as very few of them are able to go away for the vacation.

…　…

Yours sincerely,
Francis C. M. Wei

46. To Rev. E. C. Lobenstine (January 22, 1940)

Dear Dr. Lobenstine:

…　…

In the first place, my primary interest in the educational work in Hua Chung is our Christian character. Of course I am vitally concerned with the academic side of the work and will do everything possible to maintain on high standards and thorough training which have been our pride. But this could be achieved also in a national institution and other private colleges in China, should we have a few years with normal conditions to develop our higher education. But the Christian character is our special feature and it is for this that the college has been founded, and it is for this also that its cooperating Missions and friends in China as well as abroad have been supporting the college so generously.

…… ……

Secondly, I tried to bring out in our conversation the importance of a well-thought-out policy for Christian education in China which would correlate and coordinate the work of the Christian colleges and that of the Christian middle schools in each of the six regions. There is of course some necessary overlapping between the regions, but it is a pity that the Christian middle schools have not been working hard enough to send their graduates, particularly those who are Christians and from Christians homes, to the Christian college. Is it not a waste for pupils who have finished the Christian elemental schools to go largely to non-Christian middle schools so that the latter should have a number of students, who have no background in Christian training, to start the work all over again, and to have the same thing happen in the Christian colleges? Hua Chung has been making it a part of its policy to admit as many graduates from Christian middle schools as possible. Our records show that 80% to 90% of student body come from Christian middle schools. But even with this we have found it difficult to maintain the desirable percentage of Christian students in the college, because of the low percentage of Christian students in the Christian middle schools themselves. This has become more conspicuous that we begin now to draw more from the Christian middle schools in the Canton-Hong Kong region. Something must be done about this; otherwise the work in the Christian colleges, certainly in Hua Chung, will be more and more difficult.

…… ……

Fourthly, I told you something about the precarious status of our School of Education. We are the only private college which the Ministry of Education still permits to have a School of Education at all. The tendency seems that the Government is going to concentrate all training of teachers for secondary schools in Government Teachers Colleges, of which there are six in number at present. Some of the Christian colleges are not allowed to have even a department of education, and we consider it really a miracle that we can continue to have our School of Education. I interviewed the Ministry of Education in Chungking when I was there in November 1928, and the impression I got was that they would allow us to continue our School of Education, because partly of our reputation in government circles that we do not attempt anything that we could not do well, and partly because of our limited enrollment. But we are not satisfied with this uncertain situation, and so Dean P'u Hwang and Dr. HUI of the School of Education are going to Chungking during this winter vacation with instructions from the college to clarify, if possible, our position with the government as far as our School of Education is concerned. It would be a great victory if our two delegates should be able to get the status of our School of Education officially defined by the Ministry of Education.

... ...

Yours sincerely,
Francis C. M. Wei

47. To Professor Serge Elisseeff (February 15, 1940)

Dear Professor Elisseeff:

... ...

You will notice in the financial report that we have spent during the last year and half only $10,981.70 Chinese National Currency on salaries and $2,461.95 Chinese National Currency on books, stationery and sundries, totaling $13,443.65 Chinese National Currency, which is equivalent to U.S. $1,658.82. The way that we reckon the Chinese dollar in terms of U.S. currency is shown in our financial report. The average exchange for the first year was 6.165 to one, and that for the current year is 15.0185 to one.

Our first year was a very difficult year, full of uncertainties, owing to the war and our moving from Wu Chang to Kweilin in the summer of

1938 and then from Kweilin to our present site in the spring of 1939. This made it almost impossible for us to carry in on our work in any satisfactory manner, and so practically all our research projects were suspended. We come to Hsichow in Yunnan and occupied our present site in April of last year. Although lectures began on May 7 and continued until the end of July in order to complete a semester, the moving of our books and equipment from Kweilin was not completed until December of last year. In spite of that we did our best to carry on our researches and were to accomplish not a little.

…　…

Respectfully submitted,
President

48. To Rev. Arthur M. Sherman (March 18, 1940)

Dear Dr. Sherman:

…　…

At the last College Senate meeting a recommendation was made that twenty scholarships be offered to freshman students next year coming from Christian affiliated middle schools, ten of $200.00 each and ten of $150.00 each, all in national currency, to be won by competitive examinations and on the recommendation of the principals concerned. We are aware that for the welfare of the college, it is very essential to help the Christian students and to have a high percentage of Christian students all the time. The war, of course, has made it more and more difficult for the Christian families to pay the expenses of the college education for their children which are becoming higher every month. While in Wu Chang we estimated that it would cost a student in Arts and Education in our college only about $280.00 a year and $40.00 more for a science student. But here in Hsichow after we have been here for a year, the prices have gone up so much that our recent investigation shows that the minimum yearly budget for a student is at least $450.00 national currency, aside from travel and books. Books, of course, are difficult to get and are quite beyond the reach of the average student. Our students have to depend on whatever books there may be in the library or in the department, and our small enrollment reduces the hardships as far as this goes.

　　　……　……

Some of our old students went to government colleges in Kunming this last summer not for financial reasons alone. There is the notion prevalent though erroneous that graduates from government colleges would have better opportunities to find jobs. The fact is that Hua Chung, owing to our small number of graduates, has the smallest percentage of unemployed graduates. All of our last year's graduates have found jobs. We lost some of our students because they were not entirely satisfied with our Department of Economics-Commerce. We are trying our best to strengthen this department. A man with two years' postgraduate work in the London School of Economics has come to join our staff in this department since last August.

　　　……　……

Yours sincerely,
Francis C. M. Wei

49. To Mr. Robert A. Smith (June 7, 1940)

Dear Mr. Smith:

　　　……　……

PROPOSED BUDGET & SUBSIDIES. In my letter N. Y. 8 I reported on the Proposed Budget for the next academic year 1940—1941. The budget itself was sent to Mr. Lyford on April 22. A copy of this together with a copy of my letter N. Y. 8 was also sent to you in New Haven. In my letter N. Y. 8 I made comments on the budget and I hope that you have seen this and reported to the Board of Founders acting also as Directors. In N. Y. 10 I reported to Mr. Lyford and the Board of Founders through the actions taken by the Executive Committee Pro-tem on the recommendations of the Senate to give a second subsidy to the members of faculty and staff in our college who in our judgment were not able to meet the rising expense of living with their salaries. A report on the actual salaries received by each, the size of the family in Hsichow and the total subsidies given by the college was sent to Mr. Lyford, enclosed in my letter N. Y. 10. Since the Board has given the permission to the Executive Committee Pro-tem to use the balance accrued from favorable exchange to give aids to faculty members and students, we are not waiting for the approval of the Founders before we begin the second subsidy.

GRANTS FOR THIS YEAR. I have also reported that the China Foundation has made us a grant of N. C. $5,000.00 for emergency expenditures of the Yale-in-China School of Science this year. Since this grant has been made on applications for subsidy for science equipment for the School of Science, this N. C. $5,000.00 is divided among the three Departments of Biology, Chemistry and Physics, according to the old ratio of 3∶4∶3 for their equipment. The difficulty is now how to get our stuff in from abroad. But the Physics Department has practically spent all the money at its disposal, while the other two departments have been accumulating some money with which they are trying to make purchase from abroad.

We have just received the formal notice from the Ministry of Education in Chungking that our applications for subsidy from the government has been granted. The total is N. C. $20,000.00 for the present calendar year, January 1 to December 1, 1940, which is the Government fiscal year of this N. C. $20,000.00, $9,990.00 goes towards three chairs, namely, Chinese in the School of Arts, Chemistry in the School of Science and Psychology in the School of Education. The incumbents of those chairs are Professor L. P. Pao of the Chinese Department, Professor Wesley(S)Wan of the Chemistry Department and Professor I. Hu of the School of Education. It is necessary of course for the college to supplement the amount of $3,330.00 from the government for their salaries, since our scale calls for more as you may gather from our Proposed Budget. From the balance of the government grant N. C. $3,340.00 is for science equipment, which goes to

Chemistry, and N. C. $1,670.00 for Chinese books. It is the regulation of the government that money for equipment or books has to go to the department for which chairs are granted.

SCHOLARSHIPS. In the Proposed Budget for the next academic year there is a comparatively large item for Scholarships and Student Aids as called for by needs of the students under the present circumstances. I am happy to report that in reply to my letter, Mr. Li Jui, a Christian businessman, for, merely of Han Kou, has sent us N. C. $2,000.00 towards our scholarship fund for the next year. There is the income of N. C. $300.00 from the Chiu Kai-ming's mother memorial scholarship fund and I am confident that I shall be able to get one or two private friends who will give us money for the same purpose. Mr. Li Jui's gift is particularly encouraging. In the former years, he has been giving us only three hundred dollars a year for scholarship.

... ...

COMMENCEMENT. Our commencement will be on July 6. Classes are still going on. Those for the seniors and sophomores will stop on June 19 in order to give them a week of review in preparation for the intermediate examinations of the sophomores and the graduating examinations of the seniors. The freshmen and juniors will have their classes until the 26th, when all examinations will begin.

We have twenty-two candidates for the degrees in the senior class this year and it is a good class. Ever so many applications have been coming in from the affiliated middle schools for teachers and we are not graduating sufficient students to meet all the demands. Some of them, of course, are not going to teach, because they would like to join government services or to enter other walks of life, which is only natural.

... ...

Yours sincerely,
Francis C. M. Wei
President

50. To Mr. Robert A. Smith (August 13, 1940)

Dear Mr. Smith:

……

In our May and July examinations for admission we have qualified ninety-five candidates besides thirty-two recommended by the affiliated Christian middle schools for admission without examination according to the college regulations. It is difficult to tell under the circumstance how many of these 127 students will come to the freshman class next month. The uneasy situation in Indo-China may have scared quite a number away from the interior, driving them to Shanghai which people consider a safer place, much to our regret and indicating a regrettable mentality of young people accustomed to the atmosphere in Hong Kong, and it is from Hong Kong that we expect to have two-thirds of our freshman class for the next year. The Burma route is closed for the time being and it is too long a trek and too expensive for young students to come to the interior by it.

……

Yours sincerely,
Francis C. M. Wei
President

51. To Professor Serge Elisseeff (August 14, 1940)

Dear Professor Elisseeff:

……

Our difficulty in purchasing books of any kind is almost unsurmountable, especially now that transportation is more complicated by the closing of the Indo-China route and of the Burma route. Fortunately, it is easier to get books in from abroad by book post. We have been receiving all along up to the present time parcels of the book from both America and England, we should be obliged if you would buy for us books and other publications along the line of Chinese studies either in the English or the French language and mail them to us, charging the cost to the grant you are going to send to us for the coming year. If that should involve too much trouble in bookkeeping, you may send us bills and we shall send you New York checks in American currency to cover them.

… …

Yours sincerely,
Francis C. M. Wei
President

52. To Mr. Robert A. Smith (September 2, 1940)

Dear Mr. Smith:

… …

Two months of the summer vacation have gone by and in three more weeks the new term will begin. Prospects are not good for us to have a large entering class. We had hoped to have about two-thirds of our new students from Hong Kong and Macao where there are a large number of Christian middle schools, but the close of the Indo-China road and the recent rumors concerning the movements of Japanese war ships on the waters around the Indo-China peninsula have scared many away from the interior colleges. But we are unable to predict our enrollment until after registration.

… …

The government has ordered anew that all Schools of Education and Departments of Education in all the universities and colleges, with the exception of those in Peiping, Tientsin and Shanghai, stop admitting new students from this year. But the government has also sanctioned our report of admitting new students to all our departments in the college, including the School of Education. We have written to the Ministry of Education pointing out the discrepancy between the two orders we have received and asking that we may still admit new education students. We are waiting with anxiety and interest what the government will say. If our request should be refused it would not mean that our School of Education would stop work at once. The three classes now in the college will go on, and in three years' time the government may change its policy. In the meanwhile, it is necessary for us to develop our Department of Economics-Commerce into a small School of commerce, with two departments in order to maintain our status as a university which requires three schools. We had the School of Commerce in mind when we first got registered in 1930. A detailed report on this plan will be sent to the Founders later when it is ready. It will mean the adding of two more appointments in Economics, which is a subject I always want to stress.

…… ……

Yours sincerely,
Francis C. M. Wei

53. To Mr. Oliver S. Lyford (September 21, 1940)

Dear Mr. Lyford:

…… ……

Registration of students took place on September 18 and 19, and lectures will begin on Monday, September 23. Quite contrary to your expectation as indicated in the second paragraph of your letter No. 16, our enrollment this year is unusually small, smaller than any previous years since 1931. This distresses us very much, and I know it will be very disappointing to the Founders as well. It is due entirely to the development in Indo-China, during the latter part of the summer vacation. We had hoped to have a good number of students from the Christian schools in Hong Kong and Macao. We qualified a large number in our May entrance examinations. If half of those should have come, our entering class would be at least seventy-five. But the developments in Indo-China and the rumors about Yunnan and the Southwest, which had reached Hong Kong, have scared practically all the students away from the interior. And so instead of coming to unoccupied China, they have all gone to Shanghai and Peiping, which is a fact almost shameful for us Chinese to mention. It indicates the general attitude of the young people among Chinese in Hong Kong. Then the difficulty of transportation and the constant bombing in Chungking and Kweiyang have made it very difficult for students to come to us. We have heard from quite a few, both in Chungking and in Kweiyang, that their belongings had all been destroyed by the enemy bombing, and so they are not able to go to college this year.

We have just advertised again in Kunming to receive more transfer students. The National University in Kunming are on the move again and so some may want to come to us, but there is no telling since it is so late.

... ...

Yours sincerely,
Francis C. M. Wei

54. To Mr. O. S. Lyford (October 12, 1940)

Dear Mr. Lyford:

... ...

The college has a very small enrollment this term. Instead of 120 at least, as we had expected, the term opened with only 75, of whom 19 were freshmen. We counted on two-thirds of the new students from Hong Kong and Macao, as the results of our May entrance examinations for students in our affiliated Christian middle schools had indicated. In those exams we qualified 108 candidates and more than two-thirds of these were in Hong Kong and Macao. The Indo-China road was closed about the middle of August, when students would be otherwise coming in that way. Consequently only four came because they left Hong Kong earlier. I am glad my own daughter was one of them.

After registration we decided to take in more transfer students. An advertisement was put in the Kunming papers, and Professor Hsiung was sent to Kunming to examine the candidates for transfer. Only ten students have come, bringing our enrollment up to 86. A few more of the freshmen are still to arrive, some from Yali in Hunan. Transportation has been so difficult with the evacuation from Kunming that it takes an unbelievable length of time for anyone to get here from any place at all. But the spirit of the student body and of the faculty is much better this term and I feel encouraged.

I like to report that we have decided to take in a sub-freshman class this winter, and if there are qualified students, to add another mid-year freshman class. It would complicate our schedule but it is necessary. There would not be any extra budget for that.

We have started three study groups on Christianity, one conducted by the Rev. Carl Liu of the Episcopal Church, warden of the men's hostels, with my assistance, taking up the Policy and Teachings of the Anglican Communion, another by the Rev. L. Constantine, dealing with Church History, and a third by Professor Anderson, studying the Creeds. Mr. Liu has 30 in his class, Professor Constantine has 10, and Professor Anderson 15. I consider this a very encouraging sign, as the classes give no credits, being entirely extra-curricular. And I am reviving our personnel guidance scheme, about which I shall write next time.

…… ……

Yours sincerely,
Francis C. M. Wei

55. To Mr. Robert A. Smith (January 8, 1941)

Dear Mr. Smith:

…… ……

We received an order from the Ministry of Education in Chungking transmitting the request of the Generalissimo for subscriptions from our faculty and staff members to the amount of N. C. $5,000.00 towards the National Savings account. The savings are redeemable with 8% interest after years. The Ministry asked that if individual subscriptions should fail to come up to that amount the college could make it up from College Funds. The matter was first considered by the College Senate and referred to the Executive Committee pro-tem of the Directors. The President was instructed to appeal to the faculty and staff, both Chinese and missionary, for such subscriptions of their free accord. Owing to the war prices savings were, of course, very difficult and in many cases impossible for the Chinese members. The British members had their own national war funds to contribute to. But the response was very splendid. We all appreciate and admire the wonderful spirit in which the Generalissimo has been conducting the war in China and would want to do as much as possible to show our support and loyalty. The Chinese members subscribed to the amount of N. C. $1,620 and the missionary members subscribed N. C. $865. Two of the missionaries, one American and one British, took from their discretionary mission Funds N. C. $1,000.00 and N. C. $800.00 respectively, leaving the balance of N. C. $715 to be made up by the President from his own discretionary fund. So the total of N. C. $5,000.00 was subscribed without taking any money from the College Funds. I am very happy to report this to the Founders.

......

Yours sincerely,
Francis C. M. Wei
President

56. To Mr. Robert A. Smith (January 29, 1941)

Dear Mr. Smith:

......

During the vacation I am giving a short course on lectures on the Draft Constitution of the Republic of China, as I feel college students ought to know something about it and this is not taken care of by any our regular courses during term time and I happen to be making a study of it. My connection with the Political Council has revived my old interest in the study of political problems, but largely from the academic point of view. I take it only as a hobby.

The students are enjoying their winter vacation. The weather is glorious, and we have had a very good term. In almost every respect we are back to the pre-war standards. As a matter of fact, the students have been working far too hard. We have a small enrollment but ours is one of the very few institutions which have been able to carry on university work at the regular level of efficiency. This is admitted by all visitors who have come to Hsichow. The faculty have been very quiet. Formerly when I planned to leave Hsichow for a period of time some of the administrative heads always felt somewhat uneasy, but this time they all encourage me to go to Chungking. Our health records have been fine for the last year. We are still using the local hospital. But we have good prospects of having from the Han Kou Diocese Dr. Logan H. Roots and family here from Shanghai. They are being evacuated from the lower Yangtze valley. Dr. Roots is the son of Bishop Root and B. S. and M. D. of Harvard. He has been a doctor in the Episcopal Mission hospitals in Wu Chang and Anking for over ten years. Mrs. Roots is a trained nurse and so she will be a help in case of emergency. We are still waiting with anxiety to hear definitely whether the Roots will be allowed by the American consular authorities to enter free China from Shanghai via Rangoon or not. Telegrams from Shanghai, so far, are encouraging.

… …

Yours sincerely,
Francis C. M. Wei
President

57. To Rev. J. T. Addison (February 12, 1941)

Dear Thayer:

… …

For this reason I was one of those to support the idea when the Hua Chung scheme was first proposed. The work of the college for the last sixteen years, particularly since its re-organization in 1929, has proved the wisdom of the co-operative plan. We have now even on the college refugee in Hsichow a faculty of forty-two members with full training and besides in administrative staff of fourteen people. Our total budget for the current year is $201,665 Chinese national currency, U. S. $6,050 and ten foreign salaries paid directly by the cooperating missions in America and England. In the Boone days our science equipment was estimated by Bishop Gilman, at that time president of the college, to be U. S. $2,000. Now with the support of the Yale-in-China Association it has been accumulated to the total value of U. S. $150,000 at pre-war prices. Hua Chung is registered as a University under the Chinese Government and has a reputation in educational circles as one of the best of its size in the country with the highest standards. At the same time visitors representing various churches in China are of the opinion after careful observation of our work that ours is the most Christian in spirit.

…… ……

Theological education has been on my mind these days. I am not satisfied with what has been going in this country along this line, which is of paramount importance for the future of the church in China. A theological school or department must be closely connected with the churches at this juncture in the development of the Christian movement in China. Its standards must be certainly not lower in scholarship than any other department of learning in the universities. More and more of the church workers ought to come up to this standard in order to put the church in a position to command respect among the thinking people of China, and to help it take root in Chinese soil. If we should have our Department of Theology in Hua Chung, we should not only train a number of students for the ministry and for lay leadership, but we would want also to give refresher courses for church ministers in service whose danger is to become stale and loose touch with theological thinking and currents thought in the modern world. We would further have a theological magazine to maintain contact with our former students and other church workers, keep a circulating library for the reading of men in the out-of-the-way isolated stations, and help to translate the best standard books in theology and other religions. Such a department on the college would keep before the students in the other department the ideal of devoting one's life and all to building of the kingdom and to remind the faculty members that one of their duties as teachers in a Christian college whatever their own field of interest is to approach every problem from the Christian point of view. Would the mission of which you are now one of the responsible officers give us the encouragement to develope along these lines? It is my belief that if we should get the men and launch out with the work on an adventure of faith, support would come to it. It is the most important that a Christian college ought to do and the mission ought to support.

I would have a small beginning for this plan and let it develop according to its usefulness. Four full time men ought to be enough. In a pinch we could get along with three, provided we got the three men we need. There ought to be a man for the Old Testament and the history of religion, a man for the New Testament and one for church History. Either the N. T. man or the History man may combine systematic theology. If we could get a man specially for the last it would be better. Postoral theology ought to be done under experienced ministers in the neighboring churches with well organized parish work. These parishes would be our "teaching parishes" where the students might spend their sixth year after the completion of the five years in the college. The course of five years would be a combined one of Arts and Theology, with about one year and a half of time devoted to theological studies and the rest to art subjects adjunct to theology and designated by the Department of Theology. In this way the students would be able to get an Arts degree recognized by the Government at the end of the fourth year and then a year entirely for theology before the year of internship in one of the teaching parishes or in an educational institution as apprentices under a designated school chaplain. Of the theological subjects I would prefer Chinese theologians to teach systematic and pastoral theology, whereas O. T. and N. T. and church history may be taught either by Chinese professors or by theologians from abroad. The contacts of theological students with men and women in the other departments in the college would be most valuable and necessary.

In Wu Chang we could have cooperation with theological seminaries under the other churches, denominational or union. There was one there before the war, not very good in standards but it could be useful to us. Others may come to join up, all on the Oxford and Cambridge plan. Men who have already taken the bachelor's degree with the required Arts subjects may spend three years on the special study of theology. These would be our prospective theologians, whereas those who had the combined course would be just the parish ministers and intelligent school chaplains or well informed lay workers. This scheme would not depend for its operation on government recognition. We could run it within government regulations as they are now.

…   …

Yours sincerely,
Francis C. M. Wei

58. To Dr. Arthur M. Sherman (April 3, 1941)

Dear Dr. Sherman:

…   …

Government Curricula: As I have written before, the government curricula, as promulgated last year, have given us quite a bit of concern. There is no prohibition of religious teaching. Therefore, although no official statement has ever been made of the attitude of the leaders in the government as expressed by the Generalissimo and Madame Chiang Kai-shek in Han Kou, as far as I know, the new curricula do not affect the teaching of religious subjects in the colleges. Curricula affect our work in so far as the courses for each major department in all the colleges and universities are so strictly prescribed, and even elective limited. It is difficult under the circumstances to find room for the teaching of religion and Christianity inside the curriculum. We are doing our best, however, to get the students interested in electing religious courses, but that is very slow work as the required courses are so heavy. To supplement it we have been giving short courses of lectures on religious subjects outside the curriculum which do not count for credits. That has its handicaps, of course, and we have been only experimenting with it.

Religious Department in Christian Colleges: It has been in my mind for many months to take this question up with Ministry of Education and to get official recognition for it. While I was in Chungking a year and a half ago, attending the fourth session of the First People's Political Council, I had a talk with the Political Vice-minister of Education on the subject, and my argument was roughly this:

Our Draft Constitution, as well as our present Provisional Constitution, provides for religious liberty of the people. Propaganda of any religion is therefore permitted. The Christian Churches in China have thousands of preachers and ministers who preach at least once a week on Sunday to their respective congregations all over the country, and who have the closet contact with the people in their parish work, taking care not only of the children, but also of the adults, in the Sunday schools and religious education as a part of their church program. These preachers and ministers are trained in theological schools which are now mostly under the care of missionaries. They are not to blame if in the theological training of the candidates for various positions in the church, Chinese culture should be slighted and the educational policy of the government ignored. Speaking from the point of view of the education program of the nation and speaking also as a nationalistic Christian, more as a nationalist in this case than as a Christian, I would advocate that theological education be recognized by the government, so that the Ministry of Education may have the right to inspect the theological schools of different grades and see to it that they are brought up to standard with minimum requirements in the theological curriculum to take care of the culture elements of the Chinese people in higher education and to conform to the educational policy of the nation.

…… ……

A Large Proportion of Christian Students and Graduates from Christian Middle Schools Desired in Christian Colleges: This is emphasized in Vote E-1125(c) 1. We agree to this most heartily, and it has been our policy in admitting students all these years since the reorganization of the college in 1929, but the practical question is how to get the Christian middle schools themselves to encourage their students to go more to the Christian colleges instead of the national universities and other private institutions. I would recommend that the individual mission boards, which support the different Christian middle schools, pay more attention to this matter, and ask for reports from the respective Christian middle schools on the percentage of their graduates who go to college and the percentage of those who go to the Christian colleges as compared with those who go to other institutions.

Responsibility of Christian college for the welfare of the Christian middle schools: That also has been our work according to our deliberate policy, while in Wu Chang, every other year we had a conference of the principals of the Christian middle schools, twenty-two altogether in the Central China region, held on our Campus, in which the president of the college and members of the School of Education always took a leading part. That helped to create an esprit de corps of the Christian middle schools in our region, and gave us the opportunity of discussing such problems as religious education in middle schools, educational policy, and school finance, as well as to consider ways and means of overcoming difficulties caused by government regulations and Christian education. Then in alternate years Hua Chung held a Christian middle school teacher's conference, and methods of teaching were considered. The outbreak of the war in China has prevented these conferences, but our School of Education is still editing a Central China Christian Middle Schools Bulletin, whereby we try to maintain our contact with the Central China Middle Schools which have moved now to Szechwan and Yunnan. In other words, as far as the Christian middle schools in the Central China region are concerned, we have for the last twelve years been functioning more as the Central China Christian Educational Association for middle schools.

Scholarships Available for Christian Students: This question is raised in the minutes Vote E-1126, 2. We always have in Hua Chung a large number of scholarships, from the cooperating missions such as the Reformed Church Mission, the London Missionary Society, and the Methodist Mission. The Yale-in-China Association has no such scholarships, and our mission, the A. C. M., gives scholarships only privately by members of the mission staff. The college has its own scholarships, and in selecting the candidates we give preference to Christian students and graduates from Christian middle schools if they fulfill the requirements for the award of such scholarships. It has been so with us for the last twelve years since 1929.

…… ……

Yours sincerely,
Francis C. M. Wei

59. To Mr. Oliver S. Lyford (May 7, 1941)

Dear Mr. Lyford:

…… ……

<u>The Summary Budget.</u> We first of all wish to point out that war prices and the falling value of the Chinese dollar forced us to increase many items in the budget. The income items remain about the same except that as reported before, the college is not charging any tuition fees or any other fees, and so the income is reduced by at least N. C. $14,000, figuring an enrollment of 120 for the next year. If all goes well, we ought to have a large enrollment than that, but with the uncertainty of the situation we dare not be to optimistic.

…… ……

"Education Budget": This budget is practically unchanged. The vacancy in Music has to be filled if the properly-qualified person is found, and we are taking steps to secure such a person.

…… ……

Yours sincerely,
Francis C. M. Wei
President

60. To Rev. A. M. Sherman (June 10, 1941)

Dear Dr. Sherman:

…… ……

It is a disappointment to us that Dr. Bingham Dai is not able to join our faculty this year to fill the vacancy of Sociology. We are making arrangements to have that chair filled either by a man who has taken his Ph. D. in Harvard University or a man in Kunming with a B. A. from Shanghai and Ph. D. from London. Miss Mary E. Johnston has written about a Dr. Chu, who has taken a Ph. D. in Political Science from the University of Illinois. We have no chair for Political Science, but since Dr. Chu has been so highly recommended as a Christian man and a scholar, I am going to take the matter up with the Academic Committee in the college, consisting of the deans, before I answer Miss Johnston's letter. Sometime it is just as important to get a good man with the proper training as to fill a chair.

······

Yours affectionately,
Francis C. M. Wei

61. To Mr. Robert A. Smith (June 10, 1941)

Dear Mr. Smith:

······

Dr. K. C. Chang of the Economics-Commerce Department is not being reappointed. We have found it very difficult to get a good economist to teach in our college, and I would like to emphasize again the need of such a man, and if at all possible, we hope the Yale-in-China Association will find him and send him out to us before September. The American Church Mission, i. e. the Department of Foreign Missions of the National Council of the Protestant Episcopal Church in the U. S., has also been trying to find us such a man, but so far in vain. It seems a little bit strange to me that with a good Economics Department in Yale and the Graduate School of Business Administration in Harvard, we should not be able to get any Christian man from either of those places to volunteer and come out and teach Economics, which is of such importance to the national policy of China in her future developments, as well as to meet the crying need of more men trained in Economics both during the war and for the national reconstruction afterwards. I know you have your problems, but there must be a way to overcome them.

… …

I am very sorry to report that of the fifteen prospective graduates, one girl has been suffering for the last week from mental disturbances. She is now being watched by Dr. Logan Roots, our resident physician, in the Hsichow General Hospital; and Professor John C. F. Lo who has had experience in psychiatric clinics in America while he was there in 1939—1940, is collaborating with Dr. Roots. It is a mild case, but it is giving us a great deal of worry. Neither Dr. Roots nor Dr. Lo has been able to get at the root cause of the matter. The girl comes from a Christian home and has always been in Christian schools. Her father is a church minister, now in Szechuan. She has been a very good student in the Department of English Literature, and quite musical. We hope that she will be able to recover completely her mental health before very long, and we are doing everything possible for her. I am planning to meet all her expenses from my Discretionary Fund, to which so many friends in America have generously contributed.

… …

We are making arrangements for commencement on Wednesday, July 2. In the morning there will be a Baccalaureate Service for the graduates with Commencement Exercises in the afternoon. The graduating class is planning to have the Class Day Exercises on July 1, and the Alumni Association will hold its meeting in the evening of July 2 to welcome the new members. It is very difficult to get a commencement speaker in this part of our country at this time, and we are thinking of inviting the president of the High Court in Tali to address the graduates. The Chapel Committee is making arrangements for the Baccalaureate Service, and the graduates are electing the preacher.

Yours sincerely,
Francis C. M. Wei

62. To Mr. Robert A. Smith (June 20, 1941)

Dear Mr. Smith:

... ...

We are still waiting eagerly for news about the Yale appointee for the college. The man we want is for the Department of Economics. We have tried every way possible to get a qualified man meeting all our requirements for that particular subject but, so far, we have had no success. If the Yale-in-China Association and the Episcopal Church in America should be able to send us each a man for Economics, our work in the department would be much strengthened. I was talking with the acting head of the department yesterday, and he agreed with me that one or two missionary appointees to that department would be a great asset and stabilizing influence. Men trained in Economics are in great demand in the country at the present time, and few with the necessary qualification are willing to teach.

... ...

Term examinations, as well as intermediate and degree examinations, will begin next Monday. There are fifteen candidates for the degrees this year, and all except one have been qualified to take their intermediate examinations in the sophomore class.

Thirteen Yali Middle School students from the graduating class this year have taken our May examinations, and two are being recommended for admission without examinations. Practically all the thirteen who have taken examinations have qualified, and there are fourteen in Fuh Hsiang Middle School for girls who have taken our entrance examinations in Yuanling. Early next week the Scholarship Committee will meet and consider the awards of scholarships to those two groups of students. I am recommending a very liberal policy so that we may have as many awards for the students in Yuanling as possible. I have written to Dr. Dwight Rugh, telling him about this and offering even extra financial assistance from my discretionary funds to the Yali and Fuh Hsiang students who have passed our examinations and who are planning to come to Hua Chung for college, but who may not be able to meet all the expenses including travel. I am sending a freshman student, who graduated from Yali last year, immediately after commencement so that he may report in person to the principals in Yuanling, and to his fellow-students, on the conditions in the college, in order to remove certain misunderstandings which have been left over from rumors about the college of two years ago. He will bring back whatever students are coming to the college for the next year. All his expenses will be paid from my discretionary funds, because to my mind his trip will bring a better understanding between Yali and the college.

…… ……

Yours sincerely,
Francis C. M. Wei

63. To Mr. Robert A. Smith (July 9, 1941)

Dear Mr. Smith:

…… ……

We had a very happy commencement season, beginning with Class Day Exercises. On the evening of July 1, the graduates showed a very cheerful and cordial spirit, and everybody enjoyed the exercises. On July 2, we had the Baccalaureate Service in the morning, with Professor John C. F. Lo preaching, and the Rev. Carl Liu conducting the Service as arranged by the Chapel Committee. In the afternoon, we had Commencement Exercises from two to four, followed by tea served by the Social Committee. The weather was fine, and there was a big attendance, including many from the local gentry. The commencement speaker was Judge Shen, president of the Branch High Court of the Province in Tali. The District magistrate was also present, and he spoke. Fifteen students graduated, five receiving their Arts degree in English Literature, four the Science degree, one in Biology and three in Physics, and six the B. Ed. degree. On the evening of July 2, the Alumni Association had a reception to initiate the new members with Dr. John Lo in the chair. Three of our graduates were present from Chennan, and they reported on the alumni activities at the Han Kou

Diocesan Union Middle School there.

The graduation examinations were conducted as usual by the Examination Committee appointed by the Ministry of Education on the recommendation of the president, who always serves according to regulations as chairman ex-officio. Both theses and examinations showed very encouraging results. One thesis was questioned, but was soon fixed up and passed. Some of the graduates did splendid work in Physics and English Literature. One paper in Physics received a mark of "99," and one in English Literature received a perfect mark. Such marks were quite unprecedented. There were two examiners from outside; one was Dr. J. S. Kunkle, principal of the Canton Union Theological College, to examine the students in English Literature, and one was Mr. Wong Mou-tsu, head of the Political Academy in Tali with an M. A. from Teachers College, Columbia, my contemporary in America as a graduate student.

After the examinations the graduating class conducted the Sunday Service on June 30. They arranged everything themselves with one of them preaching, another conducting the service, two to read the lessons, one to say the prayers, and another presiding at the organ.

On July 3, we had a Faculty Tea in honor of those members of our faculty who were leaving the college on furlough or for good. A very cordial spirit was manifested.

All of our students have had appointments of one kind or another; the majority of them are going to teach next year. We are keeping one graduate as English clerk in my office, and another probably as an assistant in the Department of English Literature, which is going to be shorthanded next year with the pre-freshman and probably a larger entering class than we had a year ago. If we should have fifty graduates, all of them would get positions; there are ever so many demands for our graduates all over the country. As a consequence, some of the graduating class have had four or five offers to choose from.

... ...

Yours sincerely,
Francis C. M. Wei

64. To Mr. Joseph I. Parker (July 11, 1941)

Dear Mr. Parker:

…… ……

We have had a very happy commencement season with a small graduating class. The number of that class has been much reduced because it represents the freshmen who entered the college immediately after the outbreak of the hostilities four years ago, and many of them left the college when the Wuhan center was threatened after the fall of Nanking in the winter of 1937. Then we moved twice, and that has had serious effects on the size of our class, but all of them have had jobs offered to them, some having several offers to choose from. All our graduates would have been placed, if we had had a class of fifty or more.

We are expecting a better and stronger faculty next year, and if all goes well, our work will continue to improve in this quiet and peaceful town of Hsichow. There is no telling how large an entering class we are going to have. That depends much upon conditions in the country and in the Far East.

…… ……

Yours sincerely,
Francis C. M. Wei

65. To Mr. Oliver S. Lyford (October 28, 1941)

Dear Mr. Lyford:

…… ……

Our enrollment is 148, including 47 women. The distribution among the four classes is as follows: Seniors 23; Juniors 16; Sophomores 15; Freshmen 94. The freshman class includes 7 pre-freshmen who were with us last spring, and three students who are repeating the freshman year; therefore there are only 84 new students in the class. These statistics do not include six of our graduates, who are taking one or more courses in the college, and sixteen theological students who are not candidates for our degrees. If we should count these 22, which strictly speaking ought to be counted, our enrollment is 170. Even when you take the undergraduates who are candidates for the Hua Chung degrees, our enrollment is 70% more than our enrollment a year ago.

…… ……

As to the reasons why our reserves ought to be kept as much intact as possible, I shall mention only a few. First, we must remember that our college has no endowment fund and the budget for every year has to be met from appropriations from the five cooperating units and from incomes in China, including a government grant and fees taken from the students. Ever since the outbreak of the war, it has become more and more difficult to charge tuition and other fees, and now they have all been remitted. Students are paying only board and lodging, which are not strictly educational expenses. Certainly they yield no income to the college; as a matter of fact board and lodging require from time to time some subsidy in order to help them make ends meet. As our income is only from year to year, it seems to me very essential that we should have some reserve funds to fall back upon in case the world crisis should come to the worst. Some of the missions may not be able to come up to their respective quota, as far as the college budget is concerned. Many of our Chinese faculty and all the missionary members of the staff are investing their lives in the work. It would not be fair for us to have severe cuts all of a sudden, which might lead to the reducing of the staff. This is the first reason why I have been wanting, as an administrative head, to have as much reserve at the disposal of the Board of Founders as possible so as to carry on the college with a reduced budget for at least two years, if every source of income should dry up. If anything, I should like to err on the side of over precaution rather than to make no adequate provision for the future.

Secondly, it has cost us C. $150,000 to move the college to Kweilin and then to Hsichow. Prices have gone up. When the war comes to an end in China and when it is time for us to move back to Wu Chang, I am afraid it will cost us at least three times as much to move back as to move out. When we were moving out, every member of our faculty and staff had still some small savings to fall back upon, and they were able to pay part of their travelling expenses. The three years of refugee have left practically everyone of us bankrupt. I do not see how our faculty and staff members are going to meet any of the expenses in moving back to Wu Chang. They will have to be moved, literally. If all goes well, the Founders and the missions may be able to find us special funds to move the college back, but "a bird in the hand is worth two in the bush," and as long as we have some little reserve we ought to cling to it as tenaciously as possible for this purpose among others of getting the college moved back to its original site. It would be gross injustice to try to shed some of our staff and faculty members if only for the simple reason of our not being able to pay their travelling expenses back. They have been refugeeing with us with the hope that they may go back to Wu Chang with the college.

Thirdly, we have left all our buildings, two-thirds of our science equipment, all the furniture, and approximately 80% of our library books in Wu Chang. Some of the more precious equipment has been stored in the Jardine warehouses in Han Kou. No one can tell what is the fate of our property left in the Wu Han cities. Some of it may be lost, some of it may be stolen, certainly some of it will have deteriorated, and all of it may be destroyed by the enemy before the end of the war. If we should not replace whatever loss of books and equipment there may be, which eventuality would certainly sadden our people, we could have to repair the buildings and replace our furniture, without which the college would not be able to operate. This would cost money. I would like to mention in this connection also the necessity of helping members of the faculty and staff to set up their homes again when they go back. Rehabilitation, therefore, is the third reason why every bit of reserve ought to be handled as carefully as possible.

Fourthly, we do not want to deceive ourselves that after the war every problem in China will be solved. As long as the war lasts, prices will be high and subsidies and salary increases will be necessary, but this cannot stop at the end of the war, if the last war in Europe has taught us anything at all. In this respect, I am a pessimist. I am afraid the hardest time will come for at least three to five years after the cessation of hostilities in China. The founders may be able to continue to raise emergency funds, but people will not believe in any emergency if it is going to last for many long years. We have to make our preparations for that kind of situation. The war in Europe and the war in China will leave every country in the world poorer, and you will certainly agree with me that it will be more difficult to raise funds after the war than to do it at the present time, difficult though it is now. This is another reason why I feel very jealous of our limited reserve and want to do everything to keep it intact.

......

Yours sincerely,
Francis C. M. Wei

66. To Rev. Arthur M. Sherman (November 6, 1941)

Dear Dr. Sherman:

......

I shall try to answer the four questions raised on page one of the report as follow:

1. As to the attitude of Hua Chung College towards the restoration or enlargement of the department of Religion, I have written more than once to you and to the Board through Mr. Smith that it is our desire to restore our former Boone Divinity School by enlarging our present Department of Philosophy, Psychology, and Religion in the college. We feel it rather odd that a Christian college should not have a share in the training of candidates for the ministry in the different churches in China and in the training of lay religious leaders. As soon as possible, probably when we return to Wu Chang after the war, we want to launch our program of theological training. In the meantime, it is necessary for us to find qualified teachers for the fundamental theological subjects. If the Rev. Edmund Hsu should return to us after the war, he would be

able to take care of Systematic Theology. Mr. Constantine can teach Church History if necessary, in addition to his present load in the college in Western History. We wish our Board to find as soon as possible the qualified people to take care of Biblical Literatures both in the New Testament and in the Old Testament.

Again, I wish to say that a man fresh from a theological seminary would not be able to meet our needs. He ought to have at least one or two years postgraduate studies in the Old Testament or the New Testament, whichever he is going to teach. As we are Literature, candidates for our chairs of Old Testament and New Testament ought to have the necessary Biblical language.

2. As to the attitude of the Chinese Government with the regard to theological training in a registered college, I can only say that so far I do not see any possibility yet of the government recognizing theology as one of the department in the college offering a degree. During my last two visits in Chungking, I had the opportunity of opening the subject with the responsible heads of the Ministry of Education, as I have reported in my previous correspondence with the Board of Founders. It is impossible to say whether their attitude will change and how it will change, but we are working out a five-year program leading to the degree of B. A. in the college with all the government requirements for the degree fulfilled, but in addition giving the students the minimum training in the theological disciplines, so as to qualify them certainly for lay work and possibly for the ministry, if they should take an additional year after leaving the college as assistants in designated teaching churches under experienced ministers. The government cannot object to such an arrangement as we are not required to report all the courses that we teach, but only those which are to be counted towards the degree.

3. As to what Hua Chung is now offering in religion in our curriculum and as to what courses are being elected, I have also reported in my letters to Mr. Lyford. We are experimenting on it just this year. For the freshmen and sophomores the Chapel Committee is sponsoring three study groups: one on "what Christianity and the Isms," the second on "Christianity and Conduct," and the third on "Christianity

and the Isms." Between forty and forty-five of the freshmen and sophomores are attending these groups, meeting one hour every Friday in the evening, as extra-curricular studies. For the juniors and seniors I am giving a course on "Christianity in the Light of Modern Knowledge," which is a combination of Philosophy of Religion, Systematic Theology, and Apologetics, with two lectures a week counting for one credit, and twenty-five of the upper class people have elected this course. As we have only thirty-nine students in the two classes, 60% of them are taking this course. If we count seventy students joining the religious study groups or taking my course, and our total enrollment is only one hundred and forty-eight, almost half of the students are enrolled in these classes. Since this is the first year that we are experimenting on this scheme, it is still early for us to report whether it is going to be a success or not, and what measure of success it will be. It is our idea that my course should alternate with another course on the Bible for juniors and seniors. We have not quite decided who is going to teach the Bible course.

4. With regard to the "Institute of Research in Religion in China," sponsored by the Council of Higher Education, I have also written on the subject after my visit to Chungking last spring. We cannot encourage research work by having an institute without personnel, without fund, and without any plan. Therefore, I have resigned from the position of vice-chairman of the Committee. The only way to encourage research in religion in China college is by building up, first of all, the Department of Religion in the Christian college, and that is what we are trying to do, and we hope our Board of Founders will lose no time in canvassing for the necessary qualified men for this department. It is with research in view that we want to emphasize the high qualifications of the prospective teachers of religion. We may hope to inspire our students to do research work in the field only when we have faculty members who take an interest in it and who do it themselves.

…… ……

It is very desirable that we should send some younger people to

America or England for further studies in the field of Theology and Religion. Our problem at present is to get proper candidates for the fellowships which the Associated Boards have in mind. As soon as we are able to find such candidates, we shall take steps to get at least one appointed to faculty and apply for a fellowship in America, through the Associated Boards, for his further training. It is not of much use to send a man over forty, and there is always a risk if we send a man who is too young. We would like to have some one around the age of thirty, with or without previous training in theological institutions in China, but he must show a keen interest in religious work and in religious studies.

…… ……

Yours affectionately,
Francis C. M. Wei

67. To Rev. A. M. Sherman (January 13, 1942)

Dear Dr. Sherman:

…… ……

Shortly before the opening of the autumn term I was asked by the Chapel Committee to offer a special credit course in the college on Christianity for the juniors and seniors. The course has been offered, and a very encouraging number of the upper class people in the college and several members of the junior staff, all Hua Chung graduates, have elected this course, which consists of two lectures a week with a limited amount of reading, as it counts for only one credit a term. It is a combination of Philosophy of Religion, Systematic Theology, and Apologetics. I am sending you an outline of the course, and I hope you will make suggestions as how it could be improved. For my lectures in the first term I have been able to get enough reading material for the students and for my own reference books, but the Canton Union Theological College library, as well as ours, is short of books on Systematic Theology, so I shall find it difficult to get enough reference material for the class next term. This is an experimental course. It is our hope that it may alternate with a course on the Bible for lay people. In this way we give an opportunity for our junior and senior students to have some systematic training on the intellectual side of the Christian religion. We are hoping that Mr. Constantine will teach the Bible course next year, as nobody else here is as well prepared as he is for this subject. It takes a man who knows the subject well in order to make it simple and attractive to lay students. A number of theological students have been taking my course and so I do not want to make it too simple, and yet not too technical.

…… ……

Yours sincerely,
Francis C. M. Wei

68. To Mr. Oliver S. Lyford (January 27, 1942)

Dear Mr. Lyford:

…… ……

The term examinations went off very well, and the winter vacation began on Saturday, January 24. We are having four-week's holiday to accommodate local customs. Many people in distant parts of the country feel a little bit apprehensive about our situation here because they do not know our particular location well. I am getting out a letter to the alumni and friends of the college, explaining to them that the war on the Pacific and even a menace to the Burma Road would not endanger our work.

Prices are so high, particularly of foodstuffs, that many of the students are feeling more and more financial pressure. We shall have to revise our scale of scholarship grants, but as we have exhausted our budget item for scholarships and financial aids, we may have to find some other means of giving extra aids to those students who feel the pressure most. I shall study the problem with John /Coe, and then bring the result to the scholarship Committee for action. This means that in making up our budget for the next academic year we shall have to increase our scholarship item.

Less than one-third of our students, and they are largely Yunnan students, have left to go home for the vacation. The rest are staying around in the college. I have been looking over the record cards. The seniors, juniors, and sophomores have done well. The freshman cards are not ready yet. Quite a few of them have not been able to stand the strain of our rigid college standards. Many of these, again largely Yunnan students, will probably plan to take their degree in five or six years, and some have even expressed their willingness to stay for eight! But a few will drop out. It is not that we are unwilling to accommodate them by lowering our standards and modifying some of our course, but the Yunnan middle schools are really too far below standard to enable their graduates to do university work of any kind of standing. A few of these students, however, have done exceptionally well, and for their sake our experiment in taking in more Yunnan students is worthwhile.

…… ……

Yours sincerely,
Francis C. M. Wei

69. To Mr. Robert A. Smith (February 11, 1942)

Dear Mr. Smith:

…… ……

I have been thinking much about the needs of the students. When you were here in October, the student board in both the men's and women's hostels cost only about N. C. $30 a month. Now it has gone up to over N. C. $90 a month, three times that of October. In October I paid at the Bachelors' Mess N. C. $55 a month for my board, and now it is over N. C. $120. Prices continue to rise. I wrote to some friends in America, asking them to renew their gifts for student help, and I hope some will come. There is a Chinese Christian friend in Chungking who is much interested in our college and has been ever since our Wu Chang days.

…… ……

We are still in our winter vacation. Only about one third of the students, largely Yunnan students, have gone home for the Chinese

New Year. The others are still remaining here. Both faculty and students are well. The weather is splendid. There is hardly any disease.

When the Vice-minister of Education was here, he promised me that all students from Hong Kong and the South Sea Islands would be treated as students from occupied areas in China in the matter of government loans, which would take care of the greater part of their board. Needy students even from Free China may get partial loans from the government upon the recommendation of the committee which has been appointed by the government in the college to review petitions for such loans. The Vice-minister also said that the Ministry may consider our request again to take in another class of students in our School of Education, if we would just modify the title of the department a little bit in order to fit in with the government policy. I do not know yet how this is to work out, but it is my hope that the People's Political Council will meet sometimes in the spring, and then I may go to Chungking and talk matters over with the Minister face-to-face. In spite of the discouraging news from the Malay States and rumors from Burma and other parts of the South Sea Islands, we still feel that Hsichow is the safest spot. As long as we are able to manage our finances, we shall be able to carry on without any interruption.

The second term will begin on February 23. Enrollment may drop down a little bit, but that is always the case in the second term.

…… ……

Yours sincerely,
Francis C. M. Wei

70. To Mr. Oliver S. Lyford (March 11, 1942)

Dear Mr. Lyford:

…… ……

Everybody in the college is safe. The enrollment this term is a pleasant surprise to me. We had 149 students at the beginning of the fall term. 14 dropped out shortly after, and three more did not finish their term exams. Of the 132 who finished the term all but three have returned. So our enrollment is now 133 which is good for the second term at any time.

Yours sincerely,
Francis C. M. Wei

71. To Dr. Joseph I. Parker (May 29, 1942)

Dear Dr. Parker:

…… ……

With our small student body and the favorable conditions in this inland town we have been able to do very satisfactory religious work both among the students and the faculty. I feel that we have been able to do more during the last two or three years than we did in Wu Chang. It is my personal desire to have our Department of Theological Training started in the college as soon as possible, but the question is to get the qualified men for the teaching staff. The Episcopal Church Mission under the leadership of my friend Dr. Addison is very eager that this work should be started for the training of future ministers and lay church workers to meet the New Day that is sure to come to challenge the churches in China after the end of the war. Circumstances are so unfavorable just at this moment that we are able to do very little along this line except that I have been teaching a course myself, which is intended more for the general college student body than those especially interested in the study of Theology.

…… ……

Yours sincerely,
Francis C. M. Wei

72. To Mr. Oliver S. Lyford (June 11, 1942)

…… ……

The seniors who are preparing for their graduation examinations during the last week of this month, beginning with June 22, are now taking their term examinations, so that they may have a period of reading for the graduation examinations in between. The sophomore students are preparing for their intermediate examinations, and so they are having their term examinations next week, in order also to have a period of reading before the intermediate examinations. Commencement will be on July 2. The Chapel Committee is arranging for the Baccalaureate Service, which will probably be either the day before Commencement or on the morning of that day. An Examining Committee for the graduating class has been formed, and the recommendation has gone to the Ministry of Education for appointment. It consists of the President Ex-officio and the heads of all the departments in which there are graduating students, together with Dr. Wai-king Tai of the Canton Union Theological College as an external examiner. Beginning with this week, all of the officers will be busy in getting things ready for commencement and the close of the term.

Everything goes on as usual in the college, and people are more-and-more confident that we are in as safe a place as we could find anywhere else in Free China. We are watching the situation very closely, so as not to run too great a risk as far as the safety of our people is concerned.

…… ……

Yours sincerely,
Francis C. M. Wei

73. To Mr. Oliver S. Lyford (September 29, 1942)

Dear Mr. Lyford:

…… ……

The old students registered yesterday, and the new ones are being registered right now. The number of each group is encouraging. There will probably be seventy-eight old students, five or six transfer to the sophomore class from the universities in Kunming, and over seventy new freshmen, making a total of over one hundred and fifty, probably up to one hundred and sixty. Our highest enrollment since moving to

Hsichow was a year ago when one hundred and forty-eight registered, so we are breaking the record this year in spite of our apprehension for a reduced enrollment of a month ago. In my last letter my estimate was only one hundred and thirty students, but the enrollment has already exceeded that up to the present moment.

On account of transportation and war conditions, the number of women students is not so high as it ought to be, so the Women's Hostel is not fully occupied, but the three men's hostels are already crowded, and we are opening a fourth hostel for men.

......

Yours sincerely,
Francis C. M. Wei

74. To Mr. Oliver S. Lyford (October 8, 1942)

Dear Mr. Lyford:

......

We have been able to fill two vacancies in the faculty for the Department of Chinese Literature. Dr. T. Y. Tsang of the Department of Economics-Commerce may not be able to return on account of his wife's health. It is very embarrassing to have to fill a vacancy after the term has already started, but we have wired to Dr. Tsang in Kunming to get one of his friends to come and teach Sociology and Commercial Law. We are also trying to connect a man in Tali with a Ph. D. from Columbia in Economics twenty years ago to be Dr. Tsang's substitute. If both men should be appointed, we are still within the budget for the Department of Economics-Commerce and that for the Department of History-Sociology. Dr. David Hsiung has returned from Szechwan, but Dr. Wesley Wan has had leave-of-absence until the middle of the month. He left Hsichow about the middle of September to send his wife and child by plane to Wanhsien down the river from Chungking where Mrs. Wan's mother and uncle live.

Dr. W. K. Tai of the Canton Union Theological College, who is staying to take care of the seven joint students and to teach some of the theological courses, is offering for us an outline course on the Bible for juniors, and five or six students have registered for this course from the two upper classes. The Rev. Leonard Constantine, the Rev. Carl Liu, and Professor Anderson are conducting three religious discussion groups for the freshmen and sophomores, and 62 students have registered for the three groups. It is a very encouraging number. Last Saturday evening we had a Rally Meeting in the chapel to present to all the new students the religious purpose of the college and our religious program under the college Chapel Committee and the three denominational fellowships. The meeting was well attended, and the result was this encouraging registration for the religious study groups.

……

Yours sincerely,
Francis C. M. Wei

75. To Mr. Oliver S. Lyford (October 13, 1942)

Dear Mr. Lyford:

……

    I do not blame you for feeling disgusted with Dr. Lin. Dr. Francis Hsu, the sociologist we got a year ago to take Dr. Lin's place, has left us, as I have already reported in my previous correspondence with you. Now we are trying to get a man as late as this from Kunming to take his place. He is Dr. Tao, a returned student from France with a doctor's degree from a French university. Dr. T. Y. Tsang has written that he is not able to return because his wife's health needs medical attention in Kunming; this may be only an excuse, but we have to accept it because there is no way out. It is very annoying that some people do not have any sense of obligation, and notify us of their inability to return to the college even after the opening of the term. We are negotiating with a man in Tali, a returned student from America of twenty-year's standing, to carry on Dr. Tsang's course in Economics, and there is every possibility that he may come. Two teachers of Chinese Literature have just arrived, and so we should be able to set up a well-balanced faculty again for the year.

    As to registration, we have at present only 150, of whom 38 are women, but 10 are on the Dean's "leave-of-absence" list, and they may be here in a day or so. Transportation is difficult, but that does not account for every case of late registration. Many of the Yunnan students have not gotten into the habit yet of being prompt. Three students from Hunan are on their way, but they may be delayed at Kweiyang.

……

Yours sincerely,
Francis C. M. Wei

76. To Mr. Oliver S. Lyford (November 5, 1942)

Dear Mr. Lyford:

……

It is very difficult to estimate what our requirement will be half a year from now, as prices may jump again and as the general situation also may change, making a great deal of difficult in drawing budget. Further, I have not been able to discuss with the Executive Committee Pro-tem as to how our budget, which begins every year from August 1st, will fit in with the new fiscal year of the Associated Board beginning with March 1st. This will require some readjustment.

After some preliminary talk with Mr. Coe we feel that the only way to present our requests for the next year to the Associated Boards will be by taking the percentage of increase in the budget of each year over that of the previous year, and then make our estimates accordingly for the year beginning from March 1943. There is no other way to prepare the budget. As soon as everything is ready, we shall communicate with Mr. Edwards in Chungking, with the original sent to the Associated Boards in New York and a copy to you.

There has been no change in our enrollment. It is 152, because after October 16 we refused to register new student who came late. So the figure has not come up to 160, as I radioed to you before registration was completed. There are at present 114 men and 38 women students.

……

Yours sincerely,
Francis C. M. Wei

77. To Dr. Edwin C. Lobenstine (November 10, 1942)

My dear Dr. Lobenstine:

……

You must have been heard that Mr. and Mrs. Miller are on their way to America, owing to Mrs. Miller's approaching blindness caused by cataracts in her eyes. They were all advised by eye specialists in Kunming during the summer to leave China so Mrs. Miller might have the attention of ophthalmologists in America. This came to them, as well as to us, as a severe blow. Their departure has weakened our Department of English Literature. Dr. John C. F. Lo, the new dean of the Faculty of Arts, has just talked to me about the necessity of getting some experienced English-speaking teachers of English to join our faculty. I am very doubtful whether it is possible for America or Great Britain to send any missionary teachers under the circumstances. I hope it will be possible for the Yale Association to find some well-qualified teachers of English and get them interested in joining our faculty here. You may know that the American Church Mission would be willing to appoint missionaries to teach in our college, even though they may not be members of Episcopal Church. You have a wide circle of friends, and you visit New Haven very often. You will be doing us a favor if you could put Dr. Addison in touch with prospective candidates for teaching positions here. I know for the present the Yale Association would not consider the appointment of an American to the Hua Chung faculty.

……

One of our difficulties is, of course, getting reading material for the different departments so as to enable them to keep up with the world. You wrote in your letter of November 8, 1941 about the possibility of a microfilm reading desk, but I do not suppose we shall be able to get one even though it may be possible to send some to this country. The colleges in Szechwan and the government institutions will probably grab them first. I have heard from reliable sources that the American government has sent some clothing material, such as serge and khaki cloth, for faculty and students in educational institutions in Free China and that some of the Christian colleges in Chengtu have received their share, but somehow we know nothing about it. If convenient, I hope you will enquire into the matter and try to get Hua Chung into the receiving list for whatever gifts may come to educational institutions in Free China. It is not so much to have the gifts as to be remembered by people while we are in this isolated place.

... ...

Yours sincerely,
Francis C. M. Wei

78. To Mr. Oliver S. Lyford (December 8, 1942)

Dear Mr. Lyford:

... ...

  A week ago on Saturday we had a Faculty Tea, and I took the opportunity of outlining to the whole faculty and staff assembled there my own dreams about the future development of the college after the war, including the project of getting some of the younger members of the faculty to America for postgraduate studies. This seems to have caught the fancy of the faculty, and they asked me to go ahead at once in planning for it.

  I realize how difficult it is at the present time to make any such plan for sending some of the younger members of the faculty, particularly our own alumni who have worked in the college very faithfully and loyally during the last five years of war, but it is a desirable thing. The Associated Boards wrote me before the war broke out on the Pacific for possible faculty members from the college to go for further studies in America. I have, however, heard from the Associated Boards that this plan will have to be held up for the balance of the war. But if we are going to make any plans at all along this line, we must not wait until the war comes to a close. I am thinking, therefore, of two possibilities; one is to lay aside, say, U. S. $500 a year to cover the travel of younger members going to America for further studies, and the other is to write to some of the universities such as Yale, Harvard, Columbia, Chicago, and Michigan to see whether they would be interested in helping us in this scheme by being willing to consider granting us a fellowship for our graduates for further study as soon as travel on the Pacific approaches normal. All this may be just "Castles in the Air" but when the future is so uncertain, something that holds out some hope to the younger members of the faculty may be a stabilizing factor.

The Episcopal Church Fellowship in the college asked me to talk to them last Sunday on my proposed plans for the development of Theological Training in the college. I talked to them, and they were all very much interested in the ideas for the development of such a department in the college. Some of the students came to me afterwards to ask about possibilities of their studying Theology. I was very much pleased with this, for the first thing is to get some of the young people interested in the ministry and in work directly for the development of the churches in China, in order to meet the great need that is bound to confront us after the war. Somehow, my thoughts have been turning in this direction during the last three or four years, and I hope it may be possible for some of my dreams to materialize. Of the things for which I would like to spend the rest of my life this would be one of the most important, and my limited years may permit me possibly to do one thing only.

…… ……

Yours sincerely,
Francis C. M. Wei

79. To Mr. Oliver S. Lyford (January 26, 1943)

Dear Mr. Lyford:

…… ……

In the meantime I may say that we feel that the college ought to be built up on a new basis for Christian higher education in the whole Central China region, whatever the policy of the churches may be for the development of Christian higher education after the war our college ought to be one of the centers. Even according to the original recommendations of the Burton Commission in 1922, Central China is to be one of the five, if not six centers. Everything points to the fact that Christian higher education in China after the war ought to be reconsidered for the country as a whole. To divide the country into five regions, each to have a Christian college, seems to be the most sensible thing and is the only thing the churches could afford.

But the thinking in the Executive Committee meeting, which has been along the same lines as my own thinking, is that if we are going to make a contribution worthy of the Christian churches in China, our higher education work must be improved and strengthened. The competition of the national universities, as experience during the war has taught us, will be entirely too keen for us unless we are going to put our colleges on a sounder basis. There is no doubt that Wuhan will be the center of the country and therefore ought to be the site of a strong Christian college. Our offering ought to be on a winder basis than it has been for the last thirteen years. That means the widening of our scope and the adding of the necessary departments as well as the strengthening of the present ones so as to attract the students of the highest caliber and to hold the best scholars for our faculty. We are not thinking of any additional professional schools or even of graduate work at the present time, but we are thinking only of the improvement of some of our departments and the expansion of others so as to do justice to the whole educational situation in China.

The only new project that we have in mind is that of Theological Training. It seems odd that a Christian college should not make its contribution directly to the church by training church ministers and other church workers. As I have written to you before, the question has been on my mind for some years, ever since we came to Hsichow. It is very clear that there is in the country a dearth of well-trained ministers and lay workers to meet the New Day after the war. It may be too much for me to say, but it is my conviction that as far as the policy of the churches and missions goes, we have been "putting the cart before the horse." We seem to have been thinking that self-support of churches is the most important thing. As long as the church is not well developed, we cannot afford to pay for the highly-trained ministers and workers. Highly-trained people have their needs to meet, and therefore low salaries cannot keep them. We may talk about self-sacrifice, but one has to educate one's children and keep a family according to one's social standing. Therefore, it may be time for us to work the other way. First get the best workers, pay them the necessary salary, and let them develop the churches. In the course of time the churches will be able to support themselves. Hence if we should put our hand to Theological Training at all, we must aim at the best standards.

…… ……

Term examinations will be finished by Thursday, and then winter vacation will begin. Miss Zenk, of the Reformed Church in the Department of Music under the School of Education, will be married to Mr. Walter Allen, of the American Church Mission in the Department of English Literature under the School of Arts, on February 1st. The ladies are busy getting ready for the wedding. I presume that after her marriage Miss Zenk will cease to be a member of the China Mission of the Reformed Church in the United States. I have written to Dr. Casselman, raising the question as to the possibility of another Reformed Church Mission representative on the faculty after Miss Zenk's status has been changed.

…… ……

We are afraid that most of our library books left in Wu Chang will be lost to us, and it will be a very serious proposition to rebuild our library again. It seems wise for the college to renew subscriptions for all the periodicals for the different departments and to have the magazines sent to one of our agents, preferably one of the mission offices in America, to be kept there until the end of the war before they are sent out to China. Similarly we are thinking of some plan of appealing to different university presses and publishing companies to get gifts of books for our library after the war, having them received by our Board of Founders in American and kept in the United States. I am asking the different departments to prepare lists as to give some indication as to what kind of books we used for our work here. It is a great pity that in moving, the college librarian failed to move out any of our reference books, of which we had a very good collection in Wu Chang. This has been a very serious handicap to us for the last four years and a half, and it will remain so until we have the reference collection rebuilt.

... ...

Yours sincerely,
Francis C. M. Wei

80. To Rev. A. M. Sherman (January 26, 1943)

Dear Dr. Sherman:

... ...

In thinking about this aspect of our work, the main difficulty is how to get the qualified teachers. As I said in my letter to Mr. Lyford, we must have Biblical scholars from the United States and Great Britain to teach the Old Testament and New Testament. I hope that Edmund H. will be able to return to us after the war and teach Systematic Theology and Christian Ethics. We must get somebody for Church History, somebody who has really the best training in the subject because it is not easy to teach Church History in China, which ought to be taught somewhat differently from the traditional method in the West. I am thinking of the approach that Professor Latourette adopts in his book, "Expansion of Christianity" in seven volumes. I have read all except the last volume, which I have not been able to get. When I was in New Heaven in 1934—1935, I discussed the matter several times with him, and it was at that time that I found that he was preparing a book very similar to the lines which I would like to see followed in the teaching of Church History in China. For Pastoral Care and Religious Education we need a Chinese teacher, and we are on the look-out all the time for such people.

I am afraid that the scheme for Theological Training that I have in mind will appear to some of the cooperating missions as too expensive, but personally I think that work along that line cannot be too expensive, because it is certainly an important thing that a Christian college like Hua Chung ought to undertake. If our own mission is willing to give a start to it and maintain it for some years, I am sure that the other missions will join in later. We may possibly get some individuals interested who will help us to raise an endowment fund. As I explained to some of the people interested in the project here in the college, I am not thinking of Union Theological Training. I would propose to follow the plan such as is found in Oxford and Cambridge. I know the situation in Oxford myself. A denominational church may maintain a group of theological scholars for the teaching of theological subjects, and other groups may do the same thing, and then all will cooperate in getting a well-rounded program. My experience in America leads me to the conclusion that Union Theological Training loses its "bite" somehow. There does not seem to be the warmth that we must have for giving a big push to the churches after the war, but a single mission may find it too much to carry on the work and develop it as it ought to be developed. So we must have the other churches working in the college cooperate. In this way we have all the subjects taken care of, but each church may have certain courses taught by teachers of its own tradition, so that there will be cooperation and yet not uniformity. I am sure this will meet with your approval.

....

Yours affectionately,
Francis, C. M. Wei

81. To Mr. Oliver S. Lyford (March 4, 1943)

Dear Mr. Lyford:

....

The second term of the year began on February 25 with registration, and lectures started on March 1st. So far according to the report of the Registrar's Office, 124 students are in the college, but six more are on leave-of-absence to come later, so the enrollment for the term may be reckoned at 130, which is 22 fewer than that of the fall term. This is quite normal. We always reckon a drop of 15% in the enrollment for the second term of every year. The drop is largely from the freshman class people who have found it difficult to keep up with the work here. At the end of the term we sent away two students because of lack of credentials for proper admission into the college, and three more for poor work. The others dropped out on their own accord.

… …

Yours sincerely,
Francis, C. M. Wei

82. To Mr. Oliver S. Lyford (May 1, 1943)

Excerpt from Dr. Wei's letter to Mr. Lyford received on May 1st

… …

I have not reported to you the enrollment for the present term, but shall do it now.

FALL TERM 1943—1944

	Men	Women	Total		
Seniors	7	6	13	Christian students	42
Juniors	10	9	19	Non-Christian	108
Sophomores	42	6	48	Total	150
Freshmen	61	9	70		
	—	—	—		
	120	30	150		
Seniors	5	6	11	Christian students	36
Juniors	8	9	17	Non-Christian	98
Sophomores	37	6	43	Total	134
Freshmen	55	6	61		
Special	—	2	2		
	—	—	—		
	105	29	134		

… …

Very soon we shall have to think about reappointment for the next year. We shall try to wait until at least the first part of May before we make these reappointments, for by that time we may have more definite news from you with regard to our proposed budget for the next year. In the meantime we have been working hard to secure properly-qualified candidates to fill some of the serious vacancies in the college faculty. We have no one to teach Chemistry at the present time. Biology is short-handed with only Sidney Hsiao carrying on. Economics is very weak. Sociology has been suspended. History has to be strengthened, and so also English.

…… ……

Yours sincerely,
Francis, C. M. Wei

83. To Dr. Frank Price (June 17, 1943)

Dear Dr. Price:

…… ……

We submit that there are three distinct classes of workers trained in Theology that are and will be needed in the churches in China.

The A class will be people with the highest training possible at present in this country. They ought to have three years of specialized training above the university bachelor's degree, which ought to be at the end of a course of prescribed essentially degree, pre-theological covering four years. They are to teach Theology, do research and writing on Theology, and lead in religious thinking among the Chinese.

The B class would be people who have had the combined Arts and Theology course of five years after Matriculation, with a year of internship during the sixth year. We reckon that during the year of internship the student ought to be able to earn his own living at least. This training would supply ministers for the leading churches, students pastors, religious directors in colleges and middle schools, Sunday school superintendents for parishes or districts, translators, writers, and teachers of theological training institutes of the C class.

The C class training should be two years devoted mainly to the study of the Bible and Practical Theology after graduation from the senior middle school or equivalent. Hua Chung plans to undertake the training of students of Class A and Class B only.

For this work six full-time teachers of theological subjects are necessary at the initial stage of our theological project. The other faculties in the college will, of course, be able to supply the non-theological courses. Later when translation and editing work have developed, when refresher courses have become a regular feature and are given every year, and when there is a greater demand by church workers and ministers in service for directed systematic reading by correspondence—all these are feature of our theological work—there must be two full-time teachers for each of the five main theological disciplines, viz. , Old Testament, New Testament, Church History, Systematic Theology and Christian Ethics. Church Policy, Parish Administration, and Homiletics, will be taught by experienced ministers and preachers of the participating churches from outside the college in our neighborhood. Well-organized and well-staffed churches, schools with good religious programs, Christian Literatures Societies, and centers of other types of Christian work will be asked to take our students as internes.

…… ……

It is our desire that from the very beginning our Theological Training work should not be entirely dominated by one church cooperating in our college. To assure a proper balance between the Episcopal Church and the Free Churches in this work, we desire that there may a definite income from non-episcopal sources, so that the college will be able to appoint from the very beginning non-episcopal teachers of Theology. In due course of time the Free Churches will send their representatives for this work. But we must have the liberty of appointing college teachers from funds outside of our cooperating missions, so that we may not have to depend entirely upon the missionaries or other teachers nominated by the mission boards. At the initial stage of our work we wish to have enough money to appoint at least two such teachers who would be Chinese. According to the plan that we are preparing for our post-war development, we want to allow for the salary of each college teacher of the senior rank the minimum of U. S. $1,200, on the assumption that shortly after the war exchange, as well as the price level, will approach the pre-war rate. For two such teachers we must have, therefore, at least U. S. $2,400 and U. S. $600 for house rent and medical care, totaling U. S. $3,000 per annum.

……

Yours sincerely,
Francis, C. M. Wei

84. To Mr. Oliver S. Lyford (August 10, 1943)

Dear Mr. Lyford:

……

We have also considered the advisability of keeping our teaching and administrative staff to the minimum. Our administrative staff has always been very small. It cannot be further reduced. As a matter of fact, for working efficiency the dean's office ought to have at least a Chinese clerk in order to deal with government matters. For the last two years we tried, much to our handicap, to cut the staffs of all the departments to "the very bone" and found that in several cases it did not work. There is a fallacy in considering the faculty-student ratio which is usually accepted as the criterion in American college, because a college in America is free in its offering of course, but we are under government regulations in China. Regardless of the number of students majoring in a department the same number of courses has to be offered in order to qualify the students for the degree, and the government is becoming more and more strict in this respect. So since we moved to Hsichow we have been carrying on with a smaller enrollment but with a large number of courses offered and actually taught. You will get the details from the report of the Dean of the General Faculty, which is accompanying my

Annual Report to be sent in a few days.

······

Yours sincerely,
Francis, C. M. Wei

85. To Mr. Oliver S. Lyford (August 24, 1943)

Dear Mr. Lyford:

······

As far as our finance for the next year go, I feel much more optimistic at present for the immediate next year, but I have many misgivings concerning the year after next. So whatever we do to increase subsidies and other expense, we always bear this in mind. I am in constant consultation with Mr. Coe, treasurer, and with Mr. Anderson, secretary of the Executive Committee Pro-tem, and I call as many meetings of the Executive Committee Pro-tem as necessary in order to plan as wisely as possible.

So far I have no encouraging news about any new teachers for the Department of Economics, which has to be strengthened in order to carry the program for the next year, neither has there been any news of any teachers whatever for the Department of Chemistry for the next semester, although there may be some chance of getting one or two for the second semester of the year. There is no possibility either of securing a well-qualified Physical Director.

······

The college will re-open on September 15. It is earlier this year because of government regulations, but registration will begin only on September 20, and lecture will commence on September 24. The fall term will be a short term this year because of the date of China New Year, but the second term will be longer. Over 300 candidates have participated in our entrance examinations in Kunming, but I have as yet no advice from Kunming how many of them have been qualified nor how many of those qualified are likely to come to us next month. The number of candidates in Hsichow was small, only eight of them having passed the examinations, some with conditions. Due to conditions in other parts of the country and to the difficulty of travel, we have not given entrance examinations in other centers, but following the new government regulations we have sent around the information that students who graduated with high grades from middle schools may come to the college and will be classified according to their academic achievement. It is, therefore, quite impossible for us to forecast how large a freshman class we are going to have until after registration. I believe it will be around seventy-five. If so, we ought to have an enrollment of about 150, the same as a year ago.

....

Yours sincerely,
Francis, C. M. Wei

86. To Mr. Oliver S. Lyford (September 7, 1943)

Dear Mr. Lyford:

....

August 13 was the anniversary of the breaking out of the hostilities between the Japanese and our troops in Shanghai six years ago. The students staying behind in the college during the summer put on a play in the local town; the gross proceeds amounted to more than N. C. $20,000. After defraying expenses, largely for kerosine for the lighting the students were able to send to the government so their contribution towards the war in the country the sum of N. C. $13,511 as net proceeds. We are very proud of the students' efforts in doing this although the money realized is very insignificant. We are always glad that the students keep in mind the great effort being put out by the government to prosecute the war.

....

Yours sincerely,
Francis, C. M. Wei

87. To Mr. Oliver S. Lyford (October 5, 1943)

Dear Mr. Lyford:

……

The new term started on September 15 in conformity with the government regulations to open earlier, but registration of students did not start until Monday, September 20, to give time for the faculty and Senate to have their meeting and for the different departments to get things ready.

Our enrollment this year is only 145, seven fewer than that of a year ago, but actually fifteen fewer than I had expected. My estimate before the term began was 85 old students and 75 new ones, making a total of 160; but the number of old students is 100, more than I expected, and there are far fewer new students than I would like to have. I cannot put my finger on the real cause of the fewer new students. The difficulty of transportation is only a partial cause. The colleges in Kunming also have fewer new students as far as I can learn, but again that does not account for our small freshman class. However, it is heartening to have more old students coming back. It shows the persistence of the Yunnan students in sticking to our college and speaks well for our growing reputation in this province.

Naturally we have fewer Christian students. No students have come from our affiliated middle schools. What I know is entirely due to the difficulty of travel on the road, as well as to the expense. The growing number of non-Christian students, however, is a challenge to our Christian work. We are doing everything possible to reach them with our Christian message. The chapel was practically filled when the Chapel Committee had a rallying meeting of the new students on Friday evening, September 24, the day on which classes began. Every Friday evening we are having a religious talk for half an hour at seven o'clock, and then the students are divided up into four small groups to discuss the topic with a faculty leader. I gave the first talk last Friday on the subject of "Christianity and the Chinese Religions" and there was a good turn-out practically filling the whole chapel. Many students and faculty members attended as well. This series of meeting will last for eight weeks so as to give an introduction of Christianity for the new students. Next Friday Dr. Taai, in charge of our Department of Religious Studies in the college, is going to talk on "The place of the Bible in Christianity."

Our faculties, particularly that of Science, are much depleted. The Faculty of Education remains intact, but under the Faculty of Arts the Department of Economics-Commerce has not been able to fill any of its vacancies. Consequently, I have been drafted by the dean of the Faculty of Arts to teach a course on "The History of Economic Thought" because the three junior members, who are all part-time as they have administrative duties, are not prepared to give that senior course. This makes my teaching load eleven lectures a week, which however I take as my recreation from the administrative duties. The Chinese Department is well staffed. We have suspended sociology.

…… ……

Yours sincerely,
Francis, C. M. Wei

88. To Mr. Oliver S. Lyford (November 9, 1943)

Dear Mr. Lyford:

…… ……

On November 1 we had our Annual Founders Day and Matriculation Exercises. The ceremony was held at ten o'clock in the morning. Professor Sidney H. Hsiao was the speaker, and he gave a splendid address for the occasion. Fifty new students were matriculated. In the afternoon the students had volleyball games as one of the festivities of the day, and then in the evening the students put on a Stunts Night with light refreshments at the end for all the faculty and staff members and student body, the money being raised by the students themselves. The whole day showed a good spirit, which was very gratifying to me. It seems that we have a very congenial fellowship among the students and faculty this year in spite of our short handedness as far as the faculty goes, we remembered of course, on that day all the Founders of the college, the cooperating missions, and all friends and past faculty members who have put so much into the building up of the institution. It is now nineteen years since Hua Chung was first organized with only three units at that time, Boone College, Wesley College, and Griffith John College. It was in the fall of 1929 that Yale-in-China and Huping College of the Reformed Church in the United States joined in to make five units altogether. Next year we ought to be celebrating the Twentieth Anniversary of the college, and I am afraid we shall have to have the celebration here in Hsichow still. Something special ought to be done in order to make this Twentieth Anniversary, and I shall bring the matter up with the Executive Committee Pro-tem of the Board of Directors in the college, as well as with the senate, as how to plan for this Twentieth Anniversary.

Just the day before our celebration of the Founders Day, Professor Fan of Peking University, now a part of the Southwestern National Associated University, arrived here to recruit students for training for two months in Kunming before going to the Chinese Army and the Armies of our Allies in China as interpreters. On Tuesday Mr. Fan addressed the students, and I was very pleasantly surprised to find that the response was so good. Thirteen students took the examinations, and ten were qualified. Even the three students, all Yunnan students of the first two years in the college, who were rejected by Mr. Fan were, according to him, more proficient in their English than many of the people who were already acting as interpreters. However, as Hua Chung was producing more than its quote, Mr. Fan qualified only ten. Four of the ten went with Mr. Fan on Thursday to Kunming for the training class, one being a senior of the Department of Economics-Commerce, two juniors of the Department of English Literature, and one freshman also of the Department of English Literature. Six have been advised by Mr. Fan to complete the year before joining the service. The faculty had a farewell party for the departing students on Wednesday afternoon, and it was a very touching occasion. As one of the professors who spoke at the meeting pointed out, Hua Chung was a college with genuine family spirit, and we are sending our students forth as our own children for war service. When the students were leaving by horse cart on Thursday morning, a large number of faculty members and of the students turned up at eight o'clock to see them off. Two of the students going away are Christians, and the other two have had the intention of being baptized in the college before Christmas. The Rev. Carl Liu is writing to the Anglican clergyman in Kunming, also one of our graduates in charge of the church there, to prepare them for baptism before Christmas. We are so glad that we are sending all Christian students to this work. It is not going to be an easy life for them because they will meet with many temptations, and by keeping in touch with them we shall be able to help them to live up to our expectations. They realize that we have already had a number of our graduates and undergraduates in the interpreter's work and they have to live up to the good reputation already established by Hua Chung students.

... ...

Yours sincerely,
Francis, C. M. Wei

89. Report of Various Conversations at Hua Chung (Late November 1943)

(The ideas in this report come from a number of people at Hua Chung with whom Dr. Fenn talked in late November 1943)

PRESIDENT WEI:

There need be only five Christian universities, or six if there are to be two in the East China field.

There is need for financial pressure, with a China office of the Associated Boards.

Policy comes before programs. There is need for real thinking in regard to basic principles.

There is no need for an engineering college, for there is no such thing as Christian engineering. One college of agriculture (at Nanking) will be enough. Commerce is important, for it deals with men.

Medicine is also essential, but it should be of better quality.

Cheeloo might well become part of Yenching; perhaps the Medical and Rural Reconstruction Colleges.

With improvement in transportation, there will be no need for a Christian college in Fukien after war.

There is no need for a woman's college. Ginling should join Nanking in the Oxford fashion.

Lingnan seems likely to become national.

There are not enough good men in all institutions to staff one first-class Christian university.

…… ……

90. Hua Chung College Plan for Development After the War Submitted by President Francis C. M. Wei (February 15, 1944)

Extracts from a letter from Dr. Wei dated February 15, 1944

During the winter vacation we had two long session of the joint meeting of the Executive Committee pro-tem and of the college Senate, mainly to consider the plan for the development of the college after the war, to which I have already made many references in my previous letters.

Now the plan is ready, and I am enclosing it to be submitted to the Board of Founders, known as Trustees of Hua Chung College, acting at present concurrently as the Board of Directors, and through them to the cooperating missions to whom I hope you will send copies. (See Exhibit B)

We started to consider the plan more than a year ago, and off and on we have discussed it. Various members of the Executive Committee made suggestions for changes in the first draft, which I submitted months ago. During this very winter vacation I had the whole thing re-written, taking into consideration all the points made by the members of the Executive Committee Pro-tem and the Senate in joint meetings, considered every point carefully with copies of the plan in their hands between the meetings. Many paragraphs have been rewritten and the joint meetings authorized the President and the Secretary of the Executive Committee Pro-tem and the Secretary of the Senate of the college to send the plan on behalf of the two bodies for submission to the Board of Founders, and through them to the cooperating missions.

You will see that what we are submitting is a very modest plan, although it calls for additional support from the Board of Founders and the cooperating missions. It is a long-term plan, looking forward to ten years after the war for the complete development of the college according to this proposed plan. The thinking behind the plan includes all our experiences since the inception of the college in 1924. What we are trying to present to the Founders and the Directors is a general picture, setting forth what our aspirations and the Director are and what ways and means we can think of to realize them. It is almost impossible and unworthy of the name of the Christian churches in China and aboard to have a college with too limited a scope and too small a student body. We must envisage a China after the war with a government putting its resources on the improvement of education. It is our conviction, however, that with this new emphasis on education in the country, the Christian forces must have their share, so that China may get on the right track in her new development. In this effort the Central China region must be properly taken care of with a stronger Christian college operating in it not only to supply churches and the Christian movement as a whole with the properly qualified leaders, but also to try to make a real impact upon the nation in its New Day.

I am sure the Board of Founders and the missions will not spend too much time on the details of the plan, which can only be worked out according to the circumstances after the war. What we would like them to do is to see the picture as a whole and approximately what amount of support we must have from abroad in order to carry on our work with confidence.

We have not counted too much on resources in China, because we have no idea what kind of resources there will be. It would be much better for us to plan more modestly than to raise undue expectations.

In carrying out the plan money alone is not the only essential. We must have the men. In January I took the liberty of sending you a copy of my article written for publication in Szechwan on "The Future of Christian Education in China" in which I tried to express some of my ideas from my long experience in Christian education. (See Exhibit A) It would be entirely out of place for me to put in many of those ideas in this plan, but the plan ought to be judged in the light of that article, which is for general consumption.

The joint meeting of the Executive Committee Pro-tem and the Senate of the college has asked me to write to you and ask you to submit the plan as soon as possible. If it should be approved at least in principle, will you please send me a cable to that effect? There are certain matters in the plan which we would like to announce to the faculty before we make the reappointments in May, such as fellowships for the younger members of the faculty and the reintroducing of sabbatical leaves for the professors and assistant professors after the war. If you could send me a cable that the official plan has been approved, the Executive Committee Pro-tem may instruct me to announce the whole thing to our faculty and students at least. That certainly would help the morale of the college. As to the details, they may be thrashed out between the Board and the college administration. Let me repeat again, it is not the details that we are concerned with at present, for after all they can only be worked out after the war.

91. To Mr. Oliver S. Lyford (February 22, 1944)

Dear Mr. Lyford:

…… ……

We have not completed our registration yet from the term because the rule of the college allows late registration as far as one week from the first day of lecture, which will be the coming Thursday. So far we have 128 students with a few still on leave, whom we expect will be back before very long. If the enrollment should get up to 130, it could be according to our expectation because every second term has an enrollment about 15% down from the first term, when we had 148.

... ...

Yours sincerely,
Francis C. M. Wei

92. To Professor Serge Elisseeff (March 9, 1944)

Dear Professor Elisseeff:

... ...

We have also considered whether it would be possible to cut our staff. Two assistant professors for Chinese History are really the minimum, because the field is so large and there are so many courses which we have to offer according to government regulations. Of the six members in the Department of Chinese Literature, which includes the branches as required for the department by the government curriculum, three of them are devoting one-half of the time to research work. Research is, of course, of only secondary importance as far as our college is concerned, because during wartime we want to maintain first of all the efficiency of our teaching, but a limited amount of research is necessary to keep the intellectual interest alive and to hold before the students some ideals of Chinese scholarship. Our normal teaching load for each member of the faculty is ten credit hours a week. Those who are doing research work have to teach six hours. When three are teaching ten hours, and three others average six hours, the total number of teaching hours for the Department of Chinese Literature is only forty-eight, which is the minimum total to keep the department going as required by the government curriculum. This is how the budget has been formulated. If necessary, we may increase the teaching load of all the members of the staff, but that would mean decreasing the efficiency. Our nearest center of higher education is Kunming, and in the government colleges there people are teaching only four to six hours as full-time; therefore we do not dare to increase our load too much on that account, although some members of our faculty are already carrying much heavier loads than that. But in formulating a budget we have to take the normal as the basis.

······

Yours sincerely,
Francis C. M. Wei

93. To Miss Rachel Dowd (March 14, 1944)

Dear Miss Dowd:

······

You will notice in our proposed budget that the total is N. C. $3,063,860 without any provision for further increase of subsides of rising prices for the non-salary items during the next academic year. These increases are sure to come. The items that we expect to pay from Yale-in-China funds will be approximately U. S. $6,100 at the present rate of exchange of approximately forty to one. If the Yale-in-China Association should continue to give us for the next year only U. S. $5,000, there would be a deficit of U. S. $1,100, which has to be taken from the Yale-in-China Association Reserve in the college, and that is becoming smaller every year. I have not been able to get properly posted whether the Yale-in-China receipts are keeping up with its expenditures, but if there should be any hope of increase, or if there should be any other possibility, I would like the Board to consider whether it is possible for the subvention for Hua Chung to be increased before the end of the war. There are surely to be some hard years ahead of us, and even after the war we expect to have two or three years of hard times, which we(must) ways and means to tide over in order to keep the college alive. Mr. Lyford is a Yale man, and he is the treasurer of our Board of Founders. No one in America I suppose knows about the Hua Chung finances better than he does, and I hope you will get all the information from him so as to present the case of Hua Chung to the Yale-in-China Board when it meets. Yale-in-China used to be one of our stronger units, but the war has cut its subvention to the college. We only hope that the time will soon come when it will show its full strength again. All these years have been struggling along with the hope that a better day will return soon.

…… ……

Yours sincerely,
Francis C. M. Wei

94. To Dr. William Fenn (March 14, 1944)

Dear Dr. Fenn:

…… ……

You will see that such a budget will be entirely inadequate if it should be approved by our board. Our books show that for 1940—1941 the total expenditure was approximately N. C. $280,000; for 1941—1942 N. C. $470,000; for 1943—1944 N. C. $1,030,000; and our present estimated total for 1943—1944 is approximately N. C. $2,000,000. Comparing these figures and the rate at which we have been forced to increase our subsidies during the present academic year since September 1943, we will probably need in addition N. C. $1,000,000 in order to carry through the next academic year 1944—1945. Therefore, our total needs for the next academic year would be approximately N. C. $4,000,000. Our present anticipated income, however, from all the sources is U. S. $58,450 and N. C. $286,000. If the special government rate should remain are approximately forty, our total expected income would be only N. C. $2,624,000, leaving still N. C. $339,860 to be found. If we should add the N. C. $1,000,000 for further increases of subsidy and rising prices, we could have to find N. C. $1,339,860, about U. S. $33,500 at the approximate rate of forty. But in spite of your advice we still entertain the hope that the government exchange rate may be increased during the next academic year of before, and so we have cabled to our Board in New York, saying that in order to meet our needs during the next year we ought to have at least U. S. $20,000 over and above our anticipated income from all sources.

…… ……

Yours sincerely,
Francis C. M. Wei

95. To Mrs. Ida Williams (April 4, 1944)

Dear Mrs. Williams:

... ...

Before the war we had a very good library for the college in Wu Chang, which had been built up by the continued efforts of Miss Mary Elizabeth Wood for many years, but when the war came, after staying a whole year in Wu Chang, in the summer of 1938 we moved into the interior by government order and with the permission of the Board of Directors. We thought that at that time the war would not last very long, and so only a very small portion of our library books was moved out. When the war started on the Pacific after Pearl Harbor all our college buildings were occupied by the Japanese, and the latest news is that everything has been looted, so that our splendid library will be entirely gone when we get back after the war is over. It is necessary, therefore, for us to build up a library fund in order to replace the books lost. It is very good of you to remember our need and to send to our library fund U.S. $10.00, which will be used with the greatest care. Please make our needs known to all friends interested in our work, which is an expression of good will of Christian friends in America and Great Britain towards the Church in China and the Chinese.

... ...

Yours sincerely,
Francis C. M. Wei

96. To Mr. Oliver S. Lyford (April 25, 1944)

Dear Mr. Lyford:

... ...

In case the exchange should be very favorable, we shall have to do something drastic in order to increase the income of our faculty and staff members here. A letter has just come from Kunming for Dr. Bien, saying that the faculty and staff members in the National University in Kunming have just got their salaries and subsidies almost doubled. A professor is now getting in Kunming N. C. $8,500 to $9,000 a month. Prices there are higher than ours, but before long we shall catch up. Further, we have to offer salaries and subsidies comparable to Kunming's before we can hope at all to get any qualified men to fill some of our vacancies here, which we must fill in order to keep the college going. I have been consulting with Mr. Coe about proposed increases of salaries and subsidies, beginning with August, so as to give about N. C. $6,500 for our high-salaried professor, and about $6,100 for professors with initial salaries. The assistant professors will receive a few hundred dollars less per month, lecturers possibly N. C. $4,200 a month, junior lecturers about $3,600 a month, and assistants still a few hundred dollars less. Should the Executive Committee Pro-tem approve this scheme, we would have to budget two-thirds of our extra million dollars for this increase alone, leaving one-third of the million to cover other items with increased prices, as well as to cover possible necessary increases during the second half of the year. If, however, we should have definite word from you or from other sources that the exchange rate is to be considerable increased, we may have to make our increase of subsidies even more liberal.

…… ……

Yours sincerely,
Francis C. M. Wei

97. To Dr. Lobenstine (May 16, 1944)

Dear Dr. Lobenstine:

…… ……

We are in touch with a number of people both missionaries and Chinese scholars for appointment to the college faculty. If they should all join us in the autumn, our teaching force would be greatly strengthened. At the present time the faculty is so depleted that while we are able to meet all the demands of the government curriculum, all of us have to carry extra loads to keep the ship of the college afloat.

…… ……

Yours sincerely,
Francis C. M. Wei

98. To Dr. Charles H. Corbett (June 22, 1944)

Dear Dr. Corbett:

…… ……

The matter of the postwar rehabilitation of the colleges is a very important one. U. S. $3,500,000 is a large sum, but if we should attempt to set up the colleges again for efficient operation after the war, the amount needed may be greater than that. I would like to point out to you that Hua Chung College will have the longest overland route to cover in order to get back to our original home, and transportation by land is always more costly than transportation by water or rail. As to how much our homeward trip will cost we have no idea at the present time as prices are rising every day, and there is no assurance whatever as to what the rate of exchange will be when peace returns.

…… ……

Yours sincerely,
Francis, C. M. Wei

99. To Mr. Oliver S. Lyford (July 31, 1944)

Dear Mr. Lyford:

…… ……

Another purpose of my going to Kunming this time was to help the Yunnan students launch a financial campaign on behalf of the college. The campaign is to raise an endowment which will bring students from Western Yunnan to the college after we move back to Wu Chang, so as to make the link between Hua Chung and Yunnan Province permanent. After a fortnight in the city I found it very difficult to advice the students as how to start the campaign. Different plans we had considered fell through, and the only way was for the students to go to their friends and to some of mine to get contributions. Up till the time I left Kunming it was entirely uncertain how much the students would be able to raise; I believe not more than half a million dollars Chinese currency. Arriving in Hsiakwan on Thursday of last week, I found a group of Yunnan students waiting for me there because a long-distance telephone message had already come from my friends in Kunming to their firm in Hsiakwan announcing my arrival. I saw the students several times and introduced them to all the important people in town. There was greater enthusiasm in Hsiakwan for the students' project than there was in Kunming. I believe that the campaign in Hsiakwan may materialize over a third of a million dollars Chinese, if not more.

　　…　…

　　Besides I had the opportunity of giving more publicity to the college, and as a result we hope that more Christian students will come to join our freshman class this year. A telegram from Mr. Richardson of the Methodist Missionary Society announced that he is bringing from Wanhsien and Chungking sixteen students, presumably all from Christian middle schools. Two students are coming from Yali, and with the possibility of the financial aids for Arts and Education students and also with our intention of starting a theological class this coming term I expect there may be some students from the Han Kou Diocesan Union Middle School now in Tsingchen. While in Kunming, I wrote to Bishop Gilman and the Rev. Mark Li, principal of the Diocesan Union Middle School, about the new scholarships and the new theological course. So there will probably be at least twenty students from Christian middle schools, and sixty to seventy students by examination in Kunming and Hsichow which will be held about the middle of August. If the freshman class should be around eighty, our enrollment for the next term will probably be one hundred and eighty. If so, it will be the highest record since our moving out from Wu Chang, but this is entirely speculation.

　　…　…

Yours sincerely,
Francis C. M. Wei

100. To Mr. Oliver S. Lyford (August 15, 1944)

Dear Mr. Lyford:

... ...

  It is still early to estimate how many new students we shall have for the coming year. Wesley Middle School has sent seventeen students from Wanhsien in Eastern Szechwan where the school is at present. It is the largest contingent of students in any one year from any one of our Christian middle schools, or any other school. It is most encouraging. Of the seventeen students, six were recommended and therefore admitted without examination. The remaining eleven are taking the examinations just now. We shall admit them all since they have come from such a long distance with Mr. Thomas Richardson, who has been master of Physics for over ten years in Wesley Middle School and therefore an old friend of ours. It is good that Mr. Richardson has come. He will be able to get first-hand knowledge of our work and environment here and to report back to all of our friends in Eastern Szechwan, particularly to those in the Wesley Middle School, which you will remember used to be in Wu Chang under the English Methodist Mission, formerly known as the Wesleyan Methodist Mission, one of our cooperating units in the college.

  Of those taking the examinations in Hsichow, we will probably qualify about half a dozen of the candidates for admission, besides the eleven Wesleyan students. It is possible that 100 of the 400 odd candidates taking the examinations in Kunming will be qualified, and of these some 60 will probably turn up for registration in the college in September. In that case we may have about 85 new students for the freshman class; and if 95 of the old students of last year should return, we may expect a total enrollment of about 180 for the new term. This, of course, is a very rough estimate.

  As to faculty, we have been able to get only Miss Burr for the English Department so far. I have written letters to Dr. Paul V. Taylor to meet him both in Raipur, India and in Kunming, asking him to return to the college and act as Dean of the Faculty during the absence of Mr. Constantine. It is not likely that Dr. Liebenthal will accept our offer to join our faculty here on the support of the American Church Mission, for which Dr. Addison has already cabled his approval. I had a talk with Dr. Liebenthal while I was in Kunming. I have tried to get Mr. Arthur March, formerly of Hangchow College, to teach Biology here, but he has wired to decline the offer. The Methodist Missionary Society is hoping that the Rev. P. Jones of the Canton District may come out from Lienhsien and join our faculty for the duration of the war. Mr. Jones is still in Lienhsien after his evacuation from Kukong with Dr. and Mrs. Kunkle of the Canton Union Theological College, and there is absolutely no telling whether he will be able to get out to Kunming under the present circumstances. So far the Methodist Missionary Society has not been able to get us any missionaries for the faculty.

… …

Yours sincerely,
Francis, C. M. Wei

101. To Mr. Oliver S. Lyford (September 14, 1944)

Dear Mr. Lyford:

… …

We are registering the old students today, and beginning with Monday, September 18, there will be a week for the freshmen, while the old students will be going to their classes. Transportation from Kunming to the college for the last two weeks has been very difficult. We hope, however, that the students will be able to find their way to the college under the circumstances. We are extending the time for late students to register by one week in order to accommodate them. As soon as we have any definite idea as to what the enrollment will be in the college for this term, I shall report at once.

… …

Yours sincerely,
Francis C. M. Wei

102. To Rev. Edwin C. Lobenstine (September 19, 1944)

Dear Dr. Lobenstine:

… …

The new year in the college has reopened, but it happens that conditions on the road during the last two weeks have been very difficult, and something like one hundred students, both old and new, have not been able to get to the college and will not be able to until possibly the end of the month, whereas classes have already started on the 18th. It is a situation which we cannot control, and we simply have to accept it. It is probable that our enrollment this year will be over two hundred; my guess is that it will be around two hundred and twenty-five.

We have been able to fill most of our vacancies on the faculty, but there are still two important vacancies in the Department of Economics which we have not been able to fill in spite of all efforts during the last year. Professor Teng Mou-tung, who had promised to come and had been writing in a very encouraging way to us up to the middle of August, has finally turned us down again, making all sorts of excuses for not being able to come from Chengtu. This is very disappointing, but some young men in China these days do not have a sense of good faith. I hope that before very long our Board and the cooperating missions in America will be able to find us a couple of good Economics teachers for the college. This is certainly at the present time our greatest need.

… …

Yours sincerely,
Francis C. M. Wei

103. To Dr. Charles H. Corbett (October 3, 1944)

Dear Dr. Corbett:

… …

Our college re-opened in September, the registration for old students starting on September 14. Ordinarily we would have closed our registration for the new students before the end of September, but conditions on the road from Kunming to our part of the country have been very difficult, and so we have decided to extend our period of registration for new students until about a week from today, if the new arrivals should be able to prove that they had left Kunming before the end of September. Sometimes now travel from Kunming by truck takes over a week.

Up to the present 180 students have already completed their registration in the college, and as far as we know some 25 or 30 students are still on their way. As far as we can estimate, our enrollment will be over 200, and it may get to over 210, which will be the highest of our enrollment we have had since moving out from Wu Chang in the summer of 1938.

We have not been able to get all our faculty vacancies filled, but the prospects are good for having a much larger faculty this year than what we had last year. A report on our faculty with information concerning the departments has been sent to Mr. Evans, upon the request of Dr. William Fenn in Chengtu.

 ……

Yours sincerely,
Francis C. M. Wei

104. To Mr. Oliver S. Lyford (October 12, 1944)

Dear Mr. Lyford:

 ……

I am writing to report, still tentatively, the enrollment for the term. So far we have registered 102 old students (83 men and 19 women), and 110 new students including transfers (86 men and 24 women). The total to date 212: 126 freshmen, 40 sophomores, 28 juniors, and 18 seniors. As far as we know, at least five more old students and a new one are still on the way. Probably those are the only extras we shall be able to take in. This large enrollment has made it necessary for us to open a new hostel for men, making a total of six hostels for men and one for women. All the hostels are well crowded.

As far as the faculty is concerned, for the English Department we have got only Miss Burr. Dr. Liebenthal is still unknown element because we are not sure whether he will be able to leave Kunming to come here before the end of this term, or at all. There is a possibility of the Methodist Mission sending a Mr. Jeffries to teach English here. Mr. Jeffries has been evacuated from Hunan as a missionary. We have added Mr. Shen Chang-hsi to the Department of Chinese Literature, and he has arrived. We have got a new teacher for History, but he is still on the way from Chengtu. There are no new appointees for the Department of Economics-Commerce because Mr. Teng Mou-tung has finally failed us at the last moment, and Mr. Ngan Tsz-min left during the summer although he had accepted reappointment as lecturer. This is all I can report on the faculty in the School of Arts, which has all the departments pretty well lined up for this year except the Department of Economics-Commerce.

In the School of Science we have added two new teachers to the Department of Biology. One is lecturer, Mr. Daniel Chen, a member of the episcopal church, and a graduate of Boone Middle School and of Hua Chung College, with a B. S. in Biology in the class of 1935. Since his graduation he has been teaching in middle schools. He has come all the way from Yuanling with his family. The other Biology teacher is Mr. Shen Shan-chuin, a graduate of Tsing Hua University, with two years as assistant research worker in the Tsing Hua Research Bureau in Kunming; Botany is his special field. He is not a Christian, but he is related to the Acting President of Soochow University, Mr. Shen Ti-lan.

Of the five Chemistry teachers we have appointed, only Chu Fu-hua has arrived. Mr. Chu has been appointed a lecturer. He is also an episcopalian, a graduate of Boone Middle School, and Hua Chung College, B. S. Chemistry 1938. For the last six years he has been engaged in government industrial work, the last position he held was head of an oil-refining factory in Henyang, which has been lost to the

Japanese. We are expecting Professor George Bien, Ph. D. Brown, and two of his assistants who are both university graduates, to arrive from Lanchow, Kansu. Presumably he has already reached Chungking. He may be here before the end of this month. Dr. Chang Shaolin may not be able to get here until after Christmas. In Chemistry we shall have two professors, one lecturer, and two junior lecturers. The teaching staff in the Physics Department remains the same as last year. So does also the Department of Mathematics.

The School of Education has the same faculty as last year except that Mrs. Allen's vacancy has not been filled. Mrs. David Anderson is taking care of the piano students, as well as her own local students.

We have already started a series of discussion meetings on Religion for sophomores and freshman students, the first being on last Friday and it was very well attended. Among some of the new students a very good number are Christian, and there are over ten new students who are preparing for baptism.

…… ……

Yours sincerely,
Francis C. M. Wei

105. A Paragraph from Dr. Wei's Letter N. Y. 98 of November 9, 1944

…… ……

As to addition to the faculty, we are still waiting for the chemists to come from Kansu. All we know is that Se. George Bien has already left Lanchow and is on his way with his family. We hope he is bringing with him two of his assistants. We have at the present time only Mr. Chu Fu-hua to carry on the department. I have already reported on Mr. Chu's qualifications and experience. He is one of our alumni, B. S. Chemistry, 1938.

…… ……

Yours sincerely,
Francis C. M. Wei

106. To Mr. Oliver S. Lyford (February 22, 1945)

Dear Mr. Lyford:

…… ……

  It should not be difficult for us to present a good care for our college because although we have increases our enrollment from 150 to 215 for the first term of this year, we have not gotten back to our highest enrollment of 240 odd which we had during the first year of the war in Wu Chang. Also, as you say, whatever additional appointments we have to make to strengthen our faculty, they are only due to the inadequacy of our staff in the last two or three years. If there have been expanding activities in the other Christian colleges, Hua Chung certainly can plead not guilty. Should any fair-minded person look into the programs of the different Christian colleges ever since the outbreak of the war, he would see we have been most reasonable in our program and our expenditure. If there are some college which have gone ahead in expansion and have been allowed to carry on with an inflated program, and then we are called upon to stop at this particular moment when we are trying to build up towards our pre-war strength both in student enrollment and in faculty appointments, it would not seem quite fair. This ought to be pointed out to all people concerned with U. C. R. financial assistance to the Christian colleges.

  We have had a very good term, which ended on the 9th of February, and we shall reopen again on February 23, but classes will begin again only on March 5. This makes a long first term and a comparatively short second term, because in a rural town like ours we have to make adjustments to accommodate the Chinese New Year, which falls this year on February 13.

…… ……

Yours sincerely,
Francis C. M. Wei

107. To Mr. Oliver S. Lyford (March 20, 1945)

Dear Mr. Lyford:

...   ...

We have a good staff for the Chemistry Department now with Dr. George Bien heading it up as professor. He has one lecturer and two junior lecturers as his assistants. It would be better if we should be able to have at least a man of an assistant-professor's qualifications, but so far we have not been able to get one for the department. I have already reported on the arrival of Dr. Wu as college physician; she is the wife of Professor George Bien, a P. U. M. C. graduate. The Methodist Mission is sending us Dr. and Mrs. Pinoff. We had already appointed Dr. Wu before we knew anything about the coming of Dr. Pinoff, who was evacuated from Wenchow in East China.

...   ...

In a cablegram to you several days ago I mentioned the fact that Dean Lo had reported the possibility of having to close down the entire Department of Economics-Commerce on account of the short-handedness of staff. It would be a pity if that should have to eventualize, because it is the most popular and the largest department in the whole college, but we have now only one part-time assistant professor in Mr. T'an Jen-i, who is also assistant treasurer, and a junior lecturer who graduated from the college only a year and a half ago. Again, I have to teach the course on "The History of Economic Thought," for the juniors and seniors, although it is not my subject, but it is a course required by the government, and no one is willing to handle it. I hope it may be possible for you to canvass the country as secure permission from Washington to send out before September at least one qualified teacher in Economics and Accounting. We have combed the whole country for the last two years to find a teacher for the department, but all our efforts have been in vain. It seems that a man trained in Economics and Commerce will go into government service or into some more lucrative job instead of teaching.

...   ...

Yours sincerely,
Francis C. M. Wei

108. To Rev. Earle H. Ballou (March 20, 1945)

Dear Mr. Ballou:

... ...

  I hope you will keep our faculty needs in mind. We have found it very difficult, practically impossible, to find any qualified Chinese to teach Economics and English. If there is any possibility of your getting a good man or woman for Economics to come out immediately to join our faculty here, it may mean the saving of our whole department, which is so desperately shorthanded in staff at the present time that it looks as if we may have to close it next year, and it is the largest department we have in the college. Before the war we had only missionaries to teach English Language and Literature in the college. Now every missionary going on furlough means one out, as far as the college is concerned, for the duration of the war, and yet if we are going to maintain in any way our wartime standards of English we must have a sufficient number of English-speaking teachers whose mother tongue is English. If by any chance you should get any candidates to teach Economics or English, please let Mr. Lyford or Dr. Thayer Addison know about it, and cable us at the same time.

  Another need of ours is a Music teacher. Our department of Music is reduced to only one teacher, Mrs. Anderson, who is going on furlough with her husband this summer. The work in the department has to be given up unless we are able to get a Music teacher before September. For the last seven years we have been following the policy of retrenchment, but there is a limit to it. If we are going to hold together at all, we have to replenish our depleted faculty in order to do justice to our students. I realize how difficult it is to secure passports and travel facilities for any westerner coming out from the United States or Great Britain, but let us hope that there may be a change before the summer as far as that is concerned, and that the Associated Boards and our cooperating missions may be able to send us out more help. It is very strange indeed that the British authorities should have given three hundred and fifty passages to missionaries going overseas, and yet none for China. That must have been due to the change in the situation in December. The tide is beginning to turn, and I hope that both the British and American authorities will take that into consideration.

……

Yours sincerely,
Francis C. M. Wei

109. To Miss. Rachel A. Dowd (April 19, 1945)

Dear Miss Dowd:

……

You may have heard about the possibility of my going to America and teaching in Union Theological Seminary for a year. The matter has been reported to the Executive Committee Pro-tem, but since arrangement have not been completed for me to go, I have not yet cable my acceptance of the invitation to Union or to the Board of Founders.

I wrote sometime ago before my illness, to Mr. Lyford in regard to the need of certain microfilms of magazines for the college. The following is the list of magazines that we would list to have sent to us as soon as possible:

"Psychologic Abstracts" beginning from January 1945.

"American Journal of Sociology" beginning from January 1945.

"Annual Review of Psychology" Vol. I to date.

"Physiological Review" Vol. 20 to date.

"Journal of the American Chemical Society" 1944—1945, 1945.

"The Physical Review" 1944—1945, 1945.

"Journal of the American Medical Association" 1945—1946.

……

Yours sincerely,
Francis C. M. Wei

110. To Dr. Charles H. Corbett (April 19, 1945)

Dear Dr. Corbett:

							… …

Indeed it is one thing to turn out students from the college and another thing to try to give them a good education. From our experience during these war years we have found that four years is not too long to educate a student in the college, even with the present lower standards. Education, of course, is not training. Trying could be hurried up, but education has a time element. Further, to give no vacations or shorten the vacations for the students is one thing, but to shorten the vacations for the teaching staff would have disastrous results, especially when most of us are already overburdened. The four-term arrangement, such as is in practice at Chicago University, requires a large faculty so that the teachers may take turns for their vacations. This, however, is impractical in China where all the college faculties are already shorthanded.

							… …

							Yours sincerely,
							Francis C. M. Wei

111. To Mr. Oliver S. Lyford (May 4, 1945)

Dear Mr. Lyford:

							… …

Things are going on smoothly in the college. A new lecturer has been added to the Department of History-Sociology to teach Western History, which has not been properly taken care of since Mr. Constanine left Hsichow last July. This new lecturer is Mr. Hsu Yen-liang. He is a native of Shantung province, about thirty years in age, and a graduate of ten-years' standing from the Catholic University in Peiping, but he himself is not a Christian. He seems to be well trained and fits in well with the atmosphere here. He not only knows life in the

Catholic University in Peiping, but also had a year in the preparatory course at Cheloo University before he entered college. His salary has been on the budget. He was actually appointed last autumn, but he could not get here until after the winter vacation. He had to come all the way from Chengtu.

…… ……

Yours sincerely,
Francis C. M. Wei

112. To Rev. James Thayer Addison (June 19, 1945)

Dear Thayer:

…… ……

This last proposition would be the more suitable for our convenience in Hua Chung. It looks as if we are getting a number of short-time teachers of English, mostly refugee missionaries, for the next year. As soon as the war is over in China, all of them will leave us. Miss Bleakley, who has been the veteran teacher of English in Hua Chung, will probably not return to the college until we move back to Wu Chang. This would leave us in the lurch. So if Miss Burr should be able to stay with us for the third year 1945—1947, whether in Hsichow or in Wu Chang, it would be decidedly a help.

…… ……

Yours sincerely,
Francis C. M. Wei

113. To Dr. Arthur O. Rinden (February 1, 1946)

Dear Dr. Rinden:

…… ……

Present condition of Hua Chung College. The college is still operating in Hsichow. The first term was finished before Christmas and the second term has just started, beginning on the third of January.

They expect to finish the academic year by the end of March, shortening the year considerably in order to allow time for the college to start its moving back to Wu Chang as early as possible in April. This is done in order to avoid the rainy season in Yunnan which will set in towards the end of May and also to get back to Central China early enough so as to get our people, both faculty and students, re-acclimated for the hot climate in the summer.

For the current year we have a strong faculty in all departments except in the three major departments of the Yale-in-China School of Science, namely, Biology, Chemistry and Physics. In each of these three departments we have had only one senior man with a number of junior men of instructor and lecturer rank to help out. In the minor Department of Mathematics, which we expect to develop as soon as possible into a major department, we have two full professors in Mr. John L. Coe and Mr. C. S. Shen, but Mr. Shen has been away during the greater part of the year, and so the Physics Department has had to help out by giving some of the course in mathematics.

The enrollment for the first term was 286 students. This dropped down to 250 in the second term which is a drop to be expected every year in the college in Wu Chang as well as in Hsichow. Owing to poor work or other reasons about 15% of the students in the first term usually drop out in the second term.

The budget for the current year is approximately U. S. $60,000. About one-half of this has to come from the Association Board Sustaining Fund and the other half from the cooperating missions.

....

<u>The moving back of the college to Wu Chang.</u> As has been indicated, the college is fully planning to start its trek back to Wu Chang in April. A committee has been appointed by the executive pro tem of the Board of Directors to make all the necessary arrangements. It is proposed that the route be from Hsichow to Kunming by truck, from Kunming to Chutsin by rail, from Chutsin to Kweilin by truck, from Kweilin to Han Yang and from Han Yang to Wu Chang by rail.

....

<u>Ten-Year Plan for the development of Hua Chung after the war.</u> I gave you at the meeting last Saturday a copy of the Ten-Year Plan known as the Development of Hua Chung College after the war, and I have asked Mr. Fowler to send you thirty copies as soon as they are ready. I hope you will have this document sent to all the members of the Yale-in-China Board of Trustees, expect those who are in New York because they have received them.

This Ten-Year Plan has been approved tentatively by the Hua Chung Board of Founders and everything indicates that it is necessary for us to put into effect the Ten-Year Plan immediately when the college moves back to Wu Chang. You will see from the Plan that the first of the ten years will call for a budget of U. S. $115,000 for annual current expenditures. Judging by the present trend of things, it looks as if in five years we would have to increase the budget up to U. S. $165,000 for the annual current expenditures. If Hua Chung is going to hold its important position as the only Christian college in the Central China region, we must keep in mind the necessity of increasing the annual budget eventually to U. S. $300,000.

… …

Yours sincerely,
Francis C. M. Wei

114. To Rev. A. M. Sherman (August 28, 1946)

Dear Dr. Sherman:

… …

Since then I have been able to look over the campus, go about a little in the city of Wu Chang, and talk to many of my colleagues and students. It has been a very pleasant surprise that most of the trees are still here on the campus. I do not believe that most of the trees are still here on the campus. I do not believe that more than 15% of them have been cut down. To any stranger who did not know the place at all, it would not be noticeable that trees have been cut down at all. There are, of course, no lawns because weeds have been going in the open spaces for the last six years at least.

The buildings are in much better shape than I had expected. Not a great deal of flooring had been destroyed. Windows and doors were gone, but Dr. Taylor has been back here since December, and under very difficult condition, he has been able to do a splendid job in cooperation with Mr. Kemp, who has been doing the same thing for the middle school. The buildings and the residences are in fairly good repair now with glass window panes, but no screening. Most of the doors have no knobs nor locks, and many of the windows do not have hooks. Dr. Taylor is getting laborers to work on those things now, but all this will take a great deal of time.

....

Over 4,000 students have taken our entrance examinations here, in Changsha, and in Kunming. The Committee has not been able to read all their papers yet, but so far the report has come to me that they are of higher standard than those in Yunnan during the war years. If we should plan to have 400 students, we should be able to pick the very best, some of whom may come up to pre-war standards for admission. I believe only 100—120 old students will return, and that is natural because most of them are Yunnan students who may not want to take the long journey to Wu Chang away from home. Yesterday a telegram came to me, saying that two of our Yunnan students were in a car wreck, one of them being killed and the other severely injured.

Under these circumstances we have to be prepared to build up on our enrollment again with new students admitted here in Wu Chang. The Senate has decided to have only 350 students, but the pressure is so great that we may have to go up to 400. Whether it is 350 or 400, we shall have to use double decker beds in the dormitories. We are using the dormitory in Ingle Hall, which will accommodate 120; the old Women's Hospital at the London Mission on the same street with us where we may find sufficient accommodation for about 100; and we are hoping to have the use of our old Fu Kai Church which may accommodate 60 students. These three places will take care of 280 men students, and the Yen Hostels, old and new, will accommodate 130 girls. The men students will be crowded, but they will understand that this is still the aftermath of the war.

....

Yours sincerely,
Francis C. M. Wei

115. To Mr. Oliver S. Lyford (September 11, 1946)

Dear Mr. Lyford:

....

On September 7 the Executive Committee of the Board of Directors had a meeting in my house, and they recommended to the Directors that one-half of the N. C. $100,000,000 Rehabilitation Grant to the college by the government should be appropriated for the erection of a semi-permanent hostel for men and a set of Music Practice Rooms for the Music students. It is necessary to erect a dormitory for the men students because we expect about 280—300 men students, and 100 to 120 women students. The Yen Hostel, with the annex built in the summer of 1937, will accommodate 130 women students, and therefore the women will be well taken care of, even when we allow them to use single beds although the rooms are a little bit more crowded than before the way by having more beds put in them.

As to the men students, the situation is pretty tough. We used to have three hostels for men: part of Ingle Hall (the other part being used by the Physics and Biology Department and the Dining room), Poyu Hostel which is Methodist, and the old Divinity School Building. Before I returned, the Housing Committee had decided to use Poyu Hostel for faculty and staff families by putting some partitions in, and the old Divinity School for teachers without families. These two hostels would accommodate at the best only about 60 students, but they are not available for the next term for students since they have been assigned to faculty and staff members. So only Ingle Hall is left for student accommodations. By putting double deckers in, we figure we can accommodate 120 men students. We have rented the London Mission Woman's Hospital building only five-minute's walk from our front gate, and we can put in forty-five double deckers for 90 students. We must have, therefore, space somewhere else for about 100 men students. We have tried every possible way to get rented quart or to use some church property, but every way is blocked. So we have decided to put about 100 men students into the body of the ground floor of the Library Building, which is really for stacks. Since neither the stacks nor the books have arrived, and in the meantime we hope to be able to complete the erection of a semi-permanent building on a piece of new property right next to the property which was used before the war for the Practice School of the School of Education. This building will cost approximately N. C. $45,000,000 and will be built in such a way that we can continue to use it for the Practice School when the proper college hostels have been built.

…… ……

Yours sincerely,
Francis C. M. Wei

116. To Mr. Earl Fowler (October 7, 1946)

Dear Earl:

…… ……

Dr. Beaver changed his mind three times about coming to join Hua Chung, and when I was in England I had no way to tell whether Dr. Beaver was coming to us eventually or not. At least we could not wait for him for more than one year, and he had not given me any understanding that he would come. Therefore, when I met Mr. Gray in England and found that he was quite qualified to teach Church History, I approached him about his appointment on the support of the National Council. After serious consideration of the proposition, he accepted it and proceeded to apply for appointment by the National Council. In order to do this Mr. Gray resigned from at least two attractive offers in England because he was so very eager to come again as a missionary, particularly to teach Church History in Hua Chung. I hope that he will be able to get to Wu Chang in January, so as to start teaching in the second term which will begin early in February. Mr. Constantine is teaching his course for the first term, pending his arrival.

His appointment will not clash with Dr. Beaver's coming if Beaver should come at all. I am very glad to know that he has finally made up his mind to get to Wu Chang next summer. If possible, as to his work, he may teach the History of Liturgics, the History of Missions, and some Church History, and also the History of Doctrines if he should agree. I am going to write him separately about this.

…… ……

We have about 135 old students, of whom 23 are women; and about 310 new students, of whom about 115 are women, so our total enrollment this term will be around 440, and 137 will be women. All the hostels are full to the brim. The women students are using single beds, and the rooms are pretty well crowded. We have Ingle Hall as a men's hostel and we have rented the old London Mission Women's Hospital building as a second hostel for men, which is only about three minutes' walk from gate to gate. We are erecting with permission of the Board of Founders a semi-permanent one-storey hostel to accommodate 96 students on Ch'i P'b Kai, which is about five minutes' walk from our back gate. All the men students are using double deckers. We had about 4,000 candidates for admission this summer, and we had to admit more students than we had expected. They seem to be better prepared for college work than the students we admitted in Yunnan during the war.

…… ……

Yours sincerely,
Francis C. M. Wei

117. To Mr. Oliver S. Lyford (October 15, 1946)

Dear Mr. Lyford:

…… ……

Registration in the college is completed. We have now in the college 148 old students and 304 new ones, making a total enrollment of 452, of this number 310 are men and 142 are women. I have not been able to look carefully into the records of the old students, but the registration cards show that there are 109 Christian students among the 310 new students, which means 33% are Christians in the freshman class. This percentage is not so high as I would like, but you must remember that the percentage of Christian students in all the Christian schools has been miserably low during the war years, and so 33% Christian in our freshman class is encouraging. A year ago in Hsichow we had 282 students, and only 29% were Christians. During the second term of last year in Hsichow, the percentage of Christian students was increased to 31%. This, of course, applies to the total enrollment and not just to the freshman class. When I have time to get a report on the old students in the college now, I feel sure that the percentage will be higher, possibly 35%~36%.

We were very fortunate to get Dr. Wai-king Taai, professor of Religious Education to accept the concurrent job of Dean of Women, although she is carrying a full teaching load. The two hostels for women are full to the brim, and she is giving the girls her personal attention. We have three men's hostels: one on the campus, both within three to four minutes' walk from gate to gate. Each of the men's hostels is in the charge of one of our senior staff members, and each has also a junior staff member as an assistant. The management is not satisfactory, and perhaps during the rest of the week I shall get the heads of the three men's hostels together and put down more screws.

Since I returned, I have been addressing the study body repeatedly, emphasizing particularly the importance of discipline. The general moral of the student body is good as a whole, but it is not quite up to the pre-war standard yet. It is particularly difficult when you have two-thirds of the students body in the freshman class, but it is an abnormal year, and we have to pay special attention to the maintenance of traditions and standards of discipline. It is, however, an opportunity and a challenge. From my contact with the new students, which I get teaching two classes of Logic including more than two-thirds of the new ones, I feel that we are getting much better material than we did during the war years in Kweilin or Hsichow. Although we have only 109 Christians out of the 304 new students, many of the non-Christian students in the freshman class have come from a Christian middle school. I believe we have about 60% of the new students from the Christian middle schools. If the registration cards should show that to be true, I would feel much more assured of a successful year in spite of the overwhelmingly large freshman class.

... ...

New books from America have been arriving in small numbers almost every week. But altogether we have not had more than 500—600 books so far, and at least ten to twelve times that number should be coming very soon. We further hope that the steel stacks from America will soon arrive because otherwise we shall not be able to shelve the books when they are here.

No equipment has yet come, but shipment is very slow particularly with the strike going on in the States. Richard Bien has been corresponding with you about a power unit. We have electric current from the city, but it is very weak and not dependable. The new city power plant will probably be installed by next summer, and I understand it is going to be 15,000 kilowatt, but before that materializes we ought to have a small stand-by which could always be used by the science laboratories.

As a whole we have enough to carry on, and we carry on better than most of the colleges in China. At least we ought to feel proud that we are one of the few colleges which have started classes as early as this. Wuhan University has got very little ready for this work. If they should be able to start lectures by December 1, I would be surprised. The third college in our city, Chung Hwa University, has gone through a very difficult time. What they have now is just one empty building without any repairs except some white washing. They have no books, no equipment, and no faculty, and they are just starting their entrance examinations. I suppose they will start their work, the kind of work they used to do before the war or during the war, sometime about Christmas.

... ...

Yours sincerely,
Francis C. M. Wei

118. To Rt. Rev. William P. Roberts (November 11, 1946)

Dear Bishop Roberts:

....

  Concerning the Bawn School, may I say that we would be most happy to welcome the school to cooperate with us on our campus. I believe both our Board of Directors and our Board of Founders will give their permission to the school to erect a building on the grounds of our Women's Unit, so that it may have all the facilities and cooperation of the university, and particularly of our Women's Unit, and to cooperate with whatever theological which that may be developed in Hua Chung and in the other institutions which may be cooperating with Hua Chung in Theological Training. It seems to me that the proper procedure would be for the Board of Control of the Bawn School to make its proposition to our Board of Directors through me, and then we may take up the matter officially. It will be an independent school, but affiliated with Hua Chung in somewhat similar way that E. T. S. is affiliated with Harvard, or Union Theological School to Columbia, unless the Board of Control of the school should desire an even closer affiliation. We would wish that at least some of the students might be qualified as university students by passing our entrance examination and then while they lived in the Bawn School, they might have all the advantages and privileges of Hua Chung students, particularly when the Ministry of Education is concerned.

  It would not concern us whether the dean already appointed is a westerner or a Chinese, although we would like to see in due course of time a Chinese as its head. When the proportion is made to us for the Bawn School to be affiliated with Hua Chung, we may have a few details which can be easily worked out.

  As to the Central Theological School, we would give it the heartiest welcome if it should come to cooperate with us, as it is now tentatively cooperating with St. John's University. We have our own theological work, which will be on the strictly university level, and we are hoping that the Central China Union Theological School, supported by two or three missions working in this center, may also cooperate with us. With the Central China Union Theological School, the Bawn School, and our own theological work, we may have all the necessary faculty to cooperate with the Central Theological School and to supplement it. I am quite familiar with this kind of cooperation in theological work, as obtains in Oxford and Cambridge, and possibly some arrangement like that may be the best for all concerned. What I have said about the Bawn School would apply also to be Central Theological School. If the Board of Directors make an official proposition to our Board of Directors, I would present it to the next meeting of our Board of Directors, and put it through all the necessary "red tape." Today the Hua Chung Senate passed a resolution giving the Central Theological School the heartiest welcome to our midst.

Yours very cordially,
Francis C. M. Wei

119. To Mr. Rev. A. M. Sherman (November 12, 1946)

Excerpts from a letter of Dr. Francis C. M. Wei, President of Hua Chung University, to the Rev. A. M. Sherman

…… ……

We are getting Dr. Starratt, a member of the Episcopal Mission, to teach New Testament, beginning with next spring. The last letter from Earl Fowler reports that the Rev. Francis Gray has been appointed to teach Church History. Dr. Beaver of the Reformed Church Mission is coming next autumn to teach Church History, Liturgics, and History of Missions. I had hoped that the London Missionary Society might appoint Dr. Ackroyd to teach Old Testament, but unfortunately I received from him a letter the day before yesterday that owing to the conditions of his appointment as laid down by the London Missionary Society, he has now to withdraw his offer for foreign service, and so I am afraid he is forever lost to our service. Last spring while I was in New York the Rev. Mr. Swift was in correspondence with an army chaplain who was qualified to teach Old Testament and Semitics. Since Dr. Ackroyd is now unavailable would it be possible for Earl Fowler or the successor to Ervine Swift to explore the possibility of this particular candidate for the chair of Old Testament in Hua Chung? There may be teachers of Old Testament in the Central Theological School or in the Central China Union Theological Seminary, but I doubt very much if he would be such a specialist as we would like to have on our faculty. So it is necessary for us to continue to look for a man who is really qualified to develop the Department of Old Testament in connection with our own Theological Training.

It seems that the Central Theological School and the Central China Theological Seminary would desire particularly to train parish ministers, which is also a part of our plan, but in addition we would like to train as few students who may develop into real scholars in their own lines. Of course, the Bawn School is to train only women workers for the Church, and we would like to cooperate with it in this work.

You may be interested to know that we have three third-year men students, Episcopalians, who are taking the combined theological course, which we call the course on "Grade B" and there are four Episcopal men students, one man and one woman Presbyterian students, in the second year, who are taking the same combined course, so we have altogether nine students in the two years. It is my hope that in the next year sophomore class, we may have at least ten to take the same course. We started the term with eight students taking the first year of combined Theological and Arts course, but one man and one woman had to drop out because of the heavy work. Of the nine students we have now five are Boone graduates. This speaks well for our middle school.

… …

Yours sincerely,
Francis C. M. Wei

120. To Mr. J. Earl Fowler (November 15, 1946)

Dear Earl:

......

We had at the beginning of the term 446 students, but 20 students have already withdrawn, some to go to Wuhan University where they charge no fees, not even for food, and some for family reasons. So our enrollment at present is about 425. The two women's hostels are pretty crowded, but even with using single beds, Dr. Taai has been able to squeeze in 138 women students. All the men students are using double decker beds, and about 70 are living in the stack space on the ground floor of the library building. However, we hope soon to be able to move them out to the new hostel being completed on Ch'i P'an Kai, which you will remember is the street where is the First Boone Teachers' Compound on the way to St. Hilda's, only a few minutes from the Back Gate of the Boone campus.

It is good to know that the Rev. Frank L. Titus is succeeding Father Swift, and that you are doing everything possible to fill the National Council's quota of our faculty members. We need a good missionary who can teach particularly the commercial courses, such as accounting. Dr. Richard Bien is the only senior member in the Physics Department. That is the reason why we are so eager to have Dr. Yates, now in Sheffield, appointed on the support of the National Council to teach Physics here. I hope the National Council will make an exception to his appointment, although he is a non-Episcopalian. He has a Ph. D. from the University of Ireland and another Ph. D. from the University of Cambridge, and has had about ten-year's teaching as lecturer of Physics in Sheffield University. In the English universities a lecturer is of the same rank as an assistant professor in America.

......

Yours sincerely,
Francis C. M. Wei

121. To Mr. Oliver S. Lyford (December 3, 1946)

Dear Mr. Lyford:

………

Of our 446 students, 39 have withdrawn so far. About one-half of them have withdrawn on health grounds, as advised by the doctor. The war has done much damage to the health of our youth. Some are suffering from serious malnutrition and others from heart trouble. The other half have withdrawn in order to go to Wuhan University because that university announced its admission of candidates only about three weeks ago. This is no reflection on our work as compared with that in Wu Han University. Most of the students have been forced to go to Wu Han when they had the chance, because Wu Han as a national university charges no fees and even gives free board and lodging to their students. In normal times many people would be willing to pay for the kind of education we are able to give, but meeting with serious financial difficulties now, they naturally send their children to get a free education, even though ours may be better. However, my feeling is that this situation will not last. As soon as there is a settlement of the political situation and as soon as there is a reasonable budget for the government, the government universities will have to demand at least as much as the state universities do in America in the way of fees; that is, only tuition will be remitted or reduced.

If our 417 students should persist in the second semester, we would have a reasonable enrollment. We hope that we may be able to assimilate properly the 300 freshmen. As a matter of fact, this number has been reduced to 270. There is a good chance of our succeeding in doing so because, as the dean reported to the faculty yesterday, only four of the 270 freshmen were really not good college material. All the rest seemed to have adequate preparation for college work. This is really an encouragement. As the dean said, the students are much better than those we had in Yunnan during the war.

………

Yours sincerely,
Francis, C. M. Wei

122. To Mr. J. Earl Fowler (December 17, 1946)

Dear Earl:

　　…　…

　　We are taking steps to increase tuition and other charges, but there is always a limit. If we should increase our fees to such an extent as to keep Christian students and other worthwhile students away from our institution we may be defeating our own purpose, although we increase our income from student fees. Also, if the increase of fees should reduce considerably our enrollment, this item of our income would remain about the same. It is always questionable whether we should draw our students mainly from those families who are able to pay. Certainly it is not for this purpose that we have the Christian colleges in China. Therefore, I would like to present this matter to the consideration of the Board of Trustee of the college, as well as to the National Council of the Episcopal Church in the U. S., and I am perfectly willing to be guided by their decision. Beginning with the next term, we are charging more than twice the fees of this term, and I am waiting anxiously to see what effect this will produce.

　　…　…

Yours affectionately,
Francis C. M. Wei

123. To Rev. Arthur M. Sherman (February 12, 1947)

Dear Dr. Sherman:

　　…　…

　　<u>Need of Scholarship Funds.</u> I have already reported in a letter to Mr. Lyford for the current year. We have appropriated N. C. $14,000,000 for scholarships for students in the college. U. S. $2,000 has come from the Keformed Church with preference for Yunnan students studying in Hua Chung, second preference to Hunan

students, and failing both, for other students. We are applying this fund accordingly, and the rest has come mainly from gifts I have received from friends in America for my discretionary use, and the balance from L. M. D. M. college general funds.

<u>Teacher of Old Testament and Semitics.</u> I am glad to know that Father Swift and Mr. Titus are on the track of someone to fill this post and hope they will succeed. I am very sorry indeed that the candidate whom the London Missionary Society had in mind has withdrawn his offer, and the L. M. S. is not interested on considering another candidate.

... ...

Yours sincerely,
Francis C. M. Wei

124. To Mr. Oliver S. Lyford (March 10, 1947)

Dear Mr. Lyford:

... ...

The college re-opened for the second term on February 6th. We have now 384 students, which means 63 persons fewer than the first term. But every year, enrollment in the second term is 15% fewer than that in the first term, and so the smaller enrollment this term is nothing unusual.

... ...

Yours sincerely,
Francis C. M. Wei

125. To Mr. J. Earl Fowler (May 1, 1947)

Dear Earl:

... ...

We still need a man to teach Old Testament and another to teach Systematic Theology. It is a pity that Edmund Hsu with his training, is not able to come back to us on account of financial complications about which I can see no way to help him. If I were not so busy myself, I would like to undertake the teaching of Systematics myself which I used to do before 1927. But I am already having too much teaching in Philosophy.

Our scheme of theological training seems to be just the thing that the church needs. I was absent from the Diocesan Synod in one afternoon when they discussed the training of candidates for the ministry. Apparently they had many problems which they could not see any way to solve. In the evening of that day, they came to the university for a reception given by the Episcopal members of the faculty. I reported to them in detail our plan of theological training. When I was through, several of them said that we have solved all of their problems as far as the training of candidates for ministry was concerned.

On April 13th, there was a retreat for the Christian teachers of the eight Christian middle schools in the Wu Han cities. It was a whole day affair in Stokes Hall. I spoke on the policy of the Christian middle schools and I emphasized the importance of maintaining Christian character of the schools. This met with approval of all the principals present. In the afternoon, the question of religious education in the schools was considered. They felt strongly the need of teachers trained to do the religious work in the middle schools and they requested that Hua Chung should get up a course for the training of the teachers to do this work. This question was referred to the monthly meeting of the principals of Christian schools in the Wu Han cities in which Dean P'u Hwang and I always participated. We are going to meet on Saturday, May 3rd in Han Kou, and I expect to have a definite plan to propose to the principals for the training of their teachers for religious work. Possibly our theological teachers will lecture for two afternoons every week during term time from three to five. We would like to teach the Old and New Testaments, the principle of Religious Education and Christian teachings. If each Christian middle school in the Wu Han center should send us 2 or 3 teachers for such lectures, we may be able to have a goodly class, and if we should continue this for a number of years, there would be a large number of teachers to teach Bible classes, to conduct religious discussion groups and to guide the students in the religious thinking in the middle schools. Christian middle schools in Central China area outside of Wu Han, such as Yali Middle School and Fu-Hsiang Middle School in Changsha feel also the same need. We may have to set up short courses for the teachers of these middle schools, and we are thinking of some plans to do this.

… …

Yours affectionately,
Francis C. M. Wei

126. To Mr. Oliver S. Lyford (June 4, 1947)

Dear Mr. Lyford:

… …

In the meantime the general faculty had its regular monthly meeting and decided that students who missed their lectures on Monday must either make up the lectures or produce a letter of request for leave of absence on that day from their parents. A notice was posted out yesterday June 3, and the students who have to make up lectures are arranging with their professors for make-ups. There is no trace of any ill-feeling among the students whatsoever as far as their attitude towards the university authorities is concerned, thus another storm has blown over. We do not know what is coming next. It is quite a problem for the government to settle the affair in the Wu Han University. If our students should be absolutely left alone by external forces, I am sure they will behave well. We seem to have more respect of Chinese society for the way we have handled the situation during the last weeks.

Term examinations for seniors and sophomores are about finished and our Intermediate for sophomores and Final Examinations for seniors will begin in another week, while term examinations for freshmen and juniors will begin on June 11. We are going to have our Baccaulaureate Service for the graduates on Saturday morning, June 21, with the Rev. Stephen Chang of St. Paul's Cathedral in Han Kou as the preacher, and we are inviting the governor of Hupeh to be Commencement speaker, when we hold the graduating exercises in the afternoon of the same day. At the present moment, all students seem to be busy getting ready for the examinations and in less than three weeks summer vacation will begin, on June 21. It is very distressing that there have been strikes in several of the Christian universities and political arrests have been made in some of them. We are very thankful that we are entirely free from political complications.

…… ……

Yours sincerely,
Francis C. M. Wei

127. To Mr. J. Earl Fowler (September 15, 1947)

My dear Earl:

…… ……

The inertia in the House of Bishops tended to keep the Theological School and the Bawn School in Shanghai. To this the House of Deputies could not concur, and so a compromise was reached by deciding to keep the Central Theological School in Shanghai for the time being. I am afraid it will be there permanently. It will not be any loss to us in Hua Chung, but the church as a whole will realize the mistake in due course of time.

You may have heard that my son John has been appointed research assistant in the Physics Department in Yale Graduate School, and he is getting enough income to cover his necessary expenses.

…… ……

We are just in the rush of registering students in the new academic year. It will be another week before we know the exact enrollment, but my guess is that there will be 310 old students, and 230 new students including transfers, making a total of 540. All our hostels will be filled to the limit. One third of the student body will be women.

…… ……

Yours affectionately,
Francis C. M. Wei

128. To Mr. Oliver S. Lyford (September 26, 1947)

Dear Mr. Lyford:

…… ……

Since I returned, I have been busy getting ready for the opening of the new term, and later in the rush of registration of old and new students. I do not have to do a great deal because I have so many competent colleagues who attend to the various parts of the work; but all the time, I have to be here in the office for consultation and to make decisions on matters not covered by regulations. For the entering freshman class, 132 students had been recommended by the affiliated Christian middle schools, and 3,488 candidates not thus recommended took our entrance examinations in August in 4 centers, namely, Wu Chang, Changsha, Canton and Kunming. Only 210 of these who took the entrance examinations were admitted by the Admissions Committee with Dr. P'u Hwang as chairman. Thus 342 students were qualified to come, and the Committee, on the basis of past experience, had expected 70% of these to turn up for registration. But so far, only a little bit over 60% has actually turned up, and so there are up to this moment, 218 new students who had registered. We had at the end of last term 360 old students who had completed their year's work besides the seniors who graduated. Some of these 360 students were dropped on account of poor work, and others were advised to leave because of unsatisfactory conduct; still others have not returned, some because they had not paid on or before August 15th N.C. $200,000, as deposit to assure their return, and so have not been allowed to return by the dean. We have in the university now 312 old students, which is almost 90% of the students who had completed the work at the end of last year. It is a good percentage, judged by our past experience. The total enrollment in the university is therefore 530 students—312 old students and 218 new ones, of whom 188 are women students.

The two women's hostels are filled to the limit, and in most of the rooms, the students have to use double-deckers which they did not do during the last year. That is how we manage to squeeze in more women students, and the girls are now less comfortable. We cannot help this because so many girls want to come, and their families prefer to have them with us than somewhere else. Three men's hostels, namely, Ingle Hall, London Mission Hostel, and New Third Hostel are all opened and we have reopened also one half of the old Po Yu Hostel under the Methodist Church, by providing living quarters for four families in the new houses just completed. Three of the hostels are now full, but there are about 20 more vacancies in the Third Hostel, which is under Dr. Brank Fulton. I am glad that Fulton is here with his wife, and since he is interested in working among students, he will make a very good hostel warden.

…… ……

As to enrollment, we had just about 440 a year ago, and about 530 this year. I consider it wise to reach 600 a year from now and keep the enrollment at that number for two or three years before we increase the number to reach the maximum of 800. If we should get one new hostel for men and one new hostel for women built within the next ten months, we ought to be able to take care of the 600. But we could do that only by continuing the use of double-deckers, and double-deckers for university students are not really satisfactory. In ordinary times, a reasonable measure of comfort is necessary to university work. So if we should allow two or three years to build three more permanent hostels, so as to relieve the congestion in the hostels and to change the double-deckers into single beds, we may have enough space for 600 students. Then, and not until then, should we increase our enrollment to reach the maximum. As how to find the money for the necessary residences and hostels is for the Hua Chung Committee of the United Board to consider. I would suggest to take it from our Building Fund of which we have at present almost one third of a million American dollars. The building project I have just mentioned will probably require less than U. S. $100,000. We ought to be able to afford this, since it is a part of the permanent building program.

…… ……

Yours sincerely,
Francis C. M. Wei

129. To Mr. Oliver S. Lyford (October 18, 1947)

Dear Mr. Lyford:

…… ……

We have this term 523 students, of whom 190 are women. It is the opinion of the Senate that we should reach the enrollment of about 600 students in the fall of 1948, 400 men and 200 women, and then stop at that figure for two or three years not only for the sake of consideration but also to allow time for the building of more hostels, so as to relieve the congestion, and to get hostel life into the normal conditions which would mean two or at most four students in a room or suite planned for that number, all in single beds instead of six or eight or even ten in one room with all sleeping in double deckers. The hostel scheme ought to be one of the distinctive features of Hua Chung. This requires the provision of quarters for two faculty members near to each men's hostel. Our present buildings make the work of this scheme impossible. Hence the building of new hostels is an urgent need.

The Executive Committee meeting on Saturday also took action for the university to follow the government plan of subsidies. According to newspaper reports, the government has been considering various plans. It looks likely that they are going to adopt the one which call for 125% increase of all the salaries and the subsidies. So far we have been following the government plan since July 1946, and it has been proved the most satisfactory to all concerned. At times, it works hardships on our people when the government is slow in changing to meet the new price level, but as long as we know that the government is going to make new adjustments, we are willing to wait in spite of the hardships. I was working it out with Paul Ward yesterday and found that if the government should finally adopt this month the plan of increasing by 125% we would probably have a deficit of U.S. $2,000, when we take the lower fingers of the salary item for the year 1947—1948. But exchange may be in our favor, so as to eliminate this deficit. Even though there may be a deficit, the increase like this one is justifiable. We still have our reserve to fall back upon. You may like to keep the reserve as intact as possible, but it ought to be remembered that the greater part of the reserve has been kept just to meet a time like this. We may have three of four more years of hard time to face, but we ought to stretch our reserve to cover this expected period. We ought to keep the future in mind, but it does not seem warranted to sacrifice too much the present for the future.

… …

Even when we follow the government subsidy scheme, we have still to bear in mind the fact that professors in Wuhan University teach only 4 to 6 hours a week and are allowed to take extra jobs outside with pay, while the Hua Chung teachers have to carry 10 to 14 lectures a week and are not allowed to carry extra remunerative jobs outside. We feel proud of our arrangement, but while the financial conditions are as they have been, we ought to give some kind of recognition to the willingness of our people to maintain a good tradition at their own cost. We recommended in our joint letter dated October 7th that as long as there is the need, and as far as our resources are permitting, we should pay our men more than the government universities pay theirs. I do not know what the United Board will say about this, but as far as I know, not all the Christian universities which have joined the United Board are following the same scheme in paying salaries and subsidies to faculty and staff members.

Before I close I would like to report the following figures:

Total number of students registered this term: 536

Old students	316
New students	220
Total	536
Men students	344
Women students	192
Total	536

(Note: Of the total number, 13 students have already withdrawn, some by doctor's orders, and others to enter national universities where there are no fees charged.)

Of the total number of students, 40.8% are Christians, against

29% a year ago in Wu Chang, and 15% two years ago in Hsichow.

By departments the students are:

Chinese	30
English	80
Econ. & Com.	168
History	29
Biology	24
Chemistry	50
Physics	45
Education	97
Total	523

(Note: not counting the students who have left.)

……

Yours sincerely,
Francis C. M. Wei

130. To Mr. W. Reginald Wheeler (September 15, 1947)

Dear Mr. Wheeler:

……

We are just in the rush of registering students in the new academic year. It will be another week before we know the exact enrollment, but my guess is that there will be about 310 old students and 230 new ones, making a total of 540 students, one third being women. This will mean the full capacity of all our hostels, but we have to take in a certain number of new students because 3,488 candidates took our entrance examinations in August. Besides, 132 recommended students are expected from our affiliated Christian middle schools for admission without examination, these students being in the upper quarter of their classes.

……

Yours sincerely,
Francis C. M. Wei

131. To Professor Kenneth S. Latourette (January 17, 1948)

Dear Professor Latourette:

……

As I have said in my letter to Burton Rogers, if Burton should have other reasons for declining the offer of the Yale-in-China Association to join the Hua Chung faculty for a five year term beginning from July 1, 1948, I would not be in a position to bring much pressure to bear on his decision. But if Burton could not be persuaded to change his mind, I would like to urge you, as Chairman of Personnel Committee, to start at once to locate another man to take Burton's place on the Hua Chung faculty beginning with the Fall Term of the academic year 1948—1949. If you should be able to find a qualified man to teach English literature and composition in Hua Chung as a Yale appointee for the opening of the term after summer, it would be just fine. But I know how difficult it is sometime for any mission to get a man to teach in a definite field. To facilitate the work of your Personnel Committee, I would like to list the following fields in order of urgency in which we would like you to send us a well qualified man as a teacher:

Biology, Physics, Mathematics, Music, English, Accounting, and Sociology.

……

We do not have a Department of Sociology, because we cannot find trained sociologists to teach subject in China as it ought to be taught. You will perhaps agree that to teach Sociology as it has been developed in the west, either in America or in Europe, would not go very far in helping to develop that field in China. Sociology is one of the subjects which has particularly a strong local coloring. Therefore if you should send us a sociologist, we would like him or her to spend much time on the first hand study of the Chinese social background, social institutions, social trends and social problems, with the hope that materials may be accumulated in due course of time in the teaching of sociology in China.

……

The kind of man we want to have on our faculty ought to be a Christian with convictions, with at least one or two years' post graduate work in his own field, preferably with some teaching experience, eager to learn more both in China and during furloughs in the homeland, ready to cooperate with people of different nationalities and different church affiliations, and have a genuine respect for China and the Chinese people. Several years ago, such people were few on the faculties of Christian universities in China. I used to bemoan the fact that many of our Chinese faculty members had much better qualifications and experience in teaching than our Western colleagues sent by missions. But since our return to Wu Chang a year and a half ago, we have been able to get from the missions a goodly number of missionary teachers of the genuinely scholarly type and with fine training. In appointing additional missionaries to our staff, we would not want to lower that standard. Half of our missionary staff at present have good Ph. D. degrees from America or Great Britain, and the others have at least a good M. A. degree with a number of years of teaching experience. In my judgment, they fulfill well the description I have given you above.

…… ……

Yours sincerely,
Francis C. M. Wei

132. To Mr. Oliver S. Lyford (January 23, 1948)

Dear Mr. Lyford:

…… ……

This is the fourth day of our term examinations which will last until January 30, and the winter vacation will begin on January 31 to last until February 22 when the second term will begin.

The Senate has decided on the following charges for the next term:

I. Tuition	N. C. $1,600,000
Library, Medical, Athletics & Registration	800,000
II. Hostel Fees	300,000
Furniture Rental (in students' rooms)	40,000

III. General Breakage Deposit	200,000	
Light & Water Deposit	600,000	
Deposit for Board	2,000,000	
Total	N.C. $5,540,000	
IV. Book Rental	40,000 per course	
Laboratory		
Physics	100,000 per course	
Biology	100,000 per course	
Chemistry	150,000 per course	

Music fees have not been quite decided yet. We have been following the ratio of five times the fees of the Fall Term. Only the charges under I may be counted as income from fees for the university. If we should have 475 students next term (we always reckon about 15% drop from the enrollment of the first term; if so, the enrollment may be only 450) our income items from fees would still be met provided the exchange for the U. S. dollar would not shoot up too high. At any rate we are watching our budget very closely and try our best to keep within the limits as approved by the United Board, unless the situation should get out of control and then we would report for permission to reconsider our budget, which is not likely.

I do not propose to leave the university at all during the vacation but stay here and try to catch up with my correspondence which is very much in arrears, and also to map out my courses of lectures for the second term.

…… ……

Yours sincerely,
Francis C. M. Wei

133. To Mr. J. Earl Fowler (January 29, 1948)

My dear Earl:

…… ……

I am glad to know that we have the permission to engage a

competent architect for the preliminary planning of the campus. Architects are available, but in order to save the fees as well as to get the best work done, we are trying to get Mr. May, an English architect from the M. M. S. now visiting in China under the English Methodist Church. Mr. Constantine has already spoken to Mr. Heady about this and Mr. Heady is willing to consult Mr. May, now in Hunan, whether when he gets here in February, he will be able to help us in this planning. If he should be unavailable, then we would have to look around for a commercial architect. We shall keep you informed of the developments.

… …

It is still too early to say whether we shall be able to achieve our end. But the spirit of the fellows there was certainly good. The day before yesterday I was in Han Kou to see another of my former students in oil business. I mentioned this campaign and he promised at once to find a hundred million dollars for me. So it goes, and I cannot help feeling that education is a worthwhile business, because students would be appreciative after they had had a few years in life.

… …

Yours affectionately,
Francis C. M. Wei

134. To Mr. Oliver S. Lyford (March 9, 1948)

Dear Mr. Lyford:

… …

The second term began on February 23, with registration of students on the 23rd, 24th, and 25th, and with lectures beginning on February 26. Everything went off well and according to schedule. With scholarships and special aids to students, most of the students were able to register, but about one quarter of them had to postpone the payment of one-half their board. Board for the whole term was N. C. $4,000,000. The other fees and deposits amounted to about N. C. $3,600,000. This total is much less than the total in other private schools and colleges in our city or in Han Kou. It was because the figures were announced a week before the closing of the first term towards the end of January, and the Senate decided not to change them, except the deposit for the students board, which was only received for the student to be used by themselves.

Up-to-date we have 468 students already fully registered and now attending classes. About three or four more are on sick leave, granted by the Dean the General Faculty, and they may return in a few days. The total enrollment for the term may go up to 470.

………

As to enrollment, we had 537 in September. Every year in the second term have had a drop of 15%. On that reckoning the normal enrollment for this should be 456. However, we have four students who transferred from other colleges. Twenty-four registered for the transfer examinations and paid registration fee of $50,000 each. Only fourteen of these students came for the examinations, and four passed. Another four students have returned to us after a term or a year's leave of absence. Adding these eight to the 45 we get our present enrollment without counting the few more to come back from sick leave. This enrollment is very encouraging in view of the very severe economic conditions in our part of the country.

………

Everything seems to be going on well here. I find the students in much better spirit than ever before. They are seeking all the time for advice with regard to everything they try to do. As long as that spirit continues, we need to fear no internal trouble. It is our hope that we may be able to maintain the morale and improve it until our tradition is further consolidated in possible two to three years more, before we take the next step to increase our enrollment from about 600 to 800. If everything goes well, our enrollment ought to be approaching 600 next September. We shall not reach the final goal of 800 until perhaps five years from now. Please remember that although it is only the third year after the war in China, we are already in the fifth year as far as the implementation of the Ten-Year Plan is concerned. Now the wisest thing to do is to carry on and develop gradually instead of rushing our steps, while I hope you will consider advisable.

…… ……

Yours sincerely,
Francis C. M. Wei

135. To Mr. J. Earl Fowler (March 23, 1948)

Dear Earl:

…… ……

Enclosed please find a copy of the statistics of the enrollment for this second term of the year, as prepared by the Registrar's Office. You will find that our total enrollment is 469: 173 of them are women; and 296 men. 211 Christian students make exactly 45% of the total enrollment, but 32 students are being prepared for Baptism. When these students are baptized on Easter or shortly afterwards, we shall have more than 50% Christian students, which is encouraging. I have marked on the Statistical Report the order of the size of groups by provinces, as well as by departments, for you report to the Hua Chung Committee when it meets. You will note that 16 provinces are represented with more than half from the provinces of Hunan and Hupeh.

…… ……

Yours affectionately,
Francis C. M. Wei

136. To Mr. J. Earl Fowler (April 13, 1948)

Dear Mr. Fowler:

…… ……

It is very essential that the Overseas Department should find somebody to replace Miss Hutton because our English Department will be very shorthanded next year, especially now that there is the uncertainty about the return of Walter Allen and his wife. We ought to have really two more teachers of English from America since Miss Hutton is resigning and Walter Allen may not return.

…… ……

Yours sincerely,
Francis C. M. Wei

137. To Rev. Arthur M. Sherman (June 1, 1948)

Dear Dr. Sherman:

…… ……

While I am writing, I would like to report to you and through you to the Hua Chung Committee that things are very quiet here in Hua Chung. Today is June First, and it was this day a year ago when some of the Wu Han University students were killed by the military. For sometimes I was afraid that there might be some student disturbances on this day. The government has been taking very strict precautions, and I have been talking quietly to our own students about the seriousness of the situation. Our students are very sensible. On Sunday, that is, the day before yesterday, some of them went to Wuhan University to attend a Memorial Ceremony there and came back without getting excited. Today they are all going to classes. With this day over I am confident that we shall be able to complete the term without any mishap, unless there should be some unexpected event arising from the general situation, which is not likely.

…… ……

As ever,
Francis C. M. Wei

138. To Mr. J. Earl Fowler (July 28, 1948)

My dear Earl:

…… ……

If you refer to the size of the faculty and enrollment of students for the year 1947—1948, and compare them with the figures given in the Ten-Year Plan, you will notice that we have already completed the fifth year of the Plan, and in September we shall be on the sixth year. But if you should refer to the financial report of the treasurer, you will find that we had for the last year a budget of approximately U. S. $58,000, which will remain the same for the next year; together with 10 Sheng Kung Huei missionaries, 3 Methodist, 2 London Missionary Society, 1 Reformed Church, and 1 Yale-in-China, with salaries paid by their own boards, which are reckoned for budgeting purposes in China at the rate of U. S. $1,200 each. Also there are five missionary wives, three of whom are giving practically full time to the work in the university, and two part-time, which I count as one full-time, so that we have altogether four full-time wives. These four added to the salaries of the regular missionary workers make twenty-one; therefore the budget ought to be U. S. $25,200 for the missionaries. Adding this U. S. $25,200 to the budget of U. S. $58,000, we have only U. S. $83,200, which is much less than the budget estimated to be necessary even for the first year of the Ten-Year Plan, which is U. S. $115,000. In my report tried to point out to the Directors that:

"The budget is still U. S. $35,000 short of the estimated expenditure of the First Year of the Plan. One-third of this shortage has been borne by the library and scientific equipment items, which have, however, not felt the effect so seriously, because the rehabilitation funds have made up this shortage for the last two years; but the other two-thirds taken from the salary items has had grave consequences. Chinese members of the teaching and administrative staffs have been inadequately paid."

I know that the United Board may criticize us because we have at present over 500 students, instead of 350, but circumstances since our return to Wu Chang have made it almost impossible for us to confine ourselves to an enrollment of 350 students, or even 400. We have been very cautious in increasing our enrollment, and if you compare it with the enrollment in most of the other Christian college in China at the present time, you would find that our enrollment is reasonable. You will find action taken by the Board of Directors, "Voted #16" that the enrollment for the next academic year 1948—1949 ought to be not more than 600, with not more than 200 new students. The reasons for this act are given in the Minutes, and I hope that the Hua Chung Committee of the United Board will approve this action.

We are now having entrance examinations. Over 2,000 candidates are taking them in three centers, but we shall have to select from this number of candidates only about 120, i. e., one out of every 17, because we have already had 120 students recommended for admission without examination by the various affiliated Christian middle schools, and of this number experience teaches us that we may expect only about 70%, i. e. 84.

With regard to our faculty, I would like to say that its standard has improved since rehabilitation, not only among the Chinese, but also among the missionary members. Next year we shall have a teaching staff with 19 holding the Ph. D. degree, and about 12 the Masters degree, and the rest only the Bachelor's degree or equivalent. Everything is being done to raise the standards of the students, but when the standards in the middle schools, both Christian and non-Christian, still remain low, it means a great deal of effort in order to raise own standards.

There were about 190 sophomores during the last year; more than 40 of them did not qualify to take the intermediate examinations; of the 147 allowed to take the intermediate examinations, only 113 got clear passes; 23 of them have to take supplementary examinations in September before they will be allowed to enter the junior year. Even if all of these should pass and return to the university next term, we shall have only two-thirds of the last-year's sophomores in the junior class. Elimination is very heavy, and it shows how hard we have been working to maintain our standards.

I would like to call the attention of the Hua Chung Committee to the Language School. This is not expansion by any means. It is a type of service for the new missionaries, and it has not cost the university any money. Both the capital and the operating funds have been provided by the missions interested in the project, or from fees charged to the students.

I would also call the attention of the Hua Chung Committee to our Theological work, which we have not called a school or a department because so far every student who takes theological work has to work for his or her degree in one of the departments recognized by the Ministry of Education in Nanking. The Theological course is made possible by adding another year to the students' work so as to give the extra time required for about the equivalent of another major. We have been operating on this scheme for three years now, and in another year we shall be able to graduate students who have taken this combined and Theology course.

....

Yours sincerely,
Francis C. M. Wei

139. To Mr. J. Earl Fowler (August 16, 1948)

Dear Earl:

....

The entrance examinations are all over now, and some of the faculty members are busy reading their 2,000 papers in every subject. We have already 120 recommended students, and if 75% of them should come, there would be 85 or 90 of them. Then we will select about 110 to 120 from the 2,000 candidates to make up the 200 freshmen for this year.

Troops have not entered our compound here yet, or any of our college houses outside. We had a little bit of a tilt with the military authorities just about two weeks ago. The contractor building the five double houses on the new land was getting the foundation dug, and the military came along and said that they were going to build some pill boxes in that neighborhood, and they wanted to stop the contractor from putting in the foundation. We went to headquarters, and the day after that the soldiers came and pulled out their own stakes. Our own construction is now under way, but it will probably be the end of September before the first double houses will be completed, and the other three will probably not be too ready until the end of October. This will mean our men students will be crowded for two months before the congestion can be relieved with the moving of our families out of Po Yu Hostel.

…… ……

Yours sincerely,
Francis C. M. Wei

140. To Mr. J. Earl Fowler (October 5, 1948)

My dear Earl:

…… ……

None of us in Hua Chung is allowed to do any work outside, with or without remuneration, except with specific permission of the Senate. Miss Cox has never taught in Wuhan University. She taught a few hours during the last year in St. Hilda's School, but that was a part of the understanding when she joined the Hua Chung faculty, and it received the sanction of Bishop Gilman. Mr. Constantine and Dr. Taai gave two lectures a week during the last year in the Central China Union Theological Seminary without extra remuneration, and that arrangement was sanctioned by the Senate. Neither Mr. Mark Tseng, the Librarian, nor Mrs. Tseng Sen tse (née Miss Chen Sung, not Mark Tseng's wife), Assistant Librarian, was willing to teach part-time in the Boone Library School, and therefore we did not ask the Senate for permission for them to teach in the Boone Library School, and Mr. Tseng did not understand that.

The new term is under way with an enrollment of 572 students, which is only 35 more than the enrollment a year ago. In this term we have only 176 new students. Of this number 96 are from Christian middle schools and 80 from other schools. About one-half of the new students are Christians, and that will make the Christian percentage of all the students just about one-half too.

…… ……

Yours affectionately,
Francis C. M. Wei

141. To Dr. William P. Fenn (October 26, 1948)

Dear Dr. Fenn:

……

Now I am answering your questions in the order of the questionnaire, dated September 29, 1948.

ENROLLMENT 573. A year ago we had 537. The increase is only 36.

MEN AND WOMEN STUDENTS. The number of women students this year is 195 out of the total enrollment of 573. It is, therefore, approximately one-third.

TREND OF STUDENT INTERESTS. According to the enrollment by schools and departments, the general trend is towards greater interest in professional training. Our largest department is Economics-Commerce with 160. Next is Education with 72 in "Education" and 39 in "Teachers Training." Then comes English, with 78, and that is probably not for its cultural value, but for its practical use. The most popular courses among women students are Education and Music. We have, however, a goodly enrollment in Chinese Literature of both men and women students, and that is for cultural purposes. Pure Science is not so popular as before the war, but its importance remains as ever.

WAR-TIME HANDICAPS. Our war-time handicaps are still serious. Repairs of the buildings are uncompleted. We need more teaching equipment both in the library and in the science laboratories. We may say that in our rehabilitation of the library we have been making good progress, but there are still serious gaps in our library collection and in our science equipment. Because of our heavy losses during the war, over 90% of our books and 70% of our science equipment were lost and nor recovered.

TEACHING STAFF. Too few teachers in proportion to the size of the classes, particularly in Philosophy, the Social Science, and English. Logic, Ethics, and Introduction to Philosophy are required by the government, and the President is the only one to teach those courses in addition to his administrative duties. The Logic class is over 160 this term, and so also the course in Introduction to Philosophy, and next term the Ethics class will be even larger. Last spring it was over 180. The class in Sociology taught by Dean John C. F. Lo was 120 last term, and his class in General Psychology is always more than 100.

This year we have only one of our faculty abroad, and that is Mr. Donald Wang of the Department of English Literature. We have to omit many electives in English, in the social sciences, and second and third-year foreign languages because of inadequate staff. We are providing all the courses required by the government with, however, large classes.

As to additions to the staff this year, we have none. All new appointments are replacements.

NEW COURSES. None this year. There is only a reshuffling of courses to meet government requirements or to suit our present staff.

TUITION. For this term our tuition is on the basis of the Gold Yuan currency. Before the opening of the term we reckoned that it ought to be about 300 catties (or 400 lb.) of rice, but with the sudden increase of prices, we actually got less in terms of the new currency.

For aiding needy students we have about 120 scholarships, costing the university approximately U. S. $1800 a year. Scholarships are divided into three classes and are awarded to applicants according to their records of the previous two terms and according to their financial needs. The first-class scholarship is of the fees paid to the university (not including Board and Lodging); second-class, just the fees; third-class, 3/4 of the fees.

HEALTH OF THE STUDENTS. This is our third year after returning to Wu Chang, and there has been a steady improvement of the health of students, according to the report of our college physicians on the physical examinations. So far very few of our students are cut off from their families. Those who were originally from the Communist-occupied areas have their families now in the government-controlled regions. We have not been receiving any supplementary food from the National Student Relief Committee or any other source. We had a little bit from the students Relief Committee through the local YMCA, but that has stopped.

RELIGIOUS LIFE OF THE SCHOOL. Professor David F. Anderson, chairman of our Chapel Committee, has submitted the following report, which is being quoted in to:

1)"What religious activities do the students have?"

a. Regular morning chapel services five days a week and an hour's service on Sunday evening.

b. Fellowship group meeting every Friday night—about fifteen such groups are meeting this term in teachers' houses.

c. Communion services organized by the Fellowships — Episcopal every Sunday, Church of Christ in China and Methodist combined once a month.

d. Evening prayers in the women's hostel twice a week, London Mission Hostel once a week.

e. Service activities: 1) Chapel Choir, 2) Illiteracy classes, 3) Sunday Schools for faculty children and for outside children, 4) St. Thomas Society, 5) Assisting at Baby Clinic for mothers and babies.

f. Classes for non-Christian students in English and Chinese.

2)"What religious activities are student-led?"

Students participate in the planning of all religious activities, and take the lead in organizing the work of the Fellowships, the hostel prayers, and service activities.

3) "Is there a trend among non-Christian students to become Christian?"

This trend begun during the war is still strongly marked. Christianity is in danger of being popular. The political and economic situation engenders an attitude of pessimism and even despair, which causes students to feel acutely their own lack of faith and spiritual dynamic, and so makes them ready to consider what Christianity has to offer. Thirty-nine students were baptized in the course of the last academic year, and a number of students had already come forward asking for instruction this year.

4)"What extra-curricular religious activities are faculty-led?"

The faculty conducted the chapel services, and act as advisors in Fellowship groups which may mean either opening a discussion or taking part in one where a student had given the initial talk. Hostel prayers are largely conducted by the students themselves.

5) "Do you have a chaplain or a faculty advisory committee on student religious activities?"

We expect all Christians on the Faculty to take an active share in religious work rather than to depend largely on one chaplain. The organization of the chapel services is in the hands of a committee of whom three-quarters are students, the remainder teachers. Fellowship groups elect a student committee and faculty members are called in as advisors as required.

... ...

Yours sincerely,
Francis C. M. Wei

142. To Mr. J. Earl Fowler (November 4, 1948)

Dear Earl:

... ...

My comment on his note 11) is that we have enough organized athletics, but the present physical director is not the best man, so he has not been able to make a great deal of use of the field outside. As to his 12), the present lay-out may seem a bit topsy-turvy, but we cannot really finish the job until we have appointed a competent architect, who will give considerable time to the details. That is why from the beginning of this term I have been urging the Senate to give this matter more attention. It is quite apparent that Mr. Bergamini cannot remain our official architect, since he is much too occupied in the Philippines and cannot even take a brief visit to Wu Chang.

... ...

His note 13) with regard to publicity is much to the point. We need a publicity Secretary because the Chinese Alumni Bulletin is already keeping our alumni on the faculty busy, and the Weekly English News letter keeps the English Department busy enough. His last note with regard to the political consciousness of our students is correct. Our students are busy with their studies, and therefore do not take much interest in political activities, but from the Wall papers(on the Bulletin Boards)they are interested just the same.

... ...

We are in the midst of our mid-term examinations. Students are busy. They are particularly happy because both the men and women students have enough rice for the term, while other schools such Wuhan, Changsha, and others in this center have found it very difficult to get enough rice for the students and faculty.

... ...

Yours affectionately,
Francis C. M. Wei

143. To Mr. J. Earl Fowler (November 16, 1948)

Dear Earl:

... ...

The students have enough rice for the balance of the term, and they are having pretty decent food in both the men's and women's dining rooms. We have to begin to think about the winter vacation, which will be almost a month, and how to get rice for the students when the second term re-opens in February will be very serious problem. Many provincial schools are contemplating early closing because they have not been able to buy rice or because they have not had the money to buy rice with. Wuhan University has been on strike several times for the same reason, and I should not be surprised at all that by the beginning of January everyone of the schools here except the Christian middle schools and our college will be closed. We collected boarding fees at the beginning of the term and required the students to buy enough foodstuff for the whole term.

As to the faculty members, most of them are getting enough rice to last for at least a month, and with the increased pay they are going to store up more for the future. I am urging everyone to put as much money as possible into rice, oil, and fuel, because at least after the Chinese New Year those things will go up tremendously if they should be available in the market. I believe they will be available, but prices will be prohibitive.

... ...

Yours affectionately,
Francis C. M. Wei

144. To Mr. J. Earl Fowler (November 23, 1948)

Dear Earl:

... ...

At the present moment I have been urging our students, both men and women, to buy rice not only for this term for which they have practically enough, but also for the winter vacation and for the next term. It is quite possible that after the Chinese New Year the price of rice will shoot up again. Of course, it is difficult for many poor students to find money at the present moment to store up rice. However, the Senate may approve my proposal to advance the equivalent of about U. S. $10 to every scholarships students for buying rice, which is to be used only during the second term, and in the meantime it will be stored in one of the college buildings for safekeeping. This, of course, involves a certain amount of risk, but it is a risk that we ought to accept. Just at the present moment the price of rice is more reasonable than it has been for the last six weeks, and it may drop clarified.

... ...

As to my forecast of the situation, it is about the same as in my previous letters. I was talking with a group of men students during the last week, and they say that very few of the students would leave the University so long as the President is still here. I assured them that I had no place to go, and I had no intention of leaving. There is no question of the loyalty of the whole of the faculty and of all the students. In spite of the very disturbing circumstances, you do not see a single ripple on the surface of our calm and peaceful life.

...   ...

Yours affectionately,
Francis C. M. Wei

145. To Dr. Robert J. McMullen (December 7, 1948)

My dear Dr. McMullen:

...   ...

(2) The psychological atmosphere on our campus. Everybody says that the students are absurdly calm, and the faculty well-balanced in their judgment. It is difficult to report what the attitude of our Directors is because the Board as a whole has not met since June. As far as the whole campus is concerned, I may say that we are calm, determined, but watchful. We are prepared to accept what comes and do our best, standing however firmly on our Christian principles.

(3) So far only one woman student and two men students have left. The woman student left more than a month ago, and she went back to Chungking because her whole family left Han Kou. The two men students who have left are Overseas Chinese from Singapore. They were very reluctant to leave, but they had to go because their fathers in Singapore said to them that either they leave China, or stop their studies entirely.

(4) By action of the Council of Advice of the Bishop of Han Kou, two American wives with small babies have gone to Hong Kong to wait for further development in our part of the country. The husbands have already returned to continue with their teaching here after only nine-days' absence, to take their families to Hong Kong.

...   ...

Now as to the second part of my statement dealing with the plans for the future:

...   ...

(4) In case our program had to be discontinued and the institution closed for a period when Christian education could not be carried on any

further, then:

(a) We would make plans to protect the buildings and equipment the best we could under the circumstances confronting us. There is very little use to make preparation now because we do not know what the situation will be.

(b) Faculty. It is our idea to divide the faculty into three groups:

(1) The key people, who are only about one-quarter of the Chinese members of the faculty and staff whom we would want to maintain as long as there is the least bit of hope to revive the work after the closing by giving them whatever salaries and subsidies are possible.

(2) The second group which we would wish to have a lien on by paying them subsidies for at least two years. This would be another quarter of the Chinese members of the faculty and staff.

(3) The rest about 40%—50%, mainly clerks and assistants, for whom we would meet only our contract obligations, and most of them have only one-year appointments until the end of next July.

(c) As to students. In the eventuality of our having to discontinue our work and close the institution, most of the students would probably be gone anyway, some to discontinue their studies, and others to transfer to other institutions in the safer parts of the country. Perhaps only a few may stay with us as long as possible, and we will carry in our teaching in a sort of guerrilla fashion.

……

Yours sincerely,
Francis C. M. Wei

146. To Mr. J. Earl Fowler (December 14, 1948)

Dear Earl:

This last week has been very uneventful, although it is full of anxieties. Just to give you an idea of how I spend my time, besides my duties in the office and my teaching, I spent a week ago Monday afternoon attending a faculty meeting at which the faculty decided not give permission to our own students to study in another institution as refugee students, but if anyone should wish transfer to another college or university, we would give him or her a certificate of transfer as in usual times.

On last Tuesday there was a meeting of the Theological staff in the afternoon in the Starratt house, and we discussed mostly the Theological Bulletin in Chinese that we want to get out a first issue about the beginning of next year. On Wednesday the Theological staff met with all the Theological students, as they do every other week, to discuss some of the practical religious problems. Friday evening is the time when we have a large number of discussion groups in the different faculty houses. Because my time is so uncertain, I cannot have a group of my own, but recently different groups have been drafting me to answer questions. Last Friday I went to Richard Bien's house and discussed with his group the question of "What is Christian Faith" and whether religion is entirely subjective.

…… ……

Yours sincerely,
Francis C. M. Wei

147. To Mr. J. Earl Fowler (December 21, 1948)

Dear Earl:

…… ……

All classes are going on as usual, and visitors coming from outside would not know that there was fighting in the country and that people were so nervous in other parts of the country, if they just watched our students and talked to our faculty members here.

We have made practically every preparation necessary to meet any emergency, but of course, there may be things for which we cannot make any preparation. So far four more students have gone on account of the situation by order of their parents. Last week after I had mailed my last-week's letter to you, the principals of the Christian middle schools in the Wuhan Center had an emergency meeting and asked Dr. Huang P'u and me to be with them. After lengthy discussion it was decided to carry in all the Christian middle schools, according to schedule, and close for the winter vacation only after the middle of January. Our decision on Monday a week ago had a great deal of influence on the decision of the principals of the Christian middle schools.

... ...

Yours affectionately,
Francis C. M. Wei

148. To Dr. Robert J. McMullen (January 4, 1949)

Dear Dr. McMullen:

... ...

We have had a very happy time during the Christmas and New Year Season with the usual services, celebrations, and festivities. The morale of our faculty and students remains good. As soon as the announcement of the Senate was made three weeks ago that Hua Chung would not close the term earlier than the scheduled time, the students settled down to work, and they are now busy in their preparation for the term examinations. Only about a dozen students have so far left on account of the situation, mostly to go back to Canton and Hong Kong by order of their families. We do not permit any students to go to another institution as refugee students, as our work is going on as usual, but any students may transfer to another institution when they have finished this term. Our term examinations will begin on January 7 and finish on the 19th, with the winter vacation starting on January 20. Fortunately, at the beginning of the term adequate preparations were made for the food of the students for the whole term. Only the men students have had to pay an extra amount for board, equivalent to less than U. S. $2 per person. They have been having fairly good food, certainly much better than the students had in Hsichow during the war. The faculty members are being paid from month to month according to the bank rate of exchange, which has been rather favorable.

... ...

On December 13, I came back from a meeting with the Secretary-in-Chief of the Military Headquarters in Han Kou and reported it to our Senate meeting on the same afternoon; and it was unanimously decided by the Senate that we should carry on our work during this term according to schedule, which we are now doing. Hua Chung University is a very democratic institution, and the President has to execute all the actions taken by the Senate. Personally, I shall fully agree with the decision of the Senate, which seldom acts contrary to my advice. The most encouraging thing is that the whole faculties are of the same opinion and willing to take the same stand, the students being most cooperative.

There is little that we can do in preparation for a crisis. Members of our faculty and staff are storing up foodstuffs, in case they should become scared or difficult to get later on in the spring. The Treasurer's office is prepared to advance a reasonable amount of money for such purchases, but our people have not asked for that yet. They are doing everything possible with the monthly payments, which are made on the 25th of each month according to the exchange rate at the time.

If we should re-open at the middle of February, our enrollment would certainly be much smaller, possibly only two-thirds of our enrollment in September.

…… ……

Yours sincerely,
Francis C. M. Wei

149. To Mr. J. Earl Fowler (January 10, 1949)

Dear Earl:

…… ……

We are in the midst of our term examinations, which will be finished on the 19th. There is every reason for us to believe that we shall be able to close the term without any mishap on January 20, but whether we shall be able to re-open on February 14 and 15 for the second term is problematical.

…… ……

Perhaps 90% of the students will leave for the winter vacation; and if we should re-open on February 14, we may not have more than two-thirds of the enrollment in September. All the faculty and staff are staying during the vacation except Paul Ward, Alfred Starratt, and Walter Allen, who are going to Hong Kong to visit their families, or to bring up freight in the case of Walter Allen.

…… ……

Yours affectionately,
Francis C. M. Wei

150. To Rev. Robert J. McMullen (January 26, 1949)

Dear Dr. McMullen:

…… ……

You have more news about the situation in China perhaps than we do here but our local papers are very free in publishing news from all sources. The peace talk is going on and fighting has practically stopped on all fronts. On the other hand, one sees all signs of preparation for war; and unless one knows the background, one may easily feel scared. We are in the midst of our winter vacation, which began on January 20. 80% of the students have gone home with only 20% remaining in the hostels. All the faculty and staff members are staying for the vacation, except three American missionaries, two of whom have gone to visit their families in Hong Kong for the vacation, and a third has gone to Hong Kong to fetch his baggage, which had been shipped from America to Shanghai in the fall and redirected to Hong Kong.

We are making full preparations to start the second semester on February 14, but it is still uncertain whether circumstances will permit. My guess is that we may be able to start the second term, but with a much smaller enrollment perhaps only two-thirds that of last September. So far we have been successful in keeping the troops out from our buildings, but everyday we have to watch the situation and talk to the officers who come in to look around. The military authorities have been very cooperative, and we have placards from all of them, saying that our buildings are not to be occupied by troops.

… …

Yours sincerely,
Francis, C. M. Wei

151. To Dr. Robert J. McMullen (February 9, 1949)

Dear Dr. McMullen:

… …

In September the enrollment was 572 students, of whom 377 were men, and 195 women. Breaking the number up into the four classes, the figures were 47 seniors, 139 juniors, 195 sophomores, and 191 freshmen. During the term one junior withdrew, seven sophomores, and twenty-six freshmen, leaving 538 students who completed the term's work with term examinations. In view of the situation and the unusual circumstances, this was not at all bad record.

Of the total enrollment of 572, 261 were graduated from Christian middle schools, making 45% of the total. 269 were Christians, which was 47% of the total. This number of Christian students does not include a number of students baptized during the term.

In the whole University 324 were in the College of Arts during the last term: 43 Chinese majors, 78 English, 160 Economics, 43 History. 137 in the College of Science: 29 Biology, 53 Chemistry, 55 Physics. 111 in the College of Education: 72 Education, 39 Teacher Training.

Again during the last term there were 56 on the teaching staff as follows:

ARTS	FULL-TIME	PART-TIME
Chinese	8	0
English	7	3
Economics	4	1
History	4	0
Philosophy, Psychology, Religion, and Theology	<u>3</u>	<u>2</u>
Total	26	6

SCIENCE	FULL-TIME	PART-TIME
Physics	4	0
Chemistry	4	0
Biology	4	0
Mathematics	2	0
Total	14	0
EDUCATION	5	0
MUSIC	3	2
Total	8	2

N. B. By full-time is meant any faculty member who is giving his whole time to the University, even though he spends part of his time in Administration. For instance, the President and Treasurer, Dean and Registrar.

Of the total teaching staff, 18 hold Ph. D. or Sc. D. degrees; 12 M. A.'s; 18 B. A.'s; 8 Professional Diplomas or all old Chinese scholars.

Taking the teaching staff again, of the total of 56, 16 are salaried missionaries, 6 volunteer wives, 22 Chinese Christians, totaling 44, or 78.6%. Only 12 are non-Christian.

There are 16 full-time members of the administrative staff, including clerks. Of this number two are missionary wives, 7 Chinese Christians, together making a total of 56.3% Christians, and 7 non-Christians who are mainly clerks. We are proud of this high percentage of Christians on the faculty, and even on the administrative staff.

…………

Yours sincerely,
Francis C. M. Wei

152. To Dr. Robert J. McMullen (February 17, 1949)

My dear Bob:

…………

We registered our students during the last three days, and lectures have all ready started today in full swing. As I have written previously, we had expected only about 300 students, or perhaps 350, but the Registrar's office reported yesterday afternoon that 347 had already registered, and about a dozen more are registering today, bringing the total up to 360. About 120 students are on the dean's list of Leave of Absence for one or two weeks. I believe only about 90 of these will come in time for registration. The prospects are very good that we shall have an enrollment of 450, against 572 for the beginning of the first term. Every year we have a usual drop of 15% in the enrollment of the second term over the first. With our prospective enrollment of 450, we shall have only about 30 students fewer than we would expect on a normal year. We feel very much encouraged over this good enrollment, and I hope we may be able to carry through this semester without interruption.

....

Yours sincerely,
Francis C. M. Wei

153. To Rt. Rev. Jno. B. Bentley (February 24, 1949)

Dear Bishop Bentley:

....

Hua Chung University re-opened for the second term on February 14 with lectures starting on February 17. At present we have just about 410 students men and women, and students are still coming in everyday from distant parts. 90 students have leave of absence from the Dean's Office, and I trust that they are waiting to get their funds together in order to pay their fees, perhaps only 40 or 50 more will come to bring our enrollment this term up to 450. Last term we had 572, but even in a normal year our enrollment in the second term dropped by 15%. Based on this calculation we would have 450 students this term if things were normal, but owing to the circumstances, largely financial, the enrollment may not be higher than 450, which we would consider very good. Already 140 women are here, and perhaps 10 or 15 more will turn up within this week, retaining the proportion of one-third women for the whole enrollment.

……

Yours sincerely,
Francis C. M. Wei

154. To Dr. Robert J. McMullen (February 24, 1949)

Dear Dr. McMullen:

……

Our enrollment up-to-date is only 410, of whom about 140 are women, but there are 90 students still on the Dean's list for Leave of Absence. Owing to financial difficulties only about half of these are likely to come back within the next week. Registration closes on March 3. In ordinary times we allow the students to be late for only one week, but owing to the present situation the Senate decided a month ago to extend that period to two weeks, counting from the first day of lectures.

……

Consequently about 170 students asked for relief subsidies to pay their fees. The Senate has a committee to make the grants, and the committee met three days ago to consider all the applications. They have had to reduce the number as far as possible. They have considered all the circumstances with the help of a popular ballot done by the student organization, indicating how many would support a certain application and how many were against it. The result was that relief was granted to 125 students, varying from 1 tan of rice to 2 ½tan. The total amount required for this relief is 225 tan of rice, costing Sliver $9 per tan.

……

But many students returning during the coming week, and some others who have not received the grant, may need further help. The committee is still investigating in order to meet real needs. We are allowing students to postpone the payment of part of their fees until the end of March, and by that time perhaps further relief will be needed. The Board of Directors met on February 5 and authorized our request at the United Board for U. S. ＄1,500 for Student Relief and to make up the necessary remitting of fees in many cases. This recommendation by the Directors is among the actions included in the Minutes which are being sent to you as soon as they are mimeographed. I hope that this will meet with the approval of the Hua Chung Committee of the United Board. We hoped that this amount would at least come out of the special contribution made by the National Council of the Protestant Episcopal Church from the Presiding Bishop's Fund to the United Board, from which, according to Earl Fowler's letter received sometimes ago, we may expect as much as U. S. ＄20,000. I have written to you already about this, but no definite word has yet come from you. In your letter you said you were still waiting for the actions of the Budget Committee of the United Board.

…… ……

The faculty and students are still keeping up their splendid morale, although many are still waiting eagerly to see how the peace talks will come on. The prospect seems to be much better just at the present time than it was two weeks ago, but it is silly for our emotions to depend upon the newspaper reports which vary from day to day. I am going out this afternoon to a meeting of the local leaders, and I hope to get some "inside dope" from a person who has just returned from an important mission to the North. I am not in politics, and I take great care not to be involved in any, but it is necessary for me to maintain all my contacts, so as to keep Hua Chung in its proper place in the Wuhan community. Our reputation is getting better and better in all circles, and it looks as if we may be able to depend upon it for carrying us through a crisis if one should come.

…… ……

Yours sincerely,
Francis C. M. Wei

155. To Dr. Robert J. McMullen (March 3, 1949)

Dear Mac:

...　...

　　As I reported earlier, 170 students applied for relief funds, and grants were made a week ago by the Senate Committee, totaling 225 tan of rice or Sliver $2,000. A U. S. dollar comes to about Sliver $1.40 in exchange. This money has been raised locally, although the contributions have been very slow in coming in. Thirty more students have applied for the same relief, and the Committee is still in process of investigating their financial condition. We permit students to postpone part of the payment of their fees until the end of this month, and I am sure many students will need help by that time, possibly to the amount of U. S. $1,000. All these relief grants are necessary in order to help about one-third of our students, whose families have been hard-hit by the present situation, inflation, rising prices, and reduced income, besides the necessity of having to move by order of the government when the offices are evacuated from various places.

　　I do not know how to continue this relief plan after this term, unless conditions are to improve very rapidly. The financial strength of the families of our students will be further sapped, and I cannot go to Han Kou every term to raise money for relief funds. Perhaps the next stunt I shall try is to get some of the better-off students to help the poorer students, but again that can be done only once. Maybe the only thing is to put an item in our current budget for this purpose. After all, our work here is to give a good education to the students who come to us. It is of little use to have a good faculty and to have all the faculties without making it possible for the poor students to take advantage of all equipment and teaching.

...　...

Yours sincerely,
Francis C. M. Wei

156. To Dr. Robert J. McMullen (April 19, 1949)

Dear Mac:

… …

Yesterday we got the plan ready to give the Emergency Reserve money to our faculty and staff. Enclosed I am sending you a copy of the memorandum which was the substance of my announcement to the faculty and staff at a meeting at four o'clock yesterday afternoon. People seem to be perfectly satisfied and really grateful to the United Board for this arrangement.

… …

In spite of the tense situation, all our people here are still calm, and the students have been behaving very well. We have seen the proposals of the Yenching students to the administration. Some of the Yenching students' ideas are rather naive, but as a whole, we may be able to adapt ourselves to them, if the same ideas should be presented to us later in Hua Chung. Our policy is to wait and see. Adaption is the order of the day, but we shall stand firmly on our Christian and educational principles with the conviction that are going to survive.

… …

Last Saturday I was at a dinner party of the Wu Chang gentry to discuss ways and means of meeting the emergency when it comes. From the discussion I felt that there was very little to plan for except to get ready to police the city during an interregnum of perhaps about a day or two, and to arrange rice shops going. I have to keep in touch with the difficult groups of people in the city as a non-partisan. The day after tomorrow I am going to lecture to the officials of the province in training. In order to avoid misinterpretation, I am going to lecture on Kantian Philosophy, which is largely epistemological and therefore entirely non-political. I have to do stunts like that in order to play my part as dove and a serpent. For two consecutive weeks I have been addressing the weekly Assembly myself, and the students seem to be willing to accept what I had to say to them about the spirit of Hua

Chung and our democratic way of doing things for the last twenty years.

...　...

Yours sincerely,
Francis C. M. Wei

157. To Mr. J. Earl Fowler (April 19, 1949)

Dear Earl:

...　...

The situation will probably change in the near future. Yesterday I could together again the whole faculty and staff and asked them what plans we should make in order to meet the emergency. All of they could do was to reaffirm the appointment of two of the faculty members to make plans in connection with the students and servants of the University. Really no one expects very much fighting in this center; and if there should be any, it could not last very long. During the fighting we would simply suspend classes, so that people would be or shelter in some of our stronger buildings, and the young people would be organized to patrol the campus in order to avoid disturbances by people from outside. We are fortunate to be in the quieter part of the city, as you know, and if there should be any local commotion, we may not be seriously affected. There is the question of the drinking water for the ten families occupying the new houses outside the Old City Wall, and the Senate has decided to hire coolies to supply them with drinking water if the water supply should be cut off temporarily. There is enough rice for the students, faculty families, and servants for the whole term until the end of June. With the Emergency Reserve money distributed even for two month's to all the faculty and staff members, we ought to be able to tide over a period when the exchange may be very difficult or even impossible. If the period should last for more than three months, there would be difficulty, but we hope that arrangements may be made in that eventuality.

On Monday a week ago I raised the question with the Senate whether we should advance the graduation and intermediate examinations, in view of the situation. The Senate then decided to postpone the consideration of this question until yesterday, when they met again. Yesterday the Senate voted unanimously to make no changes in the University Calendar. That is to say, we are going to carry on as usual for as long as we can with all examinations in June.

... ...

Yours affectionately,
Francis C. M. Wei

158. To Dr. Robert J. McMullen (April 26, 1949)

Dear Bob:

... ...

So far our morale is still good, and the students are sensible and most cooperative. They are, of course, young and native. From time to time I have to give them a bit of advice, and they are always ready to take it with gratitude. Yesterday evening there was a meeting of the whole student body, faculty, and staff, and servants to discuss ways and means to meet an emergency. No really constructive ideas could come from a meeting like that. Naturally I was the first one to speak, and I had to be as clever as a serpent of the student leaders, and I felt that I had helped them to be more realistic.

... ...

We have already finished nine weeks of lectures, with one week of spring holiday, and we should be able to carry on for four more weeks, which would be a real achievement. My conjecture is that we stand a pretty good chance of going through the term and finishing according to schedule the latter part of June before there would be any chance, but that may be optimism or pessimism depending on how you look at the situation.

... ...

As to the number of workers on the campus, we are trying to reduce to the minimum, realizing that every extra worker means so much more trouble when the Union is formed, and they will be probably aggressive and difficult to deal with at least at the beginning, although so far our workers have been very faithful and reasonable.

……

At any rate we put Christian principles before human lives, and human lives before material property. Last night I told our students here that I would not want them to put up any resistance if there should be armed people coming in to loot, but if there should be a mob using no violence means, the number of young people on the campus may be able to keep them away. Sufficient measures of precautions have been taken to safeguard whatever valuable equipment we have, but there is no way to protect the library. We have fire drill but the danger of fire is very slight. The only thing that we are afraid of is just looting. The gentry in the city have been considering ways and means of keeping order in Wu Chang, in case there should be any interim period, but how effective those measures will be only the future will tell. We have experienced very little looting in Wu Chang in the past, and whenever there was any it was not in our part of the city—except when the Japanese were here, but that was a pretty thorough business when they had time to do it house-by-house.

You may have read Dr. T. C. Chao's articles on "The Christian Churches in Communist China" and "Revolution in China." I admire Dr. Chao for his courage and his Christian Faith, but I am inclined to disagree with him in many of his judgments. If I should have time during the next week or so, I may draft an article just in reply without taking side politically; but just stating the Christian way of looking at many of the problems he deals with. I do not mean to say that this way of dealing with those problems is not Christian, but there is more than one way of taking a Christian attitude. Last Friday evening the Lutheran Student Center asked me to address the Lutheran Student Fellowship, and I took as my topic, "I reply to Dr. T. C. Chao." T. C. and I are friends of the thirty years standing, and we agree on many things, but we part company most of the time on philosophical and theological questions, with, however, mutual respect as friends and fellow-workers in the Church.

......

Yours sincerely,
Francis C. M. Wei

159. To Dr. Robert J. McMullen (May 3, 1949)

Dear Bob:

......

On Sunday afternoon I met with the Wuhan Christian Students Union and all the student religious workers. The group was small because it clashed with another Christian student meeting in Wu Chang. They asked me to speak in "The Basic Teachings of the Christian Faith," which I did. I started from man's sense of insecurity, to which the Christian answer is the world and human life as God's Creature; then the mind of the Creator as reveled in the life and teaching of Jesus of Nazareth; and that after His Ascension God is still working in His Church and in all human minds which accept His Salvation; and finally the church as the Body of Christ to complete the work of Redemption in this world of ours. This may sound a bit too much orthodoxy for you, but the group of young people accepted it and asked a few questions, such as Creation and Darwinism. Well, I pointed out to them that there were Bergson and Lloyd Morgan after Darwin; and while we accepted the theory of Evolution, we must not stop with Darwin. The discussion was lively, and the group decided to have monthly meetings to discuss the Christian position and the new forces that are coming to China in times like these.

......

On May 1, Labor Day in China, we paid our college servants according to a scheme agreed upon by those directly in charge of the servants and the administrative heads in the university. Those servants who have been working since rehabilitation on the fall of 1946 have received three-month's pay in addition to their par for April. Those who have been working for over a year have received two months extra, and those who have served for less than a year only one month extra. Proportionately, the workers have got more than the staff and faculty members.

…… ……

Hot weather has already set in, and we have changed our class hours in the afternoon, starting at 1:30 instead of 1:15, so as to give a longer interval after lunch. The students say that they need a nap in the afternoon, but most of them simply play around, which is really good for them.

…… ……

We still continue our weekly Music Hour on Thursday evening. Once in a while I drop into the Assembly Room not only to enjoy the music when I can, but also to see what kind of audience there is. I was in the hall myself last Thursday, and it was pretty well filled. There was some record music played in the new gramophones with an amplifier sent by the China Christian University Association in London, and it was really a wonderful instrument. The main items on the program for the evening were really piano solos by Professor Edward R. Van Sant of the Economics Department. He is a pianist, as well as an economist, and he seems to enjoy his playing as much as we enjoy his music. It is wonderful that we can have such musical evening in the University, and music always lightens one's labors.

Religious activities are still going on as usual, mainly on Friday evening with all the fellowship meetings. Our Morning Chapel and other services remain unchanged.

…… ……

Yours sincerely,
Francis C. M. Wei

160. To Dr. Robert J. McMullen (May 10, 1949)

Dear Bob:

…… ……

Last Friday evening about ten o'clock I heard the bell alarm on the college side of the campus, signaling fire. I went out and found a considerable number of our own students, boys and girls, rushing about, knowing not exactly what to do. I took charge of the situation at once and sent a man student ahead to find out the original of the fire and where it was. It was near to two Boy Scout Camps at the eastern end of the school campus. A pile of kindling wood had been prepared for fire drill of the Boone Middle School boys for Saturday morning, but some mischievous little devil lit it at ten o'clock, and that started the alarm. As soon as that was ascertained, I ordered our own students to return to their hostels. Even in a small incident like that, apparently it required a more experienced person to assume leadership.

....

We have received all kinds of documents from various Christian bodies and individuals. The important thing is to know what the essentials of the Christian Faith are and decide with that Faith as our guiding principle what we can do and what we cannot do whenever a special situation arises. Again, I would say that as far as I can see, whatever the future has in store for us probably we are not going to have greater hardship than what we experienced in the winter of 1926—1927, for a little while at least. There may be further changes, of course, after that, but it seems sheer cowardice for us to run away from imagined danger. So here we are prepared to stick it out, trusting that God Almight will take care of us and that His Spirit will direct us as to what to say and what to do in a given set of circumstances. There are dangers, of course, but where can one now find a safe place? Security is only a relative term, but the Christian Faith is an absolute thing.

....

Yours sincerely,
Francis C. M. Wei

161. An Excerpt from a Letter from President Francis Wei (May 31, 1949)

....

Our students asked for the suspension of classes on Tuesday two weeks ago, and that request was granted for them to go out and welcome the entering armies. Practically all the students in the city went out to do the same, together with other groups of people. The behavior of our students in the street was highly commended by friends of Hua Chung University. On Wednesday, the 18th, classes were suspended again because of the heavy day on Tuesday, and the anxiety and activities in patrolling the campus from the previous Saturday. From Thursday through Saturday classes were again suspended, at the request of the students, to give them a chance to go to the streets and explain to the people in Wu Chang the principles of the new government, so as to help them get properly adjusted to the new regime. Classes were resumed on Monday of last week, May 23, but on Tuesday morning there was suspension of classes again, but since Tuesday afternoon all academic activities have been going on as usual.

…… ……

162. Excerpts from a Letter from President Wei, Hua Chung University (June 7, 1949)

The students are slowly setting down to their work, but during the last week we had quite a bit of uneasiness. At first, the Students' Self-government and the Senior Class petitioned the faculty to abolish the intermediate examinations, which are peculiar to Hua Chung in this country and are required of sophomores at the end of the second year before promotion to the Junior Class and the final examinations for the degrees which we started way back in 1931 before the old government required them of all colleges, which it did with the year 1938. At first the faculty made some modifications to these requirements, which the students did not accept, and then the commotion on the campus became worse so much so that beginning with Wednesday morning the Senior students started a strike and refused to go to classes whereas the other students went on with their work as usual. There was quite a bit of opposition between the Senior Class and the other students. Petitions came to the faculty again. The decision was made by the faculty to have the term examinations for the Sophomores and the Seniors at the same time as the other classes; to suspend for this year 1949 the intermediate examinations until we are able to clarify the whole question of examinations with the new government; and also to postpone the final examinations for the degree until a later date when clarification of the question has been made with the new educational authorities in this center.

... ...

We talked at great length on the requirements over and above the minimum requirements according to government regulations, which are not definite yet: for instance, whether it would be possible to have our intermediate examinations and final examinations for the degree in addition to the examinations required by the educational authorities of the new government. I was assured that we would have the liberty to have extra requirement so long as their purport was to maintain good standard.

... ...

We have had holidays more frequently than we had expected, but we have lost much less time on account of the political change than I had anticipated before the Liberation. Term examinations for all the students will begin next Tuesday, June 14, and the end of the term will be June 25. The Senate of the University has decided to allow the students to stay in the hostels designed for use during the summer. This has been our practice ever since our return to Wu Chang in 1946. One of our problems now is how to help some of the students who may be able to find their summer board because they are now cut off from their homes in the west or the south. I raised the question with the Senate yesterday, and the Senate decided to postpone the consideration of the matter until a later date.

... ...

163. Excerpts from a Letter from Francis Wei, Hua Chung University (July 21, 1949)

......

Fees will have to be lower than last term, and with a decreased enrollment, income from student fees will be much reduced for the next year. No one can tell how many students we shall have. Our estimate is about 300—500. Even the Christian middle schools will have much smaller enrollments next year. Many of their graduates have joined various kinds of activities, and so the number coming to join our freshman class will be much smaller than in an ordinary year. Economic conditions will make it very difficult for many of the families to pay even our reduced fees.

We are keeping the same faculty, except one change in the Department of English Literature. Arrangements are being made for a part-time teacher to offer one course in Elementary Russian as a second foreign language in the university next year, open only to junior and senior students of all the departments. Ethics will be dropped except as an elective course, so also Logic, but Philosophy will be required as before, and I have to teach it again myself. In preparation for the course in Philosophy I try to do as much reading as possible during the summer, and I find it not easy at all to teach it in such a way as to make it acceptable to all concerned.

......

Perhaps 100 of our students have joined the various training schools of the government, and a few have gone into the army for political work. Before they leave this center, they come back to see us very frequently, showing genuine affection for their old college. According to their reports, they are making a very good name for Hua Chung everywhere by their spirit of service and their willingness to cooperate.

......

164. To Dr. Arthur M. Sherman (August 11, 1949)

Dear Dr. Sherman:

………

We do not expect a large enrollment in September, perhaps it will be only about two-thirds of what we had a year ago. Many students have joined the various political institutions, and we are glad that they have a chance to do so. Perhaps in another year the number of students will increase again, but it may take a couple of years before we can get back to the high water mark reached in the autumn of 1948. Registration of candidates for the entrance examinations to be held next week is going on. Of the candidates, about one-half are women students, which is to be expected under the present circumstances.

We are fully intending to carry on our theological training here. The theological students will not decrease as far as we know.

Next Monday, August 15, we are going to have another meeting of the Preparation Committee for a larger meeting to plan out the religious activities of the various middle schools in this center. It is our desire that the intensified religious activities in the schools will lead to the formal organization of the Christian Student Volunteer Movement in the Wu Han area, to be held sometime during the winter vacation. Nothing is more urgent than to have a large number of young people trained, so that they may render voluntary service to the church in China. Paid ministers may decrease in number as the years go by; and if the church is going to go ahead, we shall have to depend largely upon people who get their living outside the church, but who may give part of their time to the service of the church, and that requires a great deal of encouragement and training. Our theological course here has been planned largely to meet that kind of situation.

………

Yours affectionately,
Francis C. M. Wei

165. Letter from President Wei, Hua Chung University (August 11, 1949)

......

We started registration of candidates for our entrance examinations on August 8, and it is still going on. The number of candidates is going to be small, perhaps not more than one-third of the number we used to have during the last three years since rehabilitation. Most of the middle school graduates have joined some of the training institutions, and they are not able to come and register for our entrance examinations in this month. It looks as if we may have to give other entrance examinations in September, if we should find the successful candidates too few to form a freshman class. There is, of course, another factor, which accounts for the small registration, and that is the Hunan students have not been able to come to the Wuhan Center as they did in previous years. We have already wired to Changsha, asking whether it would be possible to hold our entrance examination there later in the month or early in September.

Again, we have no way of estimating the enrollment for the next term. My guess is that it will be between 300 and 350. There will be a serious drop, but circumstances do not warrant any higher than that.

......

166. Letter from Francis Wei, Hua Chung University (September 2, 1949)

......

Then, in order to make our Biology Department more useful and to give more outlets to our Biology graduates, we are negotiating with the Institute of Hospital Theology, hitherto connected with the Union Hospital in Han Kou, for affiliation with Hua Chung University. The plan is still in the process of negotiation, and even our Senate has not considered it because we have to wait until the Board of the Institute of

Hospital Technology has given its approval. If it should go through, it would become an attached institute of Hua Chung University under our College of Science without any financial obligation on our part. The Institute at present has a staff of 15, including 4 missionaries supported by the various missions or foundations, and 11 members who are employed and their salaries are paid from local, largely from fees in the laboratories, which serve not only the Union Hospital, but other hospitals and private practitioners in the whole Wuhan area. The affiliation would standardize the training of the Institute of Hospital Technology and bring it up to university standard. Of course, students of the university standard would be increasing, but there will always be some students who are not candidates for university degrees. They would be classified as members of the training class. As soon as the Senate has considered the matter, it will go to the United Board for final sanction. It is not so much financial obligating that we may ask the United Board to undertake, but to undertake it as one of our institutes in the university. Its finances would be under the supervision of our Treasure, and its general conduct would be under our university administration, although the general set-up will remain the same—in the Union Hospital in Han Kou.

……

We are considering one or two minor projects along the line of our present development, and they may need U. S. $2,000—$3,000 to implement them, such as for instance the Physics Department is thinking of making itself more practical, which may mean the appointment of a practical physicist with an annual salary of about U. S. $1,100 a year plus house rent. Then, of course, we may have to add slightly to our laboratory equipment so as to give practical training to the Physics students of the last two years in college. The Chemistry Department has a similar project, but this, as well as that of the Physics Department, will be reported to you as soon as they have received the attention of our Senate.

……

Perhaps only about 200 of our own candidates will be qualified for entrance, and 50%—60% of those will come to us. Together with about 30 and 35 recommended students, we may make a freshman class of around 150, which is the limit set by the Senate and the Directors.

... ...

Local conditions remain about the same, and we are getting things ready for our re-opening on September 10, but classes will not begin until September 29, because we have to give the examinations due at the end of last term, which owing to conditions at the time were not given according to schedule.

... ...

167. Letter from Francis Wei, Hua Chung University (September 9, 1949)

... ...

We have already announced the result of our entrance examinations. Altogether 185 students are qualified for admission, with 32 on the waiting list. Besides there are about 35 recommended students, and perhaps two-thirds of them will come to register. According to our estimate, the freshman class will be probably 150, which is the maximum fixed by our Senate and our Board of Directors for this year. It is still too early to foretell the number of old students who may return, since there are so many interfering factors, of which economic conditions are the main one. Perhaps 250 to 280 old students may return, and so our total enrollment for this term may be around 400—that is, 50 higher than my previous estimate.

... ...

I hope the United Board will consider this need of our students. The request will be repeated for at least another term. If I were to analyze the economic situation minutely, it might not be appropriate. My feeling is that in order to help Christian education in China to tide over the next period of three years, more money ought to be spent on financial aids to students in colleges which are in those locations more seriously affected by the present situation than others, and Wu Chang is certainly one of those locations.

In order to maintain our standard, as well as our morale, and to keep up a reasonable enrollment for the occupation of our buildings, we have also to find some Sustaining Fund for the Christian middle schools which are our chief feeders. In the Wuhan area alone we have six Christian senior middle schools. My question is whether it is possible by some kind of international effort to give 100 scholarships in each of those six Christian middle schools, a total of 600 scholarships, at the rate of 4 tan a rice each about U. S. $7. The total amount needed would be U. S. $33,600. This figure may be too high. If we should reduce it by a half, it would still mean about $17,000, but some kind of financial help like this will be imperative. We have religious liberty and we are free to maintain our Christian schools, but only those schools which are able to compete with non-tuition schools will be able to survive.

....

168. Letter from Francis Wei, Hua Chung University (September 21, 1949)

To explain: even now we have only a very rough estimate of our enrollment for this term, but every indication is that we may have 430 to 460. The number of new students will probably be about 150—170, and so our cablegram said, new students comprise one-third of total enrollment. The Senate and the Board of Directors decided to admit only 150 of the new students this term, but as you know, it is always difficult to estimate how many of the students who passed their entrance examinations will actually turn up to register. We had 620 candidates, and 185 were qualified, with 332 on the waiting list. Ordinarily we would expect two-thirds of the qualified students to come to college and one-half of those on the waiting list, but this year any estimate is only a wild guess. Wuhan University had over 900 candidates taking the examinations, and they qualified over 700. Similarly the percentage of students who passes the examinations, for the national universities in

Peiping is also very high. The great majority of the students who passed our examinations will have very generous scholarships for board and lodging. Therefore, it is quite difficult for us to know how many of our qualified students will come until they have actually registered. The number of students who took our entrance examinations was one-third that of a year ago, whereas in other universities the percentage dropped down to one-fifth or even less.

Our registration is late this term because as I have written before, we were in the middle of our term examinations in June when the students had to go out to do propaganda work until the very end of the term. Therefore, we are now holding the examinations due during the last week, which will be September 24. Registration will begin in the middle of next week because we also have supplementary examinations to give as well. In other words, we are not skipping any step in our normal program. Whatever examination was not taken has to be taken now before the new term actually begins.

... ...

Our curriculum remains about the same except some of the courses will have to be modified. In addition, we have to give some political courses, and they are to be given by members of our own faculty. I have been asked by our Faculty Committee to teach the theological course in the political field, but I cannot do it as an extra burden, although I have been reading along the line of dialectic materialism ever since my days in London. We expect to work out all the problems, and the students seem to be still cooperative and are more willing to work than before the Liberation.

... ...

169. Letter from Francis Wei, Hua Chung University (January 31, 1950)

... ...

We in Hua Chung are not bold enough to guarantee that all the young people passing through here will live up to that high standard, but that has been always our aim, and a goodly number of our graduates will not disappoint us. At least we can say that so far as the general conduct of Hua Chung as a Christian university is concerned, our contribution is intended to be in the spirit of the Christian Gospel. If not for this, many of us would not be working here, both missionaries and our Chinese colleagues.

We are doing everything possible to permeate the entire campus with the Christian spirit, and as I have reported before, approximately 80% of our teaching staff are Christians, and the great majority of these are sincerely dedicated to Christ. We have our Sunday Worship and our Daily Chapel, except for one day in the week when we have College Assembly. We have religious courses, although most of them are primarily intended for those students taking the combined theological course, but they are open to other students as well. We have our four Christian fellowships, which meet separately or together in alternate weeks. In all our extracurricular activities we have in mind the educational value, and many of them are primarily Christian in character.

We are just finishing today our term examinations, and many of my colleagues who have been invigilating have remarked to me that there has been perfect order in the examination hall, and the students behaved wonderfully well.

Our winter vacation will begin tomorrow, and the second term will start on March 1. Only about 100 students are remaining in the hostels. They have been organizing themselves for review work, for tidying up the campus, for filling the trenches left by the Nationalist troops on the edge of our new land, and for conducting some anti-illiteracy schools for the people in the neighborhood. Last Friday the students asked me to address them and lay down the general principles for the winter plans. This I did, and according to the reports later their response to my appeal is very satisfying.

…… ……

170. Letter from President Wei, Hua Chung University (March 9, 1950)

... ...

I have heard with great interest with policy of the government with regard to Christian schools and colleges, as discussed in Peking last December. The policy to my mind is very reasonable. In substance Christian schools are to be divided into three categories:

1. Those institutions in which the democratic element is strong, comparatively progressive, and observing faithfully the regulations and orders of the Government. These should be sustained, and if necessary subsidized.

2. Those institutions which are not extremely reactionary, still faithful in observing government regulations and orders. These ought to be won over and improved.

3. Those institutions which are firmly and stubbornly reactionary. If any of them openly defy government orders or regulations, their defiance ought to be dealt with and corrected.

We are interested to notice that according to this policy, no school is to be closed for defiance and for being not progressive enough. I do not think anybody should expect a more reasonable policy from the government with regard to Christian schools in times like these. Of course, in colleges and middle schools there should be no required religious courses, and religion should be free for students and faculty. In middle schools, however, there should be no religious propaganda inside or outside of class. Of course, if there is a church in the vicinity of the Christian middle schools, students may participate in religious activities there instead of within school premises. As far as colleges and universities are concerned, religious propaganda is prohibited only in class. However, this point has not been made very clear because we have so far received so definite orders from the government yet. As far as Hua Chung goes, everything is carrying on as usual.

The churches are starting to register land and building as alien property, but the Han Kou Diocese of the Chung Hua Sheng Kung Hui has decided to turn the ownership of the property formerly known as the "Boone Compound" over to the Board Of Directors of Hua Chung University, if we should get the approval of the Government; and with the understanding that until Boone Middle School is able to move to its new site as originally planned (which is not very likely now), the school will continue to use that portion of the Boone Campus, which it has been using all these years.

171. To United Board Office (March 14 and 21, 1950)

The term is under way now, and the religious activities are going on full steam ahead. We had the first Sunday evening service of the spring term the day before yesterday, and the church was packed full. The Morning Chapel, everyday except Wednesday when we have Assembly, is also well attended; the attendance varies from 60 to 90. All the fellowships are starting their activities, but we have also the Christian students in the middle schools in the Wuhan cities to take care of.

… …

Our enrollment this term will be 346 when registration is completed, but the dean is still accepting students for registration because some of the students have found it so difficult to find money to pay their fees.

… …

172. Excerpts from a Letter from President Wei, Hua Chung University (August 29, 1950)

… …

Only about 700 students took our entrance examinations in the middle of August, and with present conditions we have to admit more than one-half of them. The standards are a little bit lower than last year, but this is the case in almost every university and college in China. About 180 students are taking our second examinations. It remains to be seen how many students we shall be able to admit after registration during the first week of September. We are expecting an enrollment of not more than 450. That will mean a new start over again. Four years ago we admitted more than 300 new students, in order to build up our student body, but the political situation has reduced our enrollment to less than 400, and so we have to build up again. With the present morale of faculty and students, we are not afraid of admitting a comparatively large freshman class this year. We are aiming at a student body of just about 500 for the next two or three years until we see the situation more clearly.

The Peking Conference is producing very encouraging results. People in the Christian institutions are feeling more encouraged, and a similar change of attitude is perceptible even in the Christian middle schools. Boone Middle School is expecting again an enrollment of 400 students, and St. Hilda's in our neighborhood hopes too for a good term this next term.

…… ……

173. Excerpts from a Letter from President Wei, Hua Chung University (November 29, 1950)

…… ……

You will be interested to know the following statistics:

				Total
I. Full-time Teaching Staff Chinese	43	Western	11	54
Part-time Teaching Staff Chinese	5	Western	1	6
Grand Total				60

II. Administrative Staff (all full-time)

				Total
Chinese	19	Western	2		21

Grand Total Teaching and Administrative Staff
 (full-time and part-time)

81

III. Of the full-time teaching staff of 54, 37 are Christian, i. e. 70%, and of the 6 part-time teachers only 2 are Christian, i. e. 33%.

Everyone of the 6 part-time teachers is teaching only three hours a week. Of the 21 full-time administrative staff, two-thirds i. e. 66% are Christian.

Ⅳ. Research Students   Men 5   Women 5 Total 10
   Fourth Year Students Men 48   Women 36 Total 84
   Third Year Students Men 28   Women 21 Total 49
   Second Year Students Men 52   Women 27 Total 79
   First Year Students Men 168 Women 98 Total 266
                                    Total Enrollment 488

You will note that the third year has the smallest number of students, because they were the freshman students at the time of Liberation in May 1949, and that class was most seriously affected.

Of the total number of 488 students, only 176 have re-opened themselves as Christians, making 36% of the total enrollment. This percentage of Christian students is about the lowest since rehabilitation four and a half years ago. Of the 176 Christian students, 50 belong to the Episcopal Church in China, 48 to the Church of Christ in China, 34 to the Methodist Church in China, 16 to the Baptist Church, 10 to the Roman Catholic Church, and the remainder are scattered among the other denominations.

……

174. Letter from President Wei, Hua Chung University (January 17, 1951)

……

Steps have been taken to reduce salaries again, and perhaps if necessary further reductions will be made. We must have at least U. S. $15,000, in order to pay the minimum salaries and meet the necessary expenses, including wages, light, water, and general operation. If the total amount of U. S. $28,050 should reach us before the end of the year, we ought to be fairly paid, but I believe the Ministry of Education will see to it that we are not going to spend one cent more than absolutely necessary in order to conserve our financial strength.

……

By stretching our cash in the banks in Han Kou (which includes the proceeds of the £700 recently sent us by the Rev. Noel B. Slater), we may be able to carry on until the end of March, but that would mean a great deal of hardship for many people working here. We are not sure whether we shall be able to have money for scholarships and work scholarships as we did up to the present time. Again, we must consult the Ministry of Education in Han Kou before we should budget any item for those purposes. The amount certainly will have to be reduced.

Conditions are changing very rapidly, and a great deal is still unknown, but largely the thought has come to me that it is still worthwhile to maintain Hua Chung if possible, as a private Christian institution, under of course the strict supervision of the Ministry of Education and of the government in general. In order to show our genuine purpose of wanting to serve the Chinese people, we ought to continue to support Hua Chung with the money that is given for this very purpose without any political design. There is still the need of a place like Wu Chang in the educational system in China, and a number of my Chinese colleagues agree with any of our own actions or by any of our failure to act in the right way. Therefore, I would strongly urge the United Board and all the mission boards to continue their contributions after this year as long as such contributions are necessary for the maintenance of the work.

……

175. Letter from Francis Wei at Hua Chung University (February 13, 1951)*

……

It is hardly possible to follow up the matter of asking Mr. Stephen Chen to come back to Hua Chung, if he is going to teach only

---

* This letter was received in New Haven March 5 through N. Y. Office of China College Board.

theological subjects alone. We may have permission from the Government for some of us teaching general subjects in the university to teach some of the theological subjects, until at least the present theological students in Hua Chung have finished their course, but it is hardly fair to use public funds for maintenance of a teacher who devotes all his time to religious teaching.

……

Yours very cordially,
Francis C. M. Wei

出版后记

韦卓民先生(1888—1976),广东珠海人,我国著名的翻译家、哲学家、教育家,曾长期担任华中大学校长(1929—1951年)。韦先生毕业于文华大学,曾留学美国、英国,先后获哈佛大学哲学硕士学位和伦敦大学哲学博士学位,精通英、德、法、俄等多种外语,学贯中西,尤其是在康德哲学、黑格尔哲学、逻辑学、宗教学方面造诣很深。他毕生致力于沟通中西文化,在西学东渐、弘扬中国传统文化方面作出了巨大贡献。整理、出版《韦卓民全集》(11卷)对全面展示、传承韦卓民先生的学术成就,弘扬他的爱国精神和教育思想具有重要的文化价值和现实意义。

华中师范大学有一批富于抢救保护学术珍品责任感的领导和学者,一直在不计得失地付出。如上世纪八九十年代,以章开沅教授为首的校领导组织成立了韦卓民遗著整理小组,与韦先生一同工作过的曹方久(已去世)教授,敬仰韦先生学问与人品的唐有伯、高新民、王宏维等教授,一直在搜集、整理韦先生的遗著。华中师范大学出版社从20世纪90年代起就开始陆续编辑出版韦卓民先生的译著系列及相关研究,出版有"韦译哲学名著研究系列"及关于韦卓民研究的重点图书260多万字,包括《康德哲学讲解》、《康德〈纯粹理性批判〉解义》、《康德哲学原著选读》及《韦卓民学术论著选》等书。其后,由于经费和人手的紧张,仍有约700万字的译稿和文章等未能整理出版。所幸2013年湖北省新闻出版广电局启动了湖北省学术著作出版专项资金资助项目,11卷本的《韦卓民全集》获得资助;一贯重视韦卓民著述出版的珠海市委宣传部对该套书的出版也给予了高度重视和经费上的有力支持;还有马敏、余子侠、高新民、刘家峰等老师也为全集的出版不计名利地做了大量工作。特别要说明的是,韦卓民先生的后人对全集出版给予了无私的帮助,他们承诺放弃稿酬。根据他们的建议,出版社和他们商定全集出版后开付的稿酬,将作为"韦卓民奖励基金",用于研究韦卓民先生著述的出版及相关的学术活动。在此,对这些一直关心、支持全集出版的所有同仁一并致以诚挚的谢意!

《韦卓民全集》的书稿形式繁多而复杂,除有大量手稿外,还有一些是从图书馆和档案馆拍摄的图片资料;手稿的大部分存放于华中师范大学档案馆,少部分保存在韦先生亲属手中,还有部分资料被收藏在英国和美国的大学图书馆。韦卓民遗著整理小组力求尽量把海内外所藏相关文献搜罗完备,整理出版。此次出版的《韦卓民全集》包括韦卓民生前已公开出版的各类作品和从未刊发的手稿、书信等,总体上分为翻译书稿和研究论著两大类,并按照哲学、逻辑、教育、宗教及文化等板块进行分卷,共11卷。

由于《韦卓民全集》绝大部分为翻译作品,如康德的《纯粹理性批判》、《康德的经验形而上学——〈纯粹理性批判〉上半部分注释》、《判断力批判》及卡斯拉的《康德〈判断力批判〉解义》、《康德哲学原著选读》,斯密的《康德〈纯粹理性批判〉解义》等,都是深奥难懂的哲学著作;加之韦卓民先生生活的年代和当时的行文习惯,书稿中有些说法和表述与现在的语言文字规范及出版规范有较大出入,但又不能按现在的要求径改,只能采取尊重历史、适当变通的原则进行特殊处理,现分述如下:

1. 关于标点符号。书稿中有很多不是分句而使用分号,不必断句而使用逗号,在"与"、"和"等之前使用标点的情况,还有在破折号前使用逗号和句号,以及括号中的内容单独列出并在句末用句号的情形等。这是当时的行文特点及作者的表达习惯,只要不影响对文意的理解,一律保持原貌;但如果导致无法理解,甚至是明显的错误,才按现在的规范予以改正。

2. 对书稿中的有些字词与现在的说法有出入的处理。如把"钥匙"写作"锁钥"、"介绍"写作"绍介"、"终究"写作"终久"等,都一仍其旧;还有一些不符合现在的用词规范的,如"已曾"、"看成是"、"涉及到"等,只要不影响对内容的理解,亦未作改动。

3. 全集的注释很多,且形式繁杂。有大量简写的,如"A713 即 B741"是指康德《纯粹理性批判》两个不同版本的页码;有很多注项不全的,如"见书之第 12 节";同一文献资料有多种说法的,典型的如华特生的 The

Philosophy of Kant Explained 一书,韦先生有时简译为《解康德》,有时译为《释康德》,更多的时候译为《康德解》等等。编审人员不宜按照现有的规范统一,注项不全的也因资料有限而没法补充完整。为了尽可能保持原貌,更为避免造成新的错误,只能大致统一。

4. 正文内容的层次复杂,很多并没按现在通行的层次表达形式。同一层次的内容,有用 A、B、C……表示的,也有用 a、b、c……表示的,还有用(1)、(2)、(3)……表示的等,甚至同一层次的内容,其表现形式也不统一。考虑到没有错误,均未径改。

5. 有些表述虽不合适,但明显属于个人的写作习惯。如书稿中经常用"而"表递进关系,还有很多"是……的"句式,但有的"是……"后面没有"的"字等。虽然改了更符合现在的规范,但文中此类表述甚多,考虑到这种表述不影响读者的理解,亦未擅改。

6. 全集中还有少部分英文内容,原稿中同一个英文单词既有英式拼写,也有美式拼写,专用词的大小写亦不统一,同一地名的写法不尽相同,还有作者在书信后的署名写法不尽一致,为了保持作品原貌,亦未全书统一,仅在同一篇章或同一书信中统一。

韦卓民先生行文的特殊性还有不少,书稿的编校需要特别对待之处也很多,在此不一一赘述。

与大多数 20 世纪上半叶人物文集整理出版的难度大一样,《韦卓民全集》书稿的整理、编审难度远远超乎我们的想象。书稿除了少部分成书外,绝大部分都是图书馆和档案馆存放多年的手稿,编校这类书稿的难度有三:一是书稿中有大量非规范的简化字、繁体字、异体字,并夹杂有德文、英文、法文、拉丁文、希腊文等外文,且字迹难以辨认;二是书稿存放时间太久而导致的字迹脱落或模糊不清;三是由于书稿的专业性太强而难于理解。这不仅给书稿的收集整理增加了难度,对编审和校对人员也是极大的挑战。为了使文集尽量保持韦先生写作的原貌,也为了最大限度减少书稿的差错,编校人员反复查阅原件,并多次到图书馆、档案馆通过复印、拍照等方式获得资料进行核对和辨认。这仅仅有负责、敬业的精神和认真、细致的态度是不够的,编辑同人是怀着对韦先生的景仰之情和对学术的敬畏之心来做这套书的。我们有理由相信,《韦卓民全集》的出版将为学术界提供一个全面研究韦卓民先生的最佳文本,也将为西方哲学、教育学和宗教学等的研究提供重要的学术资源。同时,韦卓民作为研究中西方文化的先贤,其全集的刊行也将进一步推动中西方文化的交流与合作,为我国当下的学术发展与文化建设起到积极作用。

本社
2016 年 3 月 10 日